Asoka Bandarage
Crisis in Sri Lanka and the World

De Gruyter Contemporary Social Sciences

―
Volume 30

Asoka Bandarage
Crisis in Sri Lanka and the World

—

Colonial and Neoliberal Origins:
Ecological and Collective Alternatives

DE GRUYTER

ISBN 978-3-11-120343-0
e-ISBN (PDF) 978-3-11-120345-4
e-ISBN (EPUB) 978-3-11-120407-9
ISSN 2747-5689
e-ISSN 2747-5697

Library of Congress Control Number: 2023933705

Bibliographic information published by the Deutsche Nationalbibliothek
The Deutsche Nationalbibliothek lists this publication in the Deutsche Nationalbibliografie; detailed bibliographic data are available on the internet at http://dnb.dnb.de.

© 2023 Walter de Gruyter GmbH, Berlin/Boston
Cover image: naruedom / iStock / Getty Images Plus
Printing and binding: CPI books GmbH, Leck

www.degruyter.com

Dedicated to Sri Lanka and the World

Foreword

As a fellow South Asian scholar-activist, it gives me great pleasure to write the Foreword to Professor Asoka Bandarage's latest book, *Crisis in Sri Lanka and the World: Colonial and Neoliberal Origins, Ecological and Collective Alternatives*. During the forty or more years I have known Asoka, we have supported each other in our various endeavors towards peace, justice and environmental sustainability in South Asia and the world.

Crisis in Sri Lanka and the World is a most timely book—and urgently needed for the world that is at a critical crossroads of extreme and accelerating possibilities. For alternatives that are just and sustainable, the crisis needs to be understood both historically as well as in the contemporary context. I cannot think of very many who can do that—both with scholarship and passion—with a fusion of global as well as local and holistic perspectives as Asoka Bandarage has been able to do here.

To understand the roots of the contemporary Sri Lankan crisis and explore solutions that go beyond IMF debt restructuring, broader systemic analyses are needed. *Crisis in Sri Lanka and the World* provides that much-needed systemic perspective. It focuses on the external determinants of the Sri Lankan crisis and its exemplification of a broader global existential crisis facing more and more debt trapped countries, especially in the post-colonial Global South. As the book ably illustrates, the crisis in Sri Lanka is not an isolated one unique to the island but representative of the global crisis.

The book provides an in-depth analysis of Sri Lanka's on-going political and economic crisis taking into account the island's historical evolution with an emphasis on external political and economic intervention. This extensively documented and clearly written scholarly work demonstrates that Sri Lanka's crisis is the culmination of several centuries of colonial and neo-colonial developments. The book's discussion of the introduction of the plantations and the import-export economy under British rule and the expansion of Sri Lanka's economic dependence during the post-independence era of neoliberalism and globalization with its emphasis on export production has great relevance to understanding similar developments elsewhere in the world.

Crisis in Sri Lanka and the World discusses the unequal economic and financial architecture of the global economy which set the framework for the debt and socio-economic crisis in Sri Lanka and elsewhere. Developing a broad political and economic perspective, the book explores the emergence of the crisis in Sri Lanka in the context of the accelerating geopolitical conflict between China and the USA in the Indian Ocean. Providing interesting information and important points of view which are left out in mainstream analyses, the book ponders if the debt crisis, economic collapse and political destabilization in Sri Lanka were intentionally precipitated for geopolitical reasons.

Moving beyond economic crisis and geopolitical rivalry, the book juxtaposes Sri Lanka's political-economic crisis with the broader ecological crisis of climate change and sea-level rise. As a country among the most severely affected by extreme weather events, the shift from the current trajectory of domination over nature and others to one of human partnership with each other and the rest of nature is urgently needed.

Transcending conventional capitalist as well as socialist thinking, *Crisis in Sri Lanka and the World* calls for a fundamental transformation of consciousness from a philosophy of dualism and domination to one of interdependence and partnership with nature and among humanity. The book concludes with a consideration of the ethical dilemmas behind the debt and survival crisis pointing out a range of social movements and initiatives which subscribe to collective and ecological alternatives and a Middle Path of sustainability and social justice.

Crisis in Sri Lanka and the World provides a courageous and incisive analysis and a compassionate and hopeful vision much needed in a world ridden with divisiveness, distrust, inequities, conflicts and despair. It is my hope that this work by Dr. Asoka Bandarage will receive the wide attention it deserves contributing to the discourse on the roots of global crisis and transformation toward a peaceable, just and sustainable future.

Dr. Sajed Kamal

Sajed Kamal, author of *The Renewable Revolution: How We Can Fight Climate Change, Prevent Energy Wars, Revitalize the Economy and Transition to a Sustainable Future* (Earthscan, UK, 2011), taught in the Sustainable International Development program at Brandeis University for twenty years.

Preface

A limited perspective dominates the discourse on the economic cum political crisis facing Sri Lanka and the world. In this book, I have attempted to broaden and deepen our understanding of the contemporary situation by bringing together extensive information and alternative thinking which are generally absent in the mainstream analysis. The book's discussion of the origin, processes and evolution of globalization is more relevant now than ever, in order to comprehend the necessity to turn towards bio-regional, ecological and equitable ways of living in both Sri Lanka and the world at large.

Crisis in Sri Lanka and the World: Colonial and Neoliberal Origins: Ecological and Collective Alternatives represents the culmination of work I have done on Sri Lanka and on global development for over forty years. It builds upon my earlier books, *Colonialism in Sri Lanka: The Political Economy of the Kandyan Highlands, 1833–1886* (Berlin: Mouton, 1983); *Women, Population and Global Crisis: A Political-Economic Analysis*, (London: Zed Books, 1997); *The Separatist Conflict in Sri Lanka: Terrorism, Ethnicity, Political Economy* (London: Routledge, 2009) and *Sustainability and Wellbeing: The Middle Path to Environment, Society and the Economy* (London: Palgrave Macmillan, 2013) as well as innumerable book chapters, encyclopedia entries, refereed academic papers and regular columns in *Huffington Post, Asia Times, The Island, IPS News* and other publications.

The book conveys insights and experience I have derived from teaching courses in a wide range of fields – Sociology, Asian Studies, Women's Studies, Environmental Studies, Global Development, International Relations, Public Policy, Buddhism and Philosophy – at Brandeis, Mount Holyoke, Georgetown, Colorado College, CIIS (California Institute for Integral Studies) and other educational institutions during the course of my career. The book is also informed by my field work and experience with educational and activist organizations, such as *Critical Asian Studies* and the Interfaith Moral Action on Climate.

I would like to thank all the individuals who have helped bring this book to fruition including many friends and colleagues in Sri Lanka, the US and elsewhere who have shared relevant information and ideas. My deep gratitude to Paul Mayhew for his sensitive and intelligent editing and his interest and support from the inception of this work. Without his contribution, this book is unlikely to have seen the light of day.

I would like to thank IT specialist Nipun Dakshitha Porage for valuable computer help and to my student assistants from Colorado College, Annabelle Sparks and Meredith Sheridan for their painstaking work on the illustrations in the book.

My thanks also to colleagues at the California Institute for Integral Studies, Annette Williams and Barbara Morrill for their timely support.

I would like to extend my appreciation to the De Gruyter editorial and production team, Gerhard Boomgaarden, Michaela Göbels, Adriana Stroe for their diligent work towards the timely publication of this work. My first book, *Colonialism in Sri Lanka*, based on my Yale University Ph.D. thesis, was published by De Gruyter/Mouton Publishers in 1983. It is a pleasure for me to publish again with De Gruyter.

I must express my debt of gratitude to my teachers at Visakha Vidyalaya, Colombo, the University of Peradeniya, Bryn Mawr College and Yale University for my academic education and to Mr. S.N. Goenka for training in *vippasana* meditation.

Much gratitude to my friend, Maggie Scobie for her great enthusiasm and encouragement of this book.

Thanks to my son, Maithri, for his love and support.

Last but not least, my deepest gratitude to the Buddha, his teaching-the *Dhamma* – and his lineage of disciples – the *Sangha* – for inspiration and guidance in life and work including the writing of this book.

Asoka Bandarage
Colombo, Sri Lanka
March 2023

Asoka Bandarage was educated at the University of Sri Lanka, Bryn Mawr College and Yale University where she received her Ph.D. in Sociology. She has served on the faculties of Brandeis University, Georgetown University and Mount Holyoke College where she received tenure.

Contents

Foreword —— VII

Preface —— IX

Abbreviations —— XV

Figures List —— XVII

Tables List —— XIX

Appendices List —— XXI

Chapter 1:
Introduction: Crisis in Sri Lanka and the World —— 1
    Dominant Perspectives —— 2
    A Global Political Economy Perspective —— 4
    Colonialism and Neocolonialism —— 9
    Class Inequality in Sri Lanka —— 13
    Geopolitical Rivalry and Neoliberalism —— 13
    Ecological and Social Collapse —— 16
    Ecological and Collective Alternatives —— 17
    Transformation of Consciousness —— 20

Chapter 2:
Pre-Colonial Era to Colonial Rule and Capitalism: C. 3 BCE to 1948 —— 22
    European Colonization —— 26
    Portuguese Colonialism (1505–1658) —— 28
    Dutch Colonialism (1658–1796) —— 31
    British Colonialism, Mercantile Period (1796–c. 1832) —— 34
    Conquest of Kandy (1815) —— 35
    British Colonialism and Capitalist Development, c. 1832–1948 —— 39
    Plantation Economy —— 40
    The 1848 Rebellion —— 45
    Environmental and Social Destruction —— 47
    Poverty and Disempowerment —— 49
    Ethno-Religious Stratification —— 52
    The Resurgence of Sinhalese Buddhist Activism —— 53

Self-Rule and Social Democracy, 1931–1948 —— 55
Donoughmore Reforms and Welfare State, 1931–1947 —— 57

Chapter 3:
'Flag Independence', Left-Wing Nationalism and Decolonization, 1948–1977 —— 61

Crises and Resistance, 1948–1956 —— 63
Decolonization and the Cold War —— 67
The 1956 Revolution in Sri Lanka —— 71
Return of Pro-Western Regime: 1965–1970 —— 79
Return to Left-Nationalism, 1970–1977 —— 82
Import Substitution Industrialization and Non-Alignment —— 86

Chapter 4:
Neoliberalism, Authoritarianism and Recolonization, 1977–2009 —— 90

Neoliberalism in Sri Lanka —— 91
Authoritarian State —— 92
'Open Economy' —— 94
Land and Agriculture —— 95
Labor, Manufacturing and Services —— 101
Middle East Labor Export —— 105
Tourism —— 109
Privatization and Import Liberalization —— 111
Dismantling the Welfare State —— 114
Inequality, Conflict and Political Violence —— 116
Unequal Exchange, Debt Crises: Sri Lanka and the World —— 119

Chapter 5:
Geopolitical Rivalry, Neocolonialism and Political Destabilization, 2009–2019 —— 122

Chinese Expansion —— 122
Indian Expansion —— 128
U.S. Expansion —— 134
'Yahapalanaya' Regime (2015–2019) —— 136
Millennium Challenge Corporation Compact —— 139
The Sri Lankan MCC Compact —— 140
Colonial Land Expropriation —— 141
Popular Resistance to the MCC Compact —— 144
U.S. Military Expansion —— 147
The Acquisition and Cross Services Agreement (ACSA) —— 149

The Status of Forces Agreement (SOFA) —— 150
UNHRC Resolution —— 153
Easter Sunday Attacks: Political Destabilization —— 155

Chapter 6:
Debt Colonialism, Inequality and the Crisis of Survival, 2019 – 2022 —— 158
Economic Crisis —— 161
Debt Crisis —— 168
A History of Debt —— 170
International Sovereign Bonds —— 172
Global Debt Crisis —— 175
Wealth Transfers —— 177
Protest and Regime Change —— 181
Widening Disparities —— 190
Privatization —— 193
A Multifaceted Collapse —— 198

Chapter 7:
Ecological and Collective Alternatives to Neoliberal Globalization —— 202
Transformation of Consciousness —— 203
Domination and the Market Paradigm —— 204
Partnership and the Ecological Paradigm —— 208
The Balanced Middle Path —— 210
Resistance to Economic Domination —— 214
Civic Engagement and Grassroots Struggles —— 217
Bioregionalism and Localization —— 219
System Change in Sri Lanka —— 221

Appendices —— 225
1. Declaration on the Establishment of New International Economic Order, 1974 / A_RES_3201(S-VI)-EN.pdf —— 225
2. 2832 Declaration of the Indian Ocean as a Zone of Peace, 1971 / A_RES_2832(XXVI)-EN.pdf —— 229
3. Earth Charter, 2000 / echarter_english.pdf —— 231

Selected Bibliography —— 235

Abbreviations

AAFLI:	Asian-American Free Labor Institute
ACSA:	Acquisition and Cross-Servicing Agreement
ACU:	Asian Clearing Union
ADB:	Asian Development Bank
BLPI:	Bolshevik–Leninist Party of India, Ceylon and Burma
BRI:	Belt and Road Initiative
BRICS:	Brazil, Russia, India, China and South Africa
CCCC:	China Communications Construction Company
CCEM:	Cabinet Committee on Economic Management
CFA:	Committee for a Free Asia
COPA:	Committee on Public Accounts
CP:	Communist Party
CPC:	Ceylon Petroleum Corporation
DRC:	Democratic Republic of the Congo
EEF:	Extended Fund Facility
EPZ:	Export Processing Zones
FDI:	Foreign Direct Investment
FTZ:	Free Trade Zone
GMO:	Genetically Modified Organisms
IAL:	International Alliance for Localization
IMF:	International Monetary Fund
INDOPACOM:	Indo Pacific Command
IOC:	Indian Oil Corporation
IOR:	Indian Ocean Region
IPKF:	Indian Peace Keeping Force
ISB:	International Sovereign Bond
ISI:	Industrial substitution industrialization
JEDB:	Janatha Estates Development Board
JSS:	*Jathika Sevaka Sanghamaya* (National Employees Union)
JVP:	*Janatha Vimukthi Peramuna* (People's Liberation Front)
LDO:	Land Development Ordinance
LIOC:	Lanka India Oil Company
LSPA:	Land Special Provisions Act
LSSP:	Lanka *Sama Samaja* Party (Equal Society Party)
LTTE:	Liberation Tigers of Tamil Eelam
MCC:	Millennium Challenge Corporation
MDP:	Mahaweli Development Programme
MEP:	*Mahajana Eksath Peramuna* (People's United Front)
MONLAR:	Movement for National Land Agriculture Reform
MSR:	Maritime Silk Road
NAM:	Non-Aligned Movement
NDO:	New Development Bank
NED:	National Endowment for Democracy

NGO:	Nongovernmental organization
NRT:	Net Resource Transfers
NUMC:	New urban middle class
PPP:	Public Private Partnerships
QUAD:	Quadrilateral Security Dialogue
SLFP:	Sri Lanka Freedom Party
SLPP:	Sri Lanka *Podujana Peramuna* (Sri Lanka People's Front)
SOE:	State-Owned Enterprises
SOFA:	State of Forces Agreement
SPC:	State Plantations Corporation
TNA:	Tamil National Alliance
UF:	United Front (A coalition of SLFP, LSSP and the CP)
UNCTAD:	United Nations Conference on Trade and Development
UNHRC:	United Nations Human Rights Commission
UNP:	United National Party
USAID:	US Agency for International Development
VFA:	Visiting Forces Agreement
VOC:	*Vereenigde Oost-indische Compagnie* (Dutch East India Company)

Figures List

Figure 1.1: Sri Lanka (Ceylon).
Figure 1.2: Countries in Debt Crisis.
Figure 1.3: Wealth inequality in Sri Lanka 1995–2021.
Figure 1.4: Global Psycho-Social Evolution.
Figure 1.5: Paradigm Shift: Psycho-Social Transformation.

Figure 4.1: Annual value transfer, Global South to Global North, constant 2011 dollars (1960–2017).

Figure 5.1: Indian Ocean Region and China's Belt and Road Initiative (BRI) and Maritime Silk Road.
Figure 5.2: China's Global Portfolio.
Figure 5.3: Indian lending to its neighbors. Extended lines of credit ($billion).
Figure 5.4: The National Physical Planning Department Sri Lanka physical spatial structure map for 2050.
Figure 5.5: United States overseas military bases.

Figure 6.1: Tourist arrivals and earnings from tourism.
Figure 6.2: Sri Lanka worker remittances.
Figure 6.3: Colombo Consumer Price Index (year on year percent change).
Figure 6.4: Sri Lanka's foreign debt, 1970–2020.
Figure 6.5: Sri Lankan debt stock by major lenders, US$ million.

Figure 7.1: Domination and the Market Paradigm.
Figure 7.2: Partnership and the Ecological Paradigm.
Figure 7.3: Middle Path Equilibrium Curve.

Tables List

Table 1.1: Sri Lanka: History of Lending IMF Commitments as of September 30, 2018 in thousands of SDRs.
Table 3.1: Sri Lankan population, total and increase, 1800–2020.
Table 3.2: Economic indicators, Sri Lanka, 1950–1970.
Table 3.3: Ceylon foreign debt, 1955–1972.
Table 3.4: Physical quality of life index scores and growth rates for sub-continental nations and China in the mid-1970s.
Table 4.1: Accelerated Mahaweli programme foreign funding.
Table 4.2: Total departures for foreign employment by country of destination, 2005–2009.
Table 4.3: Workers' remittances by regional corridors (%).
Table 4.4: Top twenty foreign investments in Sri Lanka (2002).
Table 4.5: Sri Lanka trade balance and external debt, 1970–2020.
Table 6.1: Details of outstanding international sovereign bonds as of September 30, 2022.
Table 6.2: Trade mis-invoicing: value gaps in trade between Sri Lanka and all trading partners, totals and percentages, 2008–2017 (US$ millions).
Table 6.3: National Endowment for Democracy (NED) Funding for Sri Lanka, 2017–2021.

Appendices List

Appendix 1: Declaration on the Establishment of a New International Economic Order, adopted May 1, 1974 (United Nations resolution 3201)
Appendix 2: Declaration of the Indian Ocean as a Zone of Peace, adopted December 16, 1971 (United Nations resolution 2832)
Appendix 3: The Earth Charter

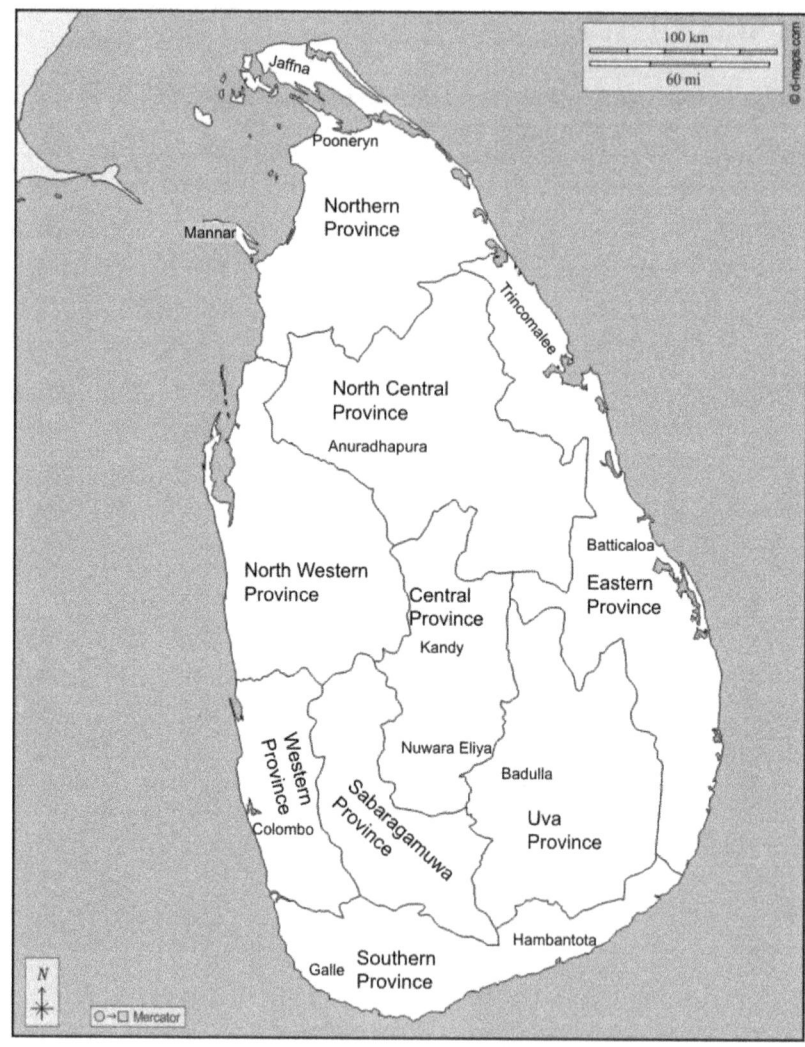

Figure 1.1: Sri Lanka (Ceylon). Source: Adapted from Asoka Bandarage, *Colonialism in Sri Lanka: The Political Economy of the Kandyan Highlands*, 1833–1886. Berlin: Mouton, 1983, xiv.

Chapter 1:
Introduction: Crisis in Sri Lanka and the World

Sri Lanka has been faced with an unprecedented political and economic crisis since the beginning of 2022. On the precipice of a foreign exchange shortage and defaulting on its foreign debt repayment on April 12, 2022, the country has been struggling to pay for its imported food, fuel, medicine, and other basic necessities. According to the dominant narratives, the collapse of the island's economy and accompanying destabilization of the state are attributed to the loss of revenue and supply chain problems associated with the COVID-19 pandemic and the Ukraine conflict; the debt crisis is attributed to China's 'debt trap diplomacy' and the destruction of the economy; and the suffering of the Sri Lankan people is overwhelmingly blamed on corruption and mismanagement by the ruling Rajapaksa family.[1]

A widespread protest movement, coordinated by NGOs, opposition political parties and citizens' groups, led to the resignations of Prime Minster Mahinda Rajapaksa on May 9 and President Gotabaya Rajapaksa on July 14, 2022. Despite the violence and chaos witnessed in the struggle, the departure of the Rajapaksas has been celebrated internationally as a victory for popular democracy.[2] Likewise, notwithstanding the austerities that would be entailed, a bail-out by the International Monetary Fund (IMF) has been accepted as the only way out of the dire economic situation.[3]

On September 1, 2022, debt-trapped Sri Lanka reached a preliminary agreement with the IMF for a 48-month Extended Fund Facility of $2.9 billion. On March 20, 2023, the agreement was finalized.[4] This amount covers only a fraction

---

[1] Ellis-Petersen, Hannah. "'The Family Took over': How a Feuding Ruling Dynasty Drove Sri Lanka to Ruin." *The Guardian*, July 7, 2022, sec. World news. Accessed July 8, 2022. https://www.theguardian.com/world/2022/jul/07/the-family-took-over-how-a-feuding-ruling-dynasty-drove-sri-lanka-to-ruin.
[2] Fonseka, Bhavani. "Sri Lanka's Crisis and the Power of Citizen Mobilization." Carnegie Endowment for International Peace, June 30, 2022. Accessed July 15, 2022. https://carnegieendowment.org/2022/06/30/sri-lanka-s-crisis-and-power-of-citizen-mobilization-pub-87416.
[3] Narayanan, Krithiga. "Why Sri Lanka Defaulted on Its Foreign Debt." dw.com, April 14, 2022. Accessed April 15, 2022. https://www.dw.com/en/sri-lankas-foreign-debt-default-why-the-island-nation-went-under/a-61475596.
[4] "IMF Staff Reaches Staff-Level Agreement on an Extended Fund Facility Arrangement with Sri Lanka." Press Release, September 1, 2022. Accessed November 15, 2022. https://www.imf.org/en/News/Articles/2022/09/01/pr22295-imf-reaches-staff-level-agreement-on-an-extended-fund-facility-arrangement-with-sri-lanka. Uditha Jayasinghe and Andrea Shalal 'Sri Lanka closes in on $2.9 bln IMF deal after China support' Reuters, March 8, 2023. https://www.reuters.com/markets/asia/sri-lanka-says-positive-news-coming-imf-29-bln-package-2023-03-07/ accessed March 16, 2023

https://doi.org/10.1515/9783111203454-007

of the country's outstanding total foreign debt of approximately $50 billion, let alone its immediate survival needs. Despite positive coverage in the international media, the IMF bail-out is a band-aid solution, which will only deepen the country's debt bondage and continue the vicious cycle of external dependence that made it so vulnerable in the first place. This is abundantly clear when one ignores the media amnesia and simply examines the sixteen earlier IMF bail-outs of Sri Lanka since the 1960s (Table 1.1) and the dozens (if not hundreds) of other IMF-driven restructurings that have occurred in ex-colonial countries over the last half century.

Dominant Perspectives

The dominant crisis narrative of rapid news cycles and mainstream media with regard to both Sri Lanka and other debt-trapped countries lacks historical and critical perspective, leaving out a host of complex factors underlying the acceleration of debt crises and economic and social collapse as well as environmental destruction. Instead, it focuses exclusively on the inefficiency and corruption of local leaders which precipitated the crisis and fails to see any solutions beyond IMF restructuring and continuation of the current financial and economic system. Failure to see the global political- economic roots of the crisis contributes to exacerbation of internal conflicts and polarization.

A myopic ethno-nationalist analysis has dominated academic and policy approaches to Sri Lanka for decades.[5] It identifies the roots of the current crisis in terms of ethno-religious politics rather than economics, namely Sinhalese Buddhist nationalism of the Rajapaksa regime and its "corruption, nepotism and short-termism."[6] This perspective also fails to see the relevance of the corruption

---

[5] Bandarage, Asoka. *The Separatist Conflict in Sri Lanka: Terrorism, Ethnicity, Political Economy.* London: Routledge/Taylor & Francis Group, 2009, 5.
[6] DeVotta, Neil. "Behind the Crisis in Sri Lanka – How Political and Economic Mismanagement Combined to Plunge Nation into Turmoil." The Conversation, July 18, 2022. Accessed July 19, 2022. http://theconversation.com/behind-the-crisis-in-sri-lanka-how-political-and-economic-mismanagement-combined-to-plunge-nation-into-turmoil-187137; DeVotta, Neil. "Sri Lanka's Road to Ruin Was Political, Not Economic." Foreign Policy, July 12, 2022. Accessed July 19, 2022. https://foreignpolicy.com/2022/07/12/sri-lanka-crisis-politics-economics-rajapaksa-protest/; Sappenfield, Mark. "The Limits of Ethnic and Religious Nationalism." The Christian Science Monitor, May 12, 2022. Accessed May 19, 2022. https://www.csmonitor.com/Daily/2022/20220512/The-limits-of-ethnic-and-religious-nationalism; Gajaweera, Nalika. "Sri Lanka's Dual Crisis: Ethnic Conflict & the Debt Economy." Jamhoor, May 4, 2022. Accessed May 5, 2022. https://www.jamhoor.org/read/sri-lankas-dual-crisis-ethnic-conflict-the-debt-economy.

Table 1.1: Sri Lanka: History of Lending IMF Commitments as of September 30, 2018 in thousands of SDRs.

Facility	Date of Arrangement	Expiration Date 4/	Amount Agreed	Amount Drawn	Amount Outstanding
Extended Fund Facility	Jun 03, 2016	Jun 02, 2019	1,070,780	715,230	715,230
Standby Arrangement	Jul 24, 2009	Jul 23, 2012	1,653,600	1,653,600	0
Extended Fund Facility	Apr 18, 2003	Apr 17, 2006	144,400	20,670	0
Extended Credit Facility	Apr 18, 2003	Apr 17, 2006	269,000	38,390	0
Standby Arrangement	Apr 20, 2001	Sep 19, 2002	200,000	200,000	0
Extended Credit Facility	Sep 13, 1991	Jul 31, 1995	336,000	280,000	0
Structural Adjustment Facility Commitment	Mar 09, 1988	Mar 08, 1991	156,170	156,170	0
Standby Arrangement	Sep 14, 1983	Jul 31, 1984	100,000	50,000	0
Extended Fund Facility	Jan 01, 1979	Dec 31, 1981	260,300	260,300	0
Standby Arrangement	Dec 02, 1977	Dec 01, 1978	93,000	93,000	0
Standby Arrangement	Apr 30, 1974	Apr 29, 1975	24,500	7,000	0
Standby Arrangement	Mar 18, 1971	Mar 17, 1972	24,500	24,500	0
Standby Arrangement	Aug 12, 1969	Aug 11, 1970	19,500	19,500	0
Standby Arrangement	May 06, 1968	May 05, 1969	19,500	19,500	0
Standby Arrangement	Jun 15, 1966	Jun 14, 1967	25,000	25,000	0
Standby Arrangement	Jun 15, 1965	Jun 14, 1966	30,000	22,500	0
Total			4,426,250	3,585,360	715,230

Source: History of IMF Lending Commitments: Sri Lanka. Available online at: https://www.imf.org/external/np/fin/tad/extarr2.aspx?memberKey1=895&date1key=2018-09-30

in both the government and private sectors and elites of all communities including the US backed pre-Rajapaksa *yahapalanaya* (good governance) regime discussed in Chapter 5. Unfortunately, these oversimplified and binary analyses, built on the duality of 'self versus other' and the assumption that cultural identity is inevitably the root of crises, ironically perpetuate division and inhibit the development of the unity needed to overcome the suffering of all ethno-religious communities due to the crisis.[7]

Both the narrow IMF economic perspective and the identity based political perspective inevitably fail to see the Sri Lankan crisis as an illustrative example of convergent global debt, food, fuel and energy crises facing much of the world. While the details differ from country to country, the patterns of exploitation and subordination which have given rise to global crises are the same. The crisis in Sri Lanka and the world are not separate but one.

Given the depth of the on-going economic collapse in Sri Lanka and other countries, the world is desperate for a fundamental rethinking of not only debt, but the dominant worldview and policies of profit-, technology- and market-driven globalization that are the continuation of colonialist ideology.

A Global Political Economy Perspective

Based on an in-depth Sri Lanka case study, *Crisis in Sri Lanka and the World* demonstrates that these recurring debt and socio-economic crises are rules and not exceptions to our globalized 'culture'. The book places the island's debt and the survival crisis in a broader historical context as the culmination of several centuries of colonial and neo-colonial developments and the disastrous capitalist paradigm of endless growth and profit. It develops a global economy perspective that sees debt not as, "a straightforward number but a social relation embedded in unequal power relations, discourses and moralities…and…institutionalized power."[8]

The debt induced crisis and the socio-economic and environmental collapse is not unique to Sri Lanka. It is a global crisis. In January 2022, the international NGO, Debt Justice pointed out that 54 countries were experiencing debt crises and that debt payments were undermining governments' ability to meet the basic economic and social needs of their citizens (Figure 1.2).[9] The United Nations Conference on

---

[7] Bandarage, Asoka. *The Separatist Conflict in Sri Lanka: Terrorism, Ethnicity, Political Economy.* London: Routledge/Taylor & Francis Group, 2009, 5; Bandarage, Asoka. "Ethno-Religious Tension in the World." In *Global Political Economy and the Wealth of Nations: Performance, Institutions, Problems, and Policies*, edited by Phillip Anthony O'Hara. Routledge Frontiers of Political Economy. London: Routledge, 2004.

[8] Sorg, Christoph. *Social Movements and the Politics of Debt: Transnational Resistance against Debt on Three Continents.* Protest and Social Movements. Amsterdam: Amsterdam University Press, 2022, 18.

[9] Jones, Tim. "Growing Global Debt Crisis to Worsen with Interest Rate Rises." *International Debt Charity | Debt Justice (formerly Jubilee Debt Campaign)*, January 23, 2022. Accessed February 19, 2022. https://debtjustice.org.uk/press-release/growing-debt-crisis-to-worsen-with-interest-rate-rises.

Trade and Development (UNCTAD) Report of 2022 stated that 60 percent of low-income countries and 30 percent of emerging market economies are 'in or near debt distress.'[10] In October 2022, the IMF itself warned that a 'wave of debt crises' may be coming to the Global South in the wake of war, interest rate hikes and the overvalued dollar.[11] Ghana suspended many of its external debt payments in December 2022 following the same by Lebanon, Suriname, Ukraine and Zambia.[12]

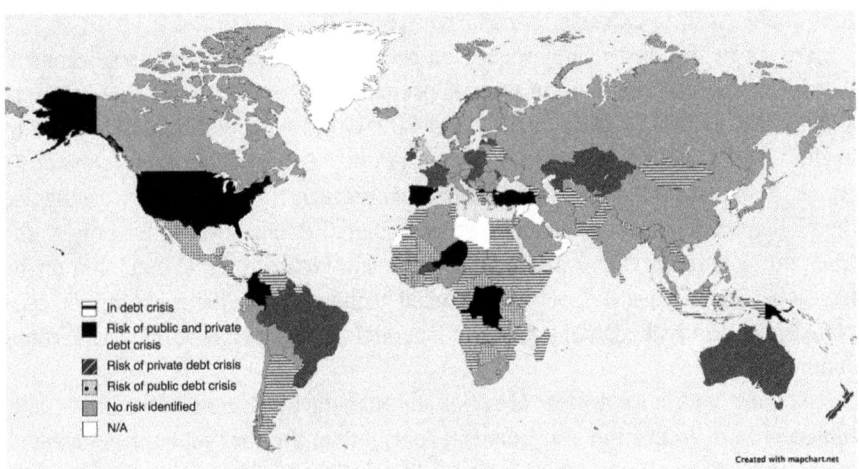

Figure 1.2: Countries in Debt Crisis. Source: Debt Justice, 2022. https://debtjustice.org.uk/countries-in-crisis

As *Crisis in Sri Lanka and the World* discusses, the transfer of financial and resource wealth from poor countries in the global South to the rich countries in the North is not a new phenomenon. It has been an enduring feature throughout centuries of both classical and neo-colonialism. Between 1980 and 2017, developing countries paid out over $4.2 trillion *solely in interest payments*, dwarfing the financial aid they received from the developed countries during that period.[13]

---

10 "Trade and Development Report 2022." *United Nations Conference on Trade and Development*, 2022. https://unctad.org/system/files/official-document/tdr2022_en.pdf.
11 Norton, Ben. "IMF Warns of 'wave of Debt Crises' Coming in Global South, with War, Interest Rate Hikes, Overvalued Dollar." *Multipolarista*, November 13, 2022. Accessed November 14, 2022. https://multipolarista.com/2022/11/13/imf-debt-crises-global-south-interest-dollar/.
12 Larry Elliott, *The Guardian*, 8, January 2023, https://www.theguardian.com/business/2023/jan/08/hedge-funds-holding-up-vital-debt-relief-for-crisis-hit-sri-lanka-warn-economists.
13 Hickel, Jason. "Aid in Reverse: How Poor Countries Develop Rich Countries," *The Guardian*, January 14, 2017, sec. Working in development, https://www.theguardian.com/global-development-pro

The effects of the COVID-19 crisis and the war in the Ukraine have simultaneously worsened the high debt burdens of developing countries whilst vastly increasing the profits of the global financial, technological, food, pharmaceutical and military corporations, deepening global economic inequality, especially in terms of the North-South divide.[14] A 2022 Oxfam Report, *Profiting From Pain*, notes that while the wealth of the world's billionaire class rose as much in 24 months during the Covid crisis as they did in 23 years, over a quarter of a billion of the world's poor could crash to extreme levels of poverty in 2022.[15]

Corporate and financial deregulation occurred with the rise of neoliberalism, that is, market-oriented reform policies promoted by western corporate interests and the multilateral financial institutions – the World Bank and the IMF – starting in the 1970s. It has given rise to financialization, the increasing importance of finance, financial institutions and financial markets in the integrated workings of the global economic system, combined with deindustrialization in wealthy countries and a shift to cheap production and manufacturing labor exploitation in the Global South. Thus, a 'fictitious' financial economy, money chasing money, separated from the real economy producing tangible goods and services, has become dominant.[16]

As more and more aspects of social and planetary life are commoditized and subjected to digitalization and financial speculation, the real value of nature and human activity are further lost. In an October 2022 Report, United Nations Special Rapporteur on the Right to Food, Michael Fakhri, pointed out that food prices are soaring today, not due to a problem with supply and demand but due to price speculation in highly financialized commodity markets.[17] Using 'big data' and artificial

---

fessionals-network/2017/jan/14/aid-in-reverse-how-poor-countries-develop-rich-countries. Accessed November 14, 2022.

14 "Profiting From Pain: The Urgency of Taxing the Rich amid a Surge in Billionaire Wealth and a Global Cost-of-Living Crisis." Press Release. *Oxfam*, May 23, 2022. Accessed June 14, 2022. https://www.oxfam.org/en/research/profiting-pain.

15 Ibid.; Shiva, Vandana. *Oneness vs the 1%: Shattering Illusions, Seeding Freedom*. North Geelong, Victoria: Spinifex Press, 2018.

16 Hudson, Michael. "Financial Capitalism v. Industrial Capitalism." *Michael-hudson.com*, September 3, 1998. Accessed November 02, 2022. https://michael-hudson.com/1998/09/financial-capitalism-v-industrial-capitalism/. Bandarage, Asoka. "Victims of Development." *The Women's Review of Books* 5, no. 1 (October 1987): 1. https://doi.org/10.2307/4020177.

17 Fakhri, Michael. "Interim Report of the Special Rapporteur on the Right to Food." United Nations General Assembly, July 18, 2022. https://undocs.org/A/76/237. Accessed November 14, 2022; Kamal, Baher. "Market Lords, Much More than a War, Behind World's Food Crisis." *Inter Press Service*, November 11, 2022. https://www.ipsnews.net/2022/11/market-lords-much-war-behind-worlds-food-crisis/.

intelligence, a handful of big companies, such as US-owned Cargills and Archer-Daniels-Midland and Chinese state-owned Cofco, have further increased their dominance over the global food chain in recent years.[18]

As transnational corporations develop ever more sophisticated financial and technological networks, these "world empires of the 21st century"[19] control larger shares of global resources and wealth and wield more power over people's lives than most governments. A 2011 study of 43,000 transnational corporations by systems theorists at the Swiss Federal Institute of Technology in Zurich showed that these corporations are "tied together in an extremely entangled web of control,"[20] and that "a large portion of control flows to a small core of financial institutions – among them, Barclays, JP Morgan Chase, Merrill Lynch, Credit Suisse, Goldman Sachs, and China Petrochemical Group – that can be seen as an economic 'super-entity.'"[21]

Moreover, a handful of the largest asset management companies, notably BlackRock (worth US$ 9.5 trillion) and Vanguard (worth US$ 8 trillion) control very large shares in companies operating in practically all the major sectors of the global economy: banking, technology, media, defense, energy, pharmaceuticals, food, agribusiness including seeds, and agrochemicals.[22] The $109 trillion financial

---

[18] Harvey, Fiona. "Small Number of Huge Companies Dominate Global Food Chain, Study Finds." *The Guardian*, September 22, 2022. Accessed September 22, 2022. https://www.theguardian.com/business/2022/sep/22/small-number-of-huge-companies-dominate-global-food-chain-study-finds.
Canfield, Matthew, Molly D. Anderson, and Philip McMichael. "UN Food Systems Summit 2021: Dismantling Democracy and Resetting Corporate Control of Food Systems." *Frontiers in Sustainable Food Systems* 5 (April 13, 2021): 661552. Accessed September 22, 2022. https://doi.org/10.3389/fsufs.2021.661552.
[19] Clairmont, Frederic, and John Cavanagh. "The Rise of the TNC." *Third World Resurgence*, no. 40 (1993): 19.
[20] Vitali, Stefania, James B. Glattfelder, and Stefano Battiston. "The Network of Global Corporate Control." *PloS One* 6, no. 10 (2011): e25995. Accessed September 22, 2022. https://doi.org/10.1371/journal.pone.0025995.
[21] Ibid., Abstract and Appendix, 16.
[22] Edwards, John. "Who Owns Vanguard Group?" Investopedia, September 7, 2022. Accessed October 14, 2022. https://www.investopedia.com/articles/investing/110515/who-are-owners-vanguard-group.asp; Mousseau, Frederic. "38 Billion Dollar Question – Who Is Driving the Destructive Industrial Agriculture Model?" *Oaklandinstitute.org*, September 20, 2022. Accessed October 05, 2022. https://www.oaklandinstitute.org/blog/vanguard-blackrock-driving-destructive-industrial-agriculture-model; Clapp, Jennifer. "The Rise of Financial Investment and Common Ownership in Global Agrifood Firms." *Review of International Political Economy* 26, no. 4 (July 4, 2019): 604–629. Accessed January 05, 2021. https://doi.org/10.1080/09692290.2019.1597755; Cooperman, Jeannette. "How a Company Called BlackRock Shapes Your News, Your Life, Our Future." Common Reader, September 15, 2021. Accessed October 05, 2022. https://commonreader.wustl.edu/how-a-company-called-blackrock-shapes-your-news-your-life-our-future/.

industry that manages and protects money for billionaires, conglomerates and individual shareholders is the largest industry in the world.[23] Although details of this are not available to the public, BlackRock is reportedly the biggest International Sovereign Bond (ISB) creditor of Sri Lanka. Prevention of debt crises require global corporate accountability, transparency and controls on finance capital, which are sorely lacking given the extreme deregulation that prevails.[24]

Currently, international financial institutions. notably the IMF and the World Bank, remain outside political and legal control without even 'elementary accountability'.[25] As critics from the Global South point out, "The overwhelming power of financial institutions makes a mockery of any serious effort for democratization and addressing the deteriorating socioeconomic living conditions of the people in Sri Lanka and elsewhere in the Global South."[26]

A major feature of global financial hegemony and asymmetry is the dominance of the US Federal Reserve and the US dollar in the global financial and monetary system.[27] The denomination of a large proportion of their public debt in US dollars has greatly increased the debt burden of Sri Lanka and other countries with depreciating currencies.[28]

Financial liberalization advanced further when interest rates dropped in the richer countries after the 2008 global financial crisis. It led to increased borrowing by developing countries from private international capital markets through

---

[23] Sutton, Christopher N., and Beth Jenkins. "The Role of the Financial Services Sector in Expanding Economic Opportunity." *Harvard Kennedy School*, 2007. https://www.hks.harvard.edu/sites/default/files/centers/mrcbg/programs/cri/files/report_19_EO%2BFinance%2BFinal.pdf Accessed October 05, 2022.
[24] Vieira, Luiz. "Debt Crisis Prevention: We Need to Talk about Capital Controls." *Bretton Woods Project*, December 9, 2021. Accessed November 05, 2022. https://www.brettonwoodsproject.org/2021/12/debt-crisis-prevention-we-need-to-talk-about-capital-controls/.
[25] Ananthavinayagan, Thamil Venthan. "Sri Lanka and the Neocolonialism of the IMF." *The Diplomat*, March 31, 2022. Accessed October 05, 2022. https://thediplomat.com/2022/03/sri-lanka-and-the-neocolonialism-of-the-imf/.
[26] Ibid.; Bello, Walden. "How the IMF and World Bank Turned a Pandemic into a Public Relations Stunt." *Foreign Policy In Focus*, October 12, 2020. Accessed October 15, 2022. https://fpif.org/how-the-imf-and-world-bank-turned-a-pandemic-into-a-public-relations-stunt/.
[27] Costantini, Orsola. "Dollar Dominance Is Financial Dominance." *Institute for New Economic Thinking*, November 23, 2022. https://www.ineteconomics.org/perspectives/blog/dollar-dominance-is-financial-dominance.
[28] Hudson, Michael. "Financial Capitalism v. Industrial Capitalism." *Michael-hudson.com*, September 3, 1998. Accessed October 15, 2022. https://michael-hudson.com/1998/09/financial-capitalism-v-industrial-capitalism/.

ISBs, which come with high interest rates and short maturation periods.[29] In fact, much of Sri Lanka's borrowing in recent years has not been from China, as is commonly reported, but from ISBs backed by the USA and the EU. In total, 81 percent of Sri Lanka's current debt is held by the West and its allies.[30]

IMF debt financing requires countries to meet its familiar structural adjustment conditions: privatization of state-owned enterprises (SOEs), cutbacks of social safety nets and alignment of local economic policy with US and other Western interests.[31] As this book demonstrates, the interventionist powers of the Bretton Wood institutions – the IMF and the World Bank – have "all along been rooted in empire and colonialism."[32]

Colonialism and Neocolonialism

Colonialism commonly refers to the direct physical and political-economic domination of one country by another while the related concept of imperialism broadly refers to the way one country exercises economic, military and political domination without significant permanent control of a subjugated country.[33] According to calculations of historian Philip Hoffman, by 1800, even before the Industrial Revolution, Europeans already controlled about 35 percent of the world including regions in Sri Lanka; and by 1914, they had gained control of 84 percent of the world.[34] If the 'internal colonization' of indigenous and other non-white populations within the imperialist countries in the Global North are also included, the

---

29 Vieira, Luiz. "Debt Crisis Prevention: We Need to Talk about Capital Controls." Bretton Woods Project, December 9, 2021. Accessed January 2, 2022. https://www.brettonwoodsproject.org/2021/12/debt-crisis-prevention-we-need-to-talk-about-capital-controls/.
30 *Department of External Resources.* "Foreign Debt Summary." Accessed December 25, 2022. http://www.erd.gov.lk/index.php?option=com_content&view=article&id=102&Itemid=308&lang=en. *The Dynamics of Distress and Debt in Emerging Markets: Sri Lanka's Struggling Economy.* ECornell Keynotes, 2022. Accessed November 15, 2022. https://www.youtube.com/watch?v=0CX_odCq20I.
31 IMF. "IMF Members' Quotas and Voting Power, and IMF Board of Governors." Accessed December 25, 2022. https://www.imf.org/en/About/executive-board/members-quotas.
32 Steinmetz-Jenkins, Daniel. "The Rotten Roots of the IMF and the World Bank." *The Nation,* June 15, 2022. Accessed October 25, 2022. https://www.thenation.com/article/culture/the-rotten-roots-of-global-economic-governance/.
33 Kohn, Margaret, and Kavita Reddy. "Colonialism." In *The Stanford Encyclopedia of Philosophy,* edited by Edward N. Zalta, Summer 2022. Metaphysics Research Lab, Stanford University, 2022. Accessed September 25, 2022. https://plato.stanford.edu/archives/sum2022/entries/colonialism/.
34 Hoffman, Philip T. *Why Did Europe Conquer the World?* Princeton University Press, 2015, 2–3.

extent of colonialism would be even more[35]. Neocolonialism broadly refers to continued economic and financial control of former colonies by imperialist powers (governments, corporations and multilateral institutions) without direct political control.[36]

Current realities cannot begin to be understood without a context of colonialism and neocolonialism.

Crisis in Sri Lanka and the World places the island's current crisis in the historical context of global interventions by European colonial powers, their collaboration with local elites, the instigation of ethnic and religious conflicts and the manipulation and repression (i.e., 'counter-insurgency') of local resistance. The political conquest of the island by successive European powers (the Portuguese, Dutch and British) starting in 1505, introduced a new economic order based on little but the maximization of profit for the imperial countries and a handful of local collaborators.

Exports from colonies such as Ceylon (colonial name given the island) during the mercantilist phase of European colonialism was crucial for capital accumulation and the rise of industrialism in Britain and other imperialist nations. During the mercantile period of European colonialism, the European nations were buyers of colonial produce such as spices, sugar, as well as slaves; colonial India also provided manufactured goods such as cotton textiles.

With the advance of industrialization, imperial nations were turned into sellers of machine-produced goods and the colonies were turned into suppliers of raw materials for European industry and food for European populations, while becoming markets for European goods. This process had far-reaching effects on the economies and social structures of colonial countries like Ceylon, which had been left relatively intact during the preceding centuries of European mercantilist expropriation.[37]

Chapter 2 in *Crisis in Sri Lanka and the World* discusses how the development of export agriculture and the import of food and other essentials under the British turned the island into a dependent 'peripheral' unit of the global capitalist economy. Adopting ideologies of modernization and development and theories of comparative advantage, the capitalist imperative integrated self-sustaining indigenous,

---

[35] Robert Blauner, *Racial Oppression in America*, New York: Harper and Row, 1972; Patrick D. Anderson, "Some critics argue that the Internal Colony Theory is outdated. Here's why they're wrong", MROnline, https://mronline.org/2019/06/14/some-critics-argue-that-the-internal-colony-theory-is-outdated-heres-why-theyre-wrong/.

[36] https://www.britannica.com/topic/neocolonialism.

[37] Bandarage, Asoka. *Colonialism in Sri Lanka: The Political Economy of the Kandyan Highlands, 1833–1886*. New Babylon, Studies in the Social Sciences. Berlin: Mouton, 1983, 66–67.

peasant, and regional economies into the growing global economy, through the appropriation of land, natural resources, and labor for export production.

Monocultural agriculture, mining, and other export-based production disturbed traditional patterns of crop rotation and small-scale subsistence production that were more harmonious with the regional ecosystems and cycles of nature. As the book discusses in chapter 2, plantation development contributed to deforestation, loss of biodiversity and animal habitats, for example, setting the stage for the contemporary human-elephant conflict. While small groups of the native population prospered through their cooperation with colonialism, most people became poor, indebted, and dependent on the vagaries of the global market for their sustenance.[38]

The victory of industrial capitalism over mercantilism was echoed in the economic thinking of classical economics. 'Laissez-faire et laissez-aller' became its slogan. As economist Harry Magdoff has pointed out, Adam Smith's theory, expounded in *The Wealth of Nations* in 1776, that trade restrictions did not increase, but decreased national wealth, was adopted as the official ideology of the British government in 1846, fifty-six years after Smith's death.[39] However, neither in colonial Ceylon nor elsewhere in the colonies or the imperial countries was capitalist enterprise 'free.' Close partnerships with the state as well as religious establishments and the media and academia were as central to maintaining economic hegemony then as they are today. Both colonialism and neo-colonialism are simultaneously economic, political, cultural and psychological projects of domination and subordination.

The transformation of indigenous worldviews and consciousness to forms consistent and compliant with imperialism was and is integral to colonialism. Conversion to Christianity was used by the Portuguese, Dutch and British to both justify colonial rule and to divide and control local populations in most all colonies, including Sri Lanka. It has continued to be an important tool of domination in the neo-colonial period, although foreign-funded NGOs, such as those supported by the US National Endowment for Democracy (NED) (Table 6.3, pages 181–184), and social media have become the main means of soft power and propaganda by governments and tech corporations, particularly in influencing and controlling the thinking of younger generations.

Sri Lanka's transition to accelerated capitalist development began with the introduction of the 'Open Economy' in 1977 discussed in chapter 4. In fact, Sri Lanka

---

38 Ibid., 145.
39 Magdoff, Harry. "Colonialism (c. 1450–c.1970)." In *The New Encyclopaedia Britannica*, 15th edition, 890. Chicago: Encyclopaedia Britannica, 1992.

was the first country in Asia to be subjected to neoliberalism. Foreign loans for massive infrastructure projects, the expansion of export production and tourism, an influx of foreign NGOs as well as significant outflow of 'cheap labor' to the Middle East further increased the island's economic and cultural dependence on external forces.[40] On top of this, the costly armed conflict with the separatist Liberation Tigers of Tamil Eelam (LTTE), and the corresponding militarization of the economy and society, deepened the country's debt and dependence on external political and economic interests, and continued to further divide the population.[41] As elsewhere in the militarized Global South and in the Global North, identity politics exaggerated and weaponized by vested interests diverted attention away from the common economic problems faced by people across ethnic and religious divides.[42]

In the Post-War period following the end of the 30-year armed conflict in 2009, discussed in chapter 5, the Rajapaksa regime pursued a policy of building costly infrastructure projects borrowing mostly from China. Capital financialization following the global financial crisis of 2008 increased international borrowing, encouraging overconsumption. The Central Bank bond scam, the biggest public financial fraud in the country's history, and extensive ISB borrowings during the *yahapalanaya* regime (2015–2019) added to Sri Lanka's long term debt and economic troubles. With the listing of Sri Lanka as a 'Middle-Income Country' by the World Bank in July 2019, the country also lost access to concessionary loans with lower interest given to poorer countries.[43] These developments, together with numerous loans and neoliberal policies of the IMF and global political and corporate institutions, contributed to growing debt burden as well as increased income and wealth inequality in Sri Lanka and across the world.

---

[40] Bandarage, Asoka. "Women and Capitalist Development in Sri Lanka, 1977–87." *Bulletin of Concerned Asian Scholars* 20, no. 2 (June 1, 1988): 57–81. https://doi.org/10.1080/14672715.1988.10404449.
[41] Bandarage, Asoka. *The Separatist Conflict in Sri Lanka: Terrorism, Ethnicity, Political Economy.* London: Routledge/Taylor & Francis Group, 2009, Chap. 4–6.
[42] Bandarage, Asoka. "Ethno-Religious Tension in the World." In *Global Political Economy and the Wealth of Nations: Performance, Institutions, Problems, and Policies,* edited by Phillip Anthony O'Hara. Routledge Frontiers of Political Economy. London: Routledge, 2004.
[43] Jayasinghe, Uditha. "Sri Lanka to Keep 'middle-Income' Status but Seek Concessional Loans." *Reuters,* October 11, 2022. Accessed October 15, 2022. https://www.reuters.com/markets/asia/sri-lanka-cabinet-approves-downgrade-low-income-country-2022-10-11/.

Class Inequality in Sri Lanka

Collaboration with external financial and economic interests has benefitted only a small class of elite in Sri Lanka, as it has in other countries around the world. Widespread tax evasion and foreign exchange plunder by an "incestuous business community-politicians-customs nexus" from different ethnoreligious communities has been a major cause for loss of government revenue during successive governments in Sri Lanka.[44] Global Financial Integrity, a Washington DC. based NGO, has reported that Sri Lankan businesses in the import-export trade 'plundered' US$ 36.833 billion between 2009 and 2017 through "intentional, dodgy invoicing and stashing the foreign exchange earnings offshore."[45]

According to 2020 data, the top one percent of the Sri Lankan population owns 31 percent of total personal wealth, top 10 percent own 64.4 percent, whereas the bottom 50 percent of the population own less than 4 percent of total wealth in the country, a fact that needs consideration in addressing the current crisis and worsening poverty (Figure 1.3).[46]

Geopolitical Rivalry and Neoliberalism

In reaction to the gross omissions of political, economic and historical context in the media, *Crisis in Sri Lanka and the World* explores Sri Lanka's present economic crisis – the worst since the country's political independence from the British – in the context of the accelerating neocolonial geopolitical conflict between China and

---

[44] Aponso, Revan. "The Pandora Papers and the Exposure of Sri Lanka's Elite." *The Economics Review*, February 22, 2022. Accessed October 15, 2022 https://theeconreview.com/2022/02/22/the-pandora-papers-and-the-exposure-of-sri-lankas-elite/; Alecci, Scilla. "Sri Lankan Power Couple Piled up Luxury Homes, Artworks and Cash Offshore as Ruling Family Rose and Rose." *The International Consortium of Investigative Journalists*, October 4, 2021. Accessed October 10, 2021. https://www.icij.org/investigations/pandora-papers/sri-lanka-rajapaksa-family-offshore-wealth-power/.

[45] "Financial Flows and Tax Havens: Combining to Limit the Lives of Billions of People." *Centre for Applied Research, Norwegian School of Economics; Global Financial Integrity; Jawaharlal Nehru University; Instituto de Estudos Socioeconômicos; Nigerian Institute of Social and Economic Research*, December 2015. Accessed November 2, 2022. https://www.gfintegrity.org/wp-content/uploads/2016/12/Financial_Flows-final.pdf.

[46] WID – World Inequality Database. "Sri Lanka." Accessed December 25, 2022. https://wid.world/country/sri-lanka/; Himal Southasian. "The Human Dimension to Sri Lanka's Economic Crisis," October 14, 2022. Accessed October 15, 2022. https://www.himalmag.com/sonali-deraniyagala-human-dimension-to-sri-lankas-economic-crisis-2022/.

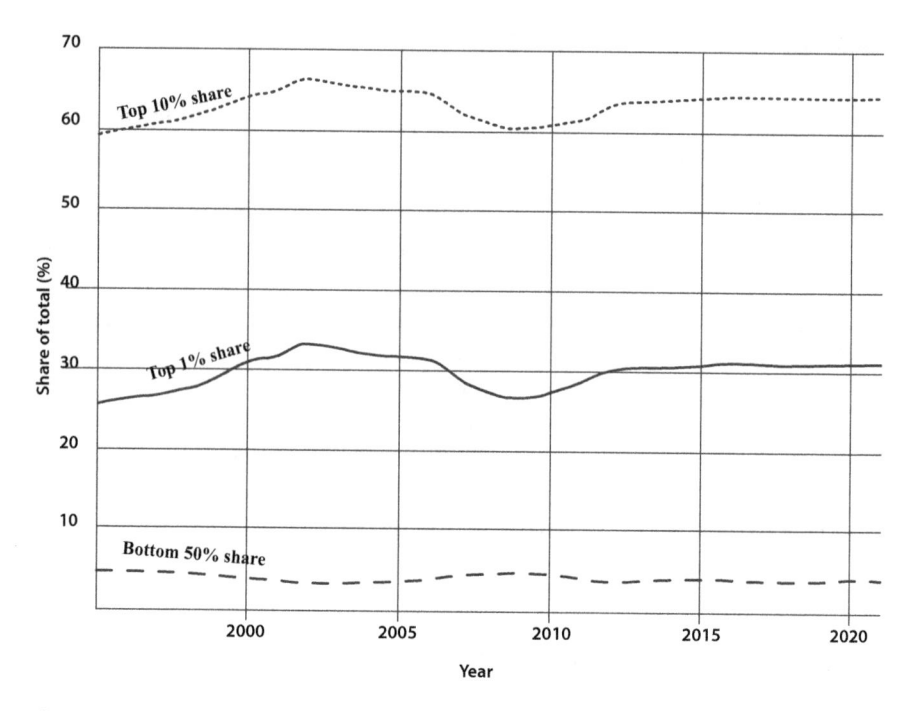

Figure 1.3: Wealth inequality in Sri Lanka 1995–2021. Source: World Inequality Database, "Wealth Inequality, Sri Lanka, 1995–2021." https://wid.world/country/sri-lanka/

the USA in the Indian Ocean.[47] Many other countries across the world are also caught in the neocolonial super power competition to control their natural resources and strategic locations.

As discussed in chapter 5, Sri Lanka has been integrated into China's massive Belt and Road Initiative since 2005, through controversial projects such as the development of Port City in Colombo and the Hambantota port. The US, in turn, seeks to include Sri Lanka in its Indo-Pacific Project through military pacts as well as the Millennium Challenge Corporation (MCC) Compact. Though the compact remains officially unsigned, its policies are clearly being pursued to accelerate the process of state land alienation and commoditization that began under the British in the early decades of the nineteenth century. More regionally, India too is seeking control over Sri Lanka's ports and natural resources for development by Indian cor-

---

[47] Bandarage, Asoka. "Neocolonialism and Geopolitical Rivalry in Sri Lanka." *Asia Times*, January 29, 2020. Accessed January 29, 2020. https://asiatimes.com/2020/01/neocolonialism-and-geopolitical-rivalry-in-sri-lanka/. Jacques, Martin. *When China Rules the World: The Rise of the Middle Kingdom and the End of the Western World.* London: Allen Lane, 2009.

porations, such as the Adani Group, with dubious environmental records. These initiatives have serious implications for Sri Lanka's sovereignty, ecology, and economic self-sufficiency.

Following the resignation of Gotabaya Rajapaksa, who came to power in 2019 in an overwhelming electoral victory, Ranil Wickramasinghe, a politician who was conclusively rejected at the last parliamentary elections, was appointed as Sri Lanka's President. Wickramasinghe is closely allied with US and western political and economic interests and is now expected to facilitate not only the IMF bail-out of the Sri Lankan economy but the greater incorporation of the island into the Indo-Pacific Strategy of the US and the western alliance.

In light of such an apparently undemocratic transition, there is much speculation as to whether the debt default and political destabilization in Sri Lanka were 'staged' or intentionally precipitated to further the US's 'Pivot to Asia' policy, the Indo-Pacific Strategy and the Quadrilateral Alliance (USA, India, Australia and Japan) in its competition to confront China's $1 trillion Belt and Road Initiative and counter China's presence in Sri Lanka.[48]

Were the people's discontent and anger at the Rajapaksa regime itself manipulated and fueled by 'digital colonialism' carried out by social media strategists backed by geopolitical interests?[49] What role was and is being played by NGOs funded by external forces, such as US and EU member embassies, or the key US 'soft power' agencies, the US Agency for International Development (USAID) and the National Endowment for Democracy (NED)?[50]

In other words, to what extent were Sri Lanka and her people victims of an externally manipulated 'shock doctrine' and a regime change operation, sold to the world as internal disintegration caused by local corruption and incapability?[51] This book is not able to provide definitive answers to this nor the other complex issues described above. However, it considers the available credible evidence to raise important questions that are fundamental to strengthening sovereignty and political and economic democracy in Sri Lanka and the world at large.

---

[48] Rajasingham-Senanayake, Darini. "A Staged Default: Sri Lanka's Sovereign Bond Debt Trap and IMF's Spring Meetings Amid Hybrid Cold War." *IDN-InDepthNews*, April 24, 2022. Accessed May 15, 2022. https://archive-2017-2022.indepthnews.info/index.php/the-world/asia-pacific/5249-a-staged-default-sri-lanka-s-sovereign-bond-debt-trap-and-imf-s-spring-meetings-amid-hybrid-cold-war-part-1.
[49] Waduge, Shenali D. "Is Sri Lanka Being Digitally Colonised?" *Sunday Observer*, June 11, 2022. Accessed October 15, 2022. https://www.sundayobserver.lk/2022/06/12/news-features/sri-lanka-being-digitally-colonised.
[50] *Red Fire*. "Sri Lanka: US Backed Colour Revolution in Colombo," July 20, 2022. Accessed July 25, 2022. https://redfireonline.com/2022/07/20/sri-lanka-us-backed-colour-revolution-in-colombo/.
[51] Klein, Naomi. *The Shock Doctrine*. New York: Henry Holt and Co., 2010.

Ecological and Social Collapse

Additional to historical and geopolitical context, *Crisis in Sri Lanka and the World* also places the island's current economic and political collapse in context of the much greater existential crisis: the ecological collapse faced by Sri Lanka and the world.

Like many other countries in the Global South with a relatively miniscule carbon footprint, according to the Global Climate Risk Index, Sri Lanka is among the countries most affected by extreme weather events. Given the predicted rise in sea level, the island is faced with massive coastal erosion, with adverse impact on nearly 55 percent of the shoreline. In a 2015 report, the Internal Displacement Monitoring Center identified Sri Lanka "as the country with the highest relative risk of being displaced by disaster in South Asia."[52] Notwithstanding these realities, destructive activities by locals and the competitive expansion of polluting industries by the world's biggest carbon polluters – i.e., China, USA and India (who are, incidentally, also nuclear powers) – continue apace, threatening the survival of the natural environment and the people.

Given the worsening crises around the world, the current trajectory of growth and development must be questioned. Can the climate crisis and environmental and social collapse be redressed within the capitalist system, driven by unbridled growth and militarism?[53] Can corporate environmentalist attempts led by the World Economic Forum and BlackRock sustain the planet, humanity and uncontrolled corporate profitmaking at the same time?[54] Can strategies to shift climate mitigation from the industrialized Global North to the poor countries of the Global South through, for example, debt-for-nature swaps suffice to avert global climate catastrophe?[55] Could the environment be protected without protecting people, their food sources, livelihoods and communities, including those in Sri Lanka?

---

52 Ginnetti, Justin, and Chris Lavell. "The Risk of Disaster-Induced Displacement in South Asia." Technical Paper. *Internal Displacement Monitoring Centre*, April 2015. Available at: https://www.internal-displacement.org/publications/the-risk-of-disaster-induced-displacement-in-south-asia.
53 Mander, Jerry. *The Capitalism Papers: Fatal Flaws of an Obsolete System*. Berkeley, CA: Counter Point, 2012.
54 World Economic Forum. "Over 120 Global Companies Adopt ESG Reporting Metrics." Accessed December 25, 2022. https://www.weforum.org/impact/stakeholder-capitalism-esg-reporting-metrics/. BlackRock. "Larry Fink's Annual 2022 Letter to CEOs." Accessed December 25, 2022. https://www.blackrock.com/corporate/investor-relations/larry-fink-ceo-letter.
55 Kessel, Andrew and Bill Mosely. "Debt-for-Nature Swaps: A Critical Approach," 2006. Accessed December 25, 2022. https://www.macalester.edu/geography/wp-content/uploads/sites/18/2012/03/kessel.pdf.

Is the transnational capitalist class attempting to create a still more advanced technocapitalist, neoliberal and neo-colonialist 'Great Reset', whereby all natural resources come under external corporate control and ordinary local people in Sri Lanka and around the world become superfluous and expendable?[56]

Ecological and Collective Alternatives

Former UK Prime Minister, Margaret Thatcher, a champion of neoliberalism, declared that "there is no alternative" to neoliberal capitalism as the world's economic system.[57] As critic Mark Fisher also observed, for many contemporary people who have not known an alternate reality, "it's easier to imagine the end of the world than the end of capitalism."[58]

Yet, if we can step back and see beyond the Overton window of our imperial age, there are indeed alternatives to the extreme neoliberal capitalism of globalization, a very short-lived phenomenon in the history of human evolution. Humanity has spent much of its history, perhaps as much as 99 percent as foragers. The low level of technological development and control over nature necessitated cooperation and equality among band members in what has been characterized as 'primitive communism'.[59] The domestication of animals and technological achievements led to settled agricultural societies – the Neolithic Revolution-some 10,000 years ago. With the evolution of social hierarchies -gender, class and ethnicity based inequalities- and states, dominant groups claimed greater rights to resources and social surplus based on heredity and religion and used institutionalized violence to maintain social control. (Figure 1.4)

The scientific revolution of the seventeenth century laid the basis for the development of western science and technology and the capitalist economy. The trajectory of development that emerged under mercantilism 500 year ago, and advanced greatly since the Industrial Revolution some 250 years later, integrated the entire world within one interconnected market and technological system.

---

[56] *World Economic Forum*. "The Great Reset." Accessed December 25, 2022. https://www.weforum.org/great-reset/.
[57] Byrne, George. "There Is No Alternative." *Sociology Lens*, January 21, 2015. Accessed March 25, 2022. https://www.sociologylens.net/article-types/opinion/there-is-no-alternative/14356.
[58] Fisher, Mark. *Capitalist Realism: Is There No Alternative?* Zero Books. Winchester, UK Washington, USA: Zero Books, 2009; Bandarage, Asoka "Women in Development: Liberalism, Marxism and Marxist-Feminism", *Development and Change*, vol. 15, no. 4, 1984, pp. 495–515.
[59] Cited in Bandarage, Asoka. *Sustainability and Well-Being: The Middle Path to Environment, Society and the Economy*. Basingstoke: Palgrave Macmillan, 2013, 36.

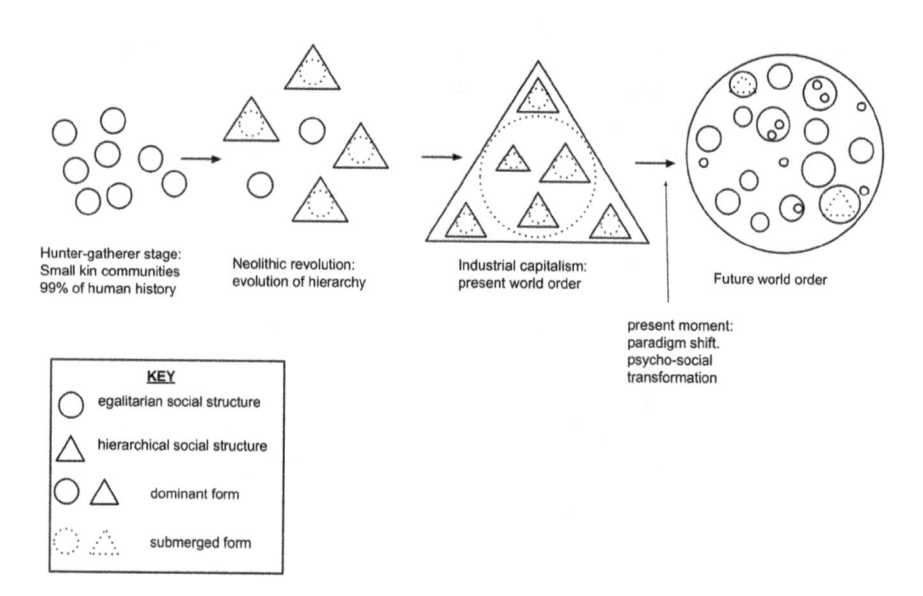

Figure 1.4: Global Psycho-Social Evolution. Source: Asoka Bandarage, Women, Population and Global Crisis: A Political-Economic Analysis. London: Zed Books, 1997, 314.

These developments undermined traditional community relations and the planet itself was reduced to a resource for exploitation. The challenge facing the world today is not a return to a foraging or feudal past but to envision and shift towards ecological and collective alternatives.[60] (Figure 1.4)

From its earliest stage, capitalist development was resisted both in the imperialist countries and the colonies by those desiring alternative, sustainable and democratic modes of social and economic organization. As discussed in chapter 2, this was the case in Sri Lanka, where peasants, Buddhist monks and others challenged the economic and cultural changes imposed by the colonial state and the plantation economy during the nineteenth century. Later, over the course of the twentieth century, labor movements and working-class struggles emerged around the world, including in Sri Lanka demanding higher wages and other benefits for the long-exploited plantation and urban workers. These ordinary histories of resistance are usually left out of history books, giving the 'victor-distorted' narrative that still underlies mainstream worldviews.

---

60 Helena Norberg-Hodge, *Ancient Futures: Learning from Ladakh.* San Francisco: Sierra Club Books, 1991, passim.

Following political independence from the British in 1948, like other newly 'independent' colonies, Sri Lanka naturally sought strategies for decolonization during the Cold War, discussed in chapter 3. Initially, policies of economic, political and cultural nationalism prevailed, including import substitution, nationalization of plantations and the abolition of the privileges of both Christian missionary schools and the English language. Despite the country's size, Sri Lanka played leadership roles in both the Non-Aligned Movement (NAM) from the 1950s to the 70s, and in UNCTAD, established in 1964, to promote developing countries' interests in global trade. In addition to external pressures, the exacerbation of ethnic rivalries set in place during the colonial era drastically disrupted the unity needed for the country to move forward.

Although scarcely reported in the local or global media, Sri Lanka's historical tradition of resistance against foreign domination and exploitation continues in the contemporary era, albeit under increasingly difficult economic conditions and political repression. As documented in chapter 5, environmental and social justice activists have challenged the wide array of controversial external interventions by China, India and the United States which threaten environmental and human wellbeing as well as the sovereignty of the country. Regrettably, the 2022 *aragalaya* (struggle, in Sinhala) protest which emerged from genuine economic grievances, failed to develop an analysis beyond the 'Gota, Go Home' demand for Gotabaya Rajapaksa to resign. Influenced by local and external interests with their own agendas, the protestors failed to develop a cohesive awareness and critique of the global political economy and the financial system at the root of the country's crisis.

Unfortunately, dominant political power in our era is about propaganda, control of narratives and exploiting ignorance and fear. *Crisis in Sri Lanka and the World* seeks to demonstrate the practical need for a fundamental questioning of the values, assumptions and misrepresentations of the neoliberal model of social and economic organization and its manifestations in Sri Lanka and the world. As such, we need a critical examination of the rhetoric of unregulated economic growth, ever-growing disparity of wealth, and technological domination as a 'false-god' solution to the problems created by the former. We also need to fundamentally rethink many of the assumptions that preceded neoliberalism; those of the Scientific Revolution, the Enlightenment and the capitalist growth model.

As discussed in this book, the current crisis in Sri Lanka as well as in the world has evolved over the last 500 or so years of European conquest and in particular the last 250 years of global capitalist development. The balance of the whole planetary organism and the survival of life are at stake. Indeed, environmental destruction, poverty and violence are not peculiar to the current period. But never have social problems been as thoroughly interconnected as they are today within the global economy and the technosphere. In order to resolve seemingly separate problems in different locations, such as Sri Lanka, we must necessarily take a global approach in addition to local approaches. Moreover, as Albert Einstein remarked, "The significant problems we have cannot be solved at the same level of thinking with which we created them".[61]

Transformation of Consciousness

Beginning in the pre-modern era, social hierarchy and domination accompanied the growth of technological and material development. The sources of the current economic crisis, in fact, lie in unbridled economic growth and the twin forces of capital and technology which also reflect the global entrenchment of a 'culture' based on social hierarchy and dominance, at the top of which are a local and global elite. A fundamental shift from the prevailing pyramidal paradigm of domination and exploitation towards a circular paradigm of partnership and balance is called for both at the local and global levels. (Figure 1.5) To help identify the social and psychological structures of the decaying paradigm and to envision the values and direction towards a sustainable paradigm are the broad objectives of this book.

This work seeks to move beyond popular, convenient and repetitive neoliberal solutions, as well as conventional left critiques of corporate capitalism and ecological critiques of globalization.

It recognizes the imperative for a reorientation of the much-neglected ethical dimension of modern economics and society. Although competition, domination, and conflict seem to characterize today's world; altruism, partnership, and harmony have been present from the first human societies. Indeed, the challenge facing both Sri Lanka and the world is to develop ethical reasoning and to incorporate it in policymaking at the local and global levels (Earth Charter, Appendix 3).[62]

Technology and the market *per se* are not the problems; it is the underlying consciousness and the intention that direct their advancement. At the root of the crisis, we face is a disconnect between the exponential growth of the profit-driven economy and a lack of development in human consciousness, i.e., in morality, empathy, and wisdom. Indeed, our challenge today is not merely political, but human and ethical; how we see and conduct ourselves personally and collectively

---

[61] Cited in Bandarage, Asoka. *Sustainability and Well-Being: The Middle Path to Environment, Society and the Economy.* Basingstoke: Palgrave Macmillan, 2013, 73.
[62] Paul, Richard, and Linda Elder. *The Miniature Guide to Understanding the Foundations of Ethical Reasoning.* Foundation for Critical Thinking, 2005, 4.

```
        Ecocrisis                              Ecology

    Domination Paradigm                  Partnership Paradigm

    Crisis in Sri Lanka and the          Harmony in Sri Lanka and
            World                               the World
```

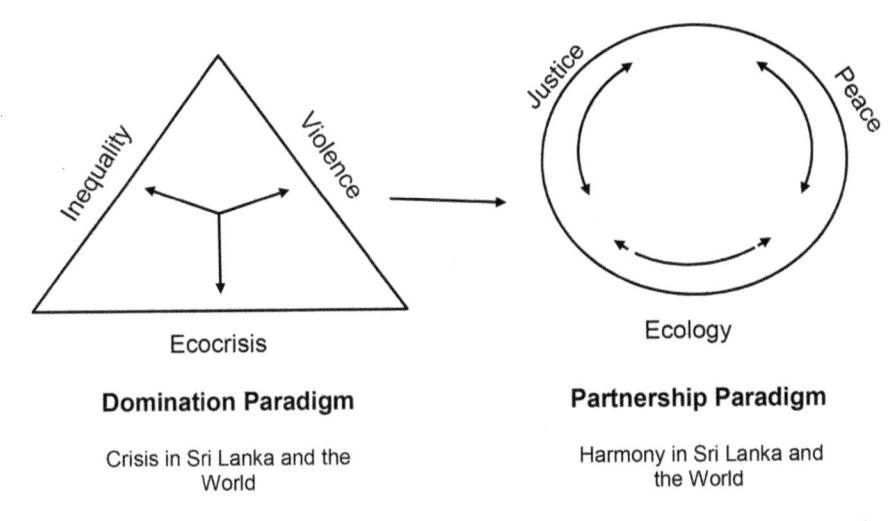

Figure 1.5: Paradigm Shift: Psycho-Social Transformation. Source: Asoka Bandarage, Women, Population and Global Crisis: A Political-Economic Analysis. London: Zed Books, 1997, 3.

toward all life and nature, other animals and each other. The central idea of the ecological and collective approach is that we are part of the Earth, not apart and separate from it just as our minds and bodies are connected and not separate.[63]

Ultimately, *Crisis in Sri Lanka and the World* identifies the deeper psychological dualism of 'self versus other', upon which all systems of domination are constructed. In chapter 7, the book emphasizes the need to rethink dualism, domination and the unregulated market paradigm to find a balanced path of human development, based on interdependence, partnership and the ecological paradigm. Such a path of development would uphold the ethical principles necessary for long-term survival: rational use of natural resources, appropriate technology, balanced consumption, equitable distribution of wealth, and livelihoods for all.[64]

---

[63] Ibid., 5.
[64] Schumacher, E. F. *Small Is Beautiful: Economics as If People Mattered.* New York: HarperCollins, 2010.

Chapter 2:
Pre-Colonial Era to Colonial Rule and Capitalism: C. 3 BCE to 1948

Most western media and academic accounts attribute the persistent and profound problems of hunger, poverty and conflict in the Global South to internal corruption, mismanagement and ignorance. This is an extension of the narrative that portrays the pre-modern histories of these regions as technologically primitive and ideologically backward. However, in many cases, the pre-colonial histories of non-western societies were highly complex and their cultures far more advanced than those of the colonizing west's values of supremacy, domination and material profit.

An enlightened philosophy of ecological and social protection accompanied the introduction of the Buddha's teaching to Sri Lanka by Arahant Mahinda, the son of the Indian emperor Asoka, in 3 BCE. The island's ancient chronicles have recorded the advice of the Arahant to the local king Devanampiyatissa who was out deer hunting in Mihintale at the time of his arrival: "O Great King, the birds of the air and the beasts have as equal a right to live and move about in any part of the land as thou. The land belongs to the people and all living beings: thou art only the guardian of it."[1]

A stone inscription found in Mihintale establishes that the king commanded the people of the area not to kill animals or destroy trees. In fact, the Mihintale Wildlife sanctuary in Sri Lanka is believed to be the first such sanctuary in the world.[2]

The ancient irrigation system of the *Raja Rata* civilization of Sri Lanka (c. 3 BCE to c. early 13 CE) was described as an "amazing system of waterworks" by Arnold Toynbee in his survey of world history.[3] Unlike modern irrigation systems, the 2000-year-old Sri Lankan system was geared for both irrigation and soil conservation. Excess monsoon rainfall was conserved in gigantic tank reser-

---

[1] Cited in Mendis, D. L. O. *Eppawala: Destruction of Cultural Heritage in the Name of Development.* 1st ed. Colombo: Sri Lanka Pugwash Group, 1999, xxviii.

[2] AmazingLanka.com. "Mihintale Sanctuary: The First Wildlife Sanctuary in the World," February 22, 2014. Accessed September 25, 2022. https://amazinglanka.com/wp/mihintale-sanctuary/.

[3] Cited in Mendis, D. L. O. *Eppawala: Destruction of Cultural Heritage in the Name of Development.* 1st ed. Colombo: Sri Lanka Pugwash Group, 1999, xxvii; see also, Seneviratna, Anuradha. *The Springs of Sinhala Civilization: An Illustrated Survey of the Ancient Irrigation System of Sri Lanka.* New Delhi: Navrang, 1989.

voirs and the soil itself through earth embankments.[4] Water from perennial rivers was diverted into the reservoirs, some of them "four thousand acres in extent" and made available for agriculture through intricately connected distributor channels.[5] "Below each tank and each great channel were hundreds of little tanks, each the nucleus of a village."[6] This system, "executed with meticulous regard for environmental concerns," was an early demonstration of the compatibility of technological and economic development and environmental conservation.[7]

The underlying principle of environmental and human protection was articulated by King Parakramabahu (1153–1186 AD) who said that "not even a little water that comes from the rain is to flow into the ocean without being made useful to man"[8] Parakramabahu, credited as "the greatest water harvesting earthworks engineer of all time,"[9] is estimated to have constructed or restored 165 dam walls, 3910 canals, 163 major and 2376 minor reservoirs and 328 stone sluices and to have repaired 1,969 embankment breaches.[10] The hydraulic system developed in this period gave rise to a prosperous economy – the 'granary of the East,'[11] enabling the early Sinhalese to cultivate their staple rice and other crops across the large flatlands of the island's dry zone for over a thousand years. Rice cultivation was considered a noble profession and the cultivator caste were given the highest status in the Sinhala caste hierarchy.[12]

An elaborate social and administrative organization based on a division of labor according to caste and service to the state (rājākariya) was employed to construct and maintain the complex irrigation system. The village tank and the village temple defined many aspects of life with Buddhist monks serving the role of educators and cultural transmitters.

---

[4] Mendis, D. L. O. *Eppawala: Destruction of Cultural Heritage in the Name of Development.* 1st ed. Colombo: Sri Lanka Pugwash Group, 1999, 2.
[5] Ibid., xxvii.
[6] Ibid., xxvii.
[7] Ibid., xxvii.
[8] Ibid., xxviii.
[9] Mackintosh, Craig. "Letters from Sri Lanka – The World's Largest Water Harvesting Earthworks Project." *The Permaculture Research Institute*, August 10, 2009. Accessed September 9, 2022. https://www.permaculturenews.org/2009/08/10/the-worlds-largest-water-harvesting-earthworks-project/.
[10] Ibid.; De Silva, Kingsley M. *History of Ceylon*, Vol. 2. Colombo: Ceylon University Press, 1960, 556.
[11] Sallay, Alvin. "Bleak Outlook for What Was Once the 'Granary of the East.'" *The Sunday Times Sri Lanka*, February 5, 2017. Accessed February 24, 2017. http://www.sundaytimes.lk/170205/business-times/bleak-outlook-for-what-was-once-the-granary-of-the-east-227053.html.
[12] Bandarage, Asoka. *Colonialism in Sri Lanka: The Political Economy of the Kandyan Highlands, 1833–1886.* New Babylon, Studies in the Social Sciences. Berlin: Mouton, 1983, Appendix 2, 363–365.

The economic surplus facilitated the development of extensive Buddhist religious edifices – monasteries, stupas, stone sculptures -and the like, built with great architectural and artistic skills and religious devotion. Sri Lanka with its advanced Buddhist culture, which first committed the Buddha's teachings into writing in 1 BCE was the center of a cosmopolitan network of collaboration across Buddhist countries in medieval Asia.[13]

The Sinhala language and *Theravada* Buddhism created a distinct culture unique to the island. There was continuous intermixture with royalty and others from India and Hindu traditions co-existed. However, Buddhism remained the only means of maintaining a distinct identity by Sri Lankan rulers.[14]

The Buddhist ethos of tolerance and equality moderated the pernicious effects of 'oriental despotism' helping legitimize the political-economic hierarchy including feudal and monastic landlordism and caste-based exploitation. Due to the Buddhist influence, the Sinhalese caste structure was spared the harsh religious sanctions prevalent within Hinduism.[15]

In addition to the arrival of peaceful Buddhist monks, traders and immigrant settlers from India and other parts of Asia, the ancient and medieval history of the island was characterized by frequent warfare among royal dynasties and violent external intervention. Due to a confluence of factors including South Indian invasions, Tamil settlements starting in 7 CE and successive civil wars, the dry zone civilization and the vast irrigation system collapsed by the 13 CE. The oppressive invasion by Magha from India with Tamil and Kerala mercenaries paved the way for Dravidian 'occupation and colonization' of northern and eastern regions and the establishment of the Jaffna Kingdom in the middle of 13 AD.[16] In the face of growing political insecurity, famine and pestilence, the Sinhala kingdoms shifted to the southwestern wet zone regions of the island.

In the wet zone, the land was cultivated without the use of the elaborate irrigation system developed in the dry zone.[17] Yet, evidence from the last independent Sinhala kingdom in the interior highlands, the Kandyan Kingdom (1473–1815), re-

---

13 Gunawardana, R. A. L. H. "Cosmopolitan Buddhism on the Move: South India and Sri Lanka in the Early Expansion of Theravāda in Southeast Asia." In *Fruits of Inspiration: Studies in Honour of Prof. J.G. de Casparis*, edited by Marijke J. Klokke and Karel R. van Kooij. Gonda Indological Studies. Groningen: Egbert Forsten, 2001.
14 Bandarage, Asoka. "Ethno-Religious Evolution in Pre-Colonial Sri Lanka." *Ethnic Studies Report* XXI, no. 2 (July 2003): 103–147, 118.
15 Ibid., 113.
16 Intirapālā, Kārttikēcu. "Dravidian Settlements in Ceylon and the Beginnings of the Kingdom of Jaffna." PhD Thesis, University of London, 1965, 32.
17 De Silva, Kingsley M. *History of Ceylon*, Vol. 2. Colombo: Ceylon University Press, 1960, 720.

veals that, at the local village level, ready access to land for wet rice and crop-rotating dry grain cultivation, systems of communal labor and relative economic autonomy and self-sufficiency were maintained.[18] A simple life of relative contentment, aligned with the rhythms of nature and ethical Buddhist teaching seems to have prevailed.[19]

As in other pre-capitalist societies, land was plentiful and labor scarce. Land per se had no value, only the expenditure of labor on the land created value.[20] A complex system of hierarchical, customary rights to land prevailed with communal rights to village land including pasture and forest, eclipsing individual rights.[21] Individuals were allowed and even encouraged to open new land for cultivation by the kings and the feudal aristocracy who could exact tribute on cultivated land.

Prior to the advent of the Europeans, there was a thriving trade network in the Indian Ocean operating across economies in Asia, Africa and Europe, a multipolar exchange network, rather than a 'single global economy.' Indian Ocean trade had a multi-ethnic composition, "with no evidence of religious animosities among the various trading groups."[22]

Sri Lanka was an important destination for Indian, Arab, and Chinese merchants. The island was known for the world's finest cinnamon along with 'gems, pearls, ivory, elephants, turtle shells, and cloth'. Ships came from across the Asian and Mediterranean worlds to obtain these products and to deliver goods brought from other countries.[23] Being a self-sufficient economy, imports were mostly limited to luxury items such as silk and velvet textiles, horses, perfumes, tobacco and wines used by the royal families.[24]

---

18 Bandarage, Asoka. *Colonialism in Sri Lanka: The Political Economy of the Kandyan Highlands, 1833–1886.* New Babylon, Studies in the Social Sciences. Berlin: Mouton, 1983, Chap. 2.
19 Saparamadu, S.D. "Introduction." In *An Historical Relation of Ceylon,* by Robert Knox, XVI–XVII, 1st ed. Ceylon Historical Journal, v. 6, July 1956–April 1957, nos. 1–4. Maharagama, Ceylon: Printed at Saman Press, 1958.
20 Knox, Robert. *An Historical Relation of Ceylon.* 1st ed. Ceylon Historical Journal, v. 6, July 1956–April 1957, nos. 1–4. Maharagama, Ceylon: Printed at Saman Press, 1958, 22.
21 Peiris, G. H. *Sri Lanka: Land Policy for Sustainable Development to Strengthen the Struggle for Survival.* First edition. Boralasgamuwa: Visidunu Publication, 2017, 41.
22 Perera, Nihal. *Decolonizing Ceylon: Colonialism, Nationalism, and the Politics of Space in Sri Lanka.* New Delhi: Oxford University Press, 1999, 21–23.
23 Hancock, James. "European Discovery & Conquest of Sri Lanka." *World History Encyclopedia,* August 31, 2022. Accessed December 15, 2022. https://www.worldhistory.org/article/2064/european-discovery-conquest-of-sri-lanka/.
24 Ellawala, H. *Social History of Early Ceylon,* Colombo: Department of Cultural Affairs, Ceylo, 1969, 141–142.

Some foreign traders settled in the beautiful island, including Arab Muslims and Indo-Arabs from the opposite coasts of India. By the beginning of 12 AD Muslims became settled communities in Sri Lanka's coastal areas.[25]

European Colonization

Beginning in the late 15 century, much of the world – the Americas, Asia, Africa and the Middle East – came under the direct control of competing European naval powers.

With the appearance of Europeans in the Indian seas as soldiers, merchants and missionaries, and the subsequent European conquest and rule of India and Sri Lanka, South Indian incursions into the island were halted. Arab expansion and Islamic conversion in Asia and the Indian Ocean region that started around 12 AD also came to a halt with the arrival of Europeans in early 16 A.D. European imperialism has dominated the Indian Ocean region and Sri Lanka ever since. The Portuguese christened the island *Ceilão*, from the Roman *Sielen*, and the British anglicized this to Ceylon. Both names were adapted from the island's ancient name, *Sihala Dipa* (*dipa* meaning island), and the Arab name, *Serendib* derived from Sihala, changed to *Selan/Seran* and *dipa* to *dib*.[26]

Geopolitical rivalry over Sri Lanka is not new. Given her strategic location in the ancient East-West maritime trade route and the military value of her natural seaports, especially Trincomalee on the east coast, Sri Lanka fell victim to conflicts between rival external powers, conflicts which had no direct relevance to the island itself. Like today, the island's conquest and subordination were not always due to the military superiority of colonizing forces. Dissension and rivalry among local rulers and intrigue and deception on the part of colonizers have always been significant factors.

Sri Lanka was subjugated by three successive European powers earning the dubious distinction of having had the longest historical experience of western colonization in Asia: Portuguese (1501–1658), Dutch (1658–1796) and British (1796–1948). It is no coincidence that Portugal, the Netherlands and Britain were also major Atlantic slave-traders who bought and transported people captured from Africa to the Americas to work as forced labor.

---

[25] Bandarage, Asoka. "Ethno-Religious Evolution in Pre-Colonial Sri Lanka." *Ethnic Studies Report* XXI, no. 2 (July 2003): 103–147, 132.
[26] Ibid., 112.

The early periods of European rule in Sri Lanka were characterized by mercantilism, essentially 'buying cheap and selling dear,' predominantly through pillage and plunder. In the later period, particularly after the British conquest and 'pacification' of the whole island, a systematic policy of capitalist economic development was introduced. From the beginning, colonial political, economic and cultural interests and policies were closely intertwined and mutually reinforced. European traders, soldiers and missionaries worked closely together and there was little differentiation between economic, political and religious spheres.

Being a tiny minority on a foreign land requires imperialists to nurture local collaboration from the start of the colonial project. As in other frontiers, a collaborator class was created through extensive use of economic incentives providing lucrative employment and social mobility. Though taking different forms, local elite collaboration remains an essential feature of neo-colonialism.

The European colonizers sought ways to control the local population and prevent unity that might undermine their power. To this end, they encouraged existing social divisions, introduced new sources of dissension and dealt harshly with individuals or groups that even remotely threatened their authority. 'Divide and conquer' – via surveillance, co-optation, provocateurism, destabilization and harsh counterinsurgency – was and remains core to imperialist policy.

Some of the early Europeans familiar with the island, such as the Englishman Robert Knox, who was detained in the Kandyan kingdom (between 1660–1679), were astounded by the genuinely liberal attitude of the island's Buddhist majority and their openness to (seemingly) contradictory religious views.[27] However, Sinhala Buddhist nationalism and its legacy of resistance against foreign invasion was seen as the greatest threat to colonial rule. Thus, a primary strategy of domination was the conversion of natives to Christianity through force or indoctrination/education, and a shift of identity and allegiance from their own history and culture to European culture and the colonial state. The transformation of consciousness that begun under colonialism continues in various forms in Sri Lanka as in other parts of the world today.

A short survey of the Sri Lankan experience of three different European colonial powers illustrates the common strategies used, each with a different flavor, but ultimately centered on a world view of superiority, domination, greed and subjugation. The discussion is meant to help understand the colonial origins of the current political and economic crisis in Sri Lanka and other neocolonial countries.

---

27 Knox, Robert. *An Historical Relation of Ceylon*. 1st ed. Ceylon Historical Journal, v. 6, July 1956–April 1957, nos. 1–4. Maharagama, Ceylon: Printed at Saman Press, 1958, 317.

Portuguese Colonialism (1505–1658)

The first European invasion of Sri Lanka in 1505 by the Portuguese was accidental when they bumped into Sri Lanka while pursuing Arab ships in the Indian Ocean 'to plunder and destroy'.[28] However, after discovering the geographical profitability of the island and her commercial value and taking advantage of conflicts among the local rulers, the Portuguese consolidated their power over Sri Lanka's maritime areas. Using their vessels, which had great firepower and speed, the Portuguese implemented a policy of military and commercial control that began to undermine the Indian Ocean region's "long-standing, relatively open trade competition."[29]

Instead of competing in existing networks, the Portuguese used force to monopolize trade by constructing their own trading system. They prevented indigenous merchants from selling goods to anyone other than themselves. Such monopolistic trading was radically new in Asia, where prior to the arrival of the Portuguese, the Indian Ocean had multiple, multi-ethnic trading networks.[30]

In Sri Lanka, Portuguese officials compiled *tombos*, or land registers, to provide detailed statements of landholdings, nature of ownership, crops grown and tax obligations. They used the existing Sinhalese caste system of service tenure to secure the essential produce of the land. Portuguese monopolies in cinnamon and elephants provided good profits, as did the trade in pepper and betel nuts (areca nuts) but the enormous pressure they put on local producers caused great hardship and popular hostility.[31] Oppressive resource extraction also resulted in extensive destruction of plant and animal life.

As historian Paul E. Peiris observed, when the Portuguese arrived in Sri Lanka, they found "a contented race, and a fairly prosperous country" but, "they succeeded in producing nothing but chaos."[32] The Portuguese introduced the use of can-

---

[28] Hancock, James. "European Discovery & Conquest of Sri Lanka." *World History Encyclopedia*, August 31, 2022. https://www.worldhistory.org/article/2064/european-discovery-conquest-of-sri-lanka/.

[29] britanica.com. "Sri Lanka – The Portuguese in Sri Lanka (1505–1658)." Accessed December 25, 2022. https://www.britannica.com/place/Sri-Lanka/The-Portuguese-in-Sri-Lanka-1505-1658.

[30] Perera, Nihal. *Decolonizing Ceylon:* op.cit, 21–23.

[31] britanica.com. "Sri Lanka – The Portuguese in Sri Lanka (1505–1658)." Accessed December 25, 2022. https://www.britannica.com/place/Sri-Lanka/The-Portuguese-in-Sri-Lanka-1505-1658.

[32] Cited in Weeraratna, Senaka. "Portuguese Era Dark Chapter in Sri Lanka's History." *Sunday Observer*, April 16, 2021. https://www.sundayobserver.lk/2021/04/18/impact/portuguese-era-dark-chapter-sri-lanka%E2%80%99s-history.

nons, as well as guns and other smaller firearms which spread quickly "once the rulers of local kingdoms grasped the significance of the new technology."[33]

Portuguese attitude towards the majority Buddhist culture as well as the minority Hindu and Muslim cultures was openly destructive. Buddhist monasteries were destroyed across the island and Roman Catholic churches were built on the very same spots. Some of the world's oldest 'university-type' centers of learning, such as, Totagamuwa and Karagala, were destroyed and their collections of invaluable books were torched and the incumbents killed.[34]

In contrast to the religious liberalism of Buddhists, religious fanaticism characterized most European Christians on the island. Portuguese on the island had instructions from Lisbon and Goa (their headquarters in Asia) "to begin by preaching, but, that failing, to proceed to the decision of the sword."[35] Incidentally, it also describes the soft power first/hard power later approach of more recent US imperialism, also rooted in European and Christian exceptionalism. This, the Portuguese did with an extreme "rapacity, bigotry, cruelty and inhumanity," unparalleled by subsequent European powers in Sri Lanka and a callousness which made "no distinction between man, woman and child."[36] As Pali scholar G.P. Malalasekara stated, "had they not been found recorded in the decades of their own friendly historians", the Portuguese atrocities on the island would be considered too revolting to have been true. … Babes were spitted on the soldiers' pikes…their mothers … were tortured to death. Men were thrown over bridges for the amusement of the troops…"[37]

It is well to remember that the Portuguese who engaged in raids to capture African slaves were also the first Europeans to buy slaves from West Africa and transport them across the Atlantic in 1526.[38] The 'Doctrine of Discovery' issued by Pope Alexander VI in 1493 and other Papal Bulls stated that any land that

---

[33] britanica.com. "Sri Lanka – Dutch Rule in Sri Lanka (1658–1796)." Accessed December 25, 2022. https://www.britannica.com/place/Sri-Lanka/Dutch-rule-in-Sri-Lanka-1658-1796.
[34] Malalasekara, G. P. *The Pāli Literature of Ceylon*. Kandy, Sri Lanka: Buddhist Publication Society, 1994, 265; Goonatilake, Susantha. *A 16th Century Clash of Civilizations: The Portuguese Presence in Sri Lanka*. 1st ed. Colombo: Vijitha Yapa Publications, 2010.
[35] Emerson Tennent quoted in Vimalananda, Tennakoon. *Buddhism in Ceylon under the Christian Powers and the Educational and Religious Policy of the British Government in Ceylon, 1797–1832*. Colombo: M.D. Gunasena & Co. Ltd., 1963, xxiv.
[36] Malalasekara, G. P. *The Pāli Literature of Ceylon*. Kandy, Sri Lanka: Buddhist Publication Society, 1994, 261.
[37] Ibid., 1261–262.
[38] *Lowcountry Digital History Initiative*. "The Trans-Atlantic Slave Trade." Accessed December 25, 2022. https://ldhi.library.cofc.edu/exhibits/show/africanpassageslowcountryadapt/introductionatlanticworld/trans_atlantic_slave_trade.

was not inhabited by Christians was available to be 'discovered,' claimed and exploited by Christian rulers.[39] This ideology supported the dehumanization of conquered people, their dispossession, forced assimilation and annihilation. It fueled white supremacy, allowing white colonizers to claim themselves as agents of divine design possessing cultural, if not genetic superiority.[40] Genocidal campaigns against non-white people conducted under Papal instructions, including in Canada and the Americas, have led to apologies by enlightened Popes in recent years. However, no such apologies have yet been forthcoming for Sri Lanka.[41]

Under the Portuguese, no offices could be held by anyone who did not profess Catholicism. All rights and privileges including government appointments, land ownership, inheritance, taxation benefits and education were granted exclusively to those who converted to Catholicism and/or attended Catholic schools.[42] Conversion to Christianity broke up the cultural unity and weakened the Sinhala Buddhists, who, until then, had maintained their Sinhala and Buddhist identities as one.

Don Juan Dharmapala, the last Sinhala king in the coastal lowlands and some members of the aristocracy and some low castes converted to Catholicism for purposes of political and economic expediency. Dharmapala lost all popular support when he abandoned his ancestral faith. Portuguese rule was hated and provoked widespread opposition in the coastal lowlands.[43] Many escaped to the independent Kandyan kingdom in the central highlands and turned to the Kandyan kings to rescue them from the brutal Portuguese.

---

[39] National Institute of Health, National Library of Medicine, Native Voices – Native Peoples' Concepts of Health and Illness. "AD 1493: The Pope Asserts Rights to Colonize, Convert, and Enslave." Accessed December 25, 2022. https://www.nlm.nih.gov/nativevoices/timeline/171.html; Gilder Lehrman Institute of American History. "The Doctrine of Discovery, 1493." Accessed December 25, 2022. https://tinyurl.com/4ffem99u.

[40] Cbc.ca. "Indigenous Activist Urges the Vatican to Revoke 500-Year-Old Documents," December 14, 2018. Accessed November 15, 2022. https://www.cbc.ca/radio/tapestry/why-religion-1.4934033/indigenous-activist-urges-the-vatican-to-revoke-500-year-old-documents-1.4940937.

[41] Povoledo, Elisabetta, and Ian Austen. "Pope Apologizes to Indigenous People of Canada." nytimes.com, April 1, 2022. Accessed December 15, 2022. https://www.nytimes.com/2022/04/01/world/europe/pope-apology-indigenous-people-canada.html.

[42] Scott, David. "Conversion and Demonism: Colonial Christian Discourse and Religion in Sri Lanka." Comparative Studies in Society and History 34 (1992), 319–320; De Silva, Chandra Richard. The Portuguese in Ceylon, 1617–1638. H. W. Cave, 1972.

[43] Nyrop, Richard F. Sri Lanka, a Country Study. 1st ed. Area Handbook Series. Washington, D.C.: Headquarters, Dept. of the Army, U.S. G.P.O., 1970; Goonewardena, K.W. The Foundation of Dutch Power in Ceylon, 1638–1658. Djambatan: Netherlands Institute for International Cultural Relations, 1958, 320.

The kings of the Kandyan Kingdom sought the help of the Dutch who were then seeking to expand their own power over the Indian Ocean. By signing a 'Treaty of Peace' with the king of Kandy in 1766, the Dutch agreed to help drive out the Portuguese in return for a Dutch monopoly of the lucrative cinnamon trade.[44] The Dutch aided the Kandyan rulers to banish the Portuguese but subsequently refused to give the captured ports and land to the Kandyan king. Instead, the Dutch East India Company established their own rule over the island's coastal lowlands. As the Sinhala proverb goes: "ginger was given only to get chilies in return."

Dutch Colonialism (1658–1796)

Dutch rule in Sri Lanka was executed by the Dutch East India Company (VOC; Vereenigde Oost-indische Compagnie), a trading company established to protect Dutch trade interests in the Indian Ocean. Founded from a grant from the state of the Netherlands, the VOC possessed significant governmental powers, including the ability to wage war and establish colonies.[45]

While continuing monopolies in the trade of cinnamon and other commodities from the island, the Dutch pursued a more systematic mercantilist policy than the Portuguese. They began the integration of Sri Lanka into the emerging world economy, developing agricultural production solely focused on external trade rather than local subsistence, including cinnamon and betel, lacquer, coconut oil and ropes of coconut fibers. Natural resources, such as gemstones from mines in the Central Highlands and pearls from fisheries on the northwestern coast as well as sea products, such as cowrie and conch shells, were also important items in the export trade. Elephants were among the most profitable items of Dutch trade given the consistently high demand in India where elephants were valued as war vehicles.[46]

Manipulating traditional caste-based *corvee* labor for purposes of export production, the Dutch put enormous pressure on the *salagama* caste to increase the

---

[44] Dewaraja, Lorna Srimathie. "Appendix: Treaty of Peace between the Dutch and the King of Kandy, 1766." In *The Kandyan Kingdom of Sri Lanka, 1707–1782*. Colombo: Lake House Investments, 1988.

[45] Ames, Glenn Joseph. *The Globe Encompassed: The Age of European Discovery, 1500–1700*. Upper Saddle River, N.J.: Pearson Prentice Hall, 2008, 102–103.

[46] britanica.com. "Sri Lanka – Dutch Rule in Sri Lanka (1658–1796)." Accessed December 25, 2022. https://www.britannica.com/place/Sri-Lanka/Dutch-rule-in-Sri-Lanka-1658-1796.

output of cinnamon, the primary Dutch export from Sri Lanka.[47] The Dutch also brought laborers from the Malabar coast in South India to expand cinnamon production. Dutch rulers in the lowlands pressured Kandyan kings to have cinnamon peeled and delivered solely to the VOC and give it monopolistic control of other products from the Kandyan territories, such as ivory, pepper, cardamom, coffee, areca nuts and beeswax.[48] The VOC encouraged the cultivation of two new cash crops – tobacco and coffee – and built canal systems to meet the need for transport to expand trade.

The policies of the Dutch Reformed Church in Sri Lanka were less barbaric than those of the Catholic Portuguese, but similarly intolerant of other faiths.[49] The ardent Calvinist Dutch proclaimed various decrees to prohibit the practice of non-Calvinist religions including Catholicism, which had been propagated by the Portuguese, and proceeded to eliminate their places of worship. Buddhist monks were not allowed to remain or officiate at Buddhist ceremonies in 'Dutch' territories.[50]

Being Christian was a 'normal condition of service' under the Dutch, as it was under the Portuguese, and largely continued to be under the British as well. Interfering in the domestic lives of the locals, the Dutch required all inhabitants in the Dutch held territories to be baptized and married according to Christian sacrament in order to ensure their hold over property, rights of inheritance and even the legitimacy of their children.[51] Sinhala officials who did not carry out these orders were severely punished.[52]

There was "tremendous and continual opposition" to Dutch policies of religious conversion and efforts to transform Sinhala society along Calvinist lines. Inspectors of Dutch churches and schools in the Galle and Matara areas, in particular, faced various forms of local resistance, non-cooperation and opposition including refusal to send children to Dutch schools and disrespect towards Dutch priests.[53]

---

[47] Scott, David. "Conversion and Demonism: Colonial Christian Discourse and Religion in Sri Lanka." Comparative Studies in Society and History 34 (1992), 331, 346.

[48] Article 8,9,10,11 in Treaty of 1766, cited in Dewaraja, Lorna Srimathie. *The Kandyan Kingdom of Sri Lanka, 1707–1782*. Colombo: Lake House Investments, 1988, 160.

[49] Vimalananda, Tennakoon. *Buddhism in Ceylon Under the Christian Powers and the Educational and Religious Policy of the British Government in Ceylon, 1797–1832*. M.D. Gunasena & Company Limited, 1963, xxxvii–xxxviii.

[50] Paranavitana, K. D. "Suppression of Buddhism and Aspects of Indigenous Culture under the Portuguese and the Dutch." *Journal of the Royal Asiatic Society of Sri Lanka* 49 (2004): 1–14.

[51] Scott, David. "Conversion and Demonism, op.cit., 325.

[52] Ibid., 332.

[53] K.W. Gunawardena, *The Foundation of Dutch Power in Ceylon, 1638–1658*, Amsterdam: Djambatan for the Netherlands Institute for International Cultural Relations, 1958, *passim*.

Recognizing the threat that Sinhala Buddhist nationalism posed to their hegemony, the Dutch sought to keep the Sinhalese in the interior and the lowlands divided and instigated conflicts between them. Although their policies did not always work, the Dutch Governor in 1674 took delight in saying that, "We have learnt the art of setting the Sinhalese in the lowlands against the highlanders so that very few of our own people need be used."[54]

Whereas hierarchical ownership rights to land had prevailed in pre-colonial Sri Lanka, the introduction of Roman-Dutch law in Dutch controlled areas (subsequently the whole country) contributed to the spread of private property rights. However, the Dutch penchant for upholding separate legal codes for different ethno-religious communities, such as the *Thesawalamai* for the Tamils in Jaffna and the Islamic law for the Muslim minority mitigated against the development of a single code of law for all subjects. The Dutch codified *Thesawalamai* as a traditional law of the Tamil inhabitants in Jaffna peninsula in 1707, which prohibited property in the region from passing on to people outside of the Jaffna Tamil community.[55] Separate legal codes helped solidify ethnic and religious differences and separatist political demands in later periods.[56] Utilizing and manipulating local cultural differences to their own political advantage, the Dutch used Muslim and Chetty (a mercantile group from South India) forces to put down Sinhala rebellions in the interior regions of Māhara, Mābolē and Kelaniya in the 1760s.[57]

The loss of Sri Lanka by the Dutch East India Company and conquest by the British East India Company was preceded by complex rivalry and battles among competing European powers. An armed confrontation known as the Battle of Trincomalee was fought over the famed seaport in the northeast between the British and the French in 1782. Subsequently, the British East India Company captured Sri Lanka from the Dutch during the wars of the French Revolution (1792–1801). When the Netherlands came under French control, the British moved into Sri Lanka from India and with the signing of the Treaty of Amiens with France in 1802, British possession of maritime Ceylon was confirmed.[58]

---

54 Cited in Dewaraja, Lorna Srimathie. *The Kandyan Kingdom of Sri Lanka, 1707–1782*. Colombo: Lake House Investments, 1988, 119.
55 https://www.britannica.com/place/Sri-Lanka/Dutch-rule-in-Sri-Lanka-1658-1796.
56 De Silva, K. M. *Managing Ethnic Tensions in Multi-Ethnic Societies: Sri Lanka, 1880–1985*. Lanham, MD: University Press of America, 1986, 17; britanica.com. "Thesavalamai." Accessed December 26, 2022. https://www.britannica.com/topic/Thesavalamai.
57 Roberts, Michael. "Ethnicity after Edward Said: Post-Orientalist Failures in Comprehending the Kandyan Period of Lankan History." In *Confrontations in Sri Lanka: Sinhalese, LTTE & Others*, 1st ed. Colombo: Vijitha Yapa Publications, 2009.
58 britanica.com. "Sri Lanka – Dutch Rule in Sri Lanka (1658–1796)." Accessed December 25, 2022.

British Colonialism, Mercantile Period (1796 – c. 1832)

At its peak, the British East India Company was the largest corporation in the world; a joint-stock company founded in 1600 to trade in the Indian Ocean region, it had its own armies and seized control of large parts of the Indian subcontinent, Southeast Asia and the Persian Gulf. Following the Indian Rebellion of 1857 against East India Company rule, the British imperial state nationalized the Company and took control over India.[59]

According to the Encyclopedia Britannica, the East India Company began using and transporting slaves in Asia and the Atlantic in the early 1620s.[60] According to the Company's archives, however, its involvement in the slave trade started in 1684, when a Captain Robert Knox was ordered to purchase and transport 250 slaves from Madagascar to St. Helena.[61] This slave trader was most likely the same Robert Knox who published *An Historical Relation of Ceylon* in 1681, following his detainment in the Kandyan Kingdom from 1660 – 1679, and died a wealthy man in Britain in 1720.[62]

Sri Lanka came under East India Company rule in 1796, but after just two years, due to local rebellions against the Company's harsh taxation policies, a dual system of rule was put in place. The Company controlled commerce while law and administration were put in the hands of a Governor accountable to both the Company and the British government.[63]

From very early on in their rule in the maritime provinces, the British sought to break what they called "the powerful combination …between the Modeliars (native chiefs) and the Principal Priests (Buddhist monks)," who they feared to be a threat to their interests.[64] Counterinsurgency took the form of a "wide extension" of Christianity, and Governor Maitland (1805 – 1812) was explicit of this objective,

---

[59] *The Diary of Samuel Pepys.* "British East India Company." Accessed December 26, 2022. https://www.pepysdiary.com/encyclopedia/2494/.
[60] britanica.com. "East India Company." Accessed December 26, 2022. https://www.britannica.com/topic/East-India-Company.
[61] Hefler, Ela. "'We Want Able Blacks': The Role of African Slavery in the East India Company, 1658 – 1757," April 12, 2017. Accessed December 15, 2022. https://vmctest.nomadcyb.org/humanities/ela-hefler/.
[62] Knox, Robert. *An Historical Relation of Ceylon.* 1st ed. Ceylon Historical Journal, v. 6, July 1956 – April 1957, nos. 1 – 4. Maharagama, Ceylon: Printed at Saman Press, 1958.
[63] Luscombe, Stephen. "Ceylon Colony." britishempire.co.uk. Accessed December 26, 2022. https://www.britishempire.co.uk/maproom/ceylon.htm.
[64] Guruge, Anaanda, ed., *Return to Righteousness: A Collection of Speeches, Essays, and Letters of the Anagarika Dharmapala* Colombo: Ministry of Education and Cultural Affairs, Ceylon, 1965, xxviii.

stating that the strategy was "inseparably connected with my political office."[65] A further British counterinsurgency strategy was the manipulation of the mistrust between the Sinhala majority and the Muslim minority with Muslims recruited as 'spies, guides and auxiliary troops' in their military campaigns against the Sinhala Kingdom in Kandy in 1803–1805 and in 1815.[66]

Conquest of Kandy (1815)

With the conquest of the Kandyan Kingdom, which covered much of the island, the entire country came under British control in 1815. The British had initially arrived offering support to a faction of the Kandyan nobility to get rid of their tyrannical king, Sri Vickrama Rajasinghe. But, once he was deposed, the British usurped the Kandyan throne for themselves, justifying their deception and claiming their commitment to protect and promote Buddhism, the religion of the people, which had been neglected by their tyrannical king.[67]

In the Kandyan Convention signed between the British and the Kandyan aristocracy in 1815, the British agreed to govern the Kandyan state according to pre-existing "Laws, Institutions and customs." Article 5 of the Convention explicitly committed the British to accord Buddhism its historical place by continuing state patronage.[68] There was vehement opposition to Article 5 from the Christian evangelical organizations, which were intimately involved in British colonial rule from its outset. However, the British colonial Governor Brownrigg astutely affirmed that, "In truth, …our possession of the country hinged upon this point….I found it nec-

---

65 Ibid., xxviii.
66 Roberts, Michael. "Ethnicity after Edward Said: Post-Orientalist Failures in Comprehending the Kandyan Period of Lankan History." In *Confrontations in Sri Lanka: Sinhalese, LTTE & Others*, 1st ed. Colombo: Vijitha Yapa Publications, 2009.
67 Bandarage, Asoka. *Colonialism in Sri Lanka: The Political Economy of the Kandyan Highlands, 1833–1886*. New Babylon, Studies in the Social Sciences. Berlin: Mouton, 1983, 47; Chandani Kirinde, "John D'Oyly's 'fake news' campaign and the fall of the Kandyan Kingdom", The Sunday Times, Feb. 4, 2018. https://www.sundaytimes.lk/180204/plus/john-doylys-fake-news-campaign-and-the-fall-of-the-kandyan-kingdom-279383.html accessed March 15, 2023.
68 Cited in Bandarage, Asoka. *Colonialism in Sri Lanka: The Political Economy of the Kandyan Highlands, 1833–1886*. New Babylon, Studies in the Social Sciences. Berlin: Mouton, 1983, 365–366; Iriyagolle, Gamini. *The Kandyan Convention: A Conditional Treaty of Cession between the Sinhalese and the British, 2nd March 1815*. Colombo: Sinhala Veera Vidahana, 2000, 4.

essary to quiet all uneasiness respecting it, by an article of guarantee couched in the most unqualified terms."[69]

British disdain for and ignorance of Sinhala Buddhist culture and the constant pressure from the Christian missionaries led to violations of the terms of the Kandyan Convention. The British abused traditional institutions, especially feudal labor services, causing great hardship to the peasantry. They super-imposed a European administrative class above the native aristocracy, damaging the latter's power and dignity. As a result, resistance spread throughout the kingdom to drive out the British. This culminated in the Great Rebellion of 1817–1818, considered to be "the most formidable insurrection" that occurred during British occupation of Sri Lanka.[70] Once the revolt began, many Kandyan chiefs joined, and before long only a few Sinhala chiefs remained loyal to the British.[71] In 1818, Muslims in the Bintenne and Wellassa provinces collaborated with 'the powerful foreigner' in quelling the rebellion and as a reward, they were freed from feudal labor obligations to the British colonial state.[72]

The freedom struggle of 1818 commonly known as the Great Rebellion invoked historical Sinhala Buddhist nationalism and united the Kandyan aristocracy, the Buddhist clergy and the Sinhala peasantry, to regain the sovereignty of the Kandyan state, the last independent local kingdom. The British managed to crush the rebellion, albeit with great difficulty, using an utterly ruthless 'scorched earth' policy. Subsequently, some British officials themselves lamented the "barbarous devastation" and depopulation the British caused the environment and people.[73] Sir Archibald Lawrie, Acting Chief Justice at the time, wrote that due to the harsh suppression of the rebellion, in many districts, the Sinhalese "lost the flower of their

---

[69] Cited in Dewaraja, Lorna Srimathie. *The Kandyan Kingdom of Sri Lanka, 1707–1782*. Colombo: Lake House Investments, 1988, 163.

[70] Bandarage, Asoka. *Colonialism in Sri Lanka: The Political Economy of the Kandyan Highlands, 1833–1886*. New Babylon, Studies in the Social Sciences. Berlin: Mouton, 1983, 51.

[71] Ibid., 51; Chandani Kirinde, 'Pride and Tears of Uva Wellassa', The Sunday Times, April 8, 2018. https://www.sundaytimes.lk/180408/plus/pride-and-tears-of-uva-wellassa-288777.html accessed March 15, 2023.

[72] Roberts, Michael. "Ethnicity after Edward Said: Post-Orientalist Failures in Comprehending the Kandyan Period of Lankan History." In *Confrontations in Sri Lanka: Sinhalese, LTTE & Others*, 1st ed. Colombo: Vijitha Yapa Publications, 2009; McGilvray, Dennis B. "Arabs, Moors Anti Muslims: Sri Lankan Muslim Ethnicity in Regional Perspective." *Contributions to Indian Sociology* 32 (1998), 446.

[73] Roberts, Michael. "Ethnicity after Edward Said: Post-Orientalist Failures in Comprehending the Kandyan Period of Lankan History." In *Confrontations in Sri Lanka: Sinhalese, LTTE & Others*, 1st ed. Colombo: Vijitha Yapa Publications, 2009; Davy, John. *An Account of the Interior of Ceylon, and of Its Inhabitants: With Travels in That Island*. Cambridge Library Collection – Travel and Exploration in Asia. Cambridge: Cambridge University Press, 2012, 330.

manhood" and that hardly any members of the leading families remained alive, with most who were lucky enough to survive sword and gun only to be killed by cholera and small pox.[74] John Davy, a surgeon in the British Army Medical Department who observed the genocide first hand, wrote:

> When a district rose in rebellion, one or more military posts were established in it; martial law was proclaimed; the dwellings of the resisting inhabitants were burnt; their fruit trees were often cut down; and the country was scoured in all directions by small detachments, who were authorised to put to death all who made opposition, or were found with arms in their hands...When one considers this rebellion and its consequences, one almost regrets, that we ever entered the Kandyan country.[75]

An apology, let alone reparations, for the atrocities committed in the Kandyan Provinces of Sri Lanka in 1818 is yet forthcoming from Britain. Back in 1818, instead of adopting a more humane approach towards the remaining population, a new bill was passed, the Proclamation of 1818, to bring the rebellious Kandyan provinces more firmly under British control, and weaken the pledge made in the Kandyan Convention of 1815 to protect Buddhism.

The new Proclamation extended general protection to all religions. In so doing, it prepared the ground for extensive proselytization by a host of evangelical Christian organizations including the Anglican Church Missionary Society and the American Missionary Society (the latter in Jaffna in the north).[76] The extensive system of English language schools established by the Christian missions became the major instrument of religious and cultural conversion.

Despite the horrors of 1818, Buddhist millenarian movements seeking to restore the historical Buddhist kingdom resurfaced in the 1820s, 1848 and the late 1880s, but were unsuccessful in driving out the British.[77] Any attempt to subvert

---

[74] John Davy cited in Iriyagolle, Gamini. *The Kandyan Convention: A Conditional Treaty of Cession between the Sinhalese and the British, 2nd March 1815*. Colombo: Sinhala Veera Vidahana, 2000, 8–11.

[75] Davy, John. *An Account of the Interior of Ceylon, and of Its Inhabitants: With Travels in That Island*. Cambridge Library Collection – Travel and Exploration in Asia. Cambridge: Cambridge University Press, 2012, 330.

[76] Ames, Michael M. "Westernization or Modernization: The Case of the Sinhalese Buddhism." *Social Compass* 20, no. 2 (May 1973): 139–170. https://doi.org/10.1177/003776867302000203, 160; Bandarage, Asoka. *Colonialism in Sri Lanka: The Political Economy of the Kandyan Highlands, 1833–1886*. New Babylon, Studies in the Social Sciences. Berlin: Mouton, 1983, 52–53; Scott, David. "Conversion and Demonism: Colonial Christian Discourse and Religion in Sri Lanka." *Comparative Studies in Society and History* 34 (1992), 349.

[77] Bandarage, Asoka. *Colonialism in Sri Lanka: The Political Economy of the Kandyan Highlands, 1833–1886*. New Babylon, Studies in the Social Sciences. Berlin: Mouton, 1983, 315–332.

British authority was considered the greatest crime – treason, no less – and subjected to the highest penalties under British law; including death, banishment and imprisonment with hard labor.

Not only were many Kandyan chiefs subjected to these punishments at various times, but Buddhist monks were also sentenced for inciting and participating in nationalist rebellions and conspiracies. Kahawatte Unnanse, a Buddhist monk from Matale, identified as the principal organizer and an active agent in a plot against the British and a Kandyan chief, Koswatte Rateralla, were hanged in 1823. Seven other rebels were deported to Mauritius and others were imprisoned. A year later, another attempt was led by a Buddhist monk in the Bintenne Laggla area. The rebels were arrested and tried in Kandy; five were ordered to be hanged, others were banished from the country or imprisoned.[78] Yet another monk was convicted for treason in 1843 in Badulla.[79]

Feudal aristocrats who refused to collaborate with the colonial enterprise lost land, titles and prestige. In contrast, extensive land grants, grandiose titles and other honors were bestowed upon the loyal collaborator class who gave evidence against nationalists and provided indispensable service to maintain colonial authority.[80] Like the Portuguese and the Dutch before them, the British depended on the hierarchy of native officials to govern both the Sinhala and the Tamil populations in the island.[81] Indeed, without the collusion with the native collaborator class, the British colonizers could not have captured, consolidated and maintained their authority over the island for 150 years.

Similarly, as we will discuss later, without the collaboration of local political leaders, NGOs and the media, external powers would not be able to continue their neo-colonial control over the island which has led to the social and economic crisis today.

---

[78] Appuhamy, Durand. *The Kandyans' Last Stand against the British.* 1st ed. Colombo: M.D. Gunasena & Co., 1995, 28–32; *Report of the Sinhala Commission.* 1st ed. Vol. 1. Colombo: National Joint Committee, 1998, 71. Karunatilake, H. N. S. *The Wars of Liberation in the Nineteenth Century.* Colombo: Centre for Demographic and Socio-economic Studies, 1999, 57.

[79] Evers, Hans-Dieter. "Buddhism and British Colonial Policy in Ceylon, 1815–1875." *Journal of Asian Studies* 11, no. 3 (December 1964), 331.

[80] Bandarage, Asoka. *Colonialism in Sri Lanka: The Political Economy of the Kandyan Highlands, 1833–1886.* New Babylon, Studies in the Social Sciences. Berlin: Mouton, 1983, 225–229.

[81] De Silva, K. M. "Education and Social Change, 1832 to c. 1900." In *History of Ceylon: From the Beginning of the Nineteenth Century to 1948*, Vol. 3. Colombo: Ceylon University Press, 1973, 166.

British Colonialism and Capitalist Development, c. 1832–1948

In colonial Ceylon, the transition from mercantilism to 'free enterprise' was represented by the comprehensive set of reforms known as the Colebrooke-Cameron Reforms introduced in 1832–1833, which laid the administrative and legal framework for Sri Lanka's capitalist economic development.

The Reforms divided the island into five administrative provinces – North, South, East, West, and Central – violating the terms of the Kandyan Treaty which bound the British to govern the Kandyan Provinces separately from the rest of the island according to pre-existing institutions and customs of the Kandyan kingdom. The Kandyan Kingdom was effectively dismembered, and its different regions attached to the artificially created new Provinces. In conjunction with the Colebrooke-Cameron Reforms, the British also brought the entire island under one highly centralized colonial administration with the locus of political control firmly based in the capital city of Colombo.[82]

Even before the Colebrooke Reforms, in the aftermath of the 1818 Rebellion, the British had begun to open up the interior highlands with an impressive system of modern roads built with forced labor in order to integrate the different regions of the island. The British exacted pre-colonial *corvee* labor services in an unusually severe manner to clear the land and build the roads, which were primarily meant for use by the plantation sector. In 1832, there were 3000 laborers in the Kandyan Provinces forced to work in the construction of public infrastructure, of which 1,000 worked on the Kandy-Trincomalee road alone.[83] The twin political and economic motives were to prevent future Kandyan rebellions and capitalist expansion.

The Colebrooke Reforms introduced a system of English schools for the explicit purpose of creating a loyal, westernized native elite who could be employed cheaply in the lower echelons of the colonial bureaucracy. The 'Minute on Education' enunciated by Thomas Macaulay, which denounced native cultures as inferior and introduced his famous educational reforms to British India in 1835, could easily have been attributed to Colebrooke, whose reforms were similar to Macaulay's in both spirit and substance, describing a strategy "...to form a class Indian in blood and color, but English in tastes, in opinions, in morals and in intellect; a class who could serve as interpreters between the government and the masses,

---

[82] Bandarage, Asoka. *The Separatist Conflict in Sri Lanka: Terrorism, Ethnicity, Political Economy.* London: Routledge/Taylor & Francis Group, 2009, 29.

[83] Bandarage, Asoka. *Colonialism in Sri Lanka: The Political Economy of the Kandyan Highlands, 1833–1886.* New Babylon, Studies in the Social Sciences. Berlin: Mouton, 1983, 176.

and who, by refining the vernaculars, would supply the means of a widespread dissemination of western learnings."[84]

Such a class, alienated from their local cultural traditions came into being in India, Sri Lanka and throughout the colonies. Subsequent generations have since become even further alienated from their cultural and ecological roots as they are absorbed into globalized western culture or, in many cases left adrift in a culturally and materially impoverished virtual reality.

The Colebrooke Reforms introduced a partial abolition of forced labor expecting that it would simultaneously create a wage labor force needed for economic expansion and also free peasants from feudal bondage. Even more importantly, the Colebrooke Reforms lifted the precolonial and mercantilist restrictions on land appropriation, encouraging the sale or grant of land held by the Crown to private buyers. The basis for private property rights and alienation of land for plantation development was thus established. As early as 1801, Frederick North, the first Governor of British Ceylon declared, "the establishment of private property is the object of all my institutions."[85] Land privatization uprooted people from their land, each other, their culture and the natural world and enabled the expansion of the export-oriented plantation economy.

From the onset of the Industrial Revolution, human lives became increasingly restricted and regimented within the time and monetary units and identities created by the confluence of the market, modern technology, and the bureaucratic state. Capitalist development took on a global character, linked closely with European imperialism from the beginning. Anthropologist Pierre Bourdieu observed that in colonial Algeria many peasants viewed the haste and speed up of life that accompanied colonialism and modernization "as a lack of decorum combined with diabolical ambition."[86] Some even referred to the clock as a 'devil's mill' that eroded dignity, freedom and humanity, an observation that equally applies to the Sri Lankan colonial transition.

Plantation Economy

Starting in 1824, the British established large scale coffee plantations in the Kandyan Highlands exacting traditional corvee labor. In the early years, the planters

---

[84] Ibid., 62.
[85] Ibid., 58.
[86] Cited in Bandarage, Asoka. *Sustainability and Well-Being: The Middle Path to Environment, Society and the Economy.* Basingstoke: Palgrave Macmillan, 2013, 38.

were mostly colonial officials known as 'planter-officials.' Pioneer road builder Governor Barnes (1824–1831) set an example to other European officials by founding a coffee plantation himself in the Kandyan Highlands.[87]

As plantations became the central institutions of the colonial economy and as state revenue became dependent on plantation coffee exports, the British planter capitalist class emerged as the most influential segment of colonial society. The Chamber of Commerce established in 1839 and the Planters Association in 1854 became their premier lobbying groups.[88] The George Steuart Company established in 1835 by James Steuart, the Master Attendant of Ports (1825–1855) – the oldest corporate house in Sri Lanka – is still one of the largest business conglomerates in the country.[89]

The most vexatious and controversial issue faced by British plantation interests in Sri Lanka was the question of native rights to land, particularly the forest, swidden and pastureland that were suited for plantation development. All uncultivated and unoccupied land in precolonial Sri Lanka was theoretically 'Crown' land belonging to the king. But, as land was plentiful and not a commodity, the king did not prohibit cultivation of 'his' lands. According to customary Kandyan law, peasant cultivators had users' rights to the highlands surrounding their villages regardless of whether the overlordship of the village was held by the king or nobility. The possession of the chenas where multi-crop swidden cultivation was practiced, "became tangible only once in seven or eight years and in the interval, the land resumed the character of ownerless jungle."[90]

In contrast, plantation development along capitalist lines presupposed absolute proprietary rights, fixed tenure, and that land was a commodity. When the colonial administration applied these modern legal terms to the former Kandyan kingdom, the old and the new systems of land tenure began to clash. During the land rush when the forests and swidden lands in the Kandyan highlands were being sold off to European planters by the colonial state, the natives began to press their customary rights and claims to land resulting in tremendous conflict between the colonizers and the colonized.[91]

With the development of the British plantation economy and the imposition of materialist values of progress and development, Sri Lanka experienced both a so-

---

[87] Ibid., 58.
[88] Perera, Nihal. *Decolonizing Ceylon: Colonialism, Nationalism, and the Politics of Space in Sri Lanka.* New Delhi: Oxford University Press, 1999, 67.
[89] *George Steuart Group of Companies.* Accessed December 26, 2022. https://georgesteuart.lk/.
[90] Cited in Bandarage, Asoka. *Colonialism in Sri Lanka: The Political Economy of the Kandyan Highlands, 1833–1886.* New Babylon, Studies in the Social Sciences. Berlin: Mouton, 1983, 29.
[91] Ibid., Chap. 5.

cial and an ecological transformation. British proclivity towards surveying and mapping of land for plantation development subordinated the natural environment and native society within a new European capitalist framework. As Urban Planning scholar Nihal Perera put it:

> ...the conflict between the 'systematic mapping of Ceylon' and the use of surveying as a tool to block out land as private property was significant. The colonial social order could neither be confirmed nor extended into so-called virgin territories without the creation of property through the quantification and mapping of space.[92]

The objective was to block out uncultivated land as Crown property to be quickly transferred to private property and make it available for sale. It is interesting to note that a similar process of surveying, mapping and registering – what some call 'land grabbing' – is now going on in Sri Lanka, led by the US Trimble Co. under the auspices of the US Millennium Challenge Corporation Compact. Its objective is to privatize remaining state land and make it available for development by private capital, mostly transnational corporations.[93] As we discuss in Chapter 5, the current IMF bail-out is also furthering privatization of state-owned lands.

The colonial state sought to resolve the conflict over the highlands once and for all through legislation. In 1840, it introduced Ordinance 12, commonly referred to as the Crown Lands Encroachment Ordinance. It's notorious Clause 6 presumed that all uncultivated and unoccupied lands belonged to the Crown:

> And it is further enacted that all Forest, Waste, Unoccupied and Uncultivated Lands shall be presumed to be the property of the Crown; until the contrary thereof be proved; and all chenas and other lands ... be deemed to belong to the Crown and not to be the property of any private person claiming the same against the Crown.[94]

By demanding ownership to a category of land which had customarily been considered communal village land, and thereby abolishing users' rights, the colonial state was able to alienate vast tracts of land and make it available for a pittance

---

[92] Perera, Nihal. *Decolonizing Ceylon: Colonialism, Nationalism, and the Politics of Space in Sri Lanka.* New Delhi: Oxford University Press, 1999, 72.

[93] *EconomyNext.* "Sri Lanka in Talks with Trimble Inc USA for Cadastral Mapping," October 8, 2017. Accessed July 15, 2022. https://economynext.com/sri-lanka-in-talks-with-trimble-inc-usa-for-cadastral-mapping-8501. Bandarage, Asoka. "Neocolonialism and Geopolitical Rivalry in Sri Lanka." *Asia Times,* January 29, 2020. Accessed January 29, 2020. https://asiatimes.com/2020/01/neocolonialism-and-geopolitical-rivalry-in-sri-lanka/.

[94] Bandarage, Asoka. *Colonialism in Sri Lanka: The Political Economy of the Kandyan Highlands, 1833–1886.* New Babylon, Studies in the Social Sciences. Berlin: Mouton, 1983, Appendix 4, 367–370.

to Europeans for plantation development. Between 1833 and 1880, an estimated 25,000 acres of crown land was sold, mostly to European capitalists, at an average of 31 shillings an acre.[95] According to the calculations of historian Patrick Peebles, crown land sales between 1833 and 1889 alone comprised roughly ten percent of the surface area of the island.[96]

Given attachment to the pursuit of paddy agriculture, which was the basis of the traditional economy and held in high esteem as a noble profession, the Sinhala peasantry did not want to become a proletariat on British owned plantations. In the earlier periods of colonial rule, the peasantry still had access to their traditional lands. Colebrooke reforms to create a free wage labor force out of the peasantry failed. Seeing the Sinhalese peasantry as superfluous to plantation agriculture and the colonial society, the British came to resent the 'independence' of the Kandyan peasantry and to regard them as a politically troublesome and indolent lot. This is evident in the statement made by colonial Governor Hercules Robinson at the opening session of the Legislative Council in 1866:

> The wants of the native population of the island are few and easily supplied by an occasional day's work in their own gardens or paddy fields. Their philosophy, their love of ease and indolence or their limited ideas, whichever may be the real cause, render them perfectly content with what they already possess.[97]

What Europeans – including Marxists – arrogantly and ethnocentrically saw as stagnation in non-Western societies were frequently ecologically sound practices and rich community traits, albeit, as social ecologist Murray Bookchin put it, "ethically and morally incompatible with the predatory dynamism of Europeans."[98]

The wholehearted commitment of the colonial state to plantation development resulted in a neglect of subsistence production. Over time, the development of plantations in the highlands cut severely into peasant chena or swidden cultivation, the safety valve of subsistence production as well as smallholder cash crop cultivation, especially what was referred to as 'peasant coffee'. The ancient irrigation works remained in disrepair and the yields from paddy cultivation were low. Yet, the British colonial state placed a huge tax burden on the peasantry to increase

---

95 Ibid., 97.
96 Patrick Peebles, 'Land Use and Population Growth in Colonial Ceylon', in Contributions to Asian Studies, ed. by James Brow, vol. 9, Leiden: E.J. Brill, 1976, 71.
97 Bandarage, Asoka. *Colonialism in Sri Lanka: The Political Economy of the Kandyan Highlands, 1833–1886*. New Babylon, Studies in the Social Sciences. Berlin: Mouton, 1983, 175.
98 Cited in Bandarage, Asoka. *Sustainability and Well-Being: The Middle Path to Environment, Society and the Economy*. Basingstoke: Palgrave Macmillan, 2013, 39.

state revenue. Only the grain crops, primarily paddy, cultivated by the peasantry were taxed whereas the 'colonial produce' for export were not.

Economic changes that were imposed also specifically disadvantaged the peasantry. A system of commutation to transfer payment from kind to its cash equivalent was introduced starting in the 1820s. A measure designed to induce the peasant sector to enter the cash nexus, it placed great hardship on the peasantry. Even Colebrooke noted the injustice of this system, which placed severe economic pressure on the most impoverished segment of the population.[99]

All the state's revenues were derived from local sources. The colonial administration received no financial support whatsoever from the imperial government, even in times of severe economic setbacks. In fact, in addition to the profits exported by the plantation enterprise, the colonial government was required to make an annual financial contribution to the home government as payment for the British garrison stationed in Ceylon.[100] In other words, the local inhabitants paid the wages of the soldiers that oppressed them.

Having failed to turn the Sinhalese into permanent wage laborers despite efforts to displace them from their beloved paddy cultivation, the British evolved a horrific system to transport hundreds of thousands of Tamils from poverty-stricken castes in South India to work on their coffee estates in Ceylon. Many died on route in conditions reminiscent of the European transatlantic slave trade. The Indians who arrived on the island – the 'coolies', as the British called them – were kept in the 'lines,' the squalid quarters built for them on Kandyan lands turned into plantations. In the 1843–1849 period a total of 48,100 laborers were imported and the number increased to 115,416 in the 1873–1886 period.[101] A class of South Indian Tamil middlemen known as the *kanganis*, who both recruited and supervised labor on the estates, profited from the sordid enterprise created by the British.[102] As historian Fred Halliday observed, the "super-exploitation of this ...immiserated class founded the fortunes of British imperialism in Ceylon ...and generated the surplus- value pumped regularly home to London."[103]

However, the resistance to British colonialism did not come from this imported labor force indentured to the planters and middlemen through debt bondage. In-

---

[99] Bandarage, Asoka. *Colonialism in Sri Lanka: The Political Economy of the Kandyan Highlands, 1833–1886.* New Babylon, Studies in the Social Sciences. Berlin: Mouton, 1983, 131.
[100] Bandarage, Asoka. *Colonialism in Sri Lanka: The Political Economy of the Kandyan Highlands, 1833–1886.* New Babylon, Studies in the Social Sciences. Berlin: Mouton, 1983, 261.
[101] Ibid., 202.
[102] Ibid., 203–210.
[103] Halliday, Fred. "The Ceylonese Insurrection." *New Left Review*, no. 69 (October 1971). https://newleftreview.org/issues/i69/articles/fred-halliday-the-ceylonese-insurrection.

stead, the resistance came from the independent and 'rebellious' Kandyan peasantry struggling to uphold Sinhala Buddhist nationalism that was continually maligned by the Europeans.

The 1848 Rebellion

In an attempt to shift the burden of the world economic depression of the mid 1840s from the plantation sector and the colonial treasury to the peasantry, Governor Torrington introduced a host of new taxes in 1848 which bore heavily on the local population.

The taxes sparked a rebellion; the most severe upheaval against the colonial state since the rebellion of 1818. While the immediate cause was taxes, the underlying cause was the growing contradiction between plantation development and peasant subsistence. Appropriation of highlands for plantations, harsh exaction of corvee labor for road construction and onerous taxes on paddy cultivation created much antipathy towards the colonial state, the white Europeans and the alien political and economic system and values they introduced.

There were several outbreaks of violence in the Kandyan areas, notably Matale and Kurunegala in July 29 and 31 1848 with rebel attacks concentrated on the installations of the colonial state, such as jails, court houses and official residences. A small group in the Kandy districts "sought to channel this discontent in an attempt to drive the British out of Kandy."[104] Given their memory of 1818 and the fear of damage to plantations and their coffee crop, the British quickly quelled the rebellion using unduly harsh suppression. In 1848, one British soldier was wounded, whereas at least 200 Kandyans lost their lives that year.

Once the rebellion was subdued, the colonial state shot dead or exiled many Sinhalese accused of sedition.[105] Kadhapolla Unnanse, a Buddhist monk, was charged with responsibility for the widespread rebellion, and was tried by Court Martial without legal defense – he had no money to pay for legal counsel – found guilty

---

[104] Bandarage, Asoka. *Colonialism in Sri Lanka: The Political Economy of the Kandyan Highlands, 1833–1886*. New Babylon, Studies in the Social Sciences. Berlin: Mouton, 1983, 317–320; see also, De Silva, Kingsley M. "The Rebellion of 1848 in Ceylon." *Ceylon Journal of Historical and Social Studies* 7, no. 2 (July 1964): 144–170.

[105] Appuhamy, Durand. *The Kandyans' Last Stand against the British*. 1st ed. Colombo: M.D. Gunasena & Co., 1995, 28–32; *Report of the Sinhala Commission*. 1st ed. Vol. 1. Colombo: National Joint Committee, 1998, 508–509.

based on flimsy evidence and the very next morning on August 26, 1848, was shot to death in his yellow robes.[106]

Although, on the surface, British rule seemed more civilized and less barbaric than the Portuguese or even the Dutch before them, any threat to its authority was harshly and unjustly dealt with as was the case in 1818, 1848 and during the 1915 communal riots. A British Parliamentary Committee appointed to investigate the 1848 rebellion revealed British suspicion that the rebellion was engineered by the Buddhist clergy and the aristocracy. This suspicion resulted in a shift of policy to attempt to incorporate the native chiefs more closely into the provincial administration of the colony. The native aristocracy in turn came to accept the permanency of British rule and to enjoy the benefits accrued to them in monetary and social status through the new partnership.

Meanwhile, coffee production in Sri Lanka collapsed in the late 1880s due to a leaf disease and the plantations were instead reappropriated to cultivate tea. More land was brought under tea cultivation and the island came to be known as 'Lipton's tea garden' and famous for its Ceylon tea. The colonial frameworks and processes put in place during the coffee period to commoditize land were expanded and strengthened during the tea period.

The passing of Ordinance No. 10 of 1856 to define and register temple properties was similar to the Waste Lands Ordinance of 1840 in that the burden of proving title to land again fell on the native landholders, in this case the Buddhist temples which held extensive monastic properties.[107] The Partition Ordinance No. 10 of 1863 lifted pre-existing restrictions and enabled the partition and sale of landed property held in common between two or more owners. The purpose was the extension of private property rights, agricultural development and the emergence of wage labor. Over time, the Ordinance became a "notorious instrument of land grabbing" for indigenous financiers and capitalists who could eject tenants whose families had held land together for centuries.[108]

The conflict between colonial and native interests over commonly held uncultivated lands continued well into the 20th century. This culminated in the enactment of Ordinance No. 1 of 1897, which firmly reiterated the Waste Lands Ordinance of 1840. stating that where no claim was made on a "forest, chena, waste

---

[106] Ibid., 483–495; *Report of the Sinhala Commission*. 1st ed. Vol. 1. Colombo: National Joint Committee, 1998, 70–71.
[107] Bandarage, Asoka. *Colonialism in Sri Lanka: The Political Economy of the Kandyan Highlands, 1833–1886*. New Babylon, Studies in the Social Sciences. Berlin: Mouton, 1983, 111.
[108] Ibid., 241–242.

and unoccupied lands," such land would be declared property of the Crown.[109] The 'Waste Lands Ordinance,' overlooked the traditional sustainable cultivation practice of letting land in fallow to maintain the natural productivity. Seeking expropriation and profits and calling uncultivated lands 'waste land', the ordinance introduced a land-grab policy decreeing that "any land or lands …. in respect of which no claim is made…be deemed the property of the Crown and may be dealt with on account of the Crown."[110]

Environmental and Social Destruction

The British colonizers were not ignorant of the inherent contradictions between their profitmaking activities and the welfare of the native people or their environment. James Steuart, the Master-Attendant of the Ports (1825–1855), and founder of the prestigious George Steuart Co. observed, "We profess to govern for the exclusive good of the natives of the country and devote our attention almost exclusively to make the culture of the soil profitable to European adventurers."[111]

The reorganization of life within the norms of economic growth and profit that came with capitalist development exerted an enormous toll both on people and the natural environment.

Plantations and infrastructure, such as roads and railway tracks, were introduced without consideration for the ecological role of forests for water balance, soil fertility, erosion prevention, and the like.[112] Monocultural coffee, tea, and rubber plantations were established and run without consideration for either the natural equilibrium of biodiversity or the watershed. To make way for plantations, the upper catchment areas of the major rivers in the Central Highlands were stripped of natural vegetation.[113]

Largely as a consequence of plantation development, Sri Lanka's forest cover declined from 82 percent in 1881 to 70 percent in 1900 to around 50 percent in 1948,

---

[109] "Ordinance No.1 of 1897, An Ordinance Relating to Claims to Forest, Chena, Waste, and Unoccupied Lands." In *The Legislative Enactments of Ceylon*, 2: 384–394. Colombo: Government Printer, 1923.
[110] Ibid.
[111] Cited in Bandarage, Asoka. *Colonialism in Sri Lanka: The Political Economy of the Kandyan Highlands, 1833–1886*. New Babylon, Studies in the Social Sciences. Berlin: Mouton, 1983, 64.
[112] Breuste, Jürgen, and Lalitha Dissanayake. "Socio-Economic and Environmental Change of Sri Lanka's Central Highlands Responses and Adaptation." In *Impact of Global Changes on Mountains*, 11–31. CRC Press, 2019.
[113] Ibid.

when the British left the island.[114] Deforestation destroyed water resources that irrigated the rivers, leaving village tanks dry. As conservationists have noted, other consequences included "landslides, heavy soil losses, soil fertility decline and reduction in crop yields, siltation of low-lying areas, frequent flooding, drying out of streams, etc."[115] These impacts continue to pose an increasing threat to the survival of the integrated ecosystem that is the entire island.

Colonialism replaced the traditional attitude of partnership with and respect of nature with an attitude of domination and conquest over nature. In violation of the Buddhist philosophy introduced to the island by Arahant Mahinda in 3 BCE, killing of animals for sport and trade became widespread under the British. The extensive killing of wild animals led to the extinction of several species.

The Elephant Department which was a highly valued unit of the pre-colonial state where elephants were used for trade and transport work was terminated by the British.[116] Instead, to the horror of the local people, the revered elephant was declared a pest and a reward of a few shillings was placed on the head of an elephant. Elephant hunting in Ceylon became world famous, especially after coffee and, later, tea plantations were opened in the central hills.

The famous hunter Sir Samuel Baker reportedly killed 104 elephants in three days. The slaughter was intense by modern sensibilities; Major Skinner, the road builder and Captain Gallwey each killed 700 elephants and Major Rogers killed 1300 elephants in three years. Another British hunter boasted killing more than 6,000 wild elephants.[117] Lest we forget, "Elephants are the largest land mammal, among the most intelligent, long lived, and sentient of nonhuman animals."[118] The colonial attitude to the destruction of such a wonderous being is a prime ex-

---

114 Perera, Bawantha. "The Destruction of Tropical Forests in Sri Lanka." Lankapura. Accessed December 27, 2022. https://lankapura.com/2011/01/destruction-tropical-forests-sri-lanka/. Butler, Rhett. "Sri Lanka Forest Information and Data." mongabay.com. Accessed December 27, 2022. https://rainforests.mongabay.com/deforestation/2000/Sri_Lanka.htm.
115 Breuste, Jürgen, and Lalitha Dissanayake. "Socio-Economic and Environmental Change of Sri Lanka's Central Highlands Responses and Adaptation." In *Impact of Global Changes on Mountains*, 11–31. CRC Press, 2019.
116 Karunatilake, H. N. S. *The Wars of Liberation in the Nineteenth Century.* Colombo: Centre for Demographic and Socio-economic Studies, 1999, 17.
117 Fernando, Kishanie S. "The Unspeakable in Pursuit of the Uneatable." *Daily Mirror*, Unknown date. Accessed December 5, 2022. https://amazinglanka.com/wp/hunting-elephants/; Godwin Witane, 'Mass Massacre of Elephants', Witane, Godwin. "Mass Massacre of Elephants in Sri Lanka." Unknown Publication, Unknown date. Accessed December 5, 2022. http://www.infolanka.com/org/srilanka/hist/37.htm.
118 Lepore, Jill. "The Elephant Who Could Be a Person." *The Atlantic*, November 16, 2021. Accessed December 15, 2021. https://www.theatlantic.com/ideas/archive/2021/11/happy-elephant-bronx-zoo-nhrp-lawsuit/620672/.

ample of the myopia of western civilization and the idea of progress based on the pursuit of "quantity and egoistic acquisition."[119] It is doubtlessly incompatible with a sustainable and long-lived culture in tune with nature.

Poverty and Disempowerment

Alienation of village common lands for plantation development, high taxes and downturns in the global economy had much to do with the increasing plight of the Kandyan peasantry. Many peasants were evicted from their paddy fields due to non-payment of taxes to the colonial state.[120] Given the need for cash in the new economy and the commoditization of land, many peasants sold their land to entrepreneurial groups from the coastal lowlands and South India for very small sums. By the mid-twentieth century, agrarian pressure had become so acute that in the Nuwara Eliya and Badulla districts, the landless peasantry were respectively 42 percent and 38 percent of the population.[121] As geographer, B.H. Farmer observed:

> ...the Crown Lands Encroachments Ordinance, and the estates that grew up because of it, have borne hard on many Kandyan villages and in doing so have accentuated an agrarian problem ... Many a Kandyan village found itself hemmed in by the estates, denied access to its customary pasture, forest and chenas (which, having been mistakenly assumed to be 'waste', had been alienated to planters) and unable to expand its paddy or other land as its population increased. ...land policy and its effects have contributed to a sense of hopelessness among the Kandyan peasantry.[122]

Overwhelming concern of the colonial administration with plantation development and export growth coincided with a neglect of rice production and the irrigation works. With the import of a large Indian labor force to work on the plantations, rice began to be imported in great quantities. Colonial authorities encouraged

---

119 Bookchin, Murray. *The Ecology of Freedom: The Emergence and Dissolution of Hierarchy.* Black Rose Books, 1991, 88.
120 Bandarage, Asoka. *Colonialism in Sri Lanka: The Political Economy of the Kandyan Highlands, 1833–1886.* New Babylon, Studies in the Social Sciences. Berlin: Mouton, 1983, 144–145.
121 Census of Ceylon and Census of Agriculture 1946 as compiled in Farmer, Bertram Hughes. *Pioneer Peasant Colonization in Ceylon: A Study in Asian Agrarian Problems.* Greenwood Press, 1976, 209.
122 Ibid., 91.

South Indian Chettiyar merchants to import rice varieties from South India familiar to the immigrant laborers, an irony in a land of historic and reverent rice culture.[123]

Increasingly, the once self-sufficient Sinhala peasantry also became dependent on imports; not only rice, but also other food and consumer goods. Rice imports to the colony increased from 798 hundredweight in the 1837–1839 period to 4,794 in the 1870–1872 period,[124] and the annual return to the colonial state from the custom duty on rice imports increased fifteen-fold between 1823 and 1876.[125] The island was increasingly integrated into the global import-export economy undermining local subsistence production – including both paddy agriculture and multi-crop dry grain agriculture – with profit-driven mono-cultural export agriculture. The previously self-sufficient population were now made dependent on the vagaries of the global economy for their very survival. The economic crisis facing Sri Lanka in 2022 is only the most recent outcome of this fundamental economic transformation that came with colonial capitalist development.

Unlike coffee, tea production required a permanent labor force and labor import from India soared. In some decades of the late 19th century, the island's population increased more from immigration from South India than by natural increase.[126] For example, during the 1871–1881 period, the natural increase was 119,792 and migration increase was 239,566 and between 1891–1901, the migration levels increased from 225,406 to 332,759.[127]

Distinct from earlier waves of immigrants from India to Sri Lanka, the more abrupt waves of immigrant laborers from South India imported by the British were not absorbed into the Sinhala caste system and society. Rather, they were defined along national, ethno-religious and social class lines and kept under tight control of the British planters on the estates, entirely separate from the majority population of Sinhala Buddhists, as well as the Tamil minority in the north.[128] To quote Halliday again, this British colonial policy "…divided the oppressed population of the island…, allowing the colonial state to manipulate and exacerbate

---

[123] Bandarage, Asoka. *Colonialism in Sri Lanka: The Political Economy of the Kandyan Highlands, 1833–1886.* New Babylon, Studies in the Social Sciences. Berlin: Mouton, 1983, 212–220.
[124] Ibid., 212.
[125] Ibid., 263.
[126] De Silva, K. M. *Managing Ethnic Tensions in Multi-Ethnic Societies: Sri Lanka, 1880–1985.* Lanham, MD: University Press of America, 1986, 19.
[127] Ibid., 19; De Silva, Kingsley M. *History of Ceylon: From the Beginning of the Nineteenth Century to 1948*, Vol. 3. Colombo: Ceylon University Press, 1959, 287.
[128] Bandarage, Asoka. *The Separatist Conflict in Sri Lanka: Terrorism, Ethnicity, Political Economy.* London: Routledge/Taylor & Francis Group, 2009, 30.

ethnic antagonisms between Tamils and Sinhalese in a classic strategy of divide and rule..."[129]

In parallel, the alcohol trade was intimately connected with colonial political-economic and plantation development. The British inherited the practice of renting arrack (a locally distilled coconut liquor) monopoly from their Dutch predecessors in the coastal lowlands and later extended it to other regions by selling the arrack franchise to the highest bidders at auctions. Members of enterprising Sinhala castes such as the *karava*, *durava* and *salagama* became wealthy from the arrack franchise and turned that wealth into social advancement.[130] However, it was the colonial state that benefited the most from the arrack as well as the opium monopolies. In the middle of the 19th century, state revenue from arrack renting was app. L 50,000 to 60,000 a year, a substantial sum at the time.[131] Similarly, the volume of opium imported by the colonial state increased from 850 lbs. in 1850 to 20,000 lbs. in 1905 and the number of shops selling it rose to 65 during that period.[132]

Drinking was introduced and popularized by colonialism as a form of social pacification and control. Robert Knox and other Europeans who knew Sinhala society intimately have remarked that the traditional Sinhalese abhorred drinking. But the taverns that were established by the British transformed Sinhalese males as well as the Indian Tamil plantation laborers into heavy drinkers, engulfing them in debt and debt servitude to money lenders, local landowners, European planters and the like. Today, consequently, Sri Lanka has a very high rate of alcohol consumption among males.[133]

Globally, alcohol helped suppress rebellions inculcating self-hatred and poverty among indigenous people. Drinking popularized by colonizers in other regions too became the escape for oppressed groups, Native Americans and Australian 'aborigines' being examples.

---

[129] Halliday, Fred. "The Ceylonese Insurrection." *New Left Review*, no. 69 (October 1971). Accessed December 25, 2022. https://newleftreview.org/issues/i69/articles/fred-halliday-the-ceylonese-insurrection.
[130] Roberts, Michael. *Caste Conflict and Elite Formation: The Rise of a Karāva Elite in Sri Lanka, 1500–1931*. Cambridge South Asian Studies. Cambridge [England]: Cambridge University Press, 1982.
[131] Bandarage, Asoka. *Colonialism in Sri Lanka: The Political Economy of the Kandyan Highlands, 1833–1886*. New Babylon, Studies in the Social Sciences. Berlin: Mouton, 1983, 265.
[132] Ibid., 265–266.
[133] Hewapathirane, Daya. "Alcohol Abuse In Sri Lanka: Grave Consequences." *Asian Tribune*, February 24, 2020. Accessed February 26, 2020. https://web.archive.org/web/20200224165952/http://www.asiantribune.com/node/93427.

Another strategy of 'divide-and-conquer' counterinsurgency, in effect, was the expansion of Christian schools for the alleged purpose of 'civilizing' heathen natives.

Ethno-Religious Stratification

As historian Ananda Wickramaratne observed: "the national system of education became in effect a system of Christian schools."[134] In 1868, 65 percent of the children enrolled in schools in Sri Lanka were Christian and only 27 percent were Buddhists. By the end of the 19th century, Christians controlled most of the recognized schools in the island, 1,117 out of 1,328 state aided schools and most of the government schools as well.[135] The Christian education imparted in these schools alienated students from their cultural traditions and endowed them with new western values and aspirations and what historian, K.M. de Silva has called, "an overpowering and seemingly indestructible Occidentalism."[136]

Conversion to Christianity under the British – conducted mainly through the educational system – was not as overtly coercive as it had been under the Portuguese and the Dutch. Nevertheless, as before, conversion continued to be a symbol of loyalty to the colonial master and the means for upward social mobility. The Christian advantage was clearly reflected in the composition of the university, the colonial administration and the modern professions. Although only 9.9 percent of the population of the island, Christians represented the highest percentage, 38.5 percent, of the student body in the University of Ceylon in 1944.[137]

The Jaffna Tamil *vellala* caste also had a decisive advantage in English language education. The colonial state's grants-in-aid provided the greater proportion of Christian missionary schools to the Northern Province. This gave the Sri Lankan Tamils, specifically the Jaffna *vellala* caste an 'intrinsic advantage' over the Sin-

---

[134] Wickremeratne, Ananda. *The Roots of Nationalism: Sri Lanka.* Colombo: Karunaratne & Sons Ltd, 1995; Ibid., xv.
[135] Ghosh, Partha S. *Ethnicity versus Nationalism: The Devolution Discourse in Sri Lanka.* New Delhi: Sage Publications, 2003, 313; Ames, Michael M. "Westernization or Modernization: The Case of the Sinhalese Buddhism." *Social Compass* 20, no. 2 (May 1973): 139–170, 148. https://doi.org/10.1177/003776867302000203.
[136] De Silva, K. M. *Managing Ethnic Tensions in Multi-Ethnic Societies: Sri Lanka, 1880–1985.* Lanham, MD: University Press of America, 1986, 37.
[137] Jennings, Ivor. "Race, Religion and Economic Opportunity in the University of Ceylon." *University of Ceylon Review*, December 194, 2.

hala majority and other minorities.[138] Next to the small Eurasian minority, the Burghers, the Ceylon Tamils were over- represented in the administrative and the modern professions relative to their proportion in the island's population. For example, in 1925, the Tamils were 11 percent of the island's population, yet constituted 30.8 percent and 20.5 percent of the government medical service and the Civil Service respectively.[139]

These 'structural imbalances' in education and modern employment and British policies of divide-and-conquer favoring the Tamil elite in political reform processes contributed to Tamil elite demands for political parity with the Sinhalese, disproportionate to their population size. The 'ethnic conflict' and the Tamil separatist movement in the post-independence period were, in large part, born out of those policies of British colonialism.[140]

The Resurgence of Sinhalese Buddhist Activism

The tremendous sense of outrage against British colonialism and the grievance felt by the Sinhala Buddhist majority found expression in new social movements in the early 20th century. Unlike the millenarian movements of the early 19th century, which sought to drive out the British and restitute the Buddhist monarchy, the Buddhist resurgence which arose in the second half of the nineteenth century was not aimed at restoring the Sinhala Buddhist state. Rather, it emerged as a social and political movement to advance Buddhists within the colonial political economy without sacrifice of their traditional religion and culture.

The lay leaders of the movement emerged from among the Sinhala entrepreneurial class mostly in the lowlands and they adopted some of the institutional strategies of the colonizers. Development of a network of English medium Buddhist schools and the temperance movement against the spread of alcohol were their primary strategies.[141]

---

138 Bandarage, Asoka. *The Separatist Conflict in Sri Lanka: Terrorism, Ethnicity, Political Economy.* London: Routledge/Taylor & Francis Group, 2009, 31.
139 Ibid., 31.
140 Ibid., 31–32.
141 Wickremeratne, Ananda. *The Roots of Nationalism: Sri Lanka.* Colombo: Karunaratne & Sons Ltd, 1995, 266; De Silva, K.M. *History of Ceylon: From the Beginning of the Nineteenth Century to 1948*, Vol. 3. Colombo: Ceylon University Press, 1973, 259; Jayasekera, P. V. J. *Confrontations with Colonialism: Resistance, Revivalism and Reform Under British Rule in Sri Lanka, 1796–1920.* Vijitha Yapa Publications, 2017.

Anagarika Dharmapala (1864–1933), the pioneer international Buddhist activist who led the struggle to restore Buddhist control of Buddha Gaya, seat of the Buddha's enlightenment in India, was also the foremost leader of the Buddhist resurgence in Sri Lanka. He was the first Sri Lankan to raise consciousness of the political, economic and cultural problems facing the country in the 20th century. He blamed the destruction of the land and the decline of the Sinhalese, on the ecological and socio-economic and cultural transformation wrought by British colonialism. In a booklet entitled *History of an Ancient Civilization* published in 1902 in Los Angeles, he wrote:

> The bureaucratic administrators, ignorant of the first principles of the natural laws of evolution, have cut down primeval forests to plant tea; have introduced opium, ganja, whiskey, arrack and other alcoholic poisons; have opened saloons and drinking taverns in every village; have killed all industries and made the people indolent...[142]

British rulers feared the resurgent Buddhist activism and the temperance movement as a threat to their political and economic dominance and took harsh action when they saw an opportunity. The most notorious example was in 1915, when communal riots broke out between a group of recent Muslim immigrants from India and some Kandyans in May 1915, over the use of loudspeakers outside of a mosque. Riots quickly spread to other parts of the country, including Colombo. Subsequent reports revealed illegal shootings of rioters by a colonial military that got "out of hand," and the group included "hot headed planters" shooting "as they pleased."[143] Colonial Secretary Stubbs "firmly believed" that the western educated Sinhalese elite were behind the organization of the rioting. Fearing the riots as a "rebellion against British rule," amidst the on-going World War 1. he "called for the most punitive measures."[144]

Martial law was declared and illegal arrests were made. Over 80 prominent Sinhalese including D. S. Senanayake (who became the country's first Prime Minister) and temperance leaders were imprisoned on charges of sedition without evidence.[145] The Anagarika Dharmapala was interned in Calcutta from June 1915 to 1920 and his younger brother Edmund Hewavitarne was imprisoned and died in

---

[142] Guruge, *Return to Righteousness: A Collection of Speeches, Essays, and Letters of the Anagarika Dharmapala.* Op.cit, 482.
[143] Fernando, P. T. M. "The British Raj and the 1915 Communal Riots in Ceylon." Modern Asian Studies 3, no. 3 (1969), 252.
[144] Fernando, P. T. M. "The British Raj and the 1915 Communal Riots in Ceylon." Modern Asian Studies 3, no. 3 (1969), 249.
[145] Ibid., 247.

prison due to lack of medical care.[146] R.A. Mirando, a leading temperance activist was killed during the riots.

Based on charges that he had shot at a group of Muslims and incited Sinhalese to riot, Edward Henry Pedris, who was attached to the Colonial Army Reserves, was convicted for treason in a three-day Field General Court Martial by passing the local legal system. A teetotaler and the twenty-seven-year-old scion of one of the island's wealthiest business families and a kinsman of Anagarika Dharmapala, he was executed on 7 July 1915.[147] The Colonial Office refused to grant an official inquiry into the unjust execution despite a concerted campaign by Sri Lankan leaders. This gruesome experience motivated the desire to get rid of British rule on the part of the Sinhala majority and hastened the movement towards social democracy in 1931 and self-rule in 1948.[148]

Self-Rule and Social Democracy, 1931–1948

The Donoughmore Commission arrived in Ceylon almost exactly a century after the last Constitutional Reform Commission, the 1832 Colebrooke Cameron Commission. Like the landmark Colebrooke Reforms which laid the legal and administrative foundation for colonial capitalist development, the Donoughmore Reforms of 1931 marked a turning point in the history of the island by providing the framework for self-rule and social democracy.

The Donoughmore Commission was appointed by socialist Sydney Webb, the first Labour Secretary of State for the Colonies. The Commissioners he appointed – Dr. Drummond Shiels, Frances Butler and Lord Donoughmore (the head of the Commission) – were also known for their egalitarian and progressive thinking. The Donoughmore Commissioners were also influenced by the on-going Great Depression and the rising power of Ceylon's labor union movement at the time.[149]

---

146 Ibid., 247; Guruge, *Return to Righteousness: A Collection of Speeches, Essays, and Letters of the Anagarika Dharmapala*, op.cit, xli.
147 Rajapathirana, Ranjith. "Judicial Assassination of Patriot Edward Henry Pedris." *Sunday Observer*, August 7, 2020. Accessed August 12, 2020. https://www.sundayobserver.lk/2020/08/09/spectrum/judicial-assassination-patriot-edward-henry-pedris.
148 Balachandran, P.K. "The Execution That Triggered the Struggle for Self-Rule." *Ceylon Today*, July 7, 2012. Accessed August 10, 2019. https://web.archive.org/web/20141221192706/http://www.ceylontoday.lk/59-9199-news-detail-the-execution-that-triggered-the-struggle-for-self-rule.html.
149 De Silva, Kingsley M. *History of Ceylon: From the Beginning of the Nineteenth Century to 1948*, Vol. 3. Colombo: Ceylon University Press, 1959, 492–493.

The Donoughmore Commission introduced universal franchise and a State Council of elected representatives thereby transferring control over domestic affairs from the British to local elites.[150] It was the first time in history that a non-white colony was granted universal franchise and control over local affairs. In 2021, on the 90th anniversary of the introduction of universal franchise to Sri Lanka, political scientist Jane Russell observed, "…Ceylon's contribution to world history in taking on universal franchise, unasked and probably prematurely, yet making it work so well for so long, has resulted in perhaps a fairer and more equal world than otherwise might have been the case."[151]

Back in 1931, threatened by the potential empowerment of the down-trodden Sinhala majority and low caste Tamils, the conservative political elite in the colony opposed the Reforms.[152] In fact, the Donoughmore Reforms resulted in divergent ethnic and social class developments. On the one hand, they communalized local politics exacerbating the Sinhala vs. Tamil conflict within the elite.[153] On the other hand, they hastened the emergence of a social welfare state beneficial to the hitherto neglected masses of citizenry.

Welfare legislation in Ceylon was first introduced to benefit the plantation sector. Unlike the earlier coffee plantations, tea plantations begun in the late 19th century, required a permanent labor force. Given the difficulties of attracting such a labor force, the British colonial state introduced minimum welfare measures in the first two decades of the 20th century in order to encourage recruitment and retention of South Indian immigrants on the tea estates. These included provision of rice at subsidized prices, minimum wage, medical facilities and exemption from the onerous poll tax borne by the indigenous population.[154] The trade unions which emerged later and began to organize the immigrant plantation workers fought for the continuation of welfare benefits. Much of the small proletariat employed

---

[150] De Silva, Leelananda. "Momentous Changes in Ceylon Instituted by the Donoughmore Commission." *Sunday Times, Sri Lanka*, July 5, 2020. Accessed August 12, 2020. https://thuppahis.com/2020/07/13/momentous-changes-in-ceylon-instituted-by-the-donoughmore-Commission/.

[151] Russell, Jane. "Complexities of Governance and Policy: 90th Anniversary of Universal Franchise in Sri Lanka." Awarelogue Initiative, Colombo, January 1, 2021. Accessed November 9, 2022. https://www.academia.edu/49945173/COMPLEXITIES_OF_GOVERNANCE_AND_POLICY_90th_Anniversary_of_Universal_Franchise_in_Sri_Lanka.

[152] De Silva, Kingsley M. *History of Ceylon: From the Beginning of the Nineteenth Century to 1948*, Vol. 3. Colombo: Ceylon University Press, 1959, 493; Ibid., 487–488.

[153] Bandarage, Asoka. *The Separatist Conflict in Sri Lanka: Terrorism, Ethnicity, Political Economy.* London: Routledge/Taylor & Francis Group, 2009, 35–37.

[154] Wickramaratne, L.A. "The Emergence of a Welfare Policy, 1931–1948", in de Silva, ed., *History of Ceylon*, vol.3, op.cit., 477.

in the modern railway, ports, tramcar services, etc. also came to be unionized and derived minimum benefits through labor agitation.[155]

The vulnerability of the colonial plantation economy, built upon the export of tea, rubber and coconut, and the import of consumer essentials, became painfully apparent during the turmoil of the Great Depression in the 1930s as it did during the two world wars. In each case, as export prices dropped and import prices soared, unemployment and poverty rose drastically. This was a precedent to Sri Lanka's many subsequent economic crises – including the 2022 crisis – all rooted in the dynamics of the colonial export-import economy.

Government subsidies for rice and flour were introduced in response to the rice shortages during the first World War and the Great Depression. This ad hoc measure was used again during the Second World War and continued well into the post-independence period, becoming a mainstay of Sri Lanka's electoral democracy and the welfare state.[156]

Clearly, more sustainable solutions than state subsidies were needed to address the problems of food shortages, growing unemployment and poverty. Starting in the last decades of the 19th century, a few colonial British Governors took initiatives to restore irrigation works and promote rice cultivation in the dry zone, but these efforts were not sufficient to bring forth food sovereignty.[157] After the introduction of the Donoughmore Constitution in 1931, a more long-term approach to meeting local survival needs came into place.

Donoughmore Reforms and Welfare State, 1931–1947

With the election of the Donoughmore State Council, control over domestic affairs passed into the hands of a Ceylonese Board of Ministers. They introduced policies explicitly to benefit the 'village poor,' newly empowered by the electoral vote.[158] This allowed some of the benefits that existed in the modern plantation and urban sectors, such as, basic medical care, rice subsidies and employment opportunities, to begin to be extended to the villages and the peasantry.

Free medical treatment was provided to the poor through the Medical Department during the Donoughmore years. These services evolved into a free comprehensive public healthcare system with the enactment of the Free Health policy in 1951. Since then, state-funded public healthcare facilities have been available

---

155 Ibid., 478.
156 De Silva, K.M.. *History of Ceylon*, Vol. 3. Colombo: Ceylon University Press, 1973, 487–488.
157 Ibid., 449–450.
158 Ibid., 484–485.

to all citizens.[159] In the post-colonial period, this system has achieved high quality of life indices in Sri Lanka, including low infant and maternal mortality and high life expectancy. However, this prized healthcare system is nearing collapse amid the current economic crisis. Patients are at risk due to power shortages, a lack of medicines, equipment shortages and other problems.[160]

Democratization and social welfare were particularly advanced by educational reform led by State Council's Minister of Education, C.W.W. Kannangara. A system of free education was introduced in 1942, establishing Central Schools to bring English education to the rural areas. The University of Ceylon, also based on the principle of free education, was inaugurated the same year.[161] The Free Education Policy which came into effect in 1945 stated that "every child above the age of 5 and not more than 16 is entitled to free education."[162] Like the free healthcare system, Sri Lanka's post-colonial free education system is now under inordinate pressure due to the effects of the Covid-19 crisis and economic collapse. Schools have been closed for long periods of time, exams have been postponed and students' futures remain uncertain.[163]

With the introduction of electoral democracy in 1931, the long-neglected issues of peasant landlessness, unemployment and poverty began to receive serious attention. Repairs began on the ancient irrigation works and landless peasants were settled in new developments in the dry zone. Under the helm of the State Council's Minister of Agriculture and Lands, D.S. Senanayake, the objectives were not only to improve the lives of the peasantry and the island's self-sufficiency in rice, but also the revival of the ancient hydraulic civilization. Between 1933 and 1948, an estimated 3,342 allotments covering 26,737 acres of land came under state sponsored settlement, mostly of landless peasantry from the highly populated wet zone to the under-

---

159 Daniel, Jasmine. "8 Facts About Healthcare in Sri Lanka." *The Borgen Project*, July 22, 2020. Accessed August 12, 2020. https://borgenproject.org/healthcare-in-sri-lanka/.

160 *UN News*. "Sri Lanka's Economic Crisis Pushes Health System to Brink of Collapse," August 17, 2022. Accessed August 22, 2022. https://news.un.org/en/story/2022/08/1124842.

161 De Silva, K. M. *History of Ceylon*, Vol. 3. Colombo: Ceylon University Press, 1973, 486; De Silva, Leelananda. "Momentous Changes in Ceylon Instituted by the Donoughmore Commission." *Sunday Times*, Sri Lanka, July 5, 2020. Accessed July 12, 2020. https://thuppahis.com/2020/07/13/momentous-changes-in-ceylon-instituted-by-the-Donoughmore-Commission/.

162 Ministry of Foreign Affairs – Sri Lanka. "Free Education Policy in Sri Lanka." Accessed December 28, 2022. https://mfa.gov.lk/cool_timeline/free-education-policy-in-sri-lanka/.

163 Mallawarachi, Bharatha. "With No Fuel and No Cash, Sri Lanka Keeps Schools Closed." AP NEWS, July 3, 2022. https://apnews.com/article/sri-lanka-foreign-debt-indian-ocean-26e667e2b510e15d8923c15c6a5c3a14.

populated dry zone. 'Colonization,' as this process was referred to since British rule, was greatly expanded in the post-colonial period.[164]

A major change to the well-established colonial approach to land policy came with the Land Development Ordinance (LDO) of 1935 which incorporated the recommendations of the Land Commission of 1929 and the terms of the Land Settlement Ordinance of 1931. As discussed earlier, the Crown Lands Encroachment Ordinance of 1840 and the Waste Lands Ordinance of 1897 were motivated by the colonial state's desire to appropriate Crown land for export-oriented plantation development. In contrast, the LDO of 1935 introduced a new national welfare approach motivated by the desire to alienate Crown land primarily to benefit villages, peasant cultivators and local food production.[165]

A Land Commissioner's Department was set up to 'map out' land for free distribution. Crown Land was given out to various categories of citizens under permits and grants, but without freehold rights. Restrictions were placed on the sale, mortgage and leasing of property granted by the state.[166] The objective of granting limited tenure with restrictions on sale was to ensure that the land remained in peasant hands and under local food production. Over the subsequent decades, the same protected form of land alienation and tenure of the LDO was continued. As a result, 80 percent of the land in Sri Lanka is still, in 2022, said to be state owned 'Crown land'.[167]

---

[164] De Silva, K.M.. *History of Ceylon*, Vol. 3. Colombo: Ceylon University Press, 1959, 460; Ellman, A.O. *Land Settlement in Sri Lanka, 1840–1975: A Review of the Major Writings on the Subject*. Colombo: Agrarian Research and Training Institute, 1976, 17.

[165] "The Land Development Ordinance: An Ordinance to Provide for the Systematic Development and Alienation of Crown Land in Ceylon. Ordinance Nos, 19 of 1935 and 3 of 1946; Act Nos, 49 of 1953 and 22 of 1955" (Ceylon State Council, October 19, 1935), [Available at: https://www.lawnet.gov.lk/land-development/]; Raji, Nabeela. "The Land Development Ordinance: Key Concerns and Ideas for Reform." Colombo: Law & Society Trust, June 2017. https://www.lstlanka.org/wp-content/uploads/2022/02/The-Land-Development-Ordinance.pdf.

[166] Ellman, A.O. Land Settlement in Sri Lanka, 1840–1975: A Review of the Major Writings on the Subject. Colombo: Agrarian Research and Training Institute, 1976, 17–18; Raji, Nabeela. "The Land Development Ordinance: Key Concerns and Ideas for Reform." Colombo: Law & Society Trust, June 2017. https://www.lstlanka.org/wp-content/uploads/2022/02/The-Land-Development-Ordinance.pdf.

[167] De Silva, Leelananda. "Momentous Changes in Ceylon Instituted by the Donoughmore Commission." *Sunday Times, Sri Lanka*, July 5, 2020. https://thuppahis.com/2020/07/13/momentous-changes-in-ceylon-instituted-by-the-donoughmore-commission/. Millennium Challenge Corporation, Sri Lanka Constraints Analysis, 2017. "Sri Lanka Constraints Analysis Report 2017." Millennium Challenge Corporation, 2017. https://assets.mcc.gov/content/uploads/constraints-analysis-sri-lanka.pdf.

During the early years following political independence from Britain, the Donoughmore influenced welfare policies on healthcare, education and land development were continued.[168] At the same time, the well-established institutions of colonialism were maintained intact. The result was a continuing clash between the goals of social democracy and those of capitalist profitmaking, a continually familiar situation in neo-colonial countries worldwide.

---

[168] Sanderatne, Nimal "Changing Scenarios: 64 Years of Lost Opportunities," *Sunday Times*, Sri Lanka, February 5, 2012. Accessed November 30, 2022. https://www.sundaytimes.lk/120205/Columns/eco.html.

Chapter 3:
'Flag Independence', Left-Wing Nationalism and Decolonization, 1948–1977

With increasing demands for further political reform towards independence, the Soulbury Constitution was introduced in 1947 to replace the Donoughmore Constitution, giving Ceylon a parliamentary electoral system. In the wake of Indian independence, the governance of the island was passed from the British to the local westernized political leaders on February 4, 1948. The imperialist power took a back seat, and placed the selected native elite in the front driving seat. As historian N. Sanmugathasan put it in 1972, "the puppets that danced on the local stage were natives, but the invisible strings that manipulated the puppets were pulled from Whitehall or Washington."[1]

The first parliamentary election was held in 1947 and was won by the conservative United National Party (UNP) headed by D.S. Senanayake. Notwithstanding his populist policies on land colonization and local agriculture, Senanayake, a wealthy owner of a graphite mining enterprise, largely represented the interests of the island's conservative landed gentry, the business community and the westernized elite. Despite a virulent anti-Marxist campaign by the conservatives, the Marxist parties – Lanka Sama Samaja Party (LSSP), Bolshevik–Leninist Party of India, Ceylon and Burma (BLPI) and the Communist Party (CP) – fared well in the 1947 election, winning 18 (20 according to some counts) out of a total 95 seats.[2] The left parties, which were supported by the urban trade unions, posed a significant threat to the interests of both western imperialism and the local "bourgeoisie."

With the political independence of 1948, D.S. Senanayake became the country's first prime minister. The signing of a defense agreement guaranteeing Britain's continued control over all the security assets of the island was a precondition for the granting of independence. The agreement, signed secretly with D.S. Senanayake on November 11, 1947, provided Britain the "use of naval and air bases,

---
[1] Sanmugathasan, N. *A Marxist Looks at the History of Ceylon*. Colombo: Sarasavi Printers, 1972, 50. 2nd ed. available at: https://www.marxists.org/history/erol/sri-lanka/ceylon-history/index.htm.
[2] Ibid., 53; "Table 31 (Gov., Parlia.) Parliament Election (1947)," Kusaka Research Institute, accessed January 2, 2023, https://www.jpp.co.jp/lanka/gov/govd/govde/gov31e.htm.

ports, military establishments and the use of telecommunication facilities ..." on the island.[3]

As the British empire receded alongside the other European imperialists – at least in the classical forms of colonialism – so rose the United States, to increase its 20th century dominance to become the unequivocal global superpower after World War II. In this role it exerted significant economic, political and cultural influence over Sri Lanka from the very start of its independence, as it did in most post-colonial countries.[4] A simple example is how John Exter, an American economist, was nominated by the Federal Reserve Board of the USA to establish a central bank for the island. Not only this; having set up the Central Bank of Ceylon, he then served as its first governor from 1950 to 1953.[5]

U.S. corporate interest was also advanced in Sri Lanka and across the developing world by the twin institutions of Bretton Woods: the IMF and World Bank, both founded in 1945, with a strategy of debt-dependency and infrastructure and economic development focused on export (i.e., plantation) economy and, ultimately, the bottom line of foreign corporate interest.[6] As the largest contributor to the IMF – with over two and a half times the quota and votes of Japan (#2), China (#3) and Germany (#4), for example, as of December 2022[7] – the US has veto power in the organization. To date, the IMF managing director is always a European and the World Bank president is always an American.[8]

---

[3] Somasunderam, Ramesh. *Strategic Significance of Srilanka.* Pannipitiya, Sri Lanka: Stamford Lake Publication, 2005, 8, 87–90.

[4] Waduge, Shenali. "US in Sri Lanka since 2015 – Turning Sri Lanka into a Neo-Colonial Military Base." LankaWeb. Accessed January 2, 2023. https://www.lankaweb.com/news/items/2019/11/01/us-in-sri-lanka-since-2015-turning-sri-lanka-into-a-neo-colonial-military-base/.

[5] *Central Bank of Sri Lanka.* "John Exter," Accessed January 2, 2023. https://www.cbsl.gov.lk/en/about/about-the-bank/bank-history/john-exter.

[6] Hudson, Michael. *Super Imperialism; the Economic Strategy of American Empire.* New York: Holt, Rinehart and Winston, 1972, 8; Steinmetz-Jenkins, Daniel. "The Rotten Roots of the IMF and the World Bank." *The Nation,* June 15, 2022. Accessed October 25, 2022. https://www.thenation.com/article/culture/the-rotten-roots-of-global-economic-governance/; Lakshman, W. D. "The IMF-World Bank Intervention in Sri Lankan Economic Policy: Historical Trends and Patterns." *Social Scientist 13,* no. 2 (1985): 3–29, 3–4. https://doi.org/10.2307/3520187.

[7] IMF. "IMF Members' Quotas and Voting Power, and IMF Board of Governors." Accessed December 30, 2022. https://www.imf.org/en/About/executive-board/members-quotas.

[8] Keating, Joshua E. "Why Is the IMF Chief Always a European?" *Foreign Policy,* May 18, 2011. Accessed October 5, 2021. https://foreignpolicy.com/2011/05/18/why-is-the-imf-chief-always-a-european/; U.S. Department of the Treasury. "International Monetary Fund." Accessed January 2, 2023. https://home.treasury.gov/policy-issues/international/international-monetary-fund.

Since its inception, the International Bank of Reconstruction and Development (IBRD) has been the 'lending arm' of the World Bank. To this day, it states in the first of its founding Articles of Agreement, clause (ii) that one of its key purposes is, "To promote private *foreign* [emphasis added] investment by means of guarantees or participations in loans and other investments made by *private* [emphasis added] investors."[9]

Although Sri Lanka's period of classical colonialism and direct political control by Britain ended with independence in 1948, the basic institutions of colonialism – the plantations, the Christian English language school system and social class and ethno-religious hierarchies – were maintained intact. Its true geopolitical, socioeconomic and cultural status post-independence (particularly between 1948 and 1956) fits what Walter Rodney, the author of the classic work, *How Europe Underdeveloped Africa* (1973) termed 'flag independence': continued colonialism under a local flag.[10]

Crises and Resistance, 1948 – 1956

Like today, in 1952, 70 years ago, Sri Lanka was faced with a foreign exchange shortage and a major food crisis due to the continuing colonial import-export economy and declining terms of trade. The rapid end of the Korean war boom led to a collapse in Sri Lanka's export prices, especially that of rubber. Other key commodities increased drastically in cost, such as the world market price of rice, which rose by 38 percent between 1951 and 1952.[11] By 1952, the government was spending 20 percent of its total revenue to bridge the gap between the world price of rice and its subsidized retail selling price in the island.[12]

Rising birth rates and decreasing death rates contributed to a dramatic increase in the population in Sri Lanka, as was the case in other parts of the

---

9 *World Bank*. "IBRD Articles of Agreement: Article I." Accessed January 4, 2023. https://www.worldbank.org/en/about/articles-of-agreement/ibrd-articles-of-agreement/article-I.
10 Rodney, Walter. *How Europe Underdeveloped Africa*. [New edition]. Brooklyn: Verso, 2018.
11 Kelegama, J.B. "The Significance of the Ceylon-China Trade Agreement of 1952 (Keynote Address at the Fiftieth Anniversary Celebrations of the Historic 'Rubber-Rice Pact' between Sri Lanka and China at the BMICH on 20 December 2002)." *The Island*, October 28, 2003. Accessed January 2, 2023. https://web.archive.org/web/20031028065224/http://www.island.lk/2002/12/22/featur06.html.
12 *Britanica.Com*. "Hartal: Ceylonese Labour Strike." Accessed January 2, 2023. https://www.britannica.com/event/hartal; De Silva, Kingsley Muthumuni. *History of Ceylon: From the Beginning of the Nineteenth Century to 1948*, Vol. 3. Colombo: Ceylon University Press, 1959, 487–488.

world.[13] Sri Lanka's total population increased from 6.7 million in 1946 to 8 million in 1953, a 21.6 percent increase with a population growth rate of 2.8 percent in 1953.[14] (Table 3.1). The dramatic population increase was partly attributable to state provisions, especially free healthcare and food subsidies, and aggravated unemployment and other socioeconomic problems.

Table 3.1: Sri Lanka population, total and increase, 1800–2020.

Year	Population	Average Annual Growth Rate
1800	1,200,000	–
1821	1,440,000	–
1849	2,210,000	–
1871	2,400,380	–
1881	2,759,738	1.4
1891	3,007,789	0.9
1901	3,565,954	1.7
1911	4,106,350	1.4
1921	4,498,605	0.9
1931	5,306,871	1.7
1946	6,657,339	1.5
1953	8,097,895	2.8
1963	10,582,064	2.7
1971	12,711,143	2.2
1981	14,846,750	1.5
1990	17,325,773	1.7
2000	18,777,601	0.8
2010	20,261,737	0.7
2020	21,413,249	0.5

Sources: Sri Lanka Department of Census and Statistics, 1974 http://www.cicred.org/Eng/Publications/pdf/c-c46.pdf and Sri Lanka Department of Census and Statistics 1971–2012 http://sis.statistics.gov.lk/statHtml/statHtml.do?orgId=144&tblId=DT_POP_SER_266&conn_path=I2 and Population of Sri Lanka from 1800 to 2020 https://www.statista.com/statistics/1067091/population-sri-lanka-historical/.

In the wake of the foreign exchange and food crises, Sri Lanka entered an agreement with China in December 1952 which came to be known as the Rubber Rice Pact. Under this agreement, China agreed to supply rice to Sri Lanka at lower than market prices and to purchase rubber at prices higher than global market

---

[13] Asoka Bandarage, *Women, Population and Global Crisis: A Political-Economic Analysis*, London: Zed Books, 1997, 5.
[14] "The Population of Sri Lanka." C.I.C.R.E.D. Series. Colombo, Sri Lanka: Department of Census & Statistics, 1974. Available at: http://cicred.org/Eng/Publications/pdf/c-c46.pdf.

prices.[15] This agreement lasted 30 years and is still considered one of the "most useful trade agreements negotiated by Sri Lanka."[16] The pact was signed amidst virulent opposition from ministers in the Ceylon Cabinet who were advised by the newly established Central Bank under John Exter. The finance minister, Junius Richard Jayawaredena (J. R., also known as 'Yankee Dickie') also vehemently opposed the pact, for its obvious challenge to US hegemony.[17]

Unsurprisingly, both Britain and the United States protested the pact and, just like current U.S. punitive policies against any country that defies its interests, the U.S. stopped a "substantial portion of its aid" to Sri Lanka and placed an embargo on the export of several items to the country in 1953.[18] Given the pro-western stance of the United National Party (UNP) that ruled at the time, despite the success of the Rubber Rice Pact, Sri Lanka did not risk establishing diplomatic relations with China at the time.[19]

On the advice of Central Bank Governor (and American) John Exter, the 1952 parliamentary elections were held ahead of time in May. He had warned of an impending economic crisis and advised "getting a fresh mandate through elections before resorting to harsh measures."[20] Accordingly, once the UNP easily won the early election, Exter then advised them to pursue austerity measures, such as cutting relief aid to the populace, in order resuscitate the economy.[21] The World Bank also advised the elimination of food subsidies.[22] Even the longstanding rice subsidy – the 'sacred cow' of the island's electoral democracy – was abolished in 1953, increasing the price of a measure of rice from 25 cents to 75 cents. Railway and postal rates were increased and even the midday bun given to schoolchildren was elim-

---

15 Kelegama, J.B. "The Significance of the Ceylon-China Trade Agreement of 1952 (Keynote Address at the Fiftieth Anniversary Celebrations of the Historic 'Rubber-Rice Pact' between Sri Lanka and China at the BMICH on 20 December 2002)." *The Island*, October 28, 2003. Accessed January 2, 2023. https://web.archive.org/web/20031028065224/http://www.island.lk/2002/12/22/featur06.html.
16 Ibid., 2.
17 Ibid., 2. Indrajith, Saman. "American Stooge JR Was Dubbed 'Yankee Dickie', Ranil Today Is 'Yankee Wickie' – Vasudeva Nanayakkara." Dbsjeyaraj.Com (blog), October 24, 2015. Accessed January 2, 2023. https://dbsjeyaraj.com/dbsj/archives/43684.
18 Rajasingham, K.T. "SRI LANKA: THE UNTOLD STORY: Chapter 15: Turbulence in Any Language." *Asia Times*, February 8, 2002. Accessed December 20, 2022. https://web.archive.org/web/20020208193722/http://www.atimes.com/ind-pak/CK17Df01.html.
19 Ibid.
20 Sanmugathasan, N. *A Marxist Looks at the History of Ceylon*. Colombo: Sarasavi Printers, 56. [2nd ed. available at: https://www.marxists.org/history/erol/sri-lanka/ceylon-history/index.htm, Accessed December 26, 2022].
21 Ibid.
22 Lakshman, W. D. "The IMF-World Bank Intervention in Sri Lankan Economic Policy: Historical Trends and Patterns." *Social Scientist 13*, no. 2 (1985): 3–29, 7. https://doi.org/10.2307/3520187.

inated.[23] Thus, like today, austerity and the burden of the economic crisis was passed on to the people.

The UNP policies of 1952/53 provoked tremendous public dissatisfaction over the rise in the cost of living, especially that of rice. Like *aragalaya* (meaning struggle in Sinhala) of today, it led to a people's struggle against the elected government, the first mass political action in the newly 'independent' country. The Marxist parties led by the Trotskyite LSSP organized civil disobedience and a *hartal* (strike) on August 12, 1953. Almost all the anti-UNP forces joined the massive country-wide protest; shops closed, work ceased and the government was paralyzed.[24] There were many outbreaks of violence and much damage to property. The government declared a state of emergency and used repressive measures to end the hartal, with ten people killed and hundreds jailed. The prime minister, Dudley Senanayake (son of D.S. Senanayake), resigned and the rice subsidy was partially restored by his cousin, the new prime minister, John Kotelawala.[25]

The hartal symbolized the growing resentment towards the UNP and its alignment with the interests of the local landed gentry, wealthy business community and westernized elite and western powers.

It is now well established that the U.S. engaged in partisan election interference prior to the pivotal 1956 election. U.S. Secretary of State John Foster Dulles and ambassador Philip K. Crowe (ex-Office of Strategic Services (OSS), the wartime precursor to the CIA) met with Prime Minister John Kotelawala and Governor General Oliver Goonetilleke to discuss political strategy and a $5 million aid package for "non-agricultural" development and technical assistance on March 11, 1956.[26] The U.S. aid package was announced in the press prior to the election with the clear description that it was conditional to curbing trade with China and the USSR.[27] 'Weaponized aid' – such as strategic pre-election announcements

---

[23] Ibid., 57.
[24] Sanmugathasan, N. *A Marxist Looks at the History of Ceylon*. Colombo: Sarasavi Printers, 1972, 55. [2nd ed. available at: https://www.marxists.org/history/erol/sri-lanka/ceylon-history/index.htm, Accessed December 26, 2022.]; Rajasingham, K. T. "Sri Lanka: The Untold Story: Chapter 15: Turbulence in Any Language." *Asia Times*, February 8, 2002. Accessed December 20, 2022. https://web.archive.org/web/20020208193722/http://www.atimes.com/ind-pak/CK17Df01.html.
[25] *Britanica.Com*. "Hartal: Ceylonese Labour Strike." Accessed January 2, 2023. https://www.britannica.com/event/hartal; https://dbsjeyaraj.com/dbsj/archives/47156.
[26] "Document 137. Memorandum of a Conversation, Colombo, March 11, 1956." In *Foreign Relations of the United States, 1955–1957, South Asia, Vol. VII*. Office of the Historian, Bureau of Public Affairs, U.S. Department of State, 2018. https://history.state.gov/historicaldocuments/frus1955-57v08.
[27] Levin, Dov. H. 'When the Great Power Gets a Vote: The Effects of Great Power Electoral Interventions on Election Results,' International Studies Quarterly (2016), 60, 189–201. Appendix 2, 2–3.

of conditional aid – were a common strategy of U.S. soft power and election interference during the Cold War and remain so today.

Despite such external efforts to sway local public opinion in favor of the conservative 'uncle-nephew' UNP, a populist left-nationalist coalition came into power in a landslide victory in the general election of April 1956. This shifted the country away from its colonial trajectory towards a socialist-nationalist direction, and reflected international desires for decolonization and resistance to neocolonialism taking place in newly independent countries across the world in the second half of the 20th century.

Decolonization and the Cold War

The term neocolonialism was articulated by pan-Africanist Kwame Nkrumah, the first president of independent Ghana (what had been called the 'Gold Coast' by European imperialists). In his 1965 book, *Neo-colonialism: The Last Stage of Imperialism*, Nkrumah described a neocolonial state as one that is "in theory, independent and has all the outward trappings of international sovereignty," but "in reality, its economic system and thus its political policy is directed from outside."[28] The concepts of neocolonialism and nonalignment in foreign policy that Nkrumah and other leaders of ex-colonial states championed in the 1950s and 1960s, despite the spin and PR of modern politics, are just as relevant today for Sri Lanka and the world, desired by the majority and equally contested by those in power who wish to retain the status quo.[29]

Decolonization of Asian and African colonies after World War II converged with the Cold War between the United States and the Soviet Union. The U.S. was increasingly concerned that as the European powers lost their colonies, Soviet-backed communist parties could come to power in the newly independent states.[30] In the feverish fear-mongering and propaganda, it is difficult to judge to what degree the USSR was pursuing global influence, intervention and dominance during

---

[28] Nkrumah, Kwame. *Neo-Colonialism, The Last Stage of Imperialism*, London: Thomas Nelson & Sons, Ltd., 1965 https://politicalanthro.files.wordpress.com/2010/08/nkrumah.pdf.

[29] Ministry of External Affairs, Government of India, *History and Evolution of Non-Aligned Movement*, August 22, 2012. Accessed December 29, 2022. https://www.mea.gov.in/in-focus-article.htm?20349/History+and+Evolution+of+NonAligned+Movement.

[30] Office of the Historian, Bureau of Public Affairs, U.S. Department of State. "Milestones: 1945–1952: Decolonization of Asia and Africa, 1945–1960." Accessed December 31, 2022. https://history.state.gov/milestones/1945-1952/asia-and-africa.

its life span. For example, in a rare, rather conservative 2016 comparison of election interference by the US and by the USSR/Russia between 1946 and 2000, Dov Levin found that 69 percent of operations were carried out by the former and 31 percent by the latter, and the budget discrepancy was far, far greater.[31] More importantly, for the US, its superficial raison d'être of rabid anti-communism served and serves as a perfect front for pursuing its true raison d'être of elitist global hegemony, crushing national liberation struggles in the process. In truth, the foreign policy of the American century was and is anti-peasant and pro-US profit far above any other values it might profess.

These national liberation struggles – initially against the old empire and then against the new – included the Indonesian struggle for independence from the Netherlands (1945–1950), the Vietnamese war against France (1945–1954), and the emergence of nationalist and socialist regimes in Egypt (1952) and Iran (1951). They buttressed U.S. fears, even when new governments did not align themselves with the Soviet Union.[32] Many of these struggles were aligned more with basic rights, survival and sovereignty than an ideological world revolution.

Documents from the U.S. government's Office of the Historian point out that, given fears of Communism, "… the United States used aid packages, technical assistance and sometimes even military intervention to encourage newly independent nations … to adopt governments that aligned with the West."[33] The same documents describe that the USSR used similar tactics to convince newly decolonized countries that "communism was an intrinsically non-imperialist economic and political ideology" in order to encourage them to join the communist bloc.[34]

In the melee, many of the new nations logically desired their own path and resisted the pressure to be drawn into the Cold War by joining the Non-Aligned Movement (NAM), which in effect began at the Bandung conference of 1955. They sought an autonomous path to internal development in keeping with their own economic needs and cultural traditions. NAM was officially founded in Belgrade, Yugoslavia in June 1961, involving Yugoslav President Josip Broz Tito, Indian Prime Minister Jawaharlal Nehru, Egyptian President Gamal Abdel Nasser and

---

[31] Levin, Dov H. "When the Great Power Gets a Vote: The Effects of Great Power Electoral Interventions on Election Results." *International Studies Quarterly* 60, no. 2 (June 2016): 189–202, Appendix 2, 2–3. https://doi.org/10.1093/isq/sqv016.
[32] Office of the Historian, Bureau of Public Affairs, U.S. Department of State. "Milestones: 1945–1952: Decolonization of Asia and Africa, 1945–1960." Accessed December 31, 2022. https://history.state.gov/milestones/1945-1952/asia-and-africa.
[33] Ibid.
[34] Ibid.

Ghanaian President Kwame Nkrumah, with Indonesian President Sukarno and Sri Lanka's Prime Minister Sirimavo Bandaranaike as its leaders.[35]

While nonaligned countries managed to maintain a nonaligned path in military terms during the Cold War, they found it exceedingly difficult to pursue sovereignty in terms of resources and economic development. A good example is Patrice Lumumba, the first prime minister of the Democratic Republic of the Congo (DRC), elected in June 1960. His attempts to bring "genuine independence and sovereign control of DRC resources threatened powerful interests."[36] Recently declassified files from U.S. and Belgian intelligence reveal that both governments collaborated with Lumumba's Congolese rivals in his brutal assassination in January 1961.[37]

Kwame Nkrumah was similarly overthrown in a military coup supported by Washington in February 1966, after he made economic development agreements with Czechoslovakia and the Soviet Union.[38] Likewise, *Ujamaa*, or 'African socialism' (derived from the Swahili word for extended family) – promoted by Tanzania's leader Julius Nyerere in the 1960s to develop villages and local food security – was harshly condemned by the West, particularly as a potential 'threat of a good example'.[39] The external opposition and internal factors contributed to Ujamaa's failure to advance community-based development over capitalism and individual-

---

[35] Ministry of External Affairs, Government of India, *History and Evolution of Non-Aligned Movement*, August 22, 2012. Accessed December 29, 2022. https://www.mea.gov.in/in-focus-article.htm?20349/History+and+Evolution+of+NonAligned+Movement; sirimavobandaranaike.org. "01–06 September 1961 – First Non-Aligned Movement Summit in Belgrade." Accessed January 2, 2023. https://sirimavobandaranaike.org/01-06-september-1961-first-non-aligned-movement-summit-in-belgrade/.

[36] Chowdhury, Anis, and Jomo Kwame Sundaram. "Africa Struggles with Neo-Colonialism." *Inter Press Service*, September 13, 2022. Accessed December 2, 2022. https://www.ipsnews.net/2022/09/africa-struggles-neo-colonialism/.

[37] Nzongola-Ntalaja, Georges. "Patrice Lumumba: The Most Important Assassination of the 20th Century" *The Guardian*. January 17, 2011. Accessed November 29th, 2022. https://amp.theguardian.com/global-development/poverty-matters/2011/jan/17/patrice-lumumba-50th-anniversary-assassination; Weissman, Stephen R. "Opening the Secret Files on Lumumba's Murder." *Washington Post*, July 21, 2002. Accessed December 30, 2022. https://www.washingtonpost.com/archive/opinions/2002/07/21/opening-the-secret-files-on-lumumbas-murder/a6cff763-335c-482f-92f4-424bf2db7742/.

[38] Chowdhury, Anis, and Jomo Kwame Sundaram. "Africa Struggles with Neo-Colonialism." *Inter Press Service*, September 13, 2022. Accessed December 2, 2022. https://www.ipsnews.net/2022/09/africa-struggles-neo-colonialism/.

[39] Dibua, J.I., and Bonny Ibhawoh. "Deconstructing Ujamaa: The Legacy of Julius Nyerere in the Quest for Social and Economic Development." *African Journal of Political Science* 8, no. 1 (2003).

ism. Ujamaa's failure deterred other African countries from charting their own paths of development.[40]

An important victory for decolonization, however, came in Egypt in 1956, when Egyptian President Gamal Abdel Nasser deterred Israel, the United Kingdom and France from removing him from office and regaining control of the Suez Canal after he nationalized the British- and French-owned Suez Canal Company, which administered the canal. Following the Suez victory, Nasser emerged a hero not only for Arab and Egyptian nationalism but also for 'Third World' nationalism around the world.[41]

Meanwhile, in Southeast Asia, the United States was heavily engaged in covert action to deter the spread of communism in Buddhist countries starting in the early 1950s. One anti-communist strategy in the region, capitalizing on the fears of communist and socialist atheism and anti-religionism, included the mobilization of Buddhist monks, as reported in Eugene Ford's book, *Cold War Monks: Buddhism and America's Secret Strategy in Southeast Asia*.[42] It represented a regional example of a broad global and domestic strategy of co-opting faith and weaponizing religion; "an approach that found numerous, if fragmentary, precedents in earlier efforts to marshal faith, often through the use of religious rhetoric, against what was perceived as an atheistic Soviet menace."[43]

As a part of this strategy, U.S. intelligence officials identified Sri Lankan Buddhist leader G. P. Malalasekera as a major obstacle. Malalasekera confounded their ideology by advocating international Buddhism as a path, not to neocolonialism, but to decolonization and "an alternative to Communism and western imperialism."[44] His main vehicle to achieve this began with the World Fellowship of Buddhists, which he founded in 1950, and which influenced the U.S. to establish the Committee for a Free Asia (CFA) in 1951 to counter Malalasekera's plans. The CFA became the Asia Foundation in 1954 and continues to fund hundreds of pro-US programs with millions of dollars across Asia.[45]

---

40 Ibid.; Boddy-Evans, Alistair. "What Was Ujamaa and How Did It Affect Tanzania?" *ThoughtCo*, August 2, 2019. Accessed December 30, 2022. https://www.thoughtco.com/what-was-ujamaa-44589.
41 *Britanica.Com*. "Suez Crisis." Accessed January 2, 2023. https://www.britannica.com/event/Suez-Crisis.
42 Ford, Eugene. *Cold War Monks: Buddhism and America's Secret Strategy in Southeast Asia*. Yale University Press, 2017.
43 Ibid., 40.
44 Ibid., 30–35.
45 Ibid., 35.

Later in the Cold War, the US weaponized the even more geopolitically potent Islamic world, with the CIA supporting and guiding the development of anti-communist pan-Islamic organizations as a means to fight the left, and by extension national liberation movements, with plenty of oil money to fuel their power.[46] These included the Muslim World League in 1962, the Islamic Centre of Geneva in 1965 and the Organization of the Islamic Conference in 1969.[47]

It was in this tumultuous environment of regional and international post-colonial and Cold War developments that Sinhala Buddhist nationalism resurged in Sri Lanka in the mid-1950s.

The 1956 Revolution in Sri Lanka

Solomon West Ridgeway Dias (S.W.R.D.) Bandaranaike, who became Prime Minister following the defeat of the right-wing UNP in 1956, was the scion of a wealthy Christian family with a long history of connection to the British colonial regime. In 1895, for example, his father Sir Solomon Dias Bandaranaike was appointed Head Mudaliyar, the highest position available to a native in the country at the time. He was also aide-de-camp to British Governor, Joseph West Ridgeway, after whom he named his son.[48]

S.W.R.D. studied at Oxford where he was secretary to the Oxford Union and excelled in oratory. The racial discrimination combined with the fervor of Indian nationalism he experienced at Oxford convinced him of the need to end the colonial subordination of his country.[49] On returning home, he became fluent in Sinhala, converted to Buddhism and donned a locally produced national garb symbolizing his personal decolonization.[50]

Bandaranaike resigned from the Western-oriented UNP and founded the nationalist Sri Lanka Freedom Party in 1951. Four years later he formed the *Mahajana Eksath Peramuna* (MEP, People's United Front), a political alliance of four na-

---

[46] Prashad, Vijay. "Part 2: The Answer to Communism Lay in the Hope of Muslim Revival." In *Washington Bullets*. New York: Monthly Review Press, 2020.
[47] Ibid.
[48] The Open University: Making Britain: Discover how South Asians shaped the nation, 1870–1950. "Solomon West Ridgeway Dias Bandaranaike." Accessed January 2, 2023. https://www.open.ac.uk/researchprojects/makingbritain/content/solomon-west-ridgeway-dias-bandaranaike.
[49] Bandaranaike, S. W. R. D. *Speeches and Writings*. Colombo, Ceylon: Information Division, Dept. of Broadcasting and Information, 1963, 77.
[50] Ibid., 287, 304; Leslie Fernando, W.T.A. "Debate: National Dress Suits Our Country, Climate and Culture." *Daily News*, January 17, 2007. Accessed January 2, 2023. http://archives.dailynews.lk/2007/01/17/fea02.asp.

tionalist-socialist parties (including the LSSP and the CP). The MEP was able to gain two-thirds majority in Parliament riding on a wave of strong Sinhala nationalist sentiment kindled by the 2500th anniversary of the Buddha's birth in 1956. And so Bandaranaike became the Prime Minister on April 12, 1956, ushering in a new era of decolonization.

Keeping with the nationalist spirit of the 1955 Bandung Conference and refusing to automatically line up with western imperialism, Bandaranaike advocated a neutral foreign policy for Sri Lanka.[51] He abrogated the defense pact with Britain, thereby terminating British military bases on the island, and established diplomatic relations with communist states. Inspired by Buddhism, Bandaranaike aimed to find a 'Middle Way' that would avoid the extremes of both capitalism and communism.

Several radical measures were carried out by the MEP regime. Despite the opposition of private interests, the island's bus transportation and the Port of Colombo were both nationalized. Additionally, the Paddy Lands Act of 1958, an agrarian reform law, was passed to give security of tenancy to rural cultivators over landowning interests. Urban workers were given greater freedom to strike and an Employee Provident Fund was introduced in 1958, still the largest social security retirement scheme in the country.[52] Though leftist, nationalist and anti-western in tone, the Bandaranaike regime was not revolutionary in that it did not seek to completely opt out of the western capitalist system.[53]

In allegiance to the strong nationalist wave that brought the MEP into office, Buddhism, the majority religion practiced by approximately 65 percent of the population at the time, was given a prominent place in the affairs of state. Likewise, in a move condemned by the English-speaking elite of all local communities, Sinhalese, the language spoken by approximately 70 percent of the population, was made the official language of the country by the Official Language Act No. 33 of 1956 (commonly referred to as the Sinhala Only Act), replacing English.[54] Tamil resistance to this policy was widespread and marked a turning point in Sinhala-

---

[51] "Final Communiqué of the Asian-African Conference, 24 April 1955." In *Asia-Africa Speak from Bandung*, 161–169. Ministry of Foreign Affairs, Indonesia, 2017. Available at: https://www.cvce.eu/en/obj/final_communique_of_the_asian_african_conference_of_bandung_24_april_1955-en-676237bd-72f7-471f-949a-88b6ae513585.html.

[52] *Employees Provident Fund, Central Bank of Sri Lanka*. "What Is EPF?" Accessed January 2, 2023. https://epf.lk/?page_id=2.

[53] Olson, Richard Stuart. "Expropriation and International Economic Coercion: Ceylon and the 'West' 1961–65." *The Journal of Developing Areas* 11, no. 2 (1977): 205–226, 215, 224.

[54] Bandarage, Asoka. *The Separatist Conflict in Sri Lanka: Terrorism, Ethnicity, Political Economy*. London: Routledge/Taylor & Francis Group, 2009, 45.

Tamil relations and a descent into violence, such as the horrific 'race riots' of 1958.[55]

In a shocking turn of events, the beleaguered prime minister was shot and assassinated on September 25, 1959. Ironically, the violent act was carried out by Talduwe Somarama, a Buddhist monk. Bandaranaike's magnanimity came through in his last message to the nation from his hospital bed before his death. Without referring to his assailant as a Buddhist monk, the Prime Minister described him "as a foolish man dressed in the robes of a monk" and called upon the government and authorities to "show compassion to this man and not try to wreak vengeance on him."[56]

It is commonly assumed that political grievance, namely Bandaranaike's alleged compromise with the Tamils, provoked his assassination. However, recent writings suggest that personal grievance, namely Bandaranaike's refusal to grant his powerful patron Buddhist monk Mapitigama Buddharakkhita a government contract for a business venture, was a major factor behind the killing.[57] In the present age of pervasive corruption of political leaders, such a refusal would be considered a huge anomaly.

Rethinking the assassination of Bandaranaike 60 years later in 2019, veteran journalist D.B.S. Jeyaraj pointed out that the ethnic dimension of Bandaranaike's policies has been exaggerated to divert attention from their radical social class dimension.[58] While his nationalist and left-leaning policies were not strictly revolutionary, they threatened powerful local as well as external interests.

Unsurprisingly, the conspiracy theory persists that the CIA was behind the assassination of Prime Minister Bandaranaike. Although no concrete evidence of

---

55 Ibid., 46–51.
56 Jeyaraj, D.B.S. "The Prime Minister is Dead!: How and Why SWRD Bandaranaike Was Assassinated Sixty Years Ago." Dbsjeyaraj.Com (blog), September 30, 2019. Accessed November 2, 2022. https://dbsjeyaraj.com/dbsj/archives/65704.
57 Thurai, T. "Buddharakkita Thera: A Modern Kingmaker." *Colombo Telegraph*, November 18, 2013. Accessed November 28, 2922. https://www.colombotelegraph.com/index.php/buddharakkita-thera-a-modern-kingmaker/; Jeyaraj, D.B.S. "The Prime Minister is Dead!: How and Why SWRD Bandaranaike Was Assassinated Sixty Years Ago." Dbsjeyaraj.Com (blog), September 30, 2019. Accessed November 2, 2022. https://dbsjeyaraj.com/dbsj/archives/65704.
58 Jeyaraj, D.B.S. "The Prime Minister is Dead!: How and Why SWRD Bandaranaike Was Assassinated Sixty Years Ago." Dbsjeyaraj.Com (blog), September 30, 2019. Accessed November 2, 2022. https://dbsjeyaraj.com/dbsj/archives/65704; Gonsalkorale, Raj. "SWRD Bandaranaike; Victim Of Sordid Politics & Unmitigated Avarice." *Colombo Telegraph*, September 25, 2020. Accessed November 2, 2022. https://www.colombotelegraph.com/index.php/swrd-bandaranaike-victim-of-sordid-politics-unmitigated-avarice/.

complicity is forthcoming, it is clear that Sri Lanka was, and of course remains, a target of US intelligence operations. For example, the preface to the Department of State's *Foreign Relations of the United States, 1958–1960, South and Southeast Asia* compendium of memos, cables and telegrams of U.S. diplomacy of this period states:

> In the Ceylon compilation, withheld material contained speculation about developments in Ceylonese politics and references to intelligence sources and methods. While the overall objectives of U.S. policy in Ceylon are clearly delineated in the compilation, the editors do not believe it reflects the full range of policy options considered by U.S. officials.[59]

One of the 'intelligence sources' redacted from these cables and memos is Princeton graduate, Donald Newton Wilber, an archaeologist and part time CIA officer, not least the propaganda chief for Operation TP-Ajax that overthrew Mohammed Mosaddeq in Iran in 1953. TP-Ajax, with a partial script inherited from the British, who were sore from losing the Anglo-Iranian Oil Company to nationalization, included bribery, disseminating propaganda and hiring foot soldiers and thugs to agitate and commit sabotage and provocateurist intimidation, including the bombing of religious leaders' houses.[60] Wilber was stationed in Colombo in 1960, as he describes in a 1986 autobiography, *Adventures in the Middle East: Excursions and Incursions*.[61] However – unlike the assassinations of Patrice Lumumba of Congo (1961), Mehdi Ben Barka of Morocco (1965), Che Guevara (1967) and Thomas Sankara of Burkina Faso (1987)[62] – there is currently no available evidence that Wilber or the CIA played a role in the Bandaranaike assassination, though we can be certain they at least paid close attention.

Following Bandaranaike's death, his widow Sirimavo Ratwatte Dias Bandaranaike, the daughter of an aristocratic Kandyan family, became the head of the Sri Lanka Freedom Party (SLFP). Despite covert electoral interventions by the U.S. in

---

[59] Office of the Historian. *Foreign Relations of the United States, 1958–1960, South and Southeast Asia*. Vol. XV. U.S. Department of State. Accessed June 15, 2020. https://history.state.gov/historicaldocuments/frus1958-60v15.

[60] Kinzer, Stephen. *Overthrow: America's Century of Regime Change from Hawaii to Iraq*. 1st ed. New York: Times Books/Henry Holt, 2006, 123.

[61] Wilber, Donald Newton. *Adventures in the Middle East: Excursions and Incursions*. Princeton, N.J.: Darwin Press, 1986.

[62] Prashad, Vijay. "Part 2: A MANUAL FOR REGIME CHANGE: 8. A Study of Assassination." In *Washington Bullets*. New York: Monthly Review Press, 2020.

support of UNP,[63] the SLFP won the July 1960 election resoundingly, electing Sirimavo Bandaranaike as prime minister. Another first in electoral democracy for Sri Lanka, she became the first female head of state in the modern world.

Mrs. Bandaranaike continued the policies begun by her late husband: leftist economic policies, neutrality in international relations and decolonization efforts in support of Buddhism and the Sinhala language.

In 1961, the government took over secondary schools, which had been inancially assisted by the state since colonial times. This move was opposed by many Catholics fearing threats to their religious identity and was considered a primary cause of the 1962 abortive coup by some top Christian officials of the Army, Navy and the Police.[64]

In contrast, under the leadership of Bad U din Mohammed, Minister of Education between 1960 and 1963, and again under the second Sirimavo Bandaranaike government between 1970 and 1977, state-funded Muslim schools were greatly expanded.[65] By 1984, there were a total of 671 Muslim schools, a category of state schools unique to Sri Lanka, with more than 8,500 teachers of whom 125 were *maha vidyalayas* (higher secondary schools), with 494 graduate staff preparing students to enter universities. As economist Ameer Ali recently observed, while this changed "the image of Muslims from a business community to a teacher or colloquially a master community," it "failed to liberate the Muslim mindset from the grips of religious conservatism."[66]

The Bandaranaike government tried to address the politically sensitive issue of the citizenship of Indian Tamils (mostly descendants of South Indian laborers brought to work on the British plantations), who were about 11 percent of the Sri Lankan population in 1963.[67] The Sirima-Shastri Pact was an agreement signed by Indian Prime Minister Lal Bahadur Shastri in 1964 that granted Ceylonese cit-

---

[63] Levin, Dov H. "When the Great Power Gets a Vote: The Effects of Great Power Electoral Interventions on Election Results." *International Studies Quarterly* 60, no. 2 (June 2016): 189–202, Appendix 2, 2–3. https://doi.org/10.1093/isq/sqv016.

[64] Liyanage, Gunadasa. "The Kataragama Factor and the 1962 Coup." The Sunday Times (Sri Lanka), August 13, 2000. Accessed December 22, 2022. https://sundaytimes.lk/000813/news3.html. Sanmugathasan, N. *A Marxist Looks at the History of Ceylon.* op.cit., https://www.marxists.org/history/erol/sri-lanka/ceylon-history/index.htm, Accessed December 26, 2022.; Leslie Fernando, W. T. A. "Schools Take over, Attempted 1962 Coup." *Sri Lanka Guardian*, January 21, 2011. Accessed August 20, 2022. http://www.srilankaguardian.org/2011/01/schools-take-over-attempted-1962-coup.html.

[65] Ali, Ameer. "Badi Revolution and Its Disappointing Aftermath." *DailyFT.* Accessed January 2, 2023. https://www.ft.lk/columns/Badi-revolution-and-its-disappointing-aftermath/4-659815.

[66] Ibid.

[67] Bandarage, Asoka. *The Separatist Conflict in Sri Lanka: Terrorism, Ethnicity, Political Economy.* London: Routledge/Taylor & Francis Group, 2009, 3.

izenship to 300,000 of the Indian population, repatriation of 525,000 to India and negotiation of the status of the remaining 150,000 Indian residents of Ceylon to be determined at a later point.[68] The pact was never fully implemented and the problem was finally resolved in 2003 when Sri Lankan citizenship was granted those of Indian origin who had lived in Sri Lanka since the signing of the Sirima-Shastri Pact in October 1964, through the enactment of the Citizenship Amendment Act, No. 16 of 2003.[69]

In economic policy, the government pursued import substitution and direct government involvement in industry, trade and finance. As a result of these nationalist policies, the size of the public sector grew to nearly 27 percent of GDP by the mid-1970s.[70] The Bandaranaike government continued the nationalization of economic enterprises started in 1956. In 1961 the Bank of Ceylon was nationalized and the People's Bank and the Insurance Corporation were established as state-owned enterprises (SOEs). Among the most controversial of these nationalist policies, perhaps unsurprisingly, was the expropriation of British and American oil companies (including Royal Dutch Shell, ESSO and CALTEX), the creation of the Ceylon Petroleum Corporation (CPC) in January 1961 and the resort to cheaper oil supplies from the Soviet Union, Romania and the United Arab Republic.[71] It is this same CPC that is now targeted for privatization under the IMF proposed debt restructuring process (see page 192).

In 1961, the Sri Lankan government pursued nationalization of the oil and petroleum industry without an agreement in place for compensation to the oil companies. As a result, the United States employed its coercive economic power against Sri Lanka by applying the Hickenlooper Amendment of 1962 to the Foreign Assistance Act of 1961, which requires suspension of foreign aid to "any country expropriating American property without compensation." On proposing this amendment to the U.S. Senate, which also prohibited aid to communist countries, Senator Bourke Hickenlooper from Iowa rationalized:

---

[68] "Agreement on Persons of Indian Origin in Ceylon" Ministry of External Affairs, Government of India, October 30, 1964. [Available at: https://mea.gov.in/bilateral-documents.htm?dtl/6426/Agreement+on+Persons+of+Indian+Origin+in+Ceylon].
[69] "Citizenship (Amendment) Act, No. 16 OF 2003." Parliament of the Democratic Republic of Sri Lanka, April 1, 2003. https://www.srilankalaw.lk/YearWisePdf/2003/CITIZENSHIP_(AMENDMENT)_ACT,_No._16_OF_2003.pdf.
[70] Kelegama, Saman. Privatization in Sri Lanka: The Experience During the Early Years of Implementation. Sri Lanka Economic Association, 1993.
[71] Olson, Richard Stuart. "Expropriation and International Economic Coercion: Ceylon and the 'West' 1961–65." The Journal of Developing Areas 11, no. 2 (1977): 205–226, 207.

> The success of expropriation in Ceylon and Brazil will stimulate expropriation in other countries. Now it is coming in Honduras, and Panama is threatening expropriation. There are bills in the legislatures of Chile and Peru – to do what? To seize American property.[72]

Keeping developing countries in line through sanctions to protect US economic interests abroad has expanded to many more countries since then. When the sanctions struck, Ceylon was already in "an extremely precarious and deteriorating economic state by 1964."[73] Ceylon's liquidity position, i.e., foreign reserves, had been weakening and unemployment had been increasing for many years (Table 3.2). As a secret CIA 'special report' from 1965 described, Ceylon is "dependent for foreign exchange on its exports of tea, rubber, and coconuts with no great prospect of expanding the foreign exchange earnings of these products."[74]
Characteristic of neocolonialism, starting early in the post-independence era, Sri Lanka had to obtain foreign loans "just to cover the interest on her foreign debt, thus increasing the debt load and requiring refinancing and further loans."[75] (Table 3.3) Like today, in 1964 the foreign exchange shortage reached a crisis point with only "45 days' worth of normal imports."[76] The expropriation conflict with the west contributed greatly to the island being declared "no longer creditworthy" after 1961.[77] In a 1977 paper in the *Journal of Developing Areas*, political economist Richard Stuart Olson observed:

> ... the coerciveness of economic sanctions against a dependent, vulnerable country resides in the fact that an economic downturn can be induced and intensified from the outside, with the resulting development of politically explosive 'relative deprivation'.[78]

This was precisely what happened in 1964–1965. In many ways, what has happened in 2022 is a repetition of the same vicious cycle: an externally dependent export-import economy; worsening terms of trade; foreign exchange shortage;

---

72 Ibid., 209; see also, American Social History Project, City University of New York. "The Hickenlooper Amendment Limits U.S. Aid to Latin America." Accessed January 2, 2023. https://shec.ashp.cuny.edu/items/show/799.
73 Olson, Richard Stuart. "Expropriation and International Economic Coercion: Ceylon and the 'West' 1961–65." *The Journal of Developing Areas* 11, no. 2 (1977): 205–226, 215.
74 "Special Report Left-Leaning Regime in Ceylon Faces Elections." Special Report. Central Intelligence Agency, March 12, 1965, 6. https://www.cia.gov/readingroom/document/cia-rdp79-00927a004800050002-5.
75 Olson, Richard Stuart. "Expropriation and International Economic Coercion: Ceylon and the 'West' 1961–65." *The Journal of Developing Areas* 11, no. 2 (1977): 205–226, 218.
76 Ibid., 214–215.
77 Ibid., 219.
78 Ibid., 222.

Table 3.2: Economic indicators, Ceylon, 1950–1970.

Year	International liquidity (in millions of us dollars)	Unemployment (per 1000 of population)	Index of agricultural production 1955–1960, 1955 = 100, 1961–1970, 1963 = 100
1950	191	8.9	n/a
1951	217	7.2	n/a
1952	164	6.4	n/a
1953	115	6.3	n/a
1954	171	6.8	n/a
1955	212	7.8	100
1956	236	8.9	102
1957	187	10.3	106
1958	176	12.2	110
1959	144	12.9	111
1960	101	13.8	114
1961	90	14.8	91
1962	85	14.5	96
1963	75	14.2	100
1964	52	14.6	105
1965	73	16.2	101
1966	43	19.7	104
1967	55	21.3	109
1968	52	22.1	114
1969	40	24.9	113
1970	43	30.5	116

Source: Richard Stuart Olson, "Expropriation and International Economic Coercion: Ceylon and the 'West' 1961–65," The Journal of Developing Areas, Jan. 1977, Vol. 11, No. 2 (Jan. 1977), 218.

debt crisis; external political pressure; shortages of food, fuel and other essentials and the resulting profound suffering of people.

The deprivations caused by the continuous budgetary deficits between 1961 and 1965 led to a decline in popular support for the SLFP government and its Marxist allies. During the 1965 election campaign, the pro-western UNP promised that if it won, the dispute with the foreign oil companies would be settled "within 24 hours."[79] The UNP (which again received U.S. covert election support) won decisively and came back to power in March 1965.[80] As self-described 'democratic so-

---

79 Ibid., 217.
80 Levin, Dov H. "When the Great Power Gets a Vote: The Effects of Great Power Electoral Interventions on Election Results." *International Studies Quarterly* 60, no. 2 (June 2016): 189–202, Appendix 2, 2–3. https://doi.org/10.1093/isq/sqv016.

Table 3.3: Ceylon's foreign debt, 1955–1972.

	A – External public debt (millions of us dollars)	B – Export receipts (millions of us dollars)	C – A/B (%)
1955	26.1	404.2	6.5
1956	39.8	361.5	11.0
1957	48.3	3.50	13.8
1958	53.7	356.5	15.1
1959	57.8	364.6	15.9
1960	61.2	361.0	17.0
1961	64.0	376.7	17.0
1962	71.9	376.9	19.1
1963	84.8	360.6	23.5
1964	85.9	405.8	21.2
1965	101.9	406.0	25.1
1966	114.3	354.2	32.3
1967	125.3	286.4	43.8
1968	182.1	344.9	52.8
1969	233.1	324.7	71.8
1970	266.2	344.6	77.2
1971	303.5	330.0	92.0
1972	322.1	287.5	112.0

Source: Richard Stuart Olson, "Expropriation and International Economic Coercion: Ceylon and the 'West' 1961–65," The Journal of Developing Areas, Jan. 1977, Vol. 11, No. 2 (Jan. 1977), 218.

cialists' at this point in time, some might be surprised of the US support that the UNP of 1965 received. In reality the CIA knew that, "although in practice the phrase may mean little more than a willingness to consider social welfare measures, the transition has brought with it a new aura of progressiveness."[81]

Return of Pro-Western Regime: 1965–1970

Immediately after winning the 1965 election, the UNP kept its promise to compensate the foreign oil companies that had been expropriated in 1961. They also further appeased powerful foreign interests by abolishing a restrictive profit remit-

---

[81] "SPECIAL REPORT LEFT-LEANING REGIME IN CEYLON FACES ELECTIONS." Special Report. Central Intelligence Agency, March 12, 1965, 5. https://www.cia.gov/readingroom/document/cia-rdp79-00927a004800050002-5.

tance law that the previous government had introduced in 1964.[82] Such profit remittance laws were attempted by many left-leaning ex-colonial countries trapped in 'bleeding out' export economies, and the Ceylon remittance law had put the British mercantile community into "a state of urgent uncertainty" upon its introduction by Bandaranaike in August 1964.[83]

Reversing the trend of the previous Bandaranaike regimes, the UNP government emphasized the development of the private sector. A new impetus was also given to food production with a "Food Production Drive."[84] The corresponding 'Green Revolution' was introduced country-wide in the mid 1960s, including development in modernized machinery, high yielding crop varieties, and increased use of fertilizers and other agrochemical inputs. It resulted in an impressive growth in output but was not sufficient to avert the ongoing import-export issues nor growing food shortages.[85]

Given the country's exhausted reserves and acute economic crisis, the US and the UK asked the World Bank to work out a stabilization agreement for Ceylon with the IMF. This led to four standby agreements between the Sri Lankan government and the IMF during the 1965–1970 period (Table 1.1; page 2). These agreements called for deflationary policies with stringent credit and decreased government spending, characteristic features of IMF and World Bank stabilization packages for Third World countries receiving their aid.[86] During this period, the Sri Lankan government was persuaded to take politically difficult steps, notably, "reducing the subsidized rice ration, increasing charges for municipal bus services, and (in 1967) devaluing the rupee."[87] These struck hard on the lower classes who were "made to sacrifice in order to stabilize the economy," as they are made to do today.[88]

---

[82] Olson, Richard Stuart. "Expropriation and International Economic Coercion: Ceylon and the 'West' 1961–65." *The Journal of Developing Areas* 11, no. 2 (1977): 205–226, 217.

[83] *The New York Times*. "Britons Criticize Ceylon Proposal; Say a Ban on Remittances Would Damage Trade," August 9, 1964, sec. Archives. Accessed December 31, 2022. https://www.nytimes.com/1964/08/09/archives/britons-criticize-geylon-proposal-say-a-ban-on-remittances-would.html.

[84] Sanderatne, Nimal. "Changing Scenarios: 64 Years of Lost Opportunities," *Sunday Times*, Sri Lanka, February 5, 2012. Accessed November 30, 2022. https://www.sundaytimes.lk/120205/Columns/eco.html.

[85] Herath, H. M. Gamini. "The Green Revolution in Rice: The Role of the Risk Factor with Special Reference to Sri Lanka." *Asian Survey* 21, no. 6 (1981): 664–675. https://doi.org/10.2307/2643794.

[86] Lakshman, W. D. "The IMF-World Bank Intervention in Sri Lankan Economic Policy: Historical Trends and Patterns." *Social Scientist* 13, no. 2 (1985): 3–29, 3–4. https://doi.org/10.2307/3520187.

[87] Olson, Richard Stuart. "Expropriation and International Economic Coercion: Ceylon and the 'West' 1961–65." *The Journal of Developing Areas* 11, no. 2 (1977), 219.

[88] Ibid., p. 219.

As promised, western aid did flow into the country after 1965 – mostly in the form of loans – but as economist W.D. Lakshman noted, "The monetarist, free-market policies promoted ... during 1965–1969 through IMF-WB intervention ....caught the country in a severe debt trap and a situation of widening disparities in the society" (Table 3.3 and Table 1.1 on page 2).[89] The debt service ratio, for example, increased from 13.1 percent in 1969 to 20.1 percent in 1970.[90] Ultimately, the lives of the poor worsened, as reflected in the acceleration of unemployment after 1965 (Table 3.2).[91]

The insecure framework of an export economy left the country highly vulnerable to world market fluctuations, such as the near 50 percent increase in the cost of rice imports in 1965, due to a worldwide shortage, and a simultaneous sharp decline in the price of Sri Lankan export commodities.[92] As the U.S. government Country Study for Sri Lanka observed, the situation became so acute that in 1966 the UNP government was compelled to declare a state of emergency to deter food riots, due to the halving of the subsidized weekly rice ration. The IMF is responsible for many documented violent public reactions to its operations, such as the so-called 'IMF food riots' caused by its painful austerity policies.[93] The rice reduction remained in place throughout the remainder of the UNP government and was a major factor in the UNP's defeat in the 1970 general elections, as it had been in its defeat in 1956.[94] A left-nationalist coalition, the United Front (UF), constituting the SLFP, LSSP and the CP and led by Sirimavo Bandaranaike, again came into power in 1970.

---

89 Lakshman, W. D. "The IMF-World Bank Intervention in Sri Lankan Economic Policy: Historical Trends and Patterns." *Social Scientist* 13, no. 2 (1985): 3–29, 16. https://doi.org/10.2307/3520187.

90 Ibid., 16.

91 Olson, Richard Stuart. "Expropriation and International Economic Coercion: Ceylon and the 'West' 1961–65." *The Journal of Developing Areas* 11, no. 2 (1977): 205–226, 219.

92 Ross, Russell R., Andrea Matles Savada, and Richard F. Nyrop. *Sri Lanka: A Country Study.* 2nd ed. Area Handbook Series. Washington, D.C.: Federal Research Division, Library of Congress: U.S. G.P.O., 1990, 48, 49. Available at: https://lccn.loc.gov/89600372.

93 Moosa, Imad A., and Nisreen Moosa. *Eliminating the IMF: An Analysis of the Debate to Keep, Reform or Abolish the Fund.* Cham: Springer International Publishing, 2019, Chap. 4.

94 Ross, Russell R., Andrea Matles Savada, and Richard F. Nyrop. *Sri Lanka: A Country Study.* 2nd ed. Area Handbook Series. Washington, D.C.: Federal Research Division, Library of Congress: U.S. G.P.O., 1990, 48, 49. Available at: https://lccn.loc.gov/89600372.

Return to Left-Nationalism, 1970–1977

As a result of electoral democracy and the social welfare state that prevailed since the Donoughmore Reforms, by the 1970s, Ceylon enjoyed a relatively high Physical Quality of Life Index (PQLI, based on average literacy, infant mortality and life expectancy rates), despite her low economic growth rate and per capita GNP. In the mid-1970s, the island had a near universal literacy rate that far exceeded her South Asian neighbors and China (Table 3.4) According to the UN, Sri Lanka's adult literacy was 92 percent in 2018.[95]

Table 3.4: Physical quality of life index scores and growth rates for sub-continental nations and China in the mid-1970s.

	GNP Per Capita 1977 (US $)	Literacy Rate (Percent)	Infant Mortality (Per 1000 Live Births)	Life Expectancy at Birth	PQLI	Average Annual Growth Rate (GNP Per Capita 1960–1977)
Nepal	110	28	150	43	28	0.2
Afghanistan	190	17	205	40	17	0.2
Bangladesh	90	26	136	46	35	-0.4
Pakistan	190	24	126	51	40	3.0
India	150	36	123	49	42	1.3
Sri Lanka	200	85	37	65	82	2.0
China	390	66	45	65	75	5.1

Source: World Bank, "World Development Report," 1979: Appendix Table I. WDR, 1983: Appendix C3.

University education had been made available in the Sinhala and Tamil languages starting in 1959, but the Sinhalese students were overwhelmingly concentrated in social studies and humanities departments, not in the science programs that led to more lucrative careers. Thus, continuing the colonial trajectory, the best jobs still went to the well-connected, English-speaking elite, and this contributed to a hardening of social class boundaries within the Sinhala community.[96]

Government social welfare policies introduced in 1950s and 1960s that were meant to benefit the Sinhala majority in fact backfired, resulting in massive dis-

---

[95] UNICEF DATA. "Literacy Rates around the World." Accessed December 31, 2022. https://data.unicef.org/topic/education/learning-and-skills/.

[96] Bandarage, Asoka. *The Separatist Conflict in Sri Lanka: Terrorism, Ethnicity, Political Economy.* London: Routledge/Taylor & Francis Group, 2009, 53–54.

content. The mobilization of discontent which had already begun during the UNP regime in the 1967–1970 period erupted into a violent insurrection against the UF left-nationalist coalition soon after it came to power in 1970.

Notwithstanding ideological differences, the leadership of the major Sinhalese political parties on the right and left and the Sri Lankan Tamil parties all "came from elite ranks, almost without exception."[97] In this class context, the *Janatha Vimukthi Peramuna* (JVP), or People's Liberation Front – led by Rohana Wijeweera, who is considered to be the first Sri Lankan politician to come from a non-elitist village background – was able to penetrate the rural areas and reach the new class of Sinhalese educated, but unemployed youth.[98] The 1971 JVP insurrection is considered unique in the history of modern revolutions, representing the first occasion when "an organized youth movement in a country, with no outside assistance, sought to seize state power by violence."[99]

The JVP's Marxist ideology was directed primarily against the Sri Lankan state and the Sinhalese ruling class. By early 1971 the JVP had over 100,000 members, many of them operating in small cells around the country. Criticizing the UF coalition and the evils of the capitalist system, Wijeweera publicly ordered JVP members to arm themselves against possible state repression. Given the unprecedented threats to order and democracy posed by the JVP, the government declared a state of emergency and instigated a curfew, giving the police and the army "full powers of arbitrary arrest and disposal of bodies without having to carry out inquests or inform the relatives of those killed."[100] With this aggressive approach to counter-insurgency, "the uprising was ruthlessly crushed in a relatively short time."[101] The Sri Lankan government received crucial military and financial assistance from a curious mix of foreign powers: Britain, India, Pakistan, Egypt, Australia, the US, the Soviet Union, Yugoslavia and China.[102]

Estimates of security personnel, JVP insurgents and civilians killed in the 1971 insurgency have varied widely from as low as 1,200 to as high as 50,000, the over-

---

97 Obeyesekere, Gananath. "Some Comments on the Social Backgrounds of the April 1971 Insurgency in Sri Lanka (Ceylon)." *The Journal of Asian Studies* 33, no. 3 (1974): 367–384. https://doi.org/10.2307/2052937.
98 Bandarage, Asoka. *The Separatist Conflict in Sri Lanka: Terrorism, Ethnicity, Political Economy.* London: Routledge/Taylor & Francis Group, 2009, 56.
99 Ibid., 54.
100 Ibid., 56.
101 Gunasēkara, Prins. *A Lost Generation: Sri Lanka in Crisis: The Untold Story.* Colombo: S. Godage & Brothers, 1998, 6.
102 Bandarage, Asoka. *The Separatist Conflict in Sri Lanka: Terrorism, Ethnicity, Political Economy.* London: Routledge/Taylor & Francis Group, 2009, 56.

whelming majority of whom were young Sinhalese Buddhist males from relatively low socioeconomic backgrounds. Bypassing the existing judicial system, the government passed the oppressive Criminal Justice Commission Act on April 6, 1972, by a two-thirds majority in parliament, allowing the admissibility of evidence without corroboration and the acceptance of hearsay evidence.[103]

With its left-wing nationalist claims thoroughly shaken by the insurrection, the government sought to both tighten its political control and speed reform to move the country in a socialist direction. With the UF's two-thirds majority in Parliament, the government was able to introduce the Constitution of May 1972, and Ceylon became the 'Socialist Republic of Sri Lanka'. In a symbolic act of decolonization, the 1972 Constitution replaced the island's colonial name Ceylon with Sri Lanka, declaring the country to be a "free, sovereign, independent and democratic socialist republic."[104]

The inclusion of a clause in the constitution giving Buddhism the "foremost place" asserting "the duty of the State to protect and foster Buddhism" was meant to redress colonial discrimination against Buddhists, but it in turn alienated the non-Buddhist minorities.[105] In another symbolic act, the US Peace Corps operation in Sri Lanka was terminated, and was not resumed until 1983.[106] Perhaps they were aware of its role in counterinsurgency and propaganda, as described by President John F Kennedy in secret memos and reports soon after the Corps was founded in 1961, that it must give "utmost attention and emphasis to programs designed to counter Communist indirect aggression"[107] and "develop agricultural pilot-projects .... with a view toward exploiting their beneficial psychological effects."[108]

After the aborted JVP insurrection, the Sri Lankan government attempted to meet the needs of disaffected Sinhalese rural youth by introducing a new affirma-

---

[103] Ibid., 57. Gunaratna, Rohan. *Sri Lanka, a Lost Revolution? The inside Story of the JVP.* Kandy, Sri Lanka: Institute of Fundamental Studies, 1990, 196, 199, 213.
[104] "The Constitution of Sri Lanka," vol. Chap. XIII, Article 105–134, 1972. Available at: https://www.parliament.lk/files/ca/4.%20The%20Constitution%20of%20Sri%20Lanka%20%20-%20%201972%20(Article%20105%20%E2%80%93134)%20Chapter%20XIII.pdf.
[105] Ibid.
[106] *Peace Corps.* "About Peace Corps Sri Lanka." Accessed January 2, 2023. https://www.peacecorps.gov/sri-lanka/about/.
[107] "72. National Security Action Memorandum No. 132," in *Foreign Relations of the United States, 1961–1963, Volume VIII, National Security Policy* (Washington D.C.: Office of the Historian, Bureau of Public Affairs, U.S. Department of State), accessed January 1, 2023, https://history.state.gov/historicaldocuments/frus1961-63v08/d72.
[108] *The Pentagon Papers: The Defense Department History of United States Decision-making on Vietnam,* The Senator Gravel Edition, vol. 2, 5 vols. (Boston: Beacon Press, 1971), 640.

tive action policy. In place of the language-based standardization policy of 1970, a district quota system was introduced in 1973 favoring students from underprivileged regions to enter university science faculties. This significantly increased the number of hitherto neglected rural Sinhalese and Sri Lankan Muslims that could enroll in university and enter the modern professions.[109]

The constitution pledged to establish a socialist democracy providing full employment through the adoption of a mixed economic framework, national control of key sectors of the economy, collective forms of ownership and ceilings on land ownership, income and other resources. State control was extended to every sector of the economy, including trade, industry and the local and foreign-owned plantations which brought in two-thirds of the island's foreign exchange.[110] The Land Reform Act of 1972, for example, placed restrictions on landholdings and house ownership.

The UF government is believed to have nationalized nearly one-fourth of the agricultural land on the island.[111] Nationalization of plantations, in particular, was approached as a major policy of decolonization. During the 1972–1973 period, the government nationalized approximately 502 privately held tea, rubber and coconut estates. In 1976, plantations came under the Janatha Estates Development Board (JEDB) and State Plantations Corporation (SPC), the two largest state-owned plantation agencies.[112]

Unfortunately, corruption – especially political patronage and mismanagement – became widespread in the state-owned plantations and in other nationalized entities.[113] Nationalization of tea plantations and political interference also led to a decline in international competitiveness and a loss of the market share of Ceylon tea. Ironically, instead of achieving greater freedom from international capital and

---

[109] Bandarage, Asoka. *The Separatist Conflict in Sri Lanka: Terrorism, Ethnicity, Political Economy*. London: Routledge/Taylor & Francis Group, 2009, 54, 58–59; https://www.ft.lk/Columnists/Badi-revolution-and-its-disappointing-aftermath/4-659815.

[110] Bandarage, Asoka. *The Separatist Conflict in Sri Lanka: Terrorism, Ethnicity, Political Economy*. London: Routledge/Taylor & Francis Group, 2009, 58.

[111] Peebles, Patrick. "Colonization and Ethnic Conflict in the Dry Zone of Sri Lanka." *The Journal of Asian Studies* 49, no. 1 (1990): 30–55, 38. https://doi.org/10.2307/2058432. Bandarage, Asoka. *The Separatist Conflict in Sri Lanka: Terrorism, Ethnicity, Political Economy*. London: Routledge/Taylor & Francis Group, 2009, 58.

[112] Poholiyadde, Sunil. "The Evolution of Sri Lanka's Plantation Sector." *Ceylon Today*, August 5, 2018. Available at: https://www.historyofceylontea.com/ceylon-publications/ceylon-tea-articles/the-evolution-of-sri-lankas-plantation-sector.html.

[113] Ibid.

financial institutions, the country accumulated more international debt (Tables 3.3 and 1.1 on pages 78 and 2).[114]

Import Substitution Industrialization and Non-Alignment

The boycott of British goods and the resuscitation of local industries and economic self-sufficiency had been the key principles of the *Swadeshi* ('of one's own land') Movement in India, which then evolved into the independence movement under Gandhi.[115] Subsequently, many ex-colonial countries adopted import substitution trade strategies after World War II, equating economic development with industrialization and capital investment.

Industrial substitution industrialization (ISI) strategies emerged from critiques of the theory of comparative advantage and the "disadvantageous pattern of specialization and trade – exporting primary commodities in exchange for imports of manufactured goods" upon which the colonial division of labor was constructed.[116] It questioned free trade as the principal path to development of poor countries, pointing out that primary product exporters would experience declining terms of trade, compelling them to export increasing amounts in exchange for decreasing amounts of manufactured imports.[117] Indeed, this was the experience of Sri Lanka and most ex-colonial countries of Latin America, Africa and Asia.

Import substitution is commonly associated with the Argentinian economist Raúl Prebisch, the first secretary general of the United Nations Conference on Trade and Development (UNCTAD), from 1964 to 1969. Sri Lankan economist Gamani Corea, who succeeded as head of UNCTAD from 1973 to 1984, also pursued better terms of trade, debt relief and other measures to support developing countries through UNCTAD.[118]

---

[114] Bandarage, Asoka. *The Separatist Conflict in Sri Lanka: Terrorism, Ethnicity, Political Economy.* London: Routledge/Taylor & Francis Group, 2009, 58.

[115] Cultural India. "History of Swadeshi Movement: Causes & Effects," July 19, 2018. Accessed December 22, 2022. https://learn.culturalindia.net/swadeshi-movement.html.

[116] Irwin, Douglas. "The Rise and Fall of Import Substitution." *Peterson Institute for International Economics*, July 8, 2020. Accessed December 22, 2022. https://www.piie.com/publications/working-papers/rise-and-fall-import-substitution.

[117] Ibid. Siddiqui, Kalim. "The 'Import-Substitution' Policy in Post-Colonial Countries: A Review." *The World Financial Review,* November 29, 2021. Accessed December 22, 2022. https://worldfinancialreview.com/the-import-substitution-policy-in-post-colonial-countries-a-review/.

[118] UNCTAD. "'True Champion of the South' Gamani Corea Honored at Tribute Seminar," March 26, 2014. Accessed December 22, 2022. https://unctad.org/news/true-champion-south-gamani-corea-honored-tribute-seminar.

Taking influence from India, UNCTAD and other developing nations, with an aim to increase national economic independence, the Sri Lankan government pursued an ISI strategy between 1970–1977. However, as experienced in many other countries, these policies faced many challenges. As Sri Lankan economist Nimal Sanderatne observed in 2012, "A small country with few raw materials, inadequate capital and technology and a very small domestic market, cannot produce quality industrial products at competitive prices."[119] Other small countries, such as Peru, Bolivia and Ecuador, and even larger countries like Argentina, were forced to stop ISI strategies for similar reasons. Lack of resources, internal corruption and mismanagement were not the only reasons for the failure of alternative paths of development in the 1970s. Global market problems such as the 1973 global oil crisis and external pressure against opting out of the neocolonial path of 'free trade' were also major factors.

The so-called Latin American debt crisis hit many countries that experimented with import substitution by the early 1980s. When they defaulted on their sovereign debt, the IMF and the World Bank responded with bailouts conditional to them replacing ISI policies with neoliberal policies and export-focused production.[120] By the 1980s, with the rise of the Washington Consensus and free trade pressure and (largely US-led) agreements, import substitution fell out of favor.[121]

The left-wing Sri Lankan government recognized that, without alternative collective efforts towards a New International Economic Order that upholds local economic autonomy and food sovereignty, the cycles of debt servitude, poverty and suffering would continue – and continue to increase in severity – in Sri Lanka and the world. This recognition was also the motivation for Sri Lanka's active participation in NAM from its inception in Bandung in 1955 and the search for alternative paths of political and economic development.

Sirimavo Bandaranaike attended the NAM inaugural summit in Belgrade in 1961 as one of its founding members. There, she proudly stated, "I am happy to attend this great conference not only as a representative of my country but also as a woman and a mother who can understand the thoughts and feelings of those mil-

---

119 Sanderatne, Nimal, "Changing Scenarios: 64 Years of Lost Opportunities," *Sunday Times*, Sri Lanka, February 5, 2012, Accessed November 30, 2022. https://www.sundaytimes.lk/120205/Columns/eco.html.
120 "Import Substitution Industrialization (ISI)," *Corporate Finance Institute*. Accessed January 1, 2023, https://corporatefinanceinstitute.com/resources/economics/import-substitution-industrialization-isi/.
121 Irwin, Douglas. "Import Substitution Is Making an Unwelcome Comeback." *Peterson Institute for International Economics*, July 8, 2020. Accessed December 22, 2022. https://www.piie.com/blogs/trade-and-investment-policy-watch/import-substitution-making-unwelcome-comeback.

lions of women .... our endeavour should be to influence world opinion to such an extent that governments, however powerful, cannot regard warfare as an alternative to negotiation."[122]

Bandaranaike attended every summit of NAM from 1961 until the fifth summit in Colombo on August 16th to 19th, 1976, when Sri Lanka was elected to head the movement, with Mrs. Bandaranaike at the helm.[123] Eighty-six countries from across the world participated in the momentous event in Colombo in 1976, bringing prestige to the country and to the nationalist-socialist government. The historic meeting resulted in the "Documents of the Fifth Conference of Heads of State or Government of Non-Aligned Countries."[124]

Prior to the 1976 NAM Colombo conference, UN declarations from 1974 also reflect the global south challenges to the Bretton Woods/Washington Consensus model of free trade and export-focused developing economies. These include the *Declaration of the Indian Ocean as a Zone of Peace*, adopted at the 2022nd plenary meeting on December 16, 1971 (resolution 2832), with the goal of the "elimination of foreign bases, military installations and logistical supply facilities") (see Appendix 2); the *Declaration on the Establishment of a New International Economic Order,* adopted May 1, 1974 (resolution 3201) "to bring about maximum economic cooperation between ...developed and developing countries , based on the principles of dignity and sovereign equality" (see Appendix 1); as well as the follow up *Programme of Action on the Establishment of a New International Economic Order,* adopted at the same meeting (resolution 3202).[125] Tellingly, despite the noble gestures of the UN, the global financial system has yet to be challenged by these idealistic declarations and has in fact entrenched its sole value of 'elite profit über alles' much further, particularly since the crumbling of the USSR

In 2023, these important declarations are more relevant than ever for Sri Lanka as the country grapples with the convergent problems of economic crisis, neocolonialism and a new phase of geopolitical rivalry.

---

[122] sirimavobandaranaike.org. "01–06 September 1961 – First Non-Aligned Movement Summit in Belgrade." Accessed January 2, 2023. https://sirimavobandaranaike.org/01-06-september-1961-first-non-aligned-movement-summit-in-belgrade/.

[123] "Documents of the Fifth Conference of Heads of State or Government of Non-Aligned Countries, Held at Colombo from 16 to 19 August 1976," August 21, 1976. Available at: http://cns.miis.edu/nam/documents/Official_Document/5th_Summit_FD_Sri_Lanka_Declaration_1976_Whole.pdf. 5th_Summit_FD_Sri_Lanka_Declaration_1976_Whole.pdf (miis.edu).

[124] Ibid.

[125] Programme of Action on the Adoption of a New Intenational Economic Order, A_RES_3202(S-VI)-EN.pdf.

The high ideals of NAM and the UN aside, to deal with the declining terms of trade and the foreign exchange crisis facing Sri Lanka in the mid-1970s, the government placed restrictions on the import of necessities such as rice, other food stuffs and cloth, and these were rationed by the state, creating a situation of endemic scarcity. This led to an entrenched top-heavy system dependent on the state and political patronage. The Sri Lankan economy became "a highly restricted and regulated or closed economy" and the growth rate fell below 3 percent and unemployment rose to almost one-quarter of the labor force in 1976.[126]

Although the UF government had come into office criticizing the former UNP regime of "uncritically accepting terms and conditions of the IMF and thereby putting the country in a severe debt trap," it now found itself in the same situation. Like today, Sri Lanka faced a food shortage and an economic crisis in 1974, and lacking foreign creditors, the country was compelled to turn to the IMF. The leftwing government signed a standby agreement with the IMF in March 1974 (Table 1.1 on page 2), accepting most of its conditions, including adjustments to the food subsidy policy.[127]

All ethnic groups were affected by the overall lack of growth and unemployment, and competition between groups increased for scarce resources and opportunities. Many of the economic grievances and state repression facing the Tamil youth in the late 1970s were similar to those of their Sinhalese counterparts. However, the Tamil struggle, spearheaded by the Tamil elite, avoided an analysis of class struggle and solidarity, as it was for the JVP, and took on a distinctly ethnic and secessionist character, exacerbating ethnic tensions and eventually leading to a separatist civil war.[128]

The 1972 constitution and university admissions policies led to increasing Tamil resistance culminating in the Vadukkodai Resolution of 1976 calling for Tamil separatism. Both the government and the Tamil political leadership failed to curb the growing violence by Tamil youth. The 1977 parliamentary elections took place amidst economic difficulties, escalating violence in the north and growing polarization across the country. This confluence of factors brought down the SLFP-led coalition, bringing the UNP back to power in a landslide victory inaugurating the period of neoliberalism and armed conflict.

---

[126] Bandarage, Asoka. *The Separatist Conflict in Sri Lanka: Terrorism, Ethnicity, Political Economy.* London: Routledge/Taylor & Francis Group, 2009, 58.
[127] Lakshman, W. D. "The IMF-World Bank Intervention in Sri Lankan Economic Policy: Historical Trends and Patterns." *Social Scientist* 13, no. 2 (1985): 3–29, 16–19. https://doi.org/10.2307/3520187.
[128] Bandarage, Asoka. *The Separatist Conflict in Sri Lanka: Terrorism, Ethnicity, Political Economy.* London: Routledge/Taylor & Francis Group, 2009, 54, 58.

Chapter 4:
Neoliberalism, Authoritarianism and Recolonization, 1977–2009

In 1973, a CIA-backed coup overthrew the democratically elected Chilean President Salvador Allende, a founder of the movement for a New International Economic Order who pursued a policy called 'La vía chilena al socialismo' ('the Chilean Way to Socialism') and installed a pro-western military regime under General Pinochet.[1] The term neoliberalism came into use in connection with Pinochet's economic reforms – as directed by 'Chicago School' economists and the US State Department – policies introduced by Margaret Thatcher in the UK and Ronald Reagan in the US in the 1980s.

Neoliberalism commonly refers to market-oriented reform policies promoted by the World Bank and the IMF which encompass deregulation, privatization, austerity and limitation of state influence in the economy.[2] Neoliberalism is a 'political project' undertaken by the global corporate elite who were intensely threatened by socialist regimes and labor movements around the world in the late 1960s and early 1970s.[3]

By the 1980s, import substitution was undermined with the rise of the 'Washington Consensus', the free trade reforms for crisis-ridden developing countries promoted by the Washington, D.C.-based institutions, namely, the IMF, the World Bank and the U.S. Department of the Treasury. The terms 'Washington Consensus', 'market fundamentalism' and 'neoliberalism' are commonly used as synonyms for strong market-based approaches to economic policymaking.[4]

---

[1] Salvador Allende, Speech to the United Nations, Dec. 4, 1972.https://www.marxists.org/archive/allende/1972/december/04.htm. Joseph, Gilbert M., and Greg Grandin. A Century of Revolution: Insurgent and Counterinsurgent Violence during Latin America's Long Cold War. Duke University Press, 2010, 27–1.

[2] Monbiot, George. "Neoliberalism – the Ideology at the Root of All Our Problems." *The Guardian*, April 15, 2016, sec. Books. Accessed November 22, 2022. https://www.theguardian.com/books/2016/apr/15/neoliberalism-ideology-problem-george-monbiot. Boas, Taylor C., and Jordan Gans-Morse. "Neoliberalism: From New Liberal Philosophy to Anti-Liberal Slogan." *Studies in Comparative International Development* 44, no. 2 (June 1, 2009): 137–161. https://doi.org/10.1007/s12116-009-9040-5.

[3] Harvey, David. *A Brief History of Neoliberalism.* Oxford University Press, 2007; Harvey, David. "Globalization: Neoliberalism Is a Political Project." *Committee for the Abolition of Illegitimate Debt*, January 2, 2023. https://www.cadtm.org/Globalization-Neoliberalism-Is-a.

[4] Global Trade Negotiations Homepage, Center for International Development at Harvard University. "Washington Consensus," April 2003. Accessed November 22, 2022. https://web.archive.org/web/20170715151421/http://www.cid.harvard.edu/cidtrade/issues/washington.html.

Along with neoliberal economic policies, U.S. interventions have included military aid and training, 'labor union imperialism' via outfits, such as, the Asian-American Free Labor Institute (AAFLI),[5] and the soft power tactics of the National Endowment for Democracy (NED), a U.S. Congress funded granting agency stalwart of soft power. With the cry of "democracy and freedom" NED-funded agencies spread U.S. corporate influence across 90 countries worldwide.[6] As Allen Weinstein of the NED's Center for Democracy said in 1991, "A lot of what we do today was done covertly 25 years ago by the CIA."[7]

Neoliberalism in Sri Lanka

With the introduction of the 'Open Economy' under the government of J. R. Jayawardena in 1977, Sri Lanka became the first country in Asia to be subjected to neoliberalism.[8] "Let the robber barons come in," was Jayawardena's rallying cry as he opened the country to foreign investors.[9] The Open Economy put an end to the socialist-nationalist project under the Bandaranaikes and transformed the political, economic, and cultural character of the island and realigned class and ethnic relations. Reversing earlier policies, the new government reinstated state assistance to private Christian schools and removed language based ethnic quotas for entry into the universities.[10]

1977 marked an acceleration of capitalist development that began with the introduction of the British colonial plantations in the 1830s. All Sri Lankan governments since 1977 have subscribed to the neoliberal path even when some promised more nationalist paths of development in their election manifestos as in the case

---

5 Shorrock, Tim, and Kathy Selvaggio. "Which Side Are You On, AAFLI?" *The Nation*; New York, February 15, 1986.
6 Swiss Policy Research. "Organizations Funded by the NED," December 2, 2019. Accessed November 2, 2022. https://swprs.org/organizations-funded-by-the-ned/.
7 Ignatius, David. "Innocence Abroad: The New World of Spyless Coups." *Washington Post*, September 22, 1991. Accessed October 10, 2021. https://www.washingtonpost.com/archive/opinions/1991/09/22/innocence-abroad-the-new-world-of-spyless-coups/92bb989a-de6e-4bb8-99b9-462c76b59a16/.
8 Kadirgamar, Ahilan, and Devaka Gunawardena. "Sri Lanka's Crisis: The Disaster of Economic Dependency." *Deccan Herald*, April 6, 2022. https://www.deccanherald.com/opinion/sri-lankas-crisis-the-disaster-of-economic-dependency-1098125.html.
9 Asiaweek.com (CNN). "Passage: Junius Richard Jayewardene." Accessed January 2, 2023. http://edition.cnn.com/ASIANOW/asiaweek/96/1115/feat7.html.
10 Bandarage, Asoka. *The Separatist Conflict in Sri Lanka: Terrorism, Ethnicity, Political Economy.* London: Routledge/Taylor & Francis Group, 2009, 91.

of Gotabaya Rajapaksa in 2019.[11] All governments since 1977 have also maintained the 1978 Constitution and the Executive Presidency introduced by J.R. Jayawardena.

Authoritarian State

The heavy dependence on foreign funding made political stability a prerequisite of the Open Economy. Political economist Mick Moore has argued that the dependence on external funding and the growing sense of economic prosperity freed the UNP government from the populist and democratic style of politics that had prevailed in the country since independence.[12] Thus, the UNP government set out to make its position secure by eliminating challenges from all opposition forces.

This objective led to the introduction of the new presidential system of government in September 1977 and the quick enactment of the new constitution in 1978, using the UNP parliamentary majority limiting public debate. The powers of government were concentrated in the new office of President which was not dependent on or constrained by the parliament. The new 'Gaullist' constitution, created principally to "attract foreign investment and to convince international aid-givers that Sri Lanka is a safe bet," elevated Jayawardena to the position of 'Executive President.'[13]

The weakening of the parliament as an institution contributed to a change in the composition of the parliament and the political culture of the island. Increased material benefits made available to members of the parliament began to attract many individuals unqualified to hold public office, subservient to the will of the president. UNP members were required to submit signed undated letters of resignation to the President, which he could use to dismiss MPs as he needed.[14] Given control and devaluation of the mass media, especially the state-owned media, there were no worthwhile debates in parliament to be reported even under the many periods of emergency between 1978 and 1989.

---

[11] "Regaining Sri Lanka: Vision and Strategy for Accelerated Development." Government of Sri Lanka, December 2002. https://planipolis.iiep.unesco.org/sites/default/files/ressources/sri_lanka_prsp_2002.pdf. Athukorala, Prema-Chandra, and Sarath Rajapatirana. "Liberalization and Industrial Transformation: Lessons from the Sri Lankan Experience." *Economic Development and Cultural Change* 48, no. 3 (2000): 543–572. https://doi.org/10.1086/452610.

[12] Mick Moore, 'Economic Liberalization versus Political Pluralism in Sri Lanka?, Modern Asian Studies Vol. 24, No. 2 (May, 1990), 371.

[13] Bandarage, The Separatist Conflict, op.cit., 95–96.

[14] Ibid., 96.

Mick Moore observed two aspects of increasing state authoritarianism and repression under Jayawardena: "the simple use of physical violence against opponents, and ... the manipulation of law and the constitution."[15] The Sinhala and Tamil democratic opposition, the media, students, the working class, union movements, and any sector or institution that posed a threat to the new political and economic order were targeted since the UNP came to power in 1977. Thugs were used routinely against groups that sought to redress grievances through public protests and peaceful demonstrations – "students, women workers on strike, nurses… Buddhist monks, joint clergy gatherings … and others."[16] Legislation restricting individual rights and emergency powers were widely used.

The UNP weakened political opposition by depriving the civil rights of Sirimavo Bandaranaike, the leader of the Sri Lanka Freedom Party (SLFP), the main opposition party, who was the Prime Minister for twelve years. These restrictions were achieved through the courts and by the enactment of new laws. Restriction of her civil rights prevented Bandaranaike from contesting the presidential elections in October 1982.[17]

Attacks were made against student opposition on practically all the university campuses in the country between 1978 and 1980. The subversion of democratic processes and popular participation was also directed at the powerful and vibrant trade union movement that had been active since the 1930s. The labor unions that were anchored in the public sector were closely allied with Marxist political parties but had remained autonomous from the state and had challenged every government since independence.[18]

State authoritarianism *vis-à-vis* the unions was largely the product of the Open Economy, which called for state protection of private investment and foreign interests. Requirements for the registration of unions were tightened, and the unions decreased in number. Unions were banned altogether from the Free Trade Zone (FTZ) in the southwestern region, a common requirement of export processing zones globally. After 1977, the left-wing unions were undermined by the UNP government-backed union, the *Jathika Sevaka Sanghamaya* (JSS), which in the late 1970s and early 1980s wielded unprecedented power through its own intelligence

---

15 Moore, 'Economic Liberalization', op.cit., 360.
16 Bandarage, Asoka. *The Separatist Conflict in Sri Lanka: Terrorism, Ethnicity, Political Economy.* London: Routledge/Taylor & Francis Group, 2009, 96.
17 Keerawella, Gamini. "Contraction of Democratic Structures after 1977" *Sri Lanka Brief,* January 16, 2020. https://srilankabrief.org/contraction-of-democratic-structures-after-1977-gamini-keerawella/.
18 Bandarage, Asoka. *The Separatist Conflict in Sri Lanka: Terrorism, Ethnicity, Political Economy.* London: Routledge/Taylor & Francis Group, 2009, 96, 97.

network and goons paid for by the state. The JSS is known to have used "brute force against anti-government unions during strikes."[19]

The harsh repression of a general strike in July 1980 virtually destroyed the trade union movement. More than 40,000 workers were dismissed from their jobs, mostly in the government sector and many of them were never reinstated. Due to this severe treatment of organized labor and other factors, such as the vast exodus of workers to the Middle East, the unions were unable to mount significant resistance. As elsewhere in the world, the processes of neoliberal economic globalization increased worker resignation to social class and transnational corporate exploitation, and that exploitation intensified culturally-based ethno-religious conflicts.

The JSS, which was controlled by Cyril Mathew, Minister of Science and Industries and considered to be the most chauvinistic Sinhala Buddhist in the Cabinet, was involved in the anti-Tamil attacks in July 1983. The new political authoritarianism and the imperious style of J.R. Jayawardena played a significant role in both the deterioration of public trust in the government and the worsening of Sinhala–Tamil relations. More than any other individual, Jayawardena has been held responsible for the institutionalization of political violence after 1977 and the repression that would transform the ethnic conflict into a civil war.[20]

'Open Economy'

The major projects of economic liberalization, the Mahaweli River Development Program, tourist expansion and labor export to the Middle East were begun several years prior to 1977. Even the FTZ, another linchpin of the Open Economy, was under consideration before 1977. It is the speedup in absorption into the western development model and the dismantling of the traditions of state welfare urged on by the World Bank and the IMF that made 1977 a turning point in the economic and social history of the island.[21]

---

[19] Ibid., 97.
[20] Ibid., 97.
[21] Ibid., 59; Herring, Ronald J. "Economic Liberalisation Policies in Sri Lanka: International Pressures, Constraints and Supports." *Economic and Political Weekly* 22, no. 8 (1987): 325–333. https://www.jstor.org/stable/4376706.

Land and Agriculture

The Mahaweli Development Programme (MDP) Sri Lanka's largest multi-purpose irrigation-based agricultural development program is also one of the largest agriculture-related development programs in the world.[22] The principal goal of the MDP was to increase power generation for expansion of manufacturing and reduce dependence on import of staple food.[23] The MDP involved the diversion of the *Mahaweli*, the longest river in the island and the settlement of landless peasantry from the densely populated wet zone in newly irrigated areas in the Dry Zone. The MDP represented a more comprehensive and costly continuation of the colonization policies started in the 1930s.

Early plans calculated that upon completion, the MDP would cover 39 percent of the whole island, allocating land among 218,000 settler families, each on 2.5 acres of irrigated farm and 0.5 acre of homestead. Upon coming into power in 1977, the UNP government sped up the MDP in the name of rapid development. The thirty-year project was telescoped into six years making it officially the Accelerated Mahaweli development Program.

The Open Economy was built upon a huge influx of foreign loans, outright grants and investments. The country's dependence on this 'explosion of aid' made satisfaction of foreign interests one of the biggest priorities of the state.[24] The massive $US 1.5 billion MDP was funded by the World Bank and a host of foreign countries including Sweden, USA Canada and Japan (Table 4.1).[25] Over time, the MDP contributed to a sharp increase in Sri Lanka's foreign indebtedness. The island's foreign debt rose from Rs. 4.96 billion in 1976 to Rs. 110 billion in 1987 of which approximately 30 percent of the increase was estimated to be due to the MDP.[26] Of all foreign assistance received for the MDP up to the end of 1986, 56.3 percent constituted loans and 43.7 percent grants.[27]

---

22 https://www.ncbi.nlm.nih.gov/pmc/articles/PMC6551383/.
23 Dunham, David, and Saman Kelegama. "Stabilisation and Adjustment: Sri Lankan Experience, 1977–1993." Economic and Political Weekly 33, no. 24 (1998): 1475–1482, 1475. https://www.jstor.org/stable/4406883.
24 Bandarage, The Separatist Conflict, op.cit., 77. Ibid., 77.
25 Karunatilake, H. N. S. *The Accelerated Mahaweli Programme and Its Impact*. Centre for Demographic and Socio-Economic Studies, 1988, 54–55, 59.
26 Ibid., 178–179.
27 Ibid., 170.

Table 4.1: Accelerated Mahaweli programme foreign funding, up to 1988.

Country/Organization	Aid Type	Amount (millions)
Sweden	Loans	Skr 256.20
	Grants	Skr 1,395.00
		Skr 1,651.20
U.S.A.	Loans	US$ 172.20
	Grants	US$ 8.00
		US$ 180.20
U.K.	Loans	£. 20.00
	Grants	£. 117.30
		£. 137.30
I.D.A. & I.B.R.D.	Loans	US$ 36.10
	Loans	SD2 101.60
Canada	Loans	Can$. 110.70
	Grants	Can$. 32.00
	Grants (Food)	Can$... 25.68
		Can$. 168.38
West Germany	Loans	DM 400.00
	Grants	DM 8.50
		DM 408.55
Saudi Arabia	Loans	S. Ri 256.00
Japan	Loans	JY 7,700.00
	Grants	JY 996.00
	Loan (Commodity)	3,300.00
	Grant (Food)	Rs. 473.00
		JY 11,996.00
		Rs. 473.00
E.E.C.	Grants	EUA 39.40
	Grants (Food)	Rs. 537.80
Kuwait	Loans	KD 12.86
UN (UNDP, UNFPA, UNTCDC, UNICEF, WFP)	Grants	US$ 41.95
A.D.B.	Loans	US$ 13.86
		SDR 10.86
Australia	Grants (Food)	Aus$ 15.00
O.P.E.C.	Loans (counterpart)	US$ 9.00
Netherlands	Loans	HFL 13.00
	Grants	HFL 1.40

Table 4.1: Accelerated Mahaweli programme foreign funding, up to 1988. *(Continued)*

Country/Organization	Aid Type	Amount (millions)
	Grants	HFL 2.10
		HFL 16.50
Belgium	Grants	Bel. Frs. 60.00
China	Loans	RMB Y 1.70

Source: Projects and Programme, Ministry of Mahaweli Development as cited in H.N.S. Karunatilake, The Accelerated Mahaweli Programme and Its Impact, Colombo: Centre for Demographic and Socio-Economic Studies, 1988, 54–55.

A significant amount of the monies received was used to pay the high salaries of foreign experts from donor countries working on Mahaweli infrastructure. Economist H.N.S. Karunatileka observed the neo-colonial character of the Mahaweli Program's payment structure:

> … Large payments were made to consultancy firms like Sir Alexander Gibbs [Partners and Ltd], Sir William Halcrow [and Partners Ltd.] and Electorwatt of Switzerland …. Some of the individual consultants of these firms were paid as much as US $150 to US $200 per hour …. These firms worked along with the Sri Lanka consultants …who were often far more qualified and competent than the expatriates, but whose rates of remuneration were a mere fraction of the less qualified expatriate technicians.[28]

Environmental and human health costs due to the faulty and hasty construction of the Mahaweli Project and chemical inputs used in agriculture were even more serious than the financial costs of the MDP. A 1993 USAID, 'Environmental Evaluation' of the MDP identified a host of environmental problems associated with the massive Project including degradation of downstream water quality, loss of natural forest cover, change in seasonal flow regimes of rivers, in-site soil loss and so on.[29]

The USAID study also identified presence of agrochemicals in runoff water, magnification of pesticides throughout natural food chains, including human consumption, crop damage from birds and large mammals due to loss of habitats and resulting physical harm to Mahaweli settlers from large mammals, such as, ele-

---

28 Ibid., 175.
29 Tolisano, Jim, Pia Abeygunewardene, Tissa Athukorala, Craig Davis, William Fleming, Kapila Goonesekera, and Tamara Rusinow. "An Environmental Evaluation of the Accelerated Mahaweli Development Program: Lessons Learned and Donor Opportunities for Improved Assistance." Bethesda, Maryland: DAI / U.S. Agency for International Development, May 1993, 20. Available at: https://pdf.usaid.gov/pdf_docs/pnabr388.pdf.

phants and boars.[30] The Green Revolution (introduced throughout the island since the mid-1960s) made agriculture in the MDP also heavily dependent on external inputs which disturbed the natural fertility of the soil and the regenerative capacity of nature.[31] Numerous studies have pointed out that the widespread chronic kidney disease among farmers in the North Central Province is likely due to the pollution of the farmlands and the river Mahaweli from widespread use of agro-chemicals. This position, however, remains highly controversial.[32]

Researchers have also pointed out that at least a third of the money allocated for the MDP was lost through graft and that political patronage, caste and class politics have given rise to a process of rapid class differentiation in the Mahaweli settlements. It was also found that the government was leasing thousands of newly irrigated Mahaweli lands to transnational corporations to cultivate export crops like tobacco using peasants as contract labor. Such developments made a mockery of the government's alleged commitment to national food self-sufficiency and the perpetuation of the smallholder peasantry.[33]

Once the Mahaweli infrastructure of dams, reservoirs, power systems, roads and other construction was completed and human settlements were established, external interests sought to advance private commercial sector development over smallholder production. External funders felt that the MDP was working against the objectives of liberalization.[34] The USAID supported initiative, the Maha-

---

[30] Ibid., 32.

[31] Fernando Sarath. "Peasants Situation and Human Rights in Sri Lanka." HURIGHTS OSAKA, December 2007. https://www.hurights.or.jp/archives/focus/section2/2007/12/peasants-situation-and-human-rights-in-sri-lanka.html.

[32] Bandara, J. M. R. S., H. V. P. Wijewardena, Y. M. a. Y. Bandara, R. G. P. T. Jayasooriya, and H. Rajapaksha. "Pollution of River Mahaweli and Farmlands under Irrigation by Cadmium from Agricultural Inputs Leading to a Chronic Renal Failure Epidemic among Farmers in NCP, Sri Lanka." Environmental Geochemistry and Health 33, no. 5 (October 2011): 439–453. https://doi.org/10.1007/s10653-010-9344-4. See also, Bandara, J. M. R. S., H. V. P. Wijewardena, J. Liyanege, M. A. Upul, and J. M. U. A. Bandara. "Chronic Renal Failure in Sri Lanka Caused by Elevated Dietary Cadmium: Trojan Horse of the Green Revolution." Toxicology Letters 198, no. 1 (September 15, 2010): 33–39. https://doi.org/10.1016/j.toxlet.2010.04.016. Bandarage, Asoka. "Political Economy of Epidemic Kidney Disease in Sri Lanka." SAGE Open 3, no. 4 (January 1, 2013): 2158244013511827. https://doi.org/10.1177/2158244013511827. Noble, A., P. Amerasinghe, H. Manthrithilake, and S. Arasalingam. "Review of Literature on Chronic Kidney Disease of Unknown Etiology (CKDu) in Sri Lanka." International Water Management Institute (IWMI)., 2014. https://doi.org/10.5337/2014.206.

[33] Bandarage, Asoka. "Women and Capitalist Development in Sri Lanka, 1977–87." *Bulletin of Concerned Asian Scholars* 20, no. 2 (June 1, 1988): 57–81, 64. https://doi.org/10.1080/14672715.1988.10404449.

[34] Levy, Brian. "Foreign Aid in the Making of Economic Policy in Sri Lanka, 1977–1983." *Policy Sciences* 22, no. 3/4 (1989): 437–461. https://www.jstor.org/stable/4532178.

weli Enterprise Development Project was introduced in the early 1990s "to promote investment and business development in agribusiness, manufacturing, tourism, minerals and services."[35]

Private sector development requires individual ownership and the right to sell land. However, these were lacking in the MDP where state owned land was granted to peasant cultivators with restrictions on sale, per the Land Development Ordinance of 1935. Since the mid-1990s, the World Bank has been pressuring the Sri Lankan government to "transform the country's land administration system from one based on deeds and documents permitting private use of state land, to one based on registration of titles"[36] and to issue freehold titles to farmers.[37] The interventionist World Bank, USAID and other institutions sought to complete the process of privatization and commoditization of state and commonly held lands that was begun by the colonial state during British rule.

In March 2001, the World Bank proposed US$ 5 million credit to Sri Lanka to begin land titling and related services that would eventually cover the entire 6.56 million hectares of land in the country of which approximately 80 percent is state owned land.[38] In its role as neo-colonial financial authority, the World Bank told the Government of Sri Lanka:

> The establishment of a legal framework and development of capacity for implementing land titling and related services, would lay the foundation for increased tenure security, efficient land transactions and administration, and effectively functioning land markets. It would build the foundation for a long-term program intended to catalyze the transformation of domestic agricultural sector...[39]

---

[35] "Mahaweli Enterprise Development, MED/EIED Project, MED/ETED 1992 Workplan." USAID, International Science and Technology Institute. INC., 1992. https://pdf.usaid.gov/pdf_docs/PDABD752.pdf.

[36] "Project Appraisal Document on a Proposed Credit in the amount of SDR 3.9 Million ($5 Million Equivalent) to the Democratic Socialist Republic of Sri Lanka for the Land Tilting and Related Services Project," The World Bank, March 22, 2001, 4. https://documents1.worldbank.org/curated/en/418081468781158319/text/multi0page.txt.

[37] Fernando Sarath. "Peasants Situation and Human Rights in Sri Lanka." HURIGHTS OSAKA, December 2007. https://www.hurights.or.jp/archives/focus/section2/2007/12/peasants-situation-and-human-rights-in-sri-lanka.html. "Regaining Sri Lanka: Vision and Strategy for Accelerated Development." Government of Sri Lanka, December 2002. https://planipolis.iiep.unesco.org/sites/default/files/ressources/sri_lanka_prsp_2002.pdf.

[38] "Project Appraisal Document on a Proposed Credit in the amount of SDR 3.9 Million ($5 Million Equivalent) to the Democratic Socialist Republic of Sri Lanka for the Land Tilting and Related Services Project," The World Bank, March 22, 2001, https://documents1.worldbank.org/curated/en/418081468781158319/text/multi0page.txt.

[39] Ibid., 4.

The objectives of this policy are "reducing government interference in the agricultural sector, and introducing land markets" for private sector development.[40] Indeed, as local activists point out given the extreme poverty and indebtedness of the farmers, outright ownership will only induce them to give up their land "even when they do not wish to."[41] The World Bank argues that "moving out of subsistence or sharecrop agriculture" would be "the path out of poverty for the rural poor" although the Bank does not say what the path out of poverty would be once the farmers lose their land.[42] Speaking against the growing aggressive efforts to advance individual land ownership and land deeds, Sarath Fernando from the Movement for National Land Agriculture Reform (MONLAR) explained,

> We have a tradition of integrated, communal land use. We must tackle poverty through other means – maybe a sustainable model for land-use based on traditional, integrated forms of farming – not initiate a process that may well push out the small farmer completely from the rural economy.[43]

In 2007, the government declared a new agricultural policy promoting domestic food production and the role of small-scale farmers. However, this policy could not be implemented in the face of mounting opposition from the international lending institutions and proponents of neoliberal economic policy.[44] Instead, as we discuss in the next Chapter, efforts to provide individual ownership to state held lands has moved ahead steadily.

---

40 Ibid., 3.
41 Dissanaike, Tharuka. "Sale or Sell out? Sri Lanka's Farmers and Land Reform." *Panos London*, March 27, 2006. https://panoslondon.panosnetwork.org/features/sale-or-sell-out-sri-lankas-farmers-and-land-reform/.
42 "Project Appraisal Document on a Proposed Credit in the amount of SDR 3.9 Million ($5 Million Equivalent) to the Democratic Socialist Republic of Sri Lanka for the Land Tilting and Related Services Project," The World Bank, March 22, 2001, https://documents1.worldbank.org/curated/en/418081468781158319/text/multi0page.txt.
43 Dissanaike, Tharuka. "Sale or Sell out? Sri Lanka's Farmers and Land Reform." *Panos London*, March 27, 2006. Accessed August 8, 2021. https://panoslondon.panosnetwork.org/features/sale-or-sell-out-sri-lankas-farmers-and-land-reform/.
44 Fernando Sarath. "Peasants Situation and Human Rights in Sri Lanka." HURIGHTS OSAKA, December 2007. https://www.hurights.or.jp/archives/focus/section2/2007/12/peasants-situation-and-human-rights-in-sri-lanka.html.

Labor, Manufacturing and Services

Since the introduction of the Open Economy in 1977 foreign investors have received the most favorable terms from the Sri Lankan state: guarantee of foreign investments by the Constitution; complete tax holidays; relief from double taxation with major countries of the world; access to telecommunications, buildings, and other infrastructure; and discouragement of labor unions.[45] The 1998 Index of Economic Freedom compiled by the Heritage Foundation and the Wall Street Journal categorized Sri Lanka as one of the 'most free' economies in the world.[46]

Under the Open Economy, fourteen FTZs have been established across the island since the first one was opened in Katunayake in 1978. FTZs, also called Export Processing Zones (EPZs), are special fenced in areas set up to attract foreign investors and manufacture goods exclusively for export using cheap local labor. The EPZs in Sri Lanka, like others elsewhere in the 'developing world', offer a liberal regulatory environment that bypasses local and international labor and environmental laws. The World Bank promotes EPZs as a source for generating employment and foreign exchange for poor countries.[47] The EPZs are a new manifestation of the colonial plantations in Sri Lanka, foreign enclaves for export production using cheap, highly controlled labor.

Most of the factories in Sri Lanka's FTZs are garment industries while there are also projects on appliance manufacturing, gem cutting, rubber-based industries, etc. Most companies are directly owned by foreign investors while others are jointly- owned or owned by local owners.[48] The FTZ manufacturing involves the assembly of raw materials and parts brought mostly from abroad.[49] As such, they do not contribute to the development of local industries or the use of local

---

[45] Bandarage, Asoka. "Women and Capitalist Development in Sri Lanka, 1977–87." *Bulletin of Concerned Asian Scholars* 20, no. 2 (June 1, 1988): 57–81, 67. https://doi.org/10.1080/14672715.1988.10404449; https://www.lexology.com/library/detail.aspx?g=855ba9c9-ffda-45b9-8730-6dd2e2c0de21.

[46] Bandarage, Asoka. *Women and Social Change in Sri Lanka: Towards a Feminist Theoretical Framework.* Working Paper (CENWOR (Organization: Sri Lanka)). Colombo, Sri Lanka: Centre for Women's Research (CENWOR), 1998, 1.

[47] *Export Processing Zones.* Policy and Research Series 20. Washington, D.C: The World Bank, 1992. Available at: https://documents1.worldbank.org/curated/en/400411468766543358/pdf/multi-page.pdf.

[48] Bandarage, Asoka. "Women and Capitalist Development in Sri Lanka, 1977–87." *Bulletin of Concerned Asian Scholars* 20, no. 2 (June 1, 1988): 57–81, 67. https://doi.org/10.1080/14672715.1988.10404449.

[49] Jayanthakumaran, Kangesu. "Trade Liberalization and Performance: The Impact of Trade Reform on Manufacturing Sector Performance: Sri Lanka 1977–89." PhD Thesis, University of Bradford, United Kingdom, 1994.

materials. Rather, they contribute to significant repatriation of profits generating relatively low net returns to the local economy.

In 2019, the apparel industry, one of the leading sectors of the island's export economy, represented 46.9 percent of total exports at US$ 9,426 million. The export destinations include the EU, US, Canada, The United Arab Emirates, Australia, and Japan.[50] The Sri Lankan garment factories produce a wide range of garments from "sportswear, lingerie, loungewear, bridal wear, workwear, swimwear to children's wear under world-renowned labels such as Victoria's Secret, Gap, Liz Claiborne, Next, Jones New York, Nike, Tommy Hilfiger, Pink, Triumph, Ann Taylor, Speedo, Abercrombie & Fitch, Land's End, Marks & Spencer, etc."[51]

Currently, the industry employs around 300,000 to 600,000 workers in 300 to 360 garment factories in the 14 FTZs around the country. Seventy-eight percent of the workers are young single women with secondary education, below twenty-five years of age performing routine work such as sewing machine operation.[52] Most women workers come from rural impoverished families, and many are their sole economic supporters. Being away from home, most women are forced to spend a substantial portion of their earnings on lodging.[53] FTZ work has contributed to significant changes in women's roles. They have released women from their rural villages and their family settings, but the modern working-class life has rarely brought economic or psychological freedom.

The pace of work and productivity norms in the factories are very high, and labor control is extremely authoritarian. Attendance is strictly monitored, and it is reported that women require permission from supervisors (some of them foreign males) even to use the toilets. Sexual harassment is not uncommon. As labor contracts are not given, workers can be dismissed at a supervisor's whim.[54] Given the compulsory nature of overtime work in many factories, most FTZ workers put in long hours of work, often 12 hours a day, without over-time pay.[55]

---

50 Dabindu Collective. "Delegation Meeting on Minimum Wage Issues in Sri Lanka – January of 2022 A Narrative to the Apparel Sector in Sri Lanka," January 24, 2022. Accessed January 30, 2022. https://www.dabinducollective.org/delegation-meeting-on-minimum-wage-issues-in-sri-lanka-january-of-2022-a-narrative-to-the-apparel-sector-in-sri-lanka/.
51 Ibid.
52 Ibid.
53 Bandarage, Women and Capitalist Development, op.cit., 68.
54 Ibid., 69.
55 Wijethunge, Pavithra. "Overworked and Underpaid, Sri Lanka's Garment Workers Left Hanging by a Thread, Workplace Issues in the Sri Lanka Garment Sector." Solidarity Center, American Federation of Labor and Congress of Industrial Organizations, October 2021, 20. https://www.solidaritycenter.org/wp-content/uploads/2021/11/Workplace-Issues-in-the-Sri-Lanka-Garment-Sector.10.2021.FINAL_.pdf.

Precise and repetitious assembly-line work leads to general ill health and deterioration of the eyes. Occupational diseases, fatigue, and stress are quite common.

An early Survey conducted by the journal, *Voice of Women* and other researchers documented the 'super exploitation' that characterizes working conditions in the FTZ.[56] The fires and deaths in Bangladesh garment export factories in recent years has brought attention to the sordid conditions in which popular brand names are produced in the so-called Third World.[57]

Modem forms of labor protest and organizing are not alien to Sri Lanka. Since the last decades of British rule, Sri Lanka has been known for its militant labor force and trade union movement, as was evident in the 1952 *Hartal*. However, the climate in the FTZ, according to the women workers interviewed by *Voice of Women*, "did not even permit the mentioning of the words 'trade union.'"[58] Still, women workers at the Polytex garment factory won the right to a union in 1983 after a prolonged strike amidst state emergency regulations, police intimidation, and threats by the factory management.[59] Today, there is only one collective bargaining agreement in Sri Lanka's garment industry with the Free Trade Zones and General Services Employees Union.[60]

The apparel sector is a multi-billion-dollar industry bringing great profit to investors, desired goods to consumers and much-needed foreign exchange to countries like Sri Lanka. However, wages of workers is notoriously low. The international activist group, Labour Behind the Label is campaigning for the human right of a living wage, "a wage sufficient to afford a decent standard of living for a worker and their family," for the garment sector worldwide. Labour Behind the Label points out the suffering caused when corporate profit prevails over the survival needs of workers:

> When governments set minimum wages, they balance the interests of workers with what they see as the need to remain competitive in the global market and pressure from companies to keep wages low. As a result, minimum wage rates often bear no relation to the cost of living and fall far short of what we would consider a living wage. In many garment-producing coun-

---

56 Bandarage, Women and Capitalist Development, op.cit., 68.
57 Hammadi, Saad, and Matthew Taylor. "Workers Jump to Their Deaths as Fire Engulfs Factory Making Clothes for Gap." *The Guardian*, December 14, 2010, sec. World news. Accessed August 8, 2022. https://www.theguardian.com/world/2010/dec/14/bangladesh-clothes-factory-workers-jump-to-death.
58 Bandarage, Women and Capitalist Development, op.cit., 69.
59 Ibid., 69.
60 Free Trade Zones & General Services Employee Union. "OUR HISTORY." Accessed January 3, 2023. https://www.ftzunionlanka.org/Page-2.php.

tries, the minimum wage actually leaves a family below the national poverty line, even though this is also set by the government.[61]

This is certainly the case in Sri Lanka. In 2019, the basic monthly salary of a worker was approximately US$ 120–175 including over time and incentives. At the same time, the cost of living estimated for a family of four was around US$ 400 which meant that many workers had to go into debt.[62] Labour Behind the Label, shows that the gap between the legal minimum wage and a living wage is increasing around the world. In Sri Lanka, in 2019, the minimum wage was Rs.10,000 whereas the estimated living wage was Rs.75,601.[63] Studies show that conditions have worsened following Covid lockdowns and that the "overworked and underpaid, Sri Lanka's garment workers [are] left hanging by a thread."[64] These realities necessitate critical rethinking of neoliberalism's strategy of export production as the only path to poverty alleviation and human well-being.

The garment sector jobs are dead-end, short-term jobs. Upon leaving the FTZ after a few years of grueling work, like their brethren displaced from rural agriculture, the women have few options. The specialized factory work provides few marketable skills. In Thailand, South Korea, and other countries, many former FTZ workers have ended up in the sex tourism trade[65]. In Sri Lanka, one of the few options for former FTZ women workers is travel to the Middle East to work as domestic labor, an even more exploitative undertaking.

---

[61] Labour Behind the Label. "Living Wage, A Wage That Covers a Workers' Basic Needs Is a Human Right." Accessed January 3, 2023. https://labourbehindthelabel.org/living-wage/.

[62] Dabindu Collective. "Delegation Meeting on Minimum Wage Issues in Sri Lanka – January of 2022 A Narrative to the Apparel Sector in Sri Lanka," January 24, 2022. Accessed January 30, 2022. https://www.dabinducollective.org/delegation-meeting-on-minimum-wage-issues-in-sri-lanka-january-of-2022-a-narrative-to-the-apparel-sector-in-sri-lanka/.

[63] Labour Behind the Label. "Living Wage, A Wage That Covers a Workers' Basic Needs Is a Human Right." Accessed January 3, 2023. https://labourbehindthelabel.org/living-wage/.

[64] Wijethunge, Pavithra. "Overworked and Underpaid, Sri Lanka's Garment Workers Left Hanging by a Thread, Workplace Issues in the Sri Lanka Garment Sector." Solidarity Center, American Federation of Labor and Congress of Industrial Organizations, October 2021. https://www.solidaritycenter.org/wp-content/uploads/2021/11/Workplace-Issues-in-the-Sri-Lanka-Garment-Sector.10.2021.FINAL_.pdf.

[65] Bandarage, Women and Capitalist Development, op.cit., 69.

Middle East Labor Export

Since the oil boom of 1973 there was an expansion in construction and economic growth in West Asia and the Middle East. The oil-rich countries began to import migrant workers from labor-surplus countries in South and Southeast Asia. Unable to provide sufficient employment for its population at home, the Sri Lankan government encouraged labor export to the Middle East in conjunction with economic liberalization.[66]

In the following two decades, labor out-migration increased tenfold, and it was estimated that in 2009 about 1.7 million migrants worked abroad, with an annual outflow of about 250,000 with most migrants working in the Gulf states, such as, Saudi Arabia, Kuwait, Oman, Bahrain, and the United Arab Emirates (Table 4.2).[67] Thus, Sri Lanka which was a labor importing country during British colonialism became a labor exporting country in the neo-colonial era.

Table 4.2: Total departures for foreign employment by country of destination, 2005–2009.

	2005	2006	2007	2008	2009
Saudi Arabia	76,210	61,424	60,489	67,443	77,849
Qatar	35,953	31,458	38,943	39,476	43,744
Kuwait	36,157	34,697	41,028	46,941	42,000
United Arab Emirates	36,371	33,797	39,018	51,174	39,653
Jordan	8,276	8,136	8,440	10,362	9,032
Bahrain	3,751	4,400	4,975	4,650	5,929
Lebanon	16,402	6,889	6,939	4,969	5,907
Oman	3,562	4,273	3,912	4,747	5,326
Republic of Korea	4,850	3,653	2,680	6,995	3,991
Maldives	2,738	3,467	3,915	4,228	3,904
Cyprus	2,234	2,346	3,004	2,829	2,929
Malaysia	1,168	3,584	1,043	1,293	1,050
Singapore	1,017	954	947	1,079	1,026
Other Countries	2,601	2,870	3,126	4,313	4,379
Total	**231,290**	**201,948**	**218,459**	**250,499**	**247,119**

Source: Sri Lanka Bureau of Foreign Employment (2009) as cited in Situation Report, UN ESCAP, https://sitreport.unescapsdd.org/sri-lanka/out-migration.

---

[66] "National Labour Migration Ploicy for Sri Lank." Ministry for Foreign Employment Promotion and Welfare, October 2008. https://www.ilo.org/dyn/migpractice/docs/268/Policy.pdf.
[67] https://sitreport.unescapsdd.org/sri-lanka/out-migration.

The colonial state was dependent on the revenue generated by the super-exploited labor force on the plantations and Sri Lanka is still heavily dependent on the revenue generated by plantation labor. In addition, the Sri Lankan economy is now heavily dependent on the remittances of the super-exploited labor migrants in the Middle East. By 2009, remittances from migrants working abroad had become the largest source of foreign exchange for the Sri Lankan economy, surpassing earnings from the export of tea which had been the primary foreign exchange earner since the colonial era. According to estimates from the Sri Lanka Bureau of Foreign Employment, of the total amount of remittances in 2009, Rs. 230 billion (US$ 2.1 billion), or 59.9 percent, came from Sri Lankan migrant workers in Western Asia.[68] Workers remittances from Western Asia/Middle East have continued to be the largest source of remittance. (Table 4:3)

Table 4.3: Workers Remittances By Regional Corridors (USD Million % Share), 2015-2019

Corridor	2015	2016	2017	2018	2019
Middle East	54.0	53.7	51.8	51.2	51.5
European Union	17.5	17.7	18.3	18.7	18.8
Far East Asia	10.0	10.2	11.5	12.1	12.3
Europe-Other	4.4	4.6	4.6	4.4	4.2
North America	3.0	2.9	2.9	2.6	2.4
South East Asia	5.6	5.5	5.5	5.8	5.6
Australia and New Zealand	2.3	2.4	2.4	2.2	2.6
South Asia	1.4	1.5	1.5	2.2	2.0
South and Central America	0.9	0.7	0.7	0.5	0.4
Other	0.9	0.8	0.8	0.3	0.2

Source: Central Bank of Sri Lanka, Annual Report 2019, Statistical Appendix. External Sector Developments and Policies, Table 93, Available online at: https://www.cbsl.gov.lk/en/publications/economic-and-financial-reports/annual-reports

The primary and often the only reason for the migration of foreign labor into the alien and often harsh physical and social environment of the Middle East is economic. At all skilled and unskilled levels, workers can make much more money in Saudi Arabia or Kuwait than they can at home. While male migrants from Sri Lanka are spread across many skilled and unskilled categories of work (doctors,

---

[68] Cited in Ibid. see also, https://www.un.int/srilanka/sites/www.un.int/files/Sri%20Lanka/2020/July/01/speech-_sfr.pdf.

engineers, mechanics, drivers, carpenters, laborers, etc.), almost all female migrants from the country are unskilled housemaids.

Domestic service is one of the lowest paid and most demeaning categories of labor in Sri Lanka. But in the Middle East, domestic workers make the highest proportionate wage increase of any group of Sri Lankan migrant workers.[69] Female migrants from Sri Lanka accounted for as much as 75 percent of the migrant flow to the Middle East in the mid-1990s, 88 percent of them as housemaids. Like the Philippines, Sri Lanka became known in the Middle East as the land of nannies. By 2008 the number declined to a little under 50 percent due to government efforts to upskill the migrant labor force.[70]

While the far higher monetary returns in the Middle East is an incomparable lure for poor unskilled Sri Lankan women, the entire process of labor recruitment and the conditions of work abroad, are full of abuse and fraught with danger at every turn. Lacking organization and protection, male migrants, especially the unskilled, also suffer greatly at the hands of unscrupulous recruiters and employers. But the exploitation of women is much worse because it takes on a specifically domestic and sexual dimension."[71]

Once arriving in the homes of their employers, most women become virtual household slaves, often the only servant of large Arab households. They are made to do all the cooking, cleaning, and childcare from early morning to late at night. In addition to working too hard, these migrant Sri Lankan women are often denied wages, verbally and physically abused, and sexually harassed. Lacking any kind of labor protection or recourse to legal procedures, the women remain at the complete mercy of their employers during their two- to three-year (or sometimes longer) contracts.[72]

Some women have been publicly lashed, and a few women have completely 'disappeared' or committed suicide for reasons often unknown to their families back home.[73] In 2009, Sri Lankan authorities received complaints from 5 percent

---

69 Bandarage, Asoka. "Women and Capitalist Development in Sri Lanka, 1977–87." *Bulletin of Concerned Asian Scholars* 20, no. 2 (June 1, 1988): 57–81, 70. https://doi.org/10.1080/14672715.1988.10404449.
70 https://www.mei.edu/publications/sri-lankan-migration-gulf-female-breadwinners-domestic-workers; https://www.ilo.org/wcmsp5/groups/public/--asia/--ro-bangkok/--ilo-colombo/documents/publication/wcms_768676.pdf.
71 Bandarage, Asoka. "Women and Capitalist Development in Sri Lanka, 1977–87." *Bulletin of Concerned Asian Scholars* 20, no. 2 (June 1, 1988): 57–81, 70. https://doi.org/10.1080/14672715.1988.10404449.
72 Cited in Ibid., 71.
73 Ibid., 72.

of total foreign employment recruitment (most victims do not lodge complaints) and reports of 333 deaths of overseas migrants.[74]

The long absences of women from their own families in Sri Lanka have changed gender roles, weakened family bonds and created problems at home. Either the children are neglected and not attending school or the husbands are drinking, gambling, and having extramarital relations (male migrants often find that their wives have taken up with other men).[75] In spite of untold miseries they experience at work, many return to the Middle East due to lack of opportunities in Sri Lanka. Although women's groups and the Sri Lankan government's Women's Bureau have put forward suggestions for improving the situation of migrant labor and the housemaids, little has changed over the years.[76]

According to data from India, Bangladesh, Nepal and Sri Lanka, there were more than 6500 deaths of migrant workers from those countries in the period 2011–2020 in Qatar attributed to the unprecedented building program in preparation for the World Cup football tournament there.[77] Nevertheless, the World Cup was held there in 2022 amidst controversy over the inhumane treatment and deaths of migrant workers. According to the activist group, Anti-Slavery International:

> Modern slavery is all around us, often hidden in plain sight. People can become enslaved making our clothes, serving our food, picking our crops, working in factories, or working in houses as cooks, cleaners or nannies. Victims of modern slavery might face violence or threats, be forced into inescapable debt, or have their passport taken away and face being threatened with deportation. Many people have fallen into this trap because they were trying to escape poverty or insecurity, improve their lives and support their families. Now, they can't leave.[78]

---

[74] https://sitreport.unescapsdd.org/sri-lanka/out-migration.
[75] Bandarage, Asoka. "Women and Capitalist Development in Sri Lanka, 1977–87." *Bulletin of Concerned Asian Scholars* 20, no. 2 (June 1, 1988): 57–81, 72. https://doi.org/10.1080/14672715.1988.10404449.
[76] ""National Labour Migration Ploicy for Sri Lank." Ministry for Foreign Employment Promotion and Welfare, October 2008. https://www.ilo.org/dyn/migpractice/docs/268/Policy.pdf.
[77] Pattisson, Pete, Niamh McIntyre, and Imran Mukhtar. "Revealed: 6,500 Migrant Workers Have Died in Qatar since World Cup Awarded." *The Guardian*, February 23, 2021, sec. Global development. Accessed November 22, 2022. https://www.theguardian.com/global-development/2021/feb/23/revealed-migrant-worker-deaths-qatar-fifa-world-cup-2022.
[78] *Anti-Slavery International.* "Anti-Slavery International | Fighting for Freedom from Slavery." Accessed January 3, 2023. https://www.antislavery.org/.

The service sector and domestic service in particular is one of the hardest to organize, and the migrant workers continue to be without organization and political mobilization. Ultimately, it is necessary to move away from the dependence on oppressive labor export promoted by neoliberal economics towards greater local self-sufficiency and livelihoods with dignity for both men and women.

Tourism

Tourism received a tremendous boost from the economic liberalization policies of 1977.[79] Due to the predominance of low-budget package tours and 'hippie' tourism, much of the local employment generated has been in low skilled and low paid jobs, such as waiters and housekeepers.[80] High-end tourism has been promoted in recent years and following the end of the armed conflict in 2009, there was a rapid growth in tourist arrivals and earnings from tourism.

There is pressure from the tourist sector to deregulate the ownership of freehold land and promote foreign ownership of land for investment in hotels and other ventures.[81] According to the Sri Lanka Tourist Development Authority, the Sri Lankan government allows "100 percent repatriation on earnings, fees and capital, and on foreign exchange transactions."[82] While there is no available evidence to determine if tourism is repatriating more earnings than it brings into Sri Lanka, it is widely known that tourism and neocolonialism mutually reinforce each other and constrain equal exchange and development options.[83]

While sex tourism and prostitution are not as prevalent as in Bangkok, the expansion of mass tourism has contributed to an increase in prostitution in Colombo

---

[79] Bandarage, Asoka. "Women and Capitalist Development in Sri Lanka, 1977–87." *Bulletin of Concerned Asian Scholars* 20, no. 2 (June 1, 1988): 57–81, 72. https://doi.org/10.1080/14672715.1988.10404449.

[80] Ibid., 73.

[81] Sirisena, Chantal. "Sri Lanka's Tourism Industry and the Foreign Ownership Debate." *Talking Economics* (Institute of Policy Studies of Sri Lanka) (blog), August 18, 2016. Accessed November 18, 2022. https://www.ips.lk/talkingeconomics/2016/08/18/sri-lankas-tourism-industry-and-the-foreign-ownership-debate/.

[82] Kelliher, Adam. "War-Torn Sri Lanka Gambles on Casinos." *Los Angeles Times* (United Press International), July 31, 1988. Accessed October 8, 2022. https://www.latimes.com/archives/la-xpm-1988-0731-mn-10720-story.html; Sri Lanka Tourism Development Authority. "FAQs." Accessed January 3, 2023. https://sltda.gov.lk/en/faqs.

[83] Freya Higgins-desbiolles, 'The Ongoingness of Imperialism: The problem of tourism dependency and the promise of radical equality', Annals of Tourism Research, vol. 94, May 2022, https://www.sciencedirect.com/science/article/pii/S0160738322000330 accessed March 20, 2023.

and the island in general. As Shireen Samarasuriya explained in her study, *Who Needs Tourism?*, prostitution was not established on a commercial basis before the advent of mass tourism: "pimping and female and male prostitution are increasing in spite of acutely felt moral degradation proves that few other means of livelihood are open to those who engage in it."[84]

Another development related to tourism and the international traffic in women is a phenomenon referred to as 'tourist brides', the export of young women from Sri Lanka to the West and to Japan to become the brides of older men.[85] Perhaps the most degrading and extreme of all ventures in the skin trade has been the business of exporting babies. The Sri Lankan government admitted years later that, the illegal adoptions that took place in Sri Lanka during the late 1980s were "mixed together with tourism."[86] The Sri Lankan health minister admitted on a Dutch documentary program in 2017 that thousands of Sri Lankan babies had been fraudulently sold for adoption in the Netherlands (4000 in the Netherlands) and other European countries such as Sweden, Denmark, Germany and the UK.in the 1980s.[87]

Some of the babies adopted were reportedly born in 'baby farms' that sold children to the West using fake documents. 'Political connections', 'corrupt officials' and 'foreign contacts' have been implicated for cashing 'in on the predicaments of desperate women.[88] A Dutch investigation into adoptions to the Netherlands between 1967 and 1998 found that many children "had been stolen or sold, and mothers often gave up children under social pressure or coercion."[89] The Netherlands banned overseas adoptions in 2021.[90]

In response largely to the protests from feminist groups, the Sri Lankan government temporarily banned foreign adoption of babies in 1987. However, it is unlikely that the skin trade can be wiped out through mere administrative fiat. The

---

84 Samarasuriya, Shireen. Who Needs Tourism? Employment for Women in the Holiday-Industry of Sudugama, Sri Lanka. Colombo-Leiden: University of Leiden, 1982, 83.
85 Ibid., 74; see also, "Sri Lankan Mail Order Brides [2022] – Get a Bride From Sri Lanka," August 18, 2022. https://web.archive.org/web/20220818113530/https://topforeignbrides.com/sri-lankan-brides/.
86 Pathirana, Saroj. "Sri Lanka Adoption: The Babies Who Were given Away." *BBC News*, March 14, 2021. Accessed March 15, 2021. https://www.bbc.com/news/world-56390772.
87 Ibid.
88 Bandarage, Asoka. "Women and Capitalist Development in Sri Lanka, 1977–87, op.cit., 74–75; Pathirana, Saroj. "Sri Lanka Adoption: The Babies Who Were given Away." *BBC News*, March 14, 2021. Accessed March 15, 2021. https://www.bbc.com/news/world-56390772.
89 Bergsten, Susanné. "Sweden To Investigate Illegal Intercountry Adoptions." *Human Rights Watch*, February 22, 2021. https://www.hrw.org/news/2021/02/22/sweden-investigate-illegal-intercountry-adoptions.
90 Ibid.

problems are rooted in the capitalist world economy and patriarchal culture and are likely to re-emerge given worsening poverty and desperation. In such contexts, tourism reinforces neocolonial disparities between rich and poor countries as well as between men and women rather than alleviating those inequities. Clearly an ethical and just economic system that puts the wellbeing of people before profits is needed both locally and internationally.

Privatization and Import Liberalization

The process of privatizing Sri Lanka's state-owned enterprises (SOEs), long known for poor management, political patronage, heavy subsidies and losses were begun after 1977. Privatization was pursued more aggressively after 1989 during the so-called second phase of neoliberal development in Sri Lanka. In 1992, the state-owned plantations were privatized with management contracts awarded to 22 Regional Plantation Companies which constituted most of the estates held by the two hitherto state-owned plantation corporations.[91]

By mid-1994, 43 SOEs in the industrial sector and 92 depots in the public transportation sector were privatized. By 1997, the number of privatizations rose to 75, with several large utility-oriented industries such as telecommunications and gas undergoing privatization.[92] Privatization-related Foreign Direct Investment (FDI) accounted for at least one-third of FDI in the 1990s.[93] The largest 20 foreign investors (mostly joint ventures with powerful countries) which started operating in the 1990s gained control over strategic sectors, such as, telecommunications, power and ports (Table 4.4).

---

[91] Bandaranaike, Romesh. "Opinion: Pulling Back the Curtain on Privatization of Sri Lanka's Plantation Sector." Lanka Business Online, August 30, 2018. https://www.lankabusinessonline.com/opinion-pulling-back-the-curtain-on-privatization-of-sri-lankas-plantation-sector/.

[92] Salih, Rozana. "Privatisation in Sri Lanka-Economic and Social Effects." In *Privatization in South Asia: Minimizing Negative Social Effects through Restructuring*, by Gopal Joshi (Ed.). New Delhi: South Asia Multi Disciplinary Advisory Team (SAAT), International Labor Organization (ILO), 2000, 175.

[93] Dissanayake, Kasun. "Privatization in Sri Lanka." Report for Master of Arts, Kansas State University, 2012. https://core.ac.uk/download/pdf/10652838.pdf.

Table 4.4: Top twenty foreign investments in Sri Lanka (2002).

Rank	Enterprise	Product	Home country	Cumulative investment as at end 2002 ($ million)	Ownership status
1	Sri Lanka Telecom (1997)	Fixed-line	Japan	236	Joint venture
2	Lanka Bell (1997)	Wireless telecom network	Singapore and United Kingdom	148	Joint venture
3	Colombo Power (2000)	Barge-mounted power plant	Japan	141	Wholly-owned
4	Lanka Cellular (1993)	Cellular phone	Singapore	141	Joint venture
5	South Asia Gateway terminals (1999)	Port services	Australia and United Kingdom	131	Joint venture
6	JAIC Lanka (1997)	Apartments	Japan	127	Wholly owned
7	Overseas Realty (1996)	Property development	Hong Kong and Singapore	119	Joint venture
8	Kabool Lanka (1990)	Yarn	Republic of Korea	118	Wholly owned
9	MTN Networks Cellular (1995)	Cellular phone networks	British Virgin Islands and Finland	117	Joint venture
10	AES Kelanitissa Power (Pvt) Ltd. (1999)	Power generation	United States	107	Joint venture
11	Shell (1995)	Gas	Netherlands	103	Joint venture
12	Ansell Lanka (1990)	Surgical GLOVES	Australia	96	Wholly owned
13	Air Lanka (1998)	Airline	United Arab Emirates	77	Joint venture
14	Prima Ceylon Ltd. (2001)	Food processing	Singapore	70	Joint venture
15	Asia Power (1998)	Power generation	United Kingdom	64	Wholly owned
16	Suntel (1996)	Wireless telecom network	Sweden	50	Joint venture
17	Colombo Dockyard	Port services	Japan	43	Joint venture
18	Ace Power Generation (1999)	Utility	Finland and United Kingdom	33	Joint venture

Table 4.4: Top twenty foreign investments in Sri Lanka (2002). *(Continued)*

Rank	Enterprise	Product	Home country	Cumulative investment as at end 2002 ($ million)	Ownership status
19	Orient Lanka (1996)	Trading	United Kingdom	31	Wholly owned
20	North Pole Lanka (Pte) Ltd (1992	PVC manufacture	Korea	27	Wholly owned

Source: Board of Investment, Sri Lanka (2003) (as amended by UNCTAD) as cited in Privatization in Sri Lanka, Kasun Dissanayake, Kansas State University, Manhattan, KS, 2012, 33–34.

The deluge of imported goods and the trends towards import liberalization and privatization had a negative effect on local industry and employment generation. An example is the national milk industry, which was handed over almost completely to Nestle, the Swiss transnational company, known for its controversial baby formula sales in the Third World.[94] Locally produced fresh milk was replaced almost completely by imported milk powder. Today, in the context of rising food prices and shortages, the country is faced with a severe scarcity of milk including baby formula and dependence on milk powder donations to community food banks from Nestle.[95]

Large numbers of workers lost jobs following privatization of SOEs.[96] Thousands also lost their livelihoods in agriculture, dairy farming and manufacturing due to the demise of local enterprises that could not compete with foreign imports. Many of the displaced had to find jobs in the FTZ, the Middle East or the local in-

---

[94] Bandarage, Asoka. "Women and Capitalist Development in Sri Lanka, 1977–87." *Bulletin of Concerned Asian Scholars* 20, no. 2 (June 1, 1988): 57–81, 75. https://doi.org/10.1080/14672715.1988.10404449.

[95] Sirimanna, Bandula. "Sri Lanka to Face Milk Powder Shortage." *Business Times*, February 13, 2011. Accessed October 9, 2022. https://www.sundaytimes.lk/110213/BusinessTimes/bt32.html. Kadirgamar, Ahilan. "Sri Lanka Food Crisis Has Its Roots in the Globalisation of the 1970s." *Climate Home News*, August 31, 2022. Accessed September 3, 2022. https://www.climatechangenews.com/2022/08/31/sri-lanka-food-crisis-has-its-roots-in-market-liberalisation/. *Ada Derana Biz English*. "Nestlé Lanka Contributes towards Sarvodaya Shramadana Movement's Community Food Banks," December 5, 2022. Accessed December 12, 2022. http://bizenglish.adaderana.lk/nestle-lanka-contributes-towards-sarvodaya-shramadana-movements-community-food-banks/.

[96] Salih, Rozana. "Privatisation in Sri Lanka-Economic and Social Effects." In *Privatization in South Asia: Minimizing Negative Social Effects through Restructuring*, by Gopal Joshi (Ed.). New Delhi: South Asia Multi Disciplinary Advisory Team (SAAT), International Labor Organization (ILO), 2000, 175.

formal sector. As feminist scholar Hema Gunatilleke observed, since the introduction of the Open Economy, numerous small-scale industries such as handloom and match box production were closed down as they could not compete with imported goods and by 1986, 135,000 women had lost employment in the handloom industry alone.[97]

As part of the liberalization of the economy after 1977, the local market was thrown open to all manner of imported goods and services. These included goods for economic production such as, technology and equipment, agrochemicals and fertilizer and a wide range of consumer goods ranging from luxury cars, home equipment, TVs, fine food, liquor, toiletries, cosmetics, and banking, restaurant, and travel services, etc. Consumerism and ostentatious living increasingly defined self-identity and social status weakening traditional community ties and widening economic inequality.

Dismantling the Welfare State

As discussed in Chapter 2, beginning with the introduction of electoral politics in 1931, the Sri Lankan state followed a universal welfare policy providing free education, free health care, and subsidized food items for all. It is this policy that gave Sri Lanka high scores on the Physical Quality of Life Index despite its low economic growth rates and per capita incomes (Table 3.4, page 81) Those enviable socioeconomic achievements were severely threatened when the government started to whittle away at the welfare state.

Following advice from the IMF, consultants from the Harvard Institute for International Development, and other foreign and local interests, the Sri Lankan government sharply limited the food subsidies, changing the earlier general rice ration to a food stamp program in 1979 limited to households below the official poverty line. During the period the program was in place, 1979–1982, the per capita calorie consumption is estimated to have dropped by about 8 percent among the bottom 20 percent of households.[98]

---

[97] Bandarage, Asoka. "Women and Capitalist Development in Sri Lanka, 1977–87." *Bulletin of Concerned Asian Scholars* 20, no. 2 (June 1, 1988): 57–81, 75. https://doi.org/10.1080/14672715.1988.10404449. Kuruvilla, Benny. "Sri Lanka: A Cautionary Tale of Authoritarian Neoliberalism." *Focus on the Global South*, October 17, 2022. Accessed November 3, 2022. https://focusweb.org/sri-lanka-a-cautionary-tale-of-authoritarian-neoliberalism/.
[98] Edirisinghe, Neville. "The Food Stamp Scheme in Sri Lanka: Costs, Benefits, and Options for Modification." Research Report. Washington, D.C.: International Food Policy Research Institute, March 1987. Available at: http://archive.org/details/foodstampschemei0000edir.

Capitulating to World Bank and the IMF conditionalities, per capita spending for education was also reduced from US$ 12 in 1972 to 8 in 1978, and health expenditures from US$ 6 to 5. Total government expenditures for food, education, and health declined from 42 to 26 percent of the budget from 1971 to 1978–1980. As the insulation provided by the welfare state was taken away and as unemployment and inflation rose, more and more people were pushed into poverty and insecurity.[99]

When structural adjustment policies and privatization diminished the role of the state after 1977, as in many other countries, hundreds of international and foreign-funded private nongovernmental organizations (NGOs) stepped in to fill the vacuum created by the loss of state support in Sri Lanka.[100] The substantial influx of bilateral and multilateral aid since 1977 opened up new employment in the NGO sector, which provided higher salaries than those available for government positions of comparable or higher rank. More than two-thirds of the development NGOs working in Sri Lanka in 2001 were established after 1977.[101]

As Kalinga Seneviratne observed in *The Scourge of Poverty and Proselytism*, "There is an interesting relationship between the neo-liberal economic policies espoused by the West since the early 1980s and rapid expansion in the funding and spread of 'faith based' NGOs that act not as missionaries but as development assistance or disaster relief agencies."[102]

During the George W. Bush administration in the United States (2001–2009), 'faith based' organizations received access to US official aid for 'development' projects overseas.[103] In Sri Lanka there are hundreds of Christian evangelical organizations receiving funds from the United States and South Korea as well as Islamic

---

99 Halton, Clay. "What Are Structural Adjustment Programs (SAPs)?" Investopedia, September 25, 2021. Accessed November 15, 2022. https://www.investopedia.com/terms/s/structural-adjustment.asp. Bandarage, Asoka. "Women and Capitalist Development in Sri Lanka, 1977–87." *Bulletin of Concerned Asian Scholars* 20, no. 2 (June 1, 1988): 57–81, 78. https://doi.org/10.1080/14672715.1988.10404449.
100 Goonatilake, Susantha. *Recolonisation: Foreign Funded NGOs in Sri Lanka*. SAGE Publishing India, 2006, passim.
101 Bandarage, Asoka. *The Separatist Conflict in Sri Lanka: Terrorism, Ethnicity, Political Economy*. London: Routledge/Taylor & Francis Group, 2009, 79.
102 Seneviratne, Kalinga. The Scourge of Poverty and Proselytism: Socio-Economic and Cultural Challenges Facing Buddhist Communities in Asia: A Case Study of Sri Lanka. Singapore: Lotus Communication Network, 2017, 96.
103 Ibid., 96.

social welfare and educational groups receiving funds from Saudi Arabia and other Islamic counties in the Middle East.[104]

Religious fundamentalism can provide a psychological foundation to corporate globalization and militarism by directing mass despair and anger toward inner salvation at the expense of social transformation. Christian evangelical sects thrive under poverty and dictatorship of brutal regimes, in places such as Sub-Saharan Africa, precisely because they fail to challenge them.[105] In Sri Lanka, sectarian, fundamentalist religious agendas threaten the liberal norms of pluralism and universalism supposedly promoted by the Open Economy and they contribute to dissension and conflict among local communities.[106]

Inequality, Conflict and Political Violence

The process of economic liberalization begun in 1977 gave rise to a newly rich element in Sri Lanka of "speculators, contractors, bookies, gem merchants, and Middle East job recruitment" agents as well as arms merchants who were tied to external interests.[107]

In contrast, cutbacks in the state sector and public employment worked against the rural areas and the "*swabahasha*-[local language] educated mono-lingual youth, in both the south and the north" of Sri Lanka. The expanded private sector under the Open Economy favored the English-educated graduates from the prestigious Colombo schools and the recently established international schools preparing students for college education abroad and new employment opportunities in the internationally driven corporate NGO sector.

As sociologist Siri Hettige put it, these processes of economic and cultural globalization helped the emergence of a new urban middle class (NUMC) "with strong

---

[104] Perera, Sasanka. *New Evangelical Movements and Conflict in South Asia: Sri Lanka and Nepal in Perspective.* RCSS Policy Studies. Colombo: Regional Centre for Strategic Studies, 1998. 2552/2009 *Report of the Commission Appointed to Inquire and Report on the Conversion of Buddhists in Sri Lanka to Other Religions by Immoral and Fraudulent Means.* Colombo: All Ceylon Buddhist Congress, 2012, 162–176. Bandarage, Asoka. *The Separatist Conflict in Sri Lanka: Terrorism, Ethnicity, Political Economy.* London: Routledge/Taylor & Francis Group, 2009, 81.

[105] Bandarage, Asoka. "Ethnic and Religious Tension in the World: A Political-Economic Perspective." In *Global Political Economy and the Wealth of Nations: Performance, Institutions, Problems, and Policies,* edited by Phillip Anthony O'Hara, 286–301. Routledge Frontiers of Political Economy. London: Routledge, 2004, 295.

[106] Bandarage, Asoka. *The Separatist Conflict in Sri Lanka: Terrorism, Ethnicity, Political Economy.* London: Routledge/Taylor & Francis Group, 2009, 81.

[107] Ibid., 78.

external links and ...almost totally dependent on such links for their sustenance."[108] The NUMC of all ethnic groups – Sinhala, Tamil, and Muslim – benefited from private-sector and NGO expansion. However, the majority of the country's rural youth, who looked to the state sector as their avenue for upward social mobility, saw the return of a new form of colonialism and re-enthronement of a "neo-colonial English-educated middle class as freezing their own chances for upward mobility".[109]

Sharp income disparities and absolute poverty levels are relatively new developments for Sri Lanka, which was a unique model of social welfarism and parliamentary democracy in the Third World. But the Open Economy and IMF Structural Adjustment widened economic inequalities and pushed the state in an increasingly authoritarian direction. Between 1973 and 1981–1982, the share of the highest quintile income earners rose from 46 to 57 percent of total income in the country, representing a 120 percent increase of their real mean income.[110] Nearly half of the population was pushed below the official poverty line of Rs 350 a month per household in 1982 with about 37.5 percent of Sri Lankan children suffering from malnutrition and 50 percent from nutritional anemia.[111]

Like the colonial plantation economy, the Open Economy offered new economic opportunities for some, but at the same time it increased competition between groups by deepening social class inequalities and ethnic rivalries.[112] Materialist culture advanced by economic liberalization undermined both the socialist-populist values prevailing since the introduction of democratic politics and the welfare state in the 1930s and the values of moderation and simplicity guiding the behavior of ordinary people since pre-colonial times. Both the socialist and Buddhist values

---

[108] Cited in Ibid., 79; Siri Hettige, "Economic Liberalization, Social Class and Ethnicity: Emerging Trends and Conflicts." In S. Gamage and I.B. Watson, ed. *Conflict and Community in Contemporary Sri Lanka: "Pearl of the East" or "the Island of Tears."* Studies on Contemporary South Asia. New Delhi: Sage Publications, 1999, 310.

[109] Ibid., 313–314.

[110] Bandarage, Asoka. *The Separatist Conflict in Sri Lanka*, op.cit., 79; Skanthakumar, B. "Growth with Inequality: The Political Economy of Neoliberalism in Sri Lanka." Country Paper for Crises, Vulnerability and Poverty in South Asia 2013 report. South Asia Alliance for Poverty Eradication (SAAPE), 2013. Available at: http://www.sacw.net/IMG/pdf/Skanthakumar_Growth_with_Inequality_The_Political_Economy_of_Neoliberalism_in_Sri_Lanka_Aug_2013.pdf.

[111] Bandarage, Asoka. "Women and Capitalist Development in Sri Lanka, 1977–87." *Bulletin of Concerned Asian Scholars* 20, no. 2 (June 1, 1988): 57–81, 77–78. https://doi.org/10.1080/14672715.1988.10404449.

[112] Ibid., 79–80.

and lifestyles were threatened by the new forces of economic and cultural globalization.[113]

In a context where globalization seemed an all-powerful and inexorable force and the state was becoming increasingly repressive, it became easier to direct latent hostility and resentment against the ethnic 'Other' rather than the transnational corporations or the local ruling elite. The English-educated minority representing the transnational elite tended to uphold ostensibly multicultural internationalist norms associated with liberal economics.

But the marginalized and alienated masses of youth shut out of the new economic order were mobilized, usually by elites with vested interests, more and more towards 'particularistic' tendencies upholding ethno-religious cultural identities: Sinhala Buddhist and socialist world view on the part of the majority community, and Tamil separatism on the part of the Sri Lankan Tamil minority. These competing particularistic tendencies reinforced each other while at the same time deflecting attention from the common social and economic problems facing underprivileged youth from all communities.[114] Educated unemployment was a major factor contributing to mobilization of Tamils into the separatist struggle as it was to mobilization of Sinhalese into the second JVP insurgency in the late 1980s.[115]

Tamil youth insurgency supported by the colonially privileged Tamil elite, India and the western community evolved into a massive armed conflict by the Liberation Tigers of Tamil Eelam (LTTE) terrorist organization against the Sri Lankan state. Violence exploded following the government sponsored pogrom against Tamils in 1983 devastating the society with death, destruction and suffering. (For further details, see the author's book, *The Separatist Conflict in Sri Lanka*).[116]

Between 1983 and 2009, an estimated 80,000 to 100,000 people lost their lives including 30,000 to 50,000 civilians, 27,693 LTTE cadres, 23,790 Sri Lankan army personnel, and 1,155 soldiers of the Indian Peace Keeping Force.[117] By 2007, war costs were estimated to be 30 percent of the total government budget. The internal war

---

113 Bandarage, Asoka. *The Separatist Conflict in Sri Lanka*, op.cit., 82.
114 Ibid., 82; Abeyratne, Sirimal. "Economic Roots of Political Conflict: The Case of Sri Lanka." The World Economy 27, no. 8 (2004): 1295–1314. https://doi.org/10.1111/j.1467-9701.2004.00645.x. Available at: https://taxpolicy.crawford.anu.edu.au/acde/asarc/pdf/papers/2002/WP2002_03.pdf.
115 Bandarage, Asoka. *The Separatist Conflict in Sri Lanka: Terrorism, Ethnicity, Political Economy*. London: Routledge/Taylor & Francis Group, 2009, 140.
116 Bandarage, Asoka. *The Separatist Conflict in Sri Lanka*, op.cit.
117 Balachandran, P. K. "Sri Lanka's Internal War Cost US$ 200 Billion." *The New Indian Express*. December 13, 2016. Accessed January 3, 2023. https://www.newindianexpress.com/world/2016/dec/13/sri-lankas-internal-war-cost-us-200-billion-1548433.html.

which ended in May 2009 is estimated to have cost the country around US$ 200 billion in total.[118]

Unequal Exchange, Debt Crises: Sri Lanka and the World

Sri Lanka's trade imbalance and external debt steadily increased over the course of economic liberalization (Table 4.5) The United Nations Conference on Trade and Development (UNCTAD) reported that compared to the previous two decades, the 25 years or so since 1980 saw sharply reduced economic growth, trade imbalances and decreased social progress in the vast majority of low- and middle-income countries.[119] At the beginning of 1989, developing nations owed foreign creditors $1.3 trillion, that is 'just over half their combined gross national products and two-thirds more than their combined export earnings." The annual debt service ratio approximated $200 billion.[120]

At the same time, by 1984, the flow of financial resources reversed with increasing net transfers from the developing countries in the global South to those in the developed global North. This takes place through "large net appropriation of resources and labor" and "induced price differentials in international trade." Research published in the journal, *New Political Economy* in 2021 estimated that when measured in Northern prices, "the drain amounted to $10.8 trillion in 2015, and $242 trillion over the period from 1990 to 2015" – amounting to a quarter of Northern GDP.[121]

Over 30 African and other countries compelled to accept IMF/World Bank Structural Adjustment Programs, experienced deteriorating social conditions in-

---

118 Ibid.
119 Hickel, Jason, Dylan Sullivan, and Huzaifa Zoomkawala. "Plunder in the Post-Colonial Era: Quantifying Drain from the Global South Through Unequal Exchange, 1960–2018." *New Political Economy* 26, no. 6 (November 2, 2021): 1030–1047. https://doi.org/10.1080/13563467.2021.1899153; Parfentev, Mikhail. "WTO and Neoliberalism: Summary." *Mikhailparfentev.Medium.Com* (blog), January 31, 2016. https://mikhailparfentev.medium.com/wto-and-neo-liberalism-summary-70701ef8df51.
120 Bandarage, Asoka. *Women, Population and Global Crisis: A Political-Economic Analysis*. London: Zed Books, 1997, 197; "Human Development Report 1990: Concept and Measurement of Human Development." New York: UNDP (United Nations Development Programme), 1990, 79. https://hdr.undp.org/content/human-development-report-1990.
121 Hickel, Jason, Christian Dorninger, Hanspeter Wieland, and Intan Suwandi. "Imperialist Appropriation in the World Economy: Drain from the Global South through Unequal Exchange, 1990–2015." *Global Environmental Change* 73 (March 1, 2022): 102467. https://doi.org/10.1016/j.gloenvcha.2022.102467.

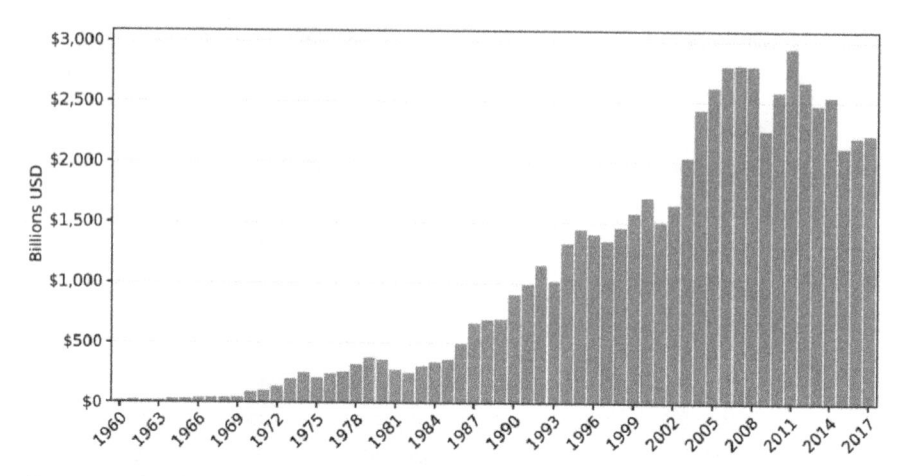

Figure 4.1: Annual Value Transfer, Global South to Global North, 1960–2017. Jason Hickel, Dylan Sullivan, Huzaifa Zoomkawala, "Plunder in the Post-Colonial Era: Quantifying Drain from the Global South Through Unequal Exchange, 1960–2018", *New Political Economy*, 30 Mar 2021: 5 https://www.tandfonline.com/doi/abs/10.1080/13563467.2021.1899153?journalCode=cnpe20))

Table 4.5: Sri Lanka trade balance and external debt, 1970–2020, (selected years).

Year	Current External Debt US $	Annual % Change	Trade Balance in Billions of US $	% of GDP
2020	$56,341,952,150	0.40 %	$-5.20B	-6.43 %
2019	$56,117,855,647	6.04 %	$-5.14B	-6.13 %
2015	$43,925,393,891	3.93 %	$-6.07B	-7.53 %
2009	$19,504,201,128	19.51 %	$-2.73B	-6.49 %
2000	$9,249,848,286	-6.97 %	$-1.73B	-10.61 %
1995	$8,395,502,197	5.46 %	$-1.36B	-10.44 %
1988	$5,209,633,063	9.57 %	$-0.75B	-10.76 %
1983	$2,890,238,573	9.81 %	$-0.78B	-15.10 %
1977	$1,141,630,268	21.23 %	$0.15B	3.66 %
1970	$435,678,442	19.41 %	$-0.07B	-3.15 %

Source: Sri Lanka External Debt 1970–2022 Microtrends, https://www.macrotrends.net/countries/LKA/sri-lanka/external-debt-stock; Sri Lanka Trade Balance 1960–2022 Microtrends, https://www.macrotrends.net/countries/LKA/sri-lanka/trade-balance-deficit

cluding increasing rates of infant or child mortality and falling ratios of primary school enrollment in the 1980–1985 period.[122]

Reflecting on four decades of free market orthodoxy, even famed economist Joseph Stiglitz, former chief economist of the World Bank and former Chairman of the (US President's) Council of Economic Advisers remarked in 2019:

> For 40 years, elites in rich and poor countries alike promised that neoliberal policies would lead to faster economic growth, and that the benefits would trickle down so that everyone, including the poorest, would be better off. Now that the evidence is in, is it any wonder that trust in elites and confidence in democracy have plummeted?[123]

---

[122] Bandarage, Asoka. *Women, Population and Global Crisis: A Political-Economic Analysis*. London: Zed Books, 1997, 201.

[123] Stiglitz, Joseph E. "The End of Neoliberalism and the Rebirth of History by Joseph E. Stiglitz." *Project Syndicate*, November 4, 2019. Accessed November 2, 2022. https://www.project-syndicate.org/commentary/end-of-neoliberalism-unfettered-markets-fail-by-joseph-e-stiglitz-2019-11.

Chapter 5:
Geopolitical Rivalry, Neocolonialism and Political Destabilization, 2009–2019

> Positioned at the geographic and political heart of the Indian Ocean, Sri Lanka is the epicenter of the 21st century struggle for regional influence. Situated between the Persian Gulf and Red Sea to the west and the Straits of Malacca and Sunda to the east, Sri Lanka is arguably the most strategically located maritime nation in the region. More than 60,000 ships – including two thirds of the world's seaborne crude oil, half of its container ships and all U.S. Navy vessels passing between the 5th and 7th Fleets – annually transit Sri Lankan waters.[1]

The above is the opening statement of the Sri Lanka *Integrated Country Strategy* approved by the U.S. State Department on April 6, 2022.

As in the era of classical colonialism, Sri Lanka is again caught amidst the growing geopolitical rivalry and external military, political, economic as well as cultural intervention. As in the era of classical colonialism, collaboration with local elites – politicians, business and NGO leaders, bureaucrats, journalists, academics – is essential for external intervention and neocolonial exploitation. In the face of overt and covert expansionist efforts of the three nuclear powers – the U.S, China and India – the political and economic sovereignty, territorial integrity, cultural identity and the very ecological survival of the beleaguered island are in jeopardy.

Chinese Expansion

As the U.S. and its allies became increasingly critical of Sri Lanka's handling of the separatist war and human rights, the Sri Lankan government under President Mahinda Rajapaksa (2005–2015) aligned itself with China and other non-Western countries like Myanmar, Iran and Libya. During the final stages of the war, in March 2009, "China blocked Western-led efforts to impose a truce through the United Nations Security Council and continued supplying arms to the Sri Lankan Government,"[2] helping to defeat the Liberation Tigers of Tamil Eelam (LTTE). In May

---

[1] "Integrated Country Strategy Sri Lanka." United States Department of State, April 6, 2022, 1. https://www.state.gov/wp-content/uploads/2022/06/ICS_SCA_Sri-Lanka_Public.pdf.
[2] Kerry, John F, Christopher J Dodd, Russell D Feingold, Barbara Boxer, Robert Menendez, Benjamin L Cardin, Robert P Casey, et al. *Sri Lanka: Recharting U.S. Strategy After the War*, Committee on

https://doi.org/10.1515/9783111203454-011

2009, Sri Lanka defeated the LTTE in what is considered "one of the few instances in modern history in which a terrorist group had been defeated militarily."[3]

While the United States and its allies pursued a human rights agenda with regard to Sri Lanka, China expanded its economic interests by providing loans "without any political strings."[4] China's soft power diplomacy and economic expansion began to transform the political and economic dynamics of Sri Lanka, the Indian Ocean Region (IOR) and the strategic environment of the world at large.[5]

China's Belt and Road Initiative (BRI), formerly known as One Belt One Road, incorporates 155 countries and organizations across Asia, Africa, the Middle East, Europe and Latin America.[6] The $4 trillion BRI-planned network of roads, railways, ports and maritime facilities is considered the "most ambitious infrastructural investment effort in history."[7] (Figure 5.1) Chinese companies such as COSCO and Hutchinson now have investment and control over approximately 100 sea ports in 63 countries around the world including Hamburg in Germany, Haifa in Israel and Piraeus in Greece as well five ports in the United States, in Miami, Houston, Long Beach, Los Angeles and Seattle (Figure 5.2).[8] Critics fear long-term potential of port control for Chinese power projection around the world fusing business, political and military interests under the Communist

---

Foreign Relations, United States Senate, One Hundred Eleventh Congress, First Session, December 7, 2009. Washington D.C.: U.S. GOVERNMENT PRINTING OFFICE, 2009, 1.
3 Ibid., p. 13.
4 Ibid., p. 13.
5 DeSilva-Ranasinghe, Sergei. "Why the Indian Ocean Matters," March 2, 2011. Accessed June 2, 2021. https://thediplomat.com/2011/03/why-the-indian-ocean-matters/.
6 *HKTDC Belt and Road Portal.* "Country Profile." Accessed January 3, 2023. https://beltandroad.hktdc.com/en/country-profiles.
7 Qinhua, Xi. "The BRI Is the Most Ambitious Infrastructure Project in History." *CGTN*, January 23, 2019. Accessed November 22, 2022. https://news.cgtn.com/news/3d3d514e77496a4d32457a6333566d54/index.html. *HKTDC Belt and Road Portal.* "The Belt and Road Initiative – A Road Map to THE FUTURE." Accessed January 3, 2023. https://beltandroad.hktdc.com/en/belt-and-road-basics. OECD. "The Belt and Road Initiative in the Global Trade, Investment and Finance Landscape." In *OECD Business and Finance Outlook 2018*, by OECD, 61–101. OECD Business and Finance Outlook. OECD, 2018. https://doi.org/10.1787/bus_fin_out-2018-6-en.
8 Xie, John. "China's Global Network of Shipping Ports Reveal Beijing's Strategy." *VOA*, September 13, 2021. Accessed September 26, 2021. https://www.voanews.com/a/6224958.html; *China Merchants Holdings International.* "China's Growing Economic Clout: The Los Angeles Port," October 5, 2022. Accessed October 12, 2022. https://www.cmhi.com.hk/chinas-growing-economic-clout-the-los-angeles-port/.

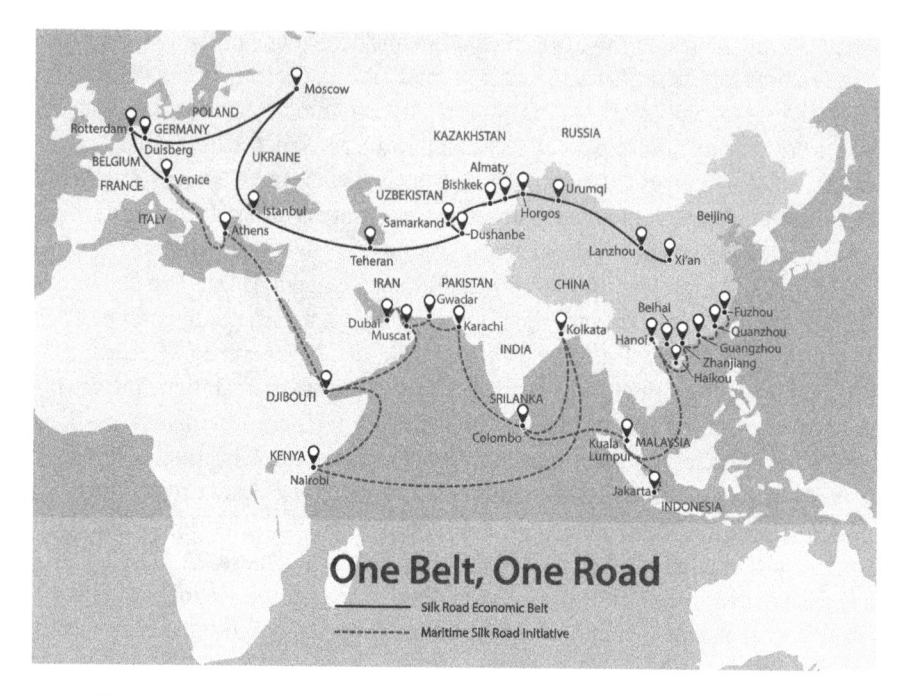

Figure 5.1: Indian Ocean Region and China's Belt and Road Initiative (BRI) and Maritime Silk Road. Source: Getty Images Data from: Reuters Photographer/Reuters.

Party umbrella.[9] Given its simultaneous control of 30 percent of global manufacturing, China wields enormous power over the availability of commodities and the survival of people in the globalized market economy.[10]

In 2013, China overtook the United States to become the world's largest trading nation, currently controlling 15 percent of global trade as opposed to 8 percent by the U.S.[11] China and the U.S. are also the leading carbon emitters in the world (27.8 percent and 15.2 percent respectively in 2022).[12] In 2013, China put forward

---

9 Tatlow, Didi Kirsten. "China's Stake in World Ports Sharpens Attention on Political Influence." *Newsweek*, October 9, 2022. Accessed October 12, 2022. https://www.newsweek.com/2022/10/14/chinas-stake-world-ports-sharpens-attention-political-influence-1749215.html.
10 *The State Council Information Office, The People's Republic of China*. "China Accounts for 30 % of Global Manufacturing Output," June 14, 2022. Accessed November 1, 2022. https://web.archive.org/web/20220614224808/http://english.scio.gov.cn/pressroom/2022-06/14/content_78269806.htm.
11 Nicita, Alessandro, and Carlos Razo. "China: The Rise of a Trade Titan." *UNCTAD*, April 27, 2021. Accessed May 5, 2021. https://unctad.org/news/china-rise-trade-titan.
12 Rapier, Robert. "The World's Top 10 Carbon Dioxide Emitters." *Forbes*, December 4, 2019. Accessed November 2, 2022. https://www.forbes.com/sites/rrapier/2019/12/04/the-worlds-top-10-carbon-dioxide-emitters/.

what is called the 21st century Maritime Silk Road (MSR) – the sea route part of the broader BRI initiative (formerly referred to as the String of Pearls). It now connects China to Southeast Asia, Africa and Europe with Chinese companies owning all the major ports along the route.[13] By 2018, China owned seaports in Pakistan, Myanmar, Dijbouti, Sri Lanka and the Maldives (Figure 5.2) in the IOR and is reportedly seeking to add a state-of the-art naval base in Bangladesh.[14]

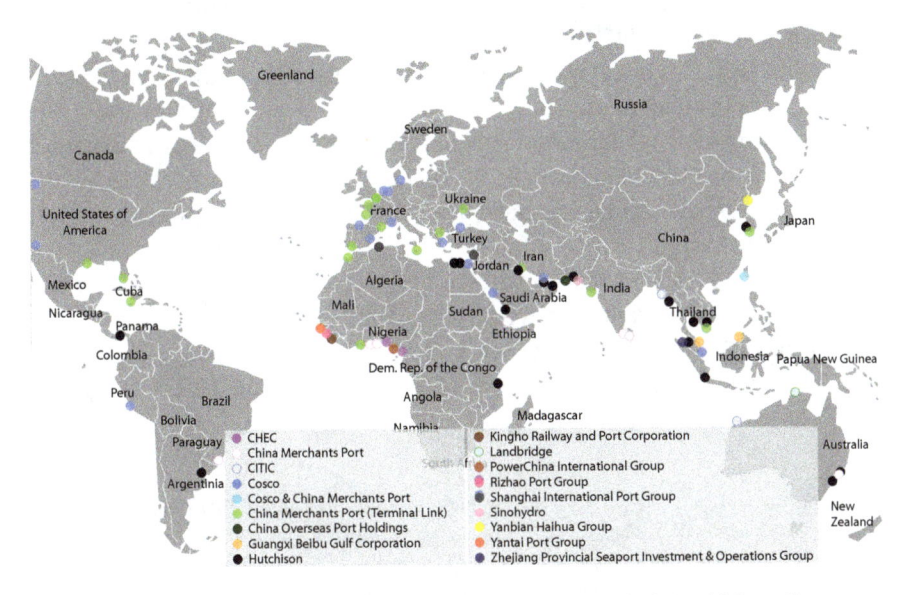

Figure 5.2: China's Global Portfolio. Source: Adapted from 'China's Stake in World Ports Sharpens Attention on Political Influence', Newsweek Magazine. October, 2022. https://www.newsweek.com/2022/10/14/chinas-stake-world-ports-sharpens-attention-political-influence-1749215.html

China has invested in infrastructure projects in Sri Lanka including a convention center, airport, hospitals, a sports stadium and the prominent BRI initiative, the International Hambantota Port. In 2010, Sri Lanka first turned to India to develop the Hambantota Port in the heart of the IOR, but when India declined the costly pro-

---

13 Xie, John. "China's Global Network of Shipping Ports Reveal Beijing's Strategy." *VOA*, September 13, 2021. Accessed September 26, 2021. https://www.voanews.com/a/6224958.html.
14 Chonkar, Kunal. "India's Policy on IOR Needs an Underwater Vision." The News 21, September 1, 2020. Accessed September 6, 2021. https://thenews21.com/pm-narendra-modis-indian-ocean-policy-sagar-needs-an-underwater-vision.

posal, Sri Lanka turned to China.[15] In January 2017, the Sri Lankan government granted China a 70 percent stake with a 99-year lease of Hambantota Port to the China Merchants Port Holdings Company for US$ 1.1 billion.[16] There was no cancellation of debt to China in exchange for the equity of an asset – a debt-equity swap – involved in the Hambantota port deal, as is commonly reported. Rather, the money earned from the port lease was used to cover soaring foreign debt service costs of sovereign bonds "which amounted to more than 40 percent of total debt service payments in 2019."[17]

Given cordial historical relations with China, such as the Rice-Rubber Pact in 1951, Sri Lankans tend to see Chinese involvement in their country as essentially benign. However, rural farming families resisted offers to sell their ancestral land to build the Chinese industrial zone next to the Hambantota port. Clashes between protesters and Sri Lankan government supporters of the project in 2017 at times turned violent.[18]

The lease of the Hambantota port has also raised concerns over the loss of a strategic state asset and the island's economic sovereignty and security. In August 2018, then-U.S. Vice President Mike Pence warned that the Hambantota port could become a military base for the Chinese Navy.[19] Both India and the U.S. are greatly

---

[15] Editor. "Japan's Indo-Pacific Strategy: The Importance of Sri Lanka." *South Asia@LSE* (blog), May 14, 2018. Accessed October 4, 2022. https://blogs.lse.ac.uk/southasia/2018/05/14/japans-indo-pacific-strategy-the-importance-of-sri-lanka/.

[16] Bandarage, Asoka. "Commentary: The Demise of Sri Lanka's Independence." *Critical Asian Studies*, February 10, 2019. https://criticalasianstudies.org/commentary/2019/2/10/the-demise-of-sri-lankas-independence. Wijayasiri, Janaka, and Nuwanthi Senaratne. "China's Belt and Road Initiative (BRI) and Sri Lanka." In *China BRI o El Nuevo Camino de La Seda*, edited by Arturo Oropeza García, 487. México, D.F: Instituto par el Desarrollo Industrial y el Crecimiento Económico Universidad Nacional Autónoma de México, Instituto de Investigaciones Jurídicas, 2018. Available here: https://archivos.juridicas.unam.mx/www/bjv/libros/12/5550/19.pdf.

[17] Moramudali, Umesh. "Is Sri Lanka Really a Victim of China's 'Debt Trap'?" *The Diplomat*, May 14, 2019. Accessed June 2, 2021. https://thediplomat.com/2019/05/is-sri-lanka-really-a-victim-of-chinas-debt-trap/.

[18] Frayer, Lauren. "In Sri Lanka, China's Building Spree Is Raising Questions About Sovereignty." NPR, December 13, 2019. Accessed December 16, 2019. https://www.npr.org/2019/12/13/784084567/i,n-sri-lanka-chinas-building-spree-is-raising-questions-about-sovereignty. Gamage, Sanath. "Over Ten People and Cops Injured during H'tota Protest." *Daily Mirror Online*, January 7, 2017. Accessed January 8, 2017. https://www.dailymirror.lk/breaking_news/Over-ten-people-and-cops-injured-during-H-tota-protest/108-121840.

[19] *Colombo Gazette*. "US Vice President Warns Sri Lanka on China Funded Port," October 6, 2018. Accessed October 22, 2018. https://colombogazette.com/2018/10/06/us-vice-president-warns-sri-lanka-on-china-funded-port/. Abeyagoonasekera, Asanga. "Maritime Security in the Indian Ocean – a Geopolitical Perspective from Sri Lanka and the Role of the EU in the Indian Ocean Region (IOR)." *Sea*

concerned over China's increasing assertiveness in the Indian Ocean, for example, the strengthening of the Chinese Navy with aircraft carriers and nuclear submarines.[20]

Among other Chinese BRI initiatives in Sri Lanka is the massive Colombo International Financial City (known as Port City until August 2016); Sri Lanka's "new Dubai" in Colombo. Construction began in 2014, with the initial phase reclaiming 269 hectares of land from the Indian Ocean. It is the largest single direct foreign investment in Sri Lankan history. This $1.4 billion project is developed by the state-owned Chinese engineering firm, China Communications Construction Company (CCCC), alleged to be "one of the most corrupt" companies in China.[21] The Port City is reported to have "its own business-friendly tax regime and regulations – and possibly a different legal system to the rest of Sri Lanka."[22]

Sri Lankan activists are concerned about the power a majority-state-owned Chinese corporation would wield as landlord of Port City. There is apprehension that only a certain class of wealthy people, mostly foreigners, would live in the expensive Financial City while services would be provided by Sri Lankans receiving little economic benefit.[23] There is fear that this represents a new form of neocolonialism that could once again make Sri Lankans second-class citizens in their own country.

Additionally, environmental activists have raised alarm that coastal sand excavation for Port City and the dumping of chemicals and other waste will cause significant ecological damage and disrupt the livelihood of those in the fishing and related industries.[24] Environmentalists, religious leaders from different communities, fishermen and others demanded that the project be halted.[25] The Human

---

Guardian Ltd, March 19, 2018. Accessed September 22, 2022. http://www.sguardian.com/2018/03/maritime-security-indian-ocean-geopolitical-perspective-sri-lanka-role-eu-indian-ocean-regionior/.

20 Gamage, Daya. "US-India Tie Strongest Military Knot on Indo-Pacific: Small Nations Tagged in." *Asian Tribune*, December 25, 2019. Accessed November 12, 2022. https://web.archive.org/web/20200226001718/http://asiantribune.com/node/93295.

21 Sabry, Hafsa. "Environment Issues of Port City Not Resolved." *Sunday Leader*, September 11, 2016. Accessed October 2, 2022. https://web.archive.org/web/20200117193338/http://www.thesundayleader.lk/2016/09/11/environment-issues-of-port-city-not-resolved/.

22 Safi, Michael. "Sri Lanka's 'New Dubai': Will Chinese-Built City Suck the Life out of Colombo?" *The Guardian*, August 2, 2018, sec. Cities. Accessed October 2, 2022. https://www.theguardian.com/cities/2018/aug/02/sri-lanka-new-dubai-chinese-city-colombo.

23 Bandarage, Asoka. "Commentary: The Demise of Sri Lanka's Independence." *Critical Asian Studies*, February 10, 2019. https://criticalasianstudies.org/commentary/2019/2/10/the-demise-of-sri-lankas-independence.

24 Ibid.

25 Ibid.

Rights Commission of Sri Lanka, in considering a petition submitted in 2015 by the Center for Environment and Nature Studies, confirmed Port City to be illegal, but the Project has moved ahead.[26]

While Sri Lankan activists have been protesting the environmental and social impact of expanding Chinese projects, the US-India-Japan alliance is aggressively seeking to involve Sri Lanka in its challenge against Chinese expansion across Asia. As a result, the island has emerged as a battleground of geopolitical rivalry and the new Cold War over the Indian Ocean.

Indian Expansion

Following the end of the separatist war with the LTTE, India has tried to consolidate its political, economic and strategic position in Sri Lanka through numerous overt and covert measures. Like China, India is seeking to incorporate other smaller neighbors like the Maldives, Myanmar, Nepal and Bhutan within its sphere of influence, especially through Prime Minister Narendra Modi's 'neighborhood first' policy.[27] Sri Lanka has old and intimate ties with India, its closest neighbor and the ancestral origin of most Sri Lankans. However, India's controversial political and military involvement during the separatist war, especially its impositions of the 13th Amendment on the Sri Lankan Constitution and the Indian Peace Keeping Force (IPKF) deployment on Sri Lankan soil, have left fear and antipathy towards India.[28]

India is seeking to counter being surrounded by pro-Chinese governments and infrastructure projects in its neighborhood that it fears could serve Beijing's military interests. India and China have fought numerous conflicts over the decades

---

26 Sabry, Hafsa. "Environment Issues of Port City Not Resolved." *Sunday Leader*, September 11, 2016. Accessed October 2, 2022. https://web.archive.org/web/20200117193338/http://www.thesundayleader.lk/2016/09/11/environment-issues-of-port-city-not-resolved/. Tharaka, Dilshan. "Writ Petition against Port City Fixed for Judgement." *Daily News*. December 12, 2019. Accessed January 3, 2023. https://www.dailynews.lk/2019/12/21/law-order/206315/writ-petition-against-port-city-fixed-judgement. https://www.chathamhouse.org/2020/03/chinese-investment-and-bri-sri-lanka-0/2-labour-and-environment.
27 Dw.com. "India's Modi Visits Sri Lanka, Maldives," June 9, 2019. Accessed June 14, 2019. https://www.dw.com/en/modi-woos-sri-lanka-maldives-as-india-fends-off-chinese-influence/a-49117835; see also, https://www.slhcindia.org/images/stories/N_images/PDF/ics%20english%20final300821.pdf.
28 Bandarage, Asoka. *The Separatist Conflict in Sri Lanka: Terrorism, Ethnicity, Political Economy.* London: Routledge/Taylor & Francis Group, 2009, Chap. 6.

including a deadly clash on their Himalayan border in 2020.[29]. Under Prime Minister Narendra Modi, the Indian government, in partnership with Indian business conglomerates, has engaged in building strategic infrastructure in neighboring countries. It has increased India's Lines of Credit (LOC) to its neighbors more than fourfold, from $3.27 billion in 2014 to $14.7 billion in 2020 (Figure 5.3). The Indian government is also building a massive bridge connecting several islands of the Maldives archipelago countering another huge bridge that China built in 2018 connecting some other islands of the Maldives.[30] The Maldivian 'India Out' campaign has expressed fears that India would turn their islands into an Indian military base.[31]

Concerned that Sri Lanka's Hambantota port could become a Chinese military base in its own backyard, India has pursued control over Sri Lanka's other strategic seaports. Japan, too, is keen for access to Sri Lankan ports, given that it is almost completely dependent on energy supplies transported across the Indian Ocean. With China in mind, Japan has provided grants to Sri Lanka to develop both the Colombo and Trincomalee ports.[32] The Colombo port is "one of the busiest ports in South Asia and an important trans-shipment hub in the region."[33] A previous plan for a terminal with a consortium of firms from Japan and India broke down in 2018 after backlash from trade unions protesting against the privatization of Sri Lanka's state assets, including those being developed by Chinese firms.[34]

---

[29] Parker, Benjamin, and Chloe Cornish. "India's Plan to Take on China as South Asia's Favourite Lender." *Financial Times*, December 1, 2022. Accessed December 2, 2022. https://www.ft.com/content/67abce3d-7313-4788-8649-abb9343a2ebc.

[30] Moorthy, N. Sathiya. "Maldives: India-Funded Sea Bridge Project Has an Ambitious Deadline." *Observer Research Foundation*, August 31, 2021. November 20, 2022. https://www.orfonline.org/expert-speak/maldives-india-funded-sea-bridge-project-has-an-ambitious-deadline/.

[31] Shivamurthy, Aditya Gowdara. "Understanding the 'India Out' Campaign in Maldives." Observer Research Foundation, October 7, 2022. November 20, 2022. https://www.orfonline.org/research/understanding-the-india-out-campaign-in-maldives/.

[32] Editor. "Japan's Indo-Pacific Strategy: The Importance of Sri Lanka." *South Asia@LSE* (blog), May 14, 2018. Accessed October 4, 2022. https://blogs.lse.ac.uk/southasia/2018/05/14/japans-indo-pacific-strategy-the-importance-of-sri-lanka/.

[33] Bandarage, Asoka. "Commentary: The Demise of Sri Lanka's Independence." *Critical Asian Studies*, February 10, 2019. https://criticalasianstudies.org/commentary/2019/2/10/the-demise-of-sri-lankas-independence.

[34] Dipanjan Roy Chaudhury, "India still to play role in Lanka Port." *Times of India*, March 19, 2018. Accessed July 15, 2022. https://economictimes.indiatimes.com/news/international/world-news/india-still-to-play-role-in-lanka-port/articleshow/63359686.cms; *World Socialist Web Site*. "Sri Lankan Riot Police Attack Colombo Port Workers," February 7, 2017. Accessed February 12, 2017. https://www.wsws.org/en/articles/2017/02/07/port-f07.html.

Country	$ billion
Bangladesh	7.9
Maldives	1.3
Mauritius	0.8
Myanmar	0.5
Nepal	1.7
Pakistan	0
Seychelles	0.1
Sri Lanka	2.1

*Data for Sri Lanka does not include latest lines of credit
Source: Ministry of External Affairs, India

Figure 5.3: Indian lending to neighboring countries. Extended lines of credit ($ billion). Source: Data from the Indian Ministry for External Affairs listed in 'India's Lines of Credit to neighbours increased more than fourfold since 2014 to $14.7 billion', The New Indian Express, March 9, 2022, https://www.newindianexpress.com/nation/2022/mar/09/indias-lines-of-credit-to-neighbours-increased-more-than-fourfold-since-2014-to-147-billion-2428131.html and 'Indian lending to its neighbors. Extended lines of credit ($billion)', Financial Times, December 1, 2022, https://www.ft.com/content/67abce3d-7313-4788-8649-abb9343a2ebc.

However, the cash-strapped Sri Lankan government finalized a $700 million deal in September 2021 with the Indian conglomerate, the Adani Group to develop a deepwater container terminal right next to the terminal at Colombo Port run by China Merchant Ports Group Co., which also runs Hambantota Port. The $14 billion Adani Group's interests span coal and energy, agribusiness, real estate, defense and other sectors across the world.[35] The Sri Lanka deal is described as a "strategic game-changer" in the battle for influence over Sri Lanka and the IOR between Beijing and New Delhi.[36] However, it does not bode well for Sri Lanka's sovereignty or en-

---

[35] Sengupta, Somini, Jacqueline Williams, and Aruna Chandrasekhar. "How One Billionaire Could Keep Three Countries Hooked on Coal for Decades." *New York Times*, August 15, 2019, sec. Climate. Accessed August 21, 2021. https://www.nytimes.com/2019/08/15/climate/coal-adani-india-australia.html.
[36] Pollard, Ruth. "Analysis | Is the Great Sri Lanka Fire Sale About to Begin?" *Washington Post*, May 30, 2022. Accessed May 31, 2022. https://www.washingtonpost.com/business/energy/is-the-great-sri-lanka-fire-sale-about-to-begin/2022/05/29/e187bc68-dfa3-11ec-ae64-6b23e5155b62_story.html.

vironmental and human well-being given Indian expansion and Adani Group's dismal record of environmental destruction and exploitation of local communities in Australia, India and Africa.[37]

In August 2022 amidst on-going debt restructuring efforts with the IMF, the Sri Lankan government gave provisional approval to two more projects of India's controversial Adani Group to build wind power projects in Mannar and Pooneryn in the Northern Province.[38] These projects to be built on strategically located sensitive ecosystems were approved without prior Environmental Impact assessments.[39]

The entire Gulf of Mannar has been declared a 'National Marine Biosphere Reserve' since 1989, the first of its kind in South and Southeast Asia.[40] It is the home of over 4,223 species of flora and fauna. One of the richest coastal regions in the world with immense ecological diversity, Gulf of Mannar harbors over 1,000 species of fish. The Gulf is also home to 133 villages and over 120,000 people.[41]

In May 2022, Sri Lankan government's Committee on Public Accounts (COPA) revealed that there are fuel and natural gas deposits in the Mannar Basin; enough to meet the entire country's needs for 60 years.[42]

---

[37] *Adani Files.* "The Adani Files, A Short History of Corruption, Destruction and Criminal Activity." Accessed January 3, 2023. http://adanifiles.com.au. "Dossier on the Adani Group's Environmental and Social Record." *AdaniWatch*, Bob Brown Foundation, September 2020. https://www.banktrack.org/download/dossier_on_the_adani_group_s_environmental_and_social_record/adani_dossier_preliminary_sept2020_intermediate_21.pdf.

[38] *Business Standard.* "Adani Group Gets Provisional Approvals for Renewable Energy Projects in SL," August 18, 2022. Accessed August 20, 2022. https://www.business-standard.com/article/companies/adani-group-gets-provisional-approvals-for-renewable-energy-projects-in-sl-122081700042_1.html.

[39] Rajasingham-Senanayake, Darini. "Privatizing Sri Lanka Ex-Ante IMF Bailout Of BlackRock: Adani Greenwash In Mannar & Pooneryn." *Colombo Telegraph*, August 20, 2022. Accessed August 21, 2022. https://www.colombotelegraph.com/index.php/privatizing-sri-lanka-ex-ante-imf-bailout-of-blackrock-adani-greenwash-in-mannar-pooneryn/.

[40] Dasgupta, KumKum. "A Gulf of Trouble for Mannar, India's Climate Change Hotspot." *Hindustan Times*, November 29, 2015. Accessed December 5, 2015. https://www.hindustantimes.com/india/climate-change-choking-gulf-of-mannar-hurting-marine-treasure/story-dVQF5q97EbNoxONs8o9EEN.html.

[41] Marirajan, T, and Vineeta Hoon. "Socio Economic Monitoring for Coastal Managers of South Asia: Field Trials and Baseline Surveys in Gulf of Mannar Region, South Tamilnadu, India Project Completion Report: NA10NOS4630055." India: Peoples Action for Development (PAD), The Centre for Action Research on Environment Science and Society (CARESS), May 2012. https://www.ncei.noaa.gov/data/oceans/coris/library/NOAA/CRCP/other/grants/International_FY10_Products/NA10NOS4630055_MannarGulf_Socmon.pdf.

[42] *ColomboPage.* "Sri Lanka: COPA Focuses on Failure to Develop a Formal Program to Explore Oil and Natural Gas in the Mannar Basin," May 6, 2022. Accessed May 12, 2022. http://www.colombopage.com/archive_22A/May06_1651842024CH.php.

Yet, the beleaguered Sri Lankan President Gotabaya Rajapaksa beholden to India for financial assistance agreed to give Adani access to Mannar to build his wind projects[43] A controversy erupted in June 2022 after the Parliament of Sri Lanka passed an amendment to the 1989 Electricity Act removing the requirement of competitive bidding when awarding power projects. This amendment is believed to have been passed to award Adani the Mannar power project without competitive bidding. M.C.C. Ferdinando, the Chairman of the Sri Lankan Electricity Board made a statement before a parliamentary committee that President Gotabaya Rajapaksa had told him that Indian Prime Minster Narendra Modi had 'pressurized' him to give Adani the deal. However, after Rajapaksa denied saying so, Ferdinando resigned from his position.[44] The controversial deal raises major issues, among them, Sri Lanka's political and economic sovereignty, India's 'neighborhood first' policy, independence of the Sri Lankan parliament and environmental sustainability of the Gulf Mannar. The Report issued by Hindenburg Research in January 2023 charging the Adani Group of accounting fraud, stock manipulation, and money laundering raise further concerns over granting Adani geopolitical power over Sri Lanka.[45]

Ever since the Indo-Lanka Accord of 1987, India has sought to develop the British colonial era Oil Tank Farm in the eastern seaport of Trincomalee through a subsidiary of the Indian Oil Corporation, India's largest commercial enterprise. Petroleum trade unions in Sri Lanka went on strike in 2017 against a deal charging that Sri Lanka would be "handing over [a] national asset" located along one of the world's busiest shipping routes to India, thereby jeopardizing the country's national security and economic independence.[46]

As noted in Chapter 3, in the 1960s, the left-wing government of Prime Minister Sirimavo Bandaranaike nationalized foreign oil companies in a controversial move asserting the island's decolonization. In January 2022, however, succumbing to Indian pressure and the need for cash, Sri Lanka signed an agreement for a joint de-

---

43 Roychaudhury, Nilova. "Sri Lankans Continue Protesting against Adani Being Favoured by PM Modi and Rajapakse." National Herald, June 24, 2022. Accessed June 26, 2022. https://www.nationalheraldindia.com/india/sri-lankans-continue-protesting-against-adani-being-favoured-by-pm-modi-and-rajapakse.
44 *Scroll.in*. "Sri Lanka Official Says Modi Insisted on Power Project Deal for Adani Group, Then Retracts Statement." Text. https://scroll.in, June 12, 2022. https://scroll.in/latest/1026026/sri-lankan-official-says-modi-insisted-power-project-deal-for-adani-group-then-retracts-statement.
45 'How The World's 3rd Richest Man Is Pulling The Largest Con In Corporate History', Hindenburg Research, January 24, 2023. https://hindenburgresearch.com/adani/accessed March 14, 2023.
46 Srinivasan, Meera. "India, Sri Lanka sign energy pact," *The Hindu*, April 28, 2017. Accessed April 30, 2017. https://www.thehindu.com/news/national/india-sri-lanka-sign-energy-pact/article18261624.ece.

velopment with the Indian Oil Corp. subsidiary in Sri Lanka taking a 49 percent stake and the Ceylon Petroleum Corp. maintaining a 51 percent stake over the Trincomalee Oil Tank Farm.[47] Critics who see this as an outcome of the new Cold War and neocolonialism argue that "The US$ 100,000 per annum, or US$ 8333.33 per month, lease for all 100 tanks in the 850 acres is not worth by any standards, given the unprecedented value of the asset in question."[48]

There have been numerous historic sea battles among rival powers to control Trincomalee, the second deepest natural harbor in the world. Of great strategic military value, it has been controlled in turn by the Portuguese, Dutch, French and English. As noted earlier, its capture by the British in 1782 paved the way for Britain's colonization of the entire island. In 1942, while Sri Lanka was still a British colony, Japan attacked Trincomalee harbor, sinking three British warships, one of which was raised in 2018. In addition to its strategic value, Sri Lankan researchers believe the area contains large deposits of thorium and titanium, likely further reason for the interest of external powers in Trincomalee.[49] The U.S. is also likely interested in Trincomalee as a naval base.[50]

A secret U.S. document declassified in January 2021, titled "U.S Strategic Framework for the Indo-Pacific" states the objective to "Accelerate India's rise and capacity to serve as a net provider of security and Major Defense Partner," and to "Strengthen the capacity of emerging partners in South Asia, including Maldives, Bangladesh, and Sri Lanka, to contribute to a free and open order."[51] It seems Sri Lanka is unwittingly being drawn into a geopolitical strategy led by the United

---

47 Pollard, Ruth. "Analysis | Is the Great Sri Lanka Fire Sale About to Begin?" *Washington Post*, May 30, 2022. Accessed May 31, 2022. https://www.washingtonpost.com/business/energy/is-the-great-sri-lanka-fire-sale-about-to-begin/2022/05/29/e187bc68-dfa3-11ec-ae64-6b23e5155b62_story.html.
48 Weerasinghe, Ranjith. "Please Don't Sell Our Trincomalee Oil Tank Farm." *The Morning*, January 6, 2022. Visited January 8, 2022. https://web.archive.org/web/20220106063647/https://www.themorning.lk/please-dont-sell-our-trincomalee-oil-tank-farm/.
49 Rogers, James. "Raised from the Deep," *The Sun*, April 3, 2018. Visited April 20, 2018. https://www.thesun.co.uk/news/5960646/british-warship-world-war-2-ss-sagaing-sri-lanka-harbour/.
50 Anderson, David A., and Anton Wijeyesekera. "U.S. Naval Basing in Sri Lanka?" Small Wars Journal, October 15, 2011. Visited September 3, 2022. https://smallwarsjournal.com/jrnl/art/us-naval-basing-in-sri-lanka.
51 "U.S. Strategic Framework for the Indo-Pacific." *Trumpwhitehouse.archives.gov.* Accessed January 3, 2023. https://trumpwhitehouse.archives.gov/wp-content/uploads/2021/01/IPS-Final-Declass.pdf; https://www.newswire.lk/2022/10/02/factum-perspective-the-president-elaborates-on-the-geopolitics-of-two-oceans/.

States to counter the perceived 'China threat' which could potentially lead to a conflagration in Sri Lanka and the Indian Ocean.[52]

U.S. Expansion

The 2013 initiative "Pivot to Asia" by the Obama administration sought to strategically rebalance U.S. interests from Europe and the Middle East toward Asia.[53] Similarly, the Asia Reassurance Initiative Act, signed into law by President Donald Trump on December 31, 2018 sought to increase military and diplomatic engagement of the U.S. in the Indo-Pacific.[54] Divided on domestic policy but united on foreign policy, both the Democratic and Republican leaders in the U.S. define the vast oceanic area ranging from the western coast of India to the west coast of the United States as one geopolitical region. Critics, however, see the Indo-Pacific as a political construct of the United States to contain China.[55]

A significant U.S.-led initiative in this regard is the Quadrilateral Security Dialogue – the QUAD – a strategic security alliance between the United States, Australia, India and Japan begun in 2007 with parallel joint and extensive military exercises known as the Malabar Exercises. The Chinese government recently issued high level protests calling QUAD an "Indo-Pacific version of NATO," and an "Asian NATO."[56]

---

[52] Kurukulasuriya, Lasanda. "Factum Perspective: The President Elaborates on the Geopolitics of Two Oceans." NewsWire, October 2, 2022. Accessed October 4, 2022. https://www.newswire.lk/2022/10/02/factum-perspective-the-president-elaborates-on-the-geopolitics-of-two-oceans/.

[53] Shiavenza, Matt. "What Exactly Does It Mean That the U.S. Is Pivoting to Asia?" *The Atlantic*. April 15, 2013. Accessed April 30, 2013. https://www.theatlantic.com/china/archive/2013/04/what-exactly-does-it-mean-that-the-us-is-pivoting-to-asia/274936/.

[54] Xenakis, John. "World View: Trump Signs Asia Reassurance Initiative Act (ARIA) Focusing U.S. Military on China," *Breitbart.com*, January 10, 2019. Accessed January 12, 2019. https://www.breitbart.com/national-security/2019/01/10/world-view-trump-signs-asia-reassurance-initiative-act-aria-focusing-u-s-military-on-china/.

[55] Siow, Maria. "What Is the 'Indo-Pacific' and Why Does the US Keep Using This Term?" *South China Morning Post*, August 26, 2021. Accessed August 40, 2021. https://www.scmp.com/week-asia/politics/article/3146363/what-indo-pacific-region-and-why-does-us-keep-using-term.

[56] *Outlook India*. "QUAD Is 'Dangerous', Akin to NATO's Eastward Expansion In Europe: China," March 20, 2022. Accessed May 2, 2022. https://www.outlookindia.com/international/quad-is-dangerous-akin-to-nato-s-eastward-expansion-in-europe-china-news-187758. *Financial Express*. "Quad Summit 2021: Why Is China Rattled?" March 14, 2021. Accessed March 16, 2021. https://www.financialexpress.com/defence/quad-summit-2021-why-is-china-rattled/2212544/. See also, "Indo-Pacific Strategy Report: Preparedness, Partnerships, and Promoting a Networked Region." Strategy Report.

As shown in Chapters 3 and 4, the United States has been politically and economically engaged in Sri Lanka since the time of her independence from Britain.[57] Recognizing the new political realities in the IOR at the end of the separatist war, and claiming that the United States "cannot afford to 'lose' strategically located Sri Lanka," the U.S. formulated a new policy to elevate its geopolitical involvement in the island.[58] The Committee on Foreign Relations of the United States Senate issued a report in December 2009 entitled "Sri Lanka: Re-charting U.S. Strategy after the war." It called for "... a new approach that increases U.S. leverage vis-à-vis Sri Lanka by expanding the number of tools at our disposal ... that will ultimately help secure longer-term U.S. strategic interests in the Indian Ocean ...."[59]

U. S. political, economic and military agendas towards Sri Lanka include a wide range of overt, covert, "soft" and hard power strategies. Although unreported in the mainstream media, the United States, with India's involvement, is believed to have orchestrated the 2015 regime change via the presidential elections. The elections, held on January 8, 2015, replaced Mahinda Rajapaksa who was aligned with China with Maithripala Sirisena as President and U.S. ally Ranil Wickramasinghe as the Prime Minister of Sri Lanka.[60]

Washington D.C.: Unites States Department of Defense, June 1, 2019. https://media.defense.gov/2019/Jul/01/2002152311/-1/-1/1/DEPARTMENT-OF-DEFENSE-INDO-PACIFIC-STRATEGY-REPORT-2019.PDF.

57 Waduge, Shenali. "US in Sri Lanka since 2015 – Turning Sri Lanka into a Neo-Colonial Military Base." LankaWeb. Accessed January 2, 2023. https://www.lankaweb.com/news/items/2019/11/01/us-in-sri-lanka-since-2015-turning-sri-lanka-into-a-neo-colonial-military-base/.

58 Kerry, John F., Christopher J. Dodd, Russell D. Feingold, Barbara Boxer, Robert Menendez, Benjamin L. Cardin, Robert P Casey, et al. *Sri Lanka: Recharting U.S. Strategy After the War, Committee on Foreign Relations, United States Senate, One Hundred Eleventh Congress, First Session, December 7, 2009*. Washington D.C.: U.S. Government Printing Office, 2009, 3.

59 Ibid., 3.

60 Ratnayake, K. "Evidence of India's Involvement in Regime Change in Sri Lanka." *World Socialist Web Site*, January 21, 2015. Accessed January 22, 2015. https://www.wsws.org/en/articles/2015/01/21/sril-j21.html. Ratnayake, K. "More Evidence of US Involvement in Sri Lankan Regime-Change." *World Socialist Web Site*, February 16, 2015. Accessed February 18, 2015. https://www.wsws.org/en/articles/2015/02/16/slus-f16.html. Wijesiriwardena, Pani. "Washington's Intrigues against Sri Lankan President." *World Socialist Web Site*, December 1, 2014. Accessed January 2, 2015. https://www.wsws.org/en/articles/2014/12/01/sril-d01.html. Dibbert, Taylor. "What Does Regime Change in Sri Lanka Mean for the United States?" *The Diplomat*, April 30, 2015. Accessed May 22, 2015. https://thediplomat.com/2015/04/what-does-regime-change-in-sri-lanka-mean-for-the-united-states/.

'Yahapalanaya' Regime (2015 – 2019)

Soon after the new *Yahapalanaya* (good governance) government came into power in January, on February 27, 2015, Sri Lanka faced the "biggest ever public financial fraud committed" in the country's history.[61] Appallingly, the Central Bank bond scam took place while an IMF staff mission led by Todd Schneider was visiting Colombo during February 23 to March 4 to conduct Post-Program 'monitoring discussions' for ' enhanced surveillance'. Completely overlooking the grand robbery that took place under the IMF's watchful eyes, Schneider issued a statement at the end of his visit saying "We welcome the government's commitment to good governance, increased transparency, and financial discipline".[62]

The USD 65 million bond scandal, attributed to blatant abuse of power by the newly appointed Central Bank Governor Arjun Mahendran, caused a huge loss and damage to the economic prospects of the country.[63] There was yet another Central Bank bond scandal in 2016 allegedly involving Mahendran and the then Sri Lankan Finance Minister Ravi Karunanayake among others.[64] Neither case has been resolved yet. According to a Nikkei Asia Business Review in 2017:

> ... the scandal also has broader business implications, not least because it reinforces a global impression of Sri Lanka as a country where corruption remains rampant. It was a factor in Sri Lanka's fall of 12 places in the 2016 Corruption Perception Index, released annually by Transparency International, a global anti-graft watchdog, and analysts say it has complicated the government's struggle to finance foreign debt repayments.[65]

Despite the Central Bank bond scandal and other violations of the rule of law, the 2015 Sri Lanka regime change was applauded in the U.S. Congress as heralding a

---

61 Bandarage, Asoka. "Good Governance in Sri Lanka." *HuffPost*, April 17, 2015. Accessed April 17, 2015. https://www.huffpost.com/entry/good-governance-in-sri-lanka_b_7087768.
62 Press Release No.15/154 : "IMF Staff Concludes Visit to Sri Lanka, March 4, 2015. https://www.imf.org/en/News/Articles/2015/09/14/01/49/pr15154 accessed March 14, 2023.
63 *Newsfirst*. "Bond Scam: Expose of the Largest Financial Scam in the History of SL," February 3, 2018. Accessed March 2, 2022. https://www.newsfirst.lk/2018/02/03/bond-scam-expose-largest-financial-scam-history-sl/. Macan-Markar, Marwaan. "Sri Lanka Government Shakes as Bond Scandal Inquiry Ends." *Nikkei Asia*, November 24, 2017. Accessed March 2, 2022. https://asia.nikkei.com/Economy/Sri-Lanka-government-shakes-as-bond-scandal-inquiry-ends2.
64 *ColomboPage*. "Sri Lanka: Court Permits Trial of 2016 Bond Scam Case with Two Defendants in Absentia," July 20, 2021. Accessed July 22, 2021. http://www.colombopage.com/archive_21A/Jul20_1626799514CH.php.
65 Macan-Markar, Marwaan. "Sri Lanka Government Shakes as Bond Scandal Inquiry Ends." *Nikkei Asia*, November 24, 2017. Accessed March 2, 2022. https://asia.nikkei.com/Economy/Sri-Lanka-government-shakes-as-bond-scandal-inquiry-ends2.ra.

"New Era for the U.S.-Sri Lanka Relationship" and a democratic alternative to the previous corrupt and authoritarian Rajapaksa government.[66] U.S. Secretary of State John Kerry and U.S. Ambassador to the U.N. Samantha Power visited Sri Lanka to uphold the new government in May 2015 and November 2015 respectively. As Sri Lankan diplomat and critic Tamara Kunnayakam has pointed out, the role played by the Yahapalanaya in the neoliberal onslaught against Sri Lanka is "not a matter of bad management, bad governance, incompetence, incapacity, or an absence of vision. They have been placed in the positions they occupy precisely because of a shared vision."[67]

Open Society founder, hedge fund billionaire George Soros and former World Bank chief economist Joseph Stiglitz attended the high-powered Sri Lanka Economic Forum in Colombo in January 2016 organized by the influential think tank, the Institute for Policy Studies[68]. There the "key findings of a preliminary study on Sri Lanka carried out by the Harvard University's Center for International Development" were to be discussed.[69] This is likely the Constraints Analysis for the MCC Compact, discussed below. At the forum, Soros pointed out that "Money will be pouring in here, because generally the banks are pulling money out."[70] He probably was referring to increased loans from Western financial markets given to the Global South following the 2008 financial crisis. Shortly after the forum, Stiglitz wrote an op-ed, "The Rebirth of Sri Lanka," stating that "with peace and the emergence of representative political institutions, Sri Lanka today has a better opportunity than ever to make the right choices."[71]

---

66 "Hearing Before the Subcommittee on Asia and the Pacific of the Committee on Foreign Affairs House of Representatives One Hundred Fourteenth Congress, Second Session, June 9, 2016." U.S. Government Printing Office, June 9, 2016. https://www.govinfo.gov/content/pkg/CHRG-114hhrg 20381/html/CHRG-114hhrg20381.htm.
67 Kunanayakam, Tamara. "Creeping Neo-Liberal Stranglehold on Sri Lanka." *Thuppahi's Blog*, June 27, 2018. Accesd June 19, 2018. https://thuppahis.com/2018/06/27/creeping-neo-liberal-strangle hold-on-sri-lanka/.
68 Ibid.
69 *Newsfirst.* "Sustainable and Inclusive Development Take Center Stage at SL Economic Forum," January 7, 2016. Accessed June 10, 2022. https://www.newsfirst.lk/2016/01/07/sustainable-and-in clusive-development-take-center-stage-at-sl-economic-forum/123916/.
70 Sirimanna, Bandula. "Soros to Boost Sri Lankan Economy, Stiglitz to Provide 'Sound' Advice'" *Sunday Times* (Sri Lanka). January 10, 2016. Accessed February 10, 2016. http://www.sundaytimes. lk/160110/business-times/soros-to-boost-sri-lankan-economy-stiglitz-to-provide-sound-advice-177966. html. Gunadasa, Saman. "Sri Lankan Government Tries to Woo Foreign Investors." *World Socialist Web Site*, January 20, 2016. Accessed January 26, 2016. https://www.wsws.org/en/articles/2016/01/20/econ-j20-1.html.
71 Stiglitz, Joseph E. "Sri Lanka's Rebirth." *Project Syndicate*, January 25, 2016. Accessed February 10, 2016. https://www.project-syndicate.org/commentary/sri-lanka-development-growth-by-joseph-e-

In retrospect, it seems that the choices made by political leaders and top bureaucrats may have been 'right' for western interests but not Sri Lanka. A major case is the buying of controversial ISBs accelerated during the Yahapalanya regime, first under Central Bank Governor Arjun Mahendran (2015–2016) and then his successor, Indrajit Coomaraswamy (2016–2019). As discussed in Chapter 6, the maturation of those ISBs is at the heart of the debt and economic crises Sri Lanka is facing today (Table 6.1).

In September 2016, the United States signed a partnership with Sri Lanka allowing the U.S. House of Representatives to 'work with' the Sri Lankan Parliament to help develop an "accountable, effective and independent" legislature, a move that raises questions about external interference in the internal affairs of a sovereign state.[72] Sri Lanka's treatment as a client state was also evident in "unwarranted interference" by diplomats of the U.S. and its allies the U.K., Canada and the European Union during the crisis caused by the Sri Lankan President Sirisena's dismissal of Prime Minister Wickramasinghe in October 2018 (he was reinstated in December 2018).[73]

The pro-U.S. *Yahapalana* government antagonized China when it halted the Colombo Port City project (resumed in 2020) but, given desperate need for cash, leased the Hambantota Port to China for US$ 1.1 Billion in 2017.[74] Ever since the U.S. backed 2015 regime change, using its local political and NGO collaborators, the U.S. sought to exert "tremendous influence" on economic, political and military arenas to integrate Sri Lanka into the U.S. Indo-Pacific Strategy.[75] The MCC Compact, the 2017 Acquisition and Cross-Servicing Agreement (ACSA) and State of Forces Agreement (SOFA), the 2015 and subsequent United Nations Human Rights Commission (UNHRC) Resolutions and parliamentary and constitutional reform have been the major initiatives in this regard.

---

stiglitz-2016-01. "Sri Lanka Economic Forum." Accessed January 3, 2023. https://web.archive.org/web/20220712192108/http://srilankaeconomicforum.org/.
72 *Daily News*. "US House of Representatives to Work with Sri Lanka Parliament," September 17, 2016. Accessed September 20, 2016. https://www.dailynews.lk/2016/09/17/local/93425.
73 Kurukulasuriya, Lasanda. "Geopolitics of Western Interest in Sri Lanka's Political Impasse – Opinion." *Daily Mirror* (Sri Lanka). December 24, 2018. Accessed January 3, 2022. https://www.dailymirror.lk/opinion/Geopolitics-of-Western-interest-in-Sri-Lanka-s-political-impasse/172-160193.
74 Umesh Moramudali, 'Hambantota Port Deal', https://thediplomat.com/2020/01/the-hambantota-port-deal-myths-and-realities/.
75 Waduge, Shenali. "US in Sri Lanka since 2015 – Turning Sri Lanka into a Neo-Colonial Military Base." *LankaWeb*. Accessed January 2, 2023. https://www.lankaweb.com/news/items/2019/11/01/us-in-sri-lanka-since-2015-turning-sri-lanka-into-a-neo-colonial-military-base/.

Millennium Challenge Corporation Compact

The Millennium Challenge Corporation (MCC), a United States government corporation, was established by the U.S. Congress in November 2002. It is a component of the George W. Bush administration's U.S. National Security Strategy introduced after the terrorist attacks of September 11, 2001, linking economic development with defense and diplomacy.

While the MCC states its mission as "reducing poverty through growth,"[76] critics argue that the MCC's primary commitment is not to poverty reduction but to "reshape the legal, institutional, infrastructural and financial contexts of poorer countries to better suit U.S. economic interests." Thus, the MCC is seen as an instrument of the "new imperialism" pursuing "economic hegemony through the extension and ever-deepening penetration of neoliberal capitalism."[77]

As of February 2022, the MCC had "completed 83 compacts and threshold programs in 51 countries and regions across Africa, Asia, Eastern Europe, Latin America, and the Pacific."[78] But many of the countries have complained about the MCC's political interference and a number of countries including Tanzania, Ghana and the Philippines have terminated agreements with the MCC. In 2017, MCC targeted Nepal and Sri Lanka, two strategically important South Asian countries that also rejected MCC Compacts.[79] Despite official withdrawal, the MCC Compact continues to hold sway over Sri Lanka. As such, a discussion of the new Cold War and neo-colonialism in Sri Lanka requires its consideration.

---

76 *Millennium Challenge Corporation.* https://www.mcc.gov/; *Millennium Challenge Corporation.* "Compact Development Guidance Chapter 8: Guidelines for Developing Project Proposals." Accessed January 3, 2023. https://www.mcc.gov/resources/story/story-cdg-chapter-8-guidelines-for-developing-project-proposals.

77 Mawdsley, Emma. "The Millennium Challenge Account: Neo-Liberalism, Poverty and Security." Review of *International Political Economy* 14, no. 3 (July 4, 2007): 487–509. https://doi.org/10.1080/09692290701395742. Soederberg, Susanne. "American Empire and 'Excluded States': The Millennium Challenge Account and the Shift to Pre-Emptive Development." *Third World Quarterly* 25, no. 2 (March 1, 2004): 279–302. https://doi.org/10.1080/0143659042000174815.

78 *Global Times.* "Fed up with Political Malevolence, Recipient Countries Reject MCC over Questionable Terms," February 25, 2022. Accessed March 3, 2022. https://www.globaltimes.cn/page/202202/1253168.shtml.

79 Ibid.

The Sri Lankan MCC Compact

Sri Lanka was selected to develop a MCC Compact in December 2016, and the MCC Board approved a five-year compact for Sri Lanka on April 25, 2019.[80] A November 2017 "Constraints Analysis" completed by the Center for International Development at Harvard University for the compact identified policy uncertainty; poor transportation and inadequate access to land, especially "the difficulty of the private sector in accessing state owned land for commercial purposes" as the major constraints to "private investment and entrepreneurship" in Sri Lanka.

According to the Harvard "Constraints Analysis":

> Access to land is a binding constraint to growth and economic transformation as well. The state reportedly owns approximately 80 percent of the land in the country and it is held by multiple ministries. Government coordination is poor and the process of acquiring rights to develop land is slow and unclear, resulting in an inability of the government to meet the demand for land needed for new private sector investment, including for export-oriented FDI [Foreign Direct Investment] …, problems with land use and titling are prevalent throughout the country and affect manufacturing, agriculture, construction, residential and commercial development, and tourism. Restrictions on land parcel size, the absence of land titles, and longstanding laws affecting rural land use all reduce agricultural productivity and rural well-being.[81]

The MCC Compact would offer $480 million to Sri Lanka to undertake transportation and land management.[82] Article 1 of the draft agreement of the compact states that the objective of the Transport Project is to "facilitate the flow of passengers and goods between the central region of the country and ports and markets" and the objective of the Land Project is to "increase the availability of information on private land and under-utilized State Lands in order to increase land market activity."[83] As discussed in Chapter 4, the World Bank and USAID had been pushing the same neoliberal policies in Sri Lanka for decades.

---

80 "Millenium Challenge Corporation Congressional Notification." *Millennium Challenge Corporation*, April 25, 2019. https://www.mcc.gov/content/uploads/cn-042519-sri-lanka-intent-to-sign.pdf.
81 Millennium Challenge Corporation, Sri Lanka Constraints Analysis, 2017. "Sri Lanka Constraints Analysis Report 2017." Millennium Challenge Corporation, 2017. https://assets.mcc.gov/content/uploads/constraints-analysis-sri-lanka.pdf.
82 *U.S. Embassy in Sri Lanka.* "Highlights of MCC Compact," July 29, 2019. https://lk.usembassy.gov/highlights-of-mcc-compact/.
83 "Draft Agreement Between the United States of America and the Democratic Socialist Republic of Sri Lanka." Ministry of Finance, Sri Lanka, and Millennium Challenge Corporation, November 5, 2019. https://web.archive.org/web/20191207020504/. http://treasury.gov.lk/documents/10181/519892/MCC+Rescan1.pdf/a5d28fac-22cc-4139-a88e-a37311bafb6b. *Millennium Challenge Corporation.* "Com-

MCC funding is to be used to change Sri Lanka's land policy through the creation of a state land inventory based on a "Parcel Fabric Map," the conversion of paper deeds into electronic titles and a "computerized mass appraisal system" for land valuation. MCC funding would support "the creation of a digital folio for each land parcel that includes the legal records on land transactions and a linkage to spatial data that identifies the location of each land parcel where possible."[84] The goal is to speed up land privatization and commoditization by providing investors, including foreign corporations, easy digital access.

According to the Draft Agreement between the MCC and Sri Lanka's Ministry of Finance, MCC funding would be used to provide titles to state-owned land held by individuals, mostly smallholder farmers, thereby facilitating the sale of their lands to any buyer.

> ... [C]onversion of State Lands to the private domain, creating a marketable and bankable title to this land in the name of the land holder. The Government shall register the absolute land grants in the title registration system, allowing the use of land as collateral for loans and the free transfer of this land without excessive government restrictions. The Land Special Provisions Act (LSPA) is expected to define the process the Government shall use for this conversion of land rights. The availability of MCC Funding for this Activity is dependent on the enactment of the LSPA ...[85]

Colonial Land Expropriation

The MCC Compact brings to mind the early stage of capitalist development in Sri Lanka, when the British colonial state introduced legislation, infrastructure and other measures to establish the plantation economy. Those measures, discussed in Chapter 2, opened up the previously isolated Kandyan Highlands, heralding a fundamental social and economic transformation that benefitted the colonizers and a small stratum of local entrepreneurs and administrators.[86] The infamous Or-

---

pact: Sri Lanka Compact," December 29, 2020. Accessed March 12, 2021. https://www.mcc.gov/where-we-work/program/sri-lanka-compact.

84 "Draft Agreement Between the United States of America and the Democratic Socialist Republic of Sri Lanka." Ministry of Finance, Sri Lanka, and Millennium Challenge Corporation, November 5, 2019, Annex 1, 29. https://web.archive.org/web/20191207020504/. http://treasury.gov.lk/documents/10181/519892/MCC+Rescan1.pdf/a5d28fac-22cc-4139-a88e-a37311bafb6b.

85 MCC Agreement, Sri Lanka, https://www.scribd.com/document/439254064/MCC-Agreement-Sri-lanka-pdf.

86 Bandarage, Asoka. "The Establishment and Consolidation of the Plantation Economy in Sri Lanka." *Bulletin of Concerned Asian Scholars* 14, no. 3 (September 1, 1982): 2–22. https://doi.org/10.1080/14672715.1982.10412654.

dinance No. 12 of 1840: to prevent Encroachments upon Crown Lands and Ordinance No. 1 of 1897, the so-called Waste Lands Ordinance, were introduced to provide the juridical and administrative framework to expropriate land from local people who had customary rights but could not prove 'ownership' and titles to their land as required by the British.[87]

British colonial policymakers and their latter-day apologists have argued that colonial policies helped advance peasant proprietorship by giving land titles to peasants who previously lacked them. However, as this author has demonstrated in her book, *Colonialism in Sri Lanka*, the long-term results were, in fact, great confusion and conflict over land rights, large scale dispossession from ancestral land and impoverishment of the Kandyan peasantry. Subsistence agriculture and local self-sufficiency were undermined, and the natural environment was disrupted.[88]

U.S. and Sri Lankan proponents of the MCC Compact have claimed that the distribution of 1 million deeds granting outright ownership to individuals holding state land under the compact is a "poverty alleviation measure."[89] The foreign-funded, private sector-oriented think tank in Sri Lanka, the Pathfinder Foundation, a proponent of the MCC Compact, said "We, as the Pathfinder Foundation, are proud to claim that the land titling and distribution among farmers …was first publicly demanded by us… in 2007."[90] In June 2018, President Sirisena promised to provide 1 million land deeds island-wide and land deeds to all Mahaweli settlers by the end of that year.[91] While at face value this seems a humanitarian measure, the Movement for Land and Agricultural Reform (MONLAR), the National Joint Committee and other Sri Lankan organizations recognize a neocolonial agenda

---

[87] Bandarage, Asoka. *Colonialism in Sri Lanka: The Political Economy of the Kandyan Highlands, 1833–1886.* New Babylon, Studies in the Social Sciences. Berlin: Mouton, 1983, Appendix 4, 367.
[88] Ibid., passim.
[89] *Sunday Times* (Sri Lanka). "One Million Land Deeds to Be Distributed to the People in Future: Min. Karunathilaka," March 19, 2019. Accessed March 30, 2019. https://sundaytimes.lk/online/news-online/10000-land-deeds-to-be-distributed-to-the-people-in-future-min-karunathilaka/2-1077974.
"Draft Agreement Between the United States of America and the Democratic Socialist Republic of Sri Lanka." Ministry of Finance, Sri Lanka, and Millennium Challenge Corporation, November 5, 2019, Annex 1, 32. https://web.archive.org/web/20191207020504/http://treasury.gov.lk/documents/10181/519892/MCC+Rescan1.pdf/a5d28fac-22cc-4139-a88e-a37311bafb6b.
[90] Siriwardena, Luxman. "MCC Grant Dilemma – The Pathfinder Compromise." *Daily Mirror* (Sri Lanka), March 10, 2020. Accessed March 12, 2020. https://www.dailymirror.lk/features/MCC-grant-dilemma-The-Pathfinder-compromise/185-184598. ; "India Modified: Any Lessons for Sri Lanka? Meeting the Aspirations of a Rising and Impatient Middle-Class." Economic Flash. Pathfinder Foundation. N.d. Accessed January 3, 2023. https://www.pathfinderfoundation.org/images/articles/articles/economic_flash/47%20indian%20elections%20-%20lessons%20for%20sri%20lanka.pdf.
[91] *ColomboPage*. "Sri Lanka: President Promises Land Deeds to All Mahaweli Settlers by Year End," June 2, 2018. http://www.colombopage.com/archive_18A/Jun02_1527922706CH.php.

for a massive modern-day land grab, displacement and peasant pauperization: "... [L]arge multinational companies have made small time farmers bankrupt and are buying off their agricultural land ... By giving desperate people an asset that they can sell, the government has ensured that these lands will be sold off."[92]

The MCC Compact includes plans to draw land survey maps and create a digital database of 3.6 million parcels of state-owned land, a task that it proposes to contract for 15 years to Trimble Inc., a U.S.-based geological information and mapping firm. The Cabinet Committee on Economic Management (CCEM), headed by Prime Minister Wickamasinghe's senior advisor Ramalingam Paskaralingam, allegedly a highly corrupt, influential bureaucrat, approved taking a $154 million loan with a 4 percent interest for this purpose.[93]

Sri Lanka Survey Department trade unions went on strike opposing the hiring of Trimble, which they see as a threat to both their employment and national security, as well as a wasteful expenditure.[94] Again, these plans mirror the early stage of colonial plantation development, when a single British "planter-official class" determined rules on land ownership, surveyed and accessed land from the colonial state, employed cheap labor and developed highly profitable plantation companies producing exports for the global market. Moreover, as seen earlier in the case of the Mahaweli Project, hiring foreign companies and consultants instead of locals for lucrative work is a common feature of neocolonial economic development.

---

92 Kuruwita, Rathindra. "MONLAR: Land given to the Poor Will End up with Multinationals." July 8th, 2019. *LankaWeb*. Accessed January 3, 2023. https://www.lankaweb.com/news/items/2019/07/08/monlar-land-given-to-the-poor-will-end-up-with-multinationals/; Leelarathna, Hassina. "Expats in Los Angeles Campaigning against Controversial US Contracts." *Daily FT*, August 1, 2019. Accessed August 22, 2019. https://web.archive.org/web/20190903214302/. http://www.ft.lk/business/Expats-in-Los-Angeles-campaigning-against-controversial-US-contracts/34-683112. *National Joint Committee.* "Letter Sent by the National Joint Committee to Prime Minister Ranil Wickramasinghe on the Millennium Challenge Corporation Agreement," June 2, 2019. Available at: http://www.sundaytimes.lk/190602/sunday-times-2/the-land-belongs-to-the-people-and-all-living-beings-thou-art-only-the-guardian-of-it-351773.html.
93 Waduge, Shenali. "US in Sri Lanka since 2015 – Turning Sri Lanka into a Neo-Colonial Military Base." LankaWeb. Accessed January 2, 2023. https://www.lankaweb.com/news/items/2019/11/01/us-in-sri-lanka-since-2015-turning-sri-lanka-into-a-neo-colonial-military-base/. "TISL Calls on CIABOC to Investigate Assets of R. Paskaralingam," November 19, 2021. Accessed November 20, 2021. https://www.tisrilanka.org/tisl-calls-on-ciaboc-to-investigate-assets-of-r-paskaralingam/; Wijeyawickrema, C. "Paskaralingam, Charith & Malik." *LankaWeb*, October 5, 2018. Accessed November 3, 2018. https://www.lankaweb.com/news/items/2018/10/05/paskaralingam-charith-malik/.
94 *The Sunday Times* (Sri Lanka). "State Surveyors Strike to Oppose Plans to Hand over Contract to US Firm," December 17, 2017. Accessed December 20, 2017. http://www.sundaytimes.lk/171217/news/state-surveyors-strike-to-oppose-plans-to-hand-over-contract-to-us-firm-273640.html.

The Sri Lanka Physical Plan (2018–2050) and a projected Physical Spatial Structure Map for 2050 (Figure 5.4), upon which the MCC Compact is based, have also raised alarm.[95.] There is concern that the proposed "economic corridor" and highway from Trincomalee to Colombo, reported to cover 1.2 million acres, could "splinter" Sri Lanka into two separate entities. Given the relationship of the MCC to U.S. National Security Strategy there is fear that the compact could facilitate greater U.S. control, undermining Sri Lanka's sovereignty unity and territorial integrity.[96]

Popular Resistance to the MCC Compact

The struggle over the MCC Compact brings to mind the long history of popular resistance against colonial land policies in Sri Lanka. The rebellion of 1848, for example, was a nationalist revolt against imperialist policies such as the Ordinance of 1840, which helped expropriate peasant lands to develop the plantation economy. Contemporary activist groups demanding a halt to the MCC Compact were encouraged by the decision of the Sri Lanka Supreme Court on the State Land Special Provisions Act (LSPA) in July 2019, referring the act to the Provincial Councils, as it would impact and probably deter passage of land provisions envisaged in the MCC Compact.[97] As shown earlier, the LSPA is vital for the MCC Compact for conversion of land rights, i.e., land privatization and commoditization in Sri Lanka.[98]

---

95 "National Physical Planning Policy & The Plan – 2017–2050." Battaramulla, Sri Lanka: National Physical Planning Department Sri Lanka, June 2019. https://nppd.gov.lk/images/National_Physical_Plans/National_Physical%20Planning%20Policy%20and%20The%20Plan%202050.pdf.
96 Ladduwahetty, Neville. "The Millennium Challenge Corporation Compact with Sri Lanka," *The Island*, June 2, 2019. Accessed June 4, 2019. http://www.island.lk/index.php?page_cat=article-details&page=article-details&code_title=205231. See also, "'Che." "Rise-up Sri Lanka Rise-up! Destroy the Enemy Utterly as It Pivots to Mother Lanka (Part 1)." *LankaWeb*, March 12, 2019. March 14, 2019. http://www.lankaweb.com/news/items/2019/02/26/rise-up-sri-lanka-rise-up-destroy-the-enemy-as-it-pivots-to-lanka-to-build-an-electrified-eelam-border-wall-and-make-the-island-its-military-hub-in-the-indo-pacific-part-1/.
97 "Leelarathna, Hassina. "Expats in Los Angeles Campaigning against Controversial US Contracts." Daily FT, August 1, 2019. https://web.archive.org/web/20190903214302/http://www.ft.lk/business/Expats-in-Los-Angeles-campaigning-against-controversial-US-contracts/34-683112. "State Lands Special Provisions Bill to Acquire 1.2 million acres of land for economic corridor?" *Newsfirst*, July 31, 2019 https://www.newsfirst.lk/2019/07/31/state-lands-special-provisions-bill-to-acquire-1-2-mn-acres-of-land-for-economic-corridor/. "State Lands Special Provisions Bill to Acquire 1.2 million acres of land for economic corridor?" *Newsfirst*, July 31, 2019 https://www.newsfirst.lk/2019/07/31/state-lands-special-provisions-bill-to-acquire-1-2-mn-acres-of-land-for-economic-corridor/.

Popular Resistance to the MCC Compact — 145

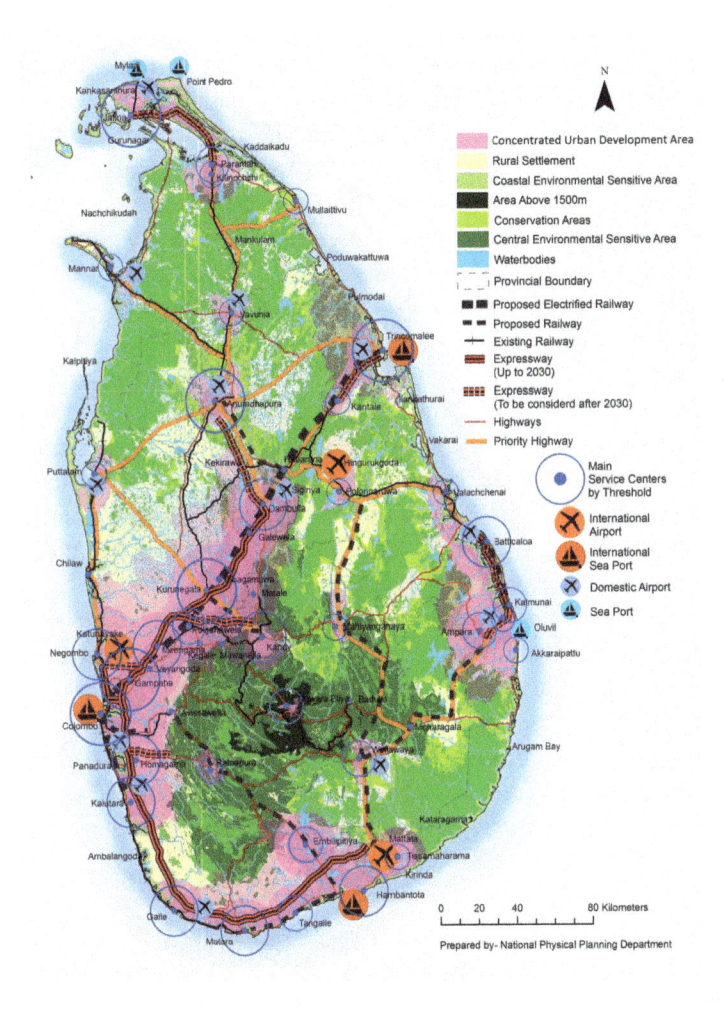

Figure 5.4: The Sri Lanka physical spatial structure map for 2050. Source: Sri Lanka National Physical Planning Department, June 2019. https://www.nppd.gov.lk/images/downloads/maps/National_Physical_Plan_2050.jpg

---

98 "Draft Agreement Between the United States of America and the Democratic Socialist Republic of Sri Lanka." Ministry of Finance, Sri Lanka, and Millennium Challenge Corporation, November 5, 2019, 30. https://web.archive.org/web/20191207020504/http://treasury.gov.lk/documents/10181/519892/MCC+Rescan1.pdf/a5d28fac-22cc-4139-a88e-a37311bafb6b; See also, Mittal, Janhavi. "Land Privatization: Why Sri Lanka Must Reject the MCC Compact." *Oaklandinstitute.org*, August 17, 2020. Accessed August 22, 2020. https://www.oaklandinstitute.org/blog/privatizing-state-land-sri-lanka.

Anticipating the electoral defeat of the U.S.-backed Sri Lankan government and in a hurry to seal the MCC Compact, the U.S. Embassy in Sri Lanka issued a statement on November 6, 2019, stating that "the United States anticipates working toward grant signing and parliamentary approval with the Government of Sri Lanka after November 16, 2019."[99] On November 6, 2019, the Government Medical Officers Association also filed a Fundamental Rights Petition seeking to stay all approvals and decisions in respect to the compact as well as the military pacts (ACSA and SOFA, discussed below) with the United States. The petitioners state that if signed or executed, the compact would violate the fundamental tenet of sovereignty of the country, which the constitution expressly upholds to be "Free, Sovereign and Independent."[100]

As in the era of classical colonialism, Buddhist monks have also been at the forefront of nationalist resistance against external powers attempting to subordinate the country. A Buddhist monk, the Venerable Ududumbara Kashyapa, for example, began a fast-unto-death on November 5, 2019, against the MCC Compact, and only abandoned it once the government decided not to sign it before the November 2019 presidential election.[101]

Gotabaya Rajapaksa promised to discard the MCC Compact during his election campaign. After his appointment as president, he appointed a cabinet subcommittee to study the compact; it advised the government not to go ahead with it.'[102] Given the massive public outrage, the MCC Board discontinued the compact with the government of Sri Lanka in December 2020.[103] However, as activist groups state, although the MCC Compact is no more, the land reforms intended to meet the imperialist and neoliberal agenda are slowly being implemented through

---

[99] U.S. Embassy Sri Lanka, "Statement on Next Steps for the Millennium Challenge Cooperation Development Assistance Grant," Nov. 6, 2019 https://lk.usembassy.gov/u-s-embassy-statement-on-next-steps-for-the-millennium-challenge-corporation-development-assistance-grant/. See also, Seneviratne, Malinda. "Opinion: A Political Reading of the US Ambassador's Angst." *Daily Mirror* (Sri Lanka), August 1, 2019. Accessed August 4, 2019. https://www.dailymirror.lk/opinion/A-POLITICAL-READING-OF-THE-US-AMBASSADORS-ANGST/172-172114.

[100] Sooriyagoda, Lakmal. "GMOA Files FR against MCC, ACSA, SOFA." *Daily News*, November 6, 2019. https://www.dailynews.lk/2019/11/06/law-order/202146/gmoa-files-fr-against-mcc-acsa-sofa.

[101] Wasala, Rohana R. "Empowerment or Entrapment? The Millennium Challenge Corporation Compact and the Message of the Fasting Monk." *LankaWeb*, November 10, 2019. Accessed November 11, 2019. https://www.lankaweb.com/news/items/2019/11/10/empowerment-or-entrapment-the-millennium-challenge-corporation-compact-and-the-message-of-the-fasting-monk/.

[102] *Daily Mirror* (Sri Lanka). "Govt. Adopting Double Standards on MCC: JVP," December 16, 2019. https://www.dailymirror.lk/breaking_news/Govt-adopting-double-standards-on-MCC-JVP/108-179692.

[103] *Millennium Challenge Corporation*. "Compact: Sri Lanka Compact," December 29, 2020. Accessed March 12, 2021. https://www.mcc.gov/where-we-work/program/sri-lanka-compact.

such measures as the transfer of control of "other state forest lands" to Divisional secretaries and the opening of lands to large-scale commercial agriculture.[104] The American Trimble Company associated with the MCC Compact continues to be active in geospatial monitoring, land development and other infrastructure projects in Sri Lanka.[105]

The U.S. Principal Deputy Assistant Secretary of State for South and Central Asian Affairs Alice Wells stated in January 2020: "Sri Lanka occupies some very important real estate in the Indo-Pacific region, and it's a country of increasing strategic importance in the Indian Ocean region,"[106]

As the General Secretary of Sri Lanka's Professionals' National Front pointed out, the MCC Compact was not a mere grant but a component of the Indo-Pacific strategy advanced by the US and India.

> The MCC is part of their strategy to use Sri Lanka and other nations for military and strategic purposes. The MCC compact does not stand alone but it should be taken with SOFA and ACSA.[107]

U.S. Military Expansion

Military engagement with the strategically located Sri Lanka is considered vital to achieving U.S. objectives in the Indo-Pacific region. In August 2016, the first joint operation between the U.S. and the Sri Lankan military took place in Jaffna with participation of Tamil National Alliance (TNA) politicians at the launching.[108] Since 2016, U.S. military ships have visited Colombo and the U.S. 7th Fleet vessels and the aircraft carrier USS John C. Stennis have visited the port of Trincomalee.

---

104 Kuruwita, Rathindra. "Professionals Warn Lanka Not to Be Lulled into Complacency over US Withdrawal of MCC." *The Island*, December 19, 2020. Accessed December 20, 2020. http://island.lk/professionals-warn-lanka-not-to-be-lulled-into-complacency-over-us-withdrawal-of-mcc/.
105 *Trimble Geospatial*. "Geospatial Customer Stories: Comprehensive Monitoring of Victoria Dam," November 1, 2019. Accessed November 12, 2022. https://geospatialresources.trimble.com/customer-story/comprehensive-monitoring-of-victoria-dam-2.
106 *Tamil Guardian*. "US and Sri Lanka 'Have Compelling Shared Interests' – Alice Wells," January 28, 2020. https://www.tamilguardian.com/content/us-and-sri-lanka-%E2%80%98have-compelling-shared-interests%E2%80%99-%E2%80%93-alice-wells.
107 Cited in Kuruwita, Rathindra. "Professionals Warn Lanka Not to Be Lulled into Complacency over US Withdrawal of MCC." The Island, December 19, 2020. Accessed December 20, 2020. http://island.lk/professionals-warn-lanka-not-to-be-lulled-into-complacency-over-us-withdrawal-of-mcc/.
108 Nesan, K. "Tamil Nationalists Hail US 'Operation Pacific Angel' in Sri Lanka." World Socialist Web Site, September 1, 2016. Accessed September 6, 2016. https://www.wsws.org/en/articles/2016/09/01/tami-s01.html.

In December 2018, the U.S. Navy announced the setting up of a "logistic hub" in Sri Lanka to secure support, supplies and services at sea.[109] Between January 24 and 29, 2019, the Bandaranaike International Airport in Sri Lanka was reportedly "used for U.S. military planes to bring in supplies, and for aircraft aboard John C. Stennis to fly in, load, and ferry them back," in possible violation of Sri Lanka's sovereignty.[110]

Military engagement with Sri Lanka has become even more urgent for the United States since the International Court of Justice ruled in February 2019 that U.S. occupation of the Indian Ocean Chagos Islands, the site of the Diego Garcia military base, is illegal, and that the islands be handed back to Mauritius within six months. The base was established after Britain, the "illegal colonial owner" of Chagos, forcibly removed its inhabitants between 1968 and 1973. Diego Garcia is one of the United States' most important and secretive military bases and has been central in launching invasions in Iraq and Afghanistan and flying missions across Asia, including over the South China Sea.[111] If the islands go back to Mauritius and the Chagossians are allowed to return, the U.S. will require an alternative base, which could be Sri Lanka.[112] Two US-Sri Lanka bilateral agreements, the ACSA and the SOFA, appear headed in this direction.

The United States and India (currently the second largest importer of weapons in the world)[113] have agreed to draw the smaller regional states, such as Sri Lanka, the Maldives and Nepal – into their military alliance. A defense and security agreement signed in September 2020 between the United States and the Maldives giving

---

[109] Ferdinando, Shamindra. "US Sets up Logistic Hub in Sri Lanka amidst Political Chaos." *Thuppahi's Blog*, December 21, 2018. Accessed December 22, 2018. https://thuppahis.com/2018/12/21/consolidation-of-an-us-logistics-hub-in-sri-lanka-amidst-the-gross-failures-of-rajapaksa-sirisena-and-wickremasinghe-on-the-un-front/.

[110] Kurukulasuriya, Lusunda. "Duplicity and Doublespeak About the US Military Logistics Hub in Sri Lanka –." Dbsjeyaraj.com, February 4, 2019. Accessed February 10, 2019. https://dbsjeyaraj.com/dbsj/archives/62829.

[111] Vine, David. "The Truth About the U.S. Military Base at Diego Garcia,"
TruthDig, June 15, 2015. Accessed December 22, 2015. https://www.truthdig.com/articles/the-truth-about-the-u-s-military-base-at-diego-garcia/.

[112] Bandarage, Asoka. "US Military Presence and Popular Resistance in Sri Lanka," *Covert Action Magazine*, August 12, 2019, Accessed August 12, 2019. https://covertactionmagazine.com/index.php/2019/08/12/u-s-military-presence-and-popular-resistance-in-sri-lanka/. See also, Pieris, Kamalika "Yahapalana and the United States of America (Part 7)," *LankaWeb*, July 30, 2019. Accessed August 10, 2019. http://www.lankaweb.com/news/items/2019/07/30/yahapalana-and-the-united-states-of-america-part-7/.

[113] Ireland, Sophie. "These Are the World's Biggest Importers Of Major Arms." CEOWORLD magazine, June 12, 2021. Accessed August 1, 2021. https://ceoworld.biz/2021/06/12/these-are-the-worlds-biggest-importers-of-major-arms/.

greater access to the US in the Indian Ocean was welcomed by India as a check on the growing Chinese dominance in South Asia.[114] Defense analysts point out that following strengthened military and defense ties and understanding between the United States and India in December 2019, smaller states like Sri Lanka that have already gone into military pacts – such as ACSA and SOFA – may be unable to move away from them.[115]

The Acquisition and Cross Services Agreement (ACSA)

Expanding on an earlier 2007 ACSA, the U.S. Defense Department and the Sri Lankan Ministry of Defense entered into a new ACSA on August 4, 2017. This 83-page military pact is considered a "part of the grand strategy of a united military front between the U.S. and India" in the Indo-Pacific.[116] It does not have a specified expiry date and provides open-ended access for U.S. military vessels to use Sri Lanka's airports and seaports. It is designed to facilitate reciprocal logistic support between the U.S. and Sri Lanka for use 'during combined exercises … or for unforeseen circumstances or exigencies in which one of the parties may have a need for Logistic Support, Supplies and Services.'"[117] Reportedly, it allows "every single security or military apparatus in the United States access to Sri Lanka," making Sri Lanka the "main supply hub for U.S. armed forces in the Indo-Pacific region."[118] Analysts argue that if fully implemented, "it will effectively undermine the Chinese share of geopolitical control in Sri Lanka, by way of military presence in the country."[119]

---

[114] Ranjan, Amit. "United States-Maldives Defence Pact: What Lies Ahead for India?" *Institute of South Asian Studies (ISAS), National University of Singapore*, October 14, 2020. Accessed October 24, 2020. https://www.isas.nus.edu.sg/papers/united-states-%c2%admaldives-defence-pact-what-lies-ahead-for-india/.
[115] Gamage, Daya. "US-India Tie Strongest Military Knot on Indo-Pacific: Small Nations Tagged in." *Asian Tribune*, December 25, 2019. Accessed November 12, 2022. https://web.archive.org/web/20200226001718/http://asiantribune.com/node/93295.
[116] Ibid.
[117] *The Sunday Times* (Sri Lanka). "Embattled President Fighting on All Fronts," May 5, 2019. Accessed May 12, 2019. http://www.sundaytimes.lk/190505/columns/embattled-president-fighting-on-all-fronts-348051.html.
[118] Ibid.
[119] Wasantha Bandara, K. M. "Indo – American Aggression for Geopolitical Control in Sri Lanka." *Sinhalanet*, June 29, 2019. Accessed November 12, 2022. https://www.sinhalanet.net/indo-american-aggression-for-geopolitical-control-in-sri-lanka.

Sri Lanka's *Yahapalanaya* Cabinet approved ACSA 2017 hastily, under pressure from the U.S. and without careful examination or discussion. It was approved without thorough study by Sri Lankan armed forces commanders and officials, who have expressed serious reservations over some of its provisions. Similarly, ACSA was not presented to the Sri Lankan Parliament[120] and the renewed ACSA has still not been made public, despite requests for transparency by opposition political parties and the president of the Bar Association of Sri Lanka (BASL), among others. The then-Joint Opposition in Parliament, the JVP and *Yuthukama* civil society organization "strongly protested against the signing of the ACSA."[121]

The Status of Forces Agreement (SOFA)

The United States has requested that the Sri Lankan Government accept a new SOFA, expanding on the original signed in 1995. On June 30, 2019, *The Sunday Times* published the new draft SOFA governing U.S. military personnel in Sri Lanka,[122] revealing that it would provide full diplomatic immunity not only to any member of U.S. armed forces but also to its contractors and employees operating in Sri Lanka. SOFA, as drafted, would allow U.S. army personnel the right to:
- Be in any part of Sri Lanka, without restriction;
- Carry arms in uniform;
- Only need U.S. identification to enter and leave Sri Lanka; i.e., would not need passports or visas;
- Exemption from Sri Lankan law, and not being liable for criminal offenses in the country;
- Exemption from all Sri Lankan taxes; and
- Exemption from customs checking at ports of entry and exit to the island.

---

120 *The Sunday Times* (Sri Lanka). "Inside Story of How Sri Lanka Fell into the ACSA-SOFA Trap," July 7, 2019. Accessed July 12, 2019. http://www.sundaytimes.lk/190707/columns/inside-story-of-how-sri-lanka-fell-into-the-acsa-sofa-trap-357287.html.

121 Ferdinando, Shamindra. "ACSA, SOFA and 2019 Prez Poll." *LankaWeb*, June 5, 2019. https://www.lankaweb.com/news/items/2019/06/05/acsa-sofa-and-2019-prez-poll/.

122 *The Sunday Times* (Sri Lanka). "Sri Lanka's sovereignty and the US," June 30, 2019. Accessed July 4, 2019. http://www.sundaytimes.lk/190630/columns/sri-lankas-sovereignty-and-the-us-355926.html.

The U.S. Department of Defense would also be allowed to operate its own telecommunication systems in Sri Lanka without cost to the U.S. Government.[123] U.S. security companies, notably Sallyport Global, have been running ads to recruit U.S. citizens with "active TOP secret clearance" to work for U.S. defense operations in Sri Lanka.[124]

There is increasing outrage over, and opposition to, the blatant violation of Sri Lanka's independence and sovereignty that SOFA, ACSA and the MCC Compact represent. It has come from all strata and sectors of Sri Lankan society: for example, the Chief of Defense staff, the Chamber of Commerce, and the president of the BASL have all warned of the dangers SOFA poses to national interests. The Sri Lanka *Podujana Peramuna* political party and the newly formed STOP USA Campaign have organized media briefings and mass rallies calling for transparency and accountability in making international agreements.

In response to widespread opposition, the U.S. 'rebranded' SOFA as a Visiting Forces Agreement (VFA). Engaged in a social media campaign to protect the agreements, U.S. Ambassador Alaina Teplitz stated in July 2019 that the U.S. has "no intention to build a military base or establish a permanent military presence in Sri Lanka."[125] However, as Sri Lankan President's Counsel (and former Ambassador to Iran) M.M. Zuhair warns, "With SOFA in hand, the Americans do not require a military "base" in Sri Lanka ... because the whole island will be a U.S. controlled super State operating above the Sri Lankan laws and State ..."[126]

While it is known that the ACSA was signed in 2017, if and when the SOFA was signed remains a secret. The only indication that it has been signed has come from Cabinet spokesman Bandula Guawardena while discussing the termination of the MCC Compact on February 28, 2020. When asked if the government would also reconsider the ACSA and the SOFA Agreements with the U.S., Gunawardena merely said the "government would not overturn any agreements that have already

---

123 Ibid. See also, Kurukulasuriya, Lasanda. "SOFA with US Threatens Lanka's Sovereignty." *Sinhalanet*, May 31, 2019. Accessed June 3, 2019. https://www.sinhalanet.net/sofa-with-us-threatens-lankas-sovereignty.
124 *The Sunday Times* (Sri Lanka). "US security firms seek Cleared American Guards for Lanka," July 7, 2019. Accessed July 8, 2019. http://www.sundaytimes.lk/190707/columns/us-security-firms-seek-cleared-american-guards-for-lanka-357298.html.
125 *Daily Mirror* (Sri Lanka). "No Intention to Build a Military Base in SL: US," July 18, 2019. July 20, 2019. https://www.dailymirror.lk/breaking_news/No-intention-to-build-a-military-base-in-SL-US/108-171333.
126 *LankaWeb*. "Ex-Top AG's Dept Officer Warns of US Trojan Horse," July 28, 2019. Accessed July 20, 2019. https://www.lankaweb.com/news/items/2019/07/28/ex-top-ags-dept-officer-warns-of-us-trojan-horse/.

152 — Chapter 5: Geopolitical Rivalry and Political Destabilization

been signed."[127] As the Sri Lankan government has not retracted the statement, can it be assumed that a SOFA has been signed with the U.S. in secret? What has happened to accountability, transparency and democracy?

A 2019 map of United States military bases around the world lists Sri Lanka as an "unconfirmed lily pad" (Figure 5.5). Lily pads, "as in a frog jumping across a pond toward its prey," constitute a new expanding U.S. military strategy to garrison the planet with "small, secretive, inaccessible facilities with limited numbers of troops, spartan amenities, and prepositioned weaponry and supplies."[128]

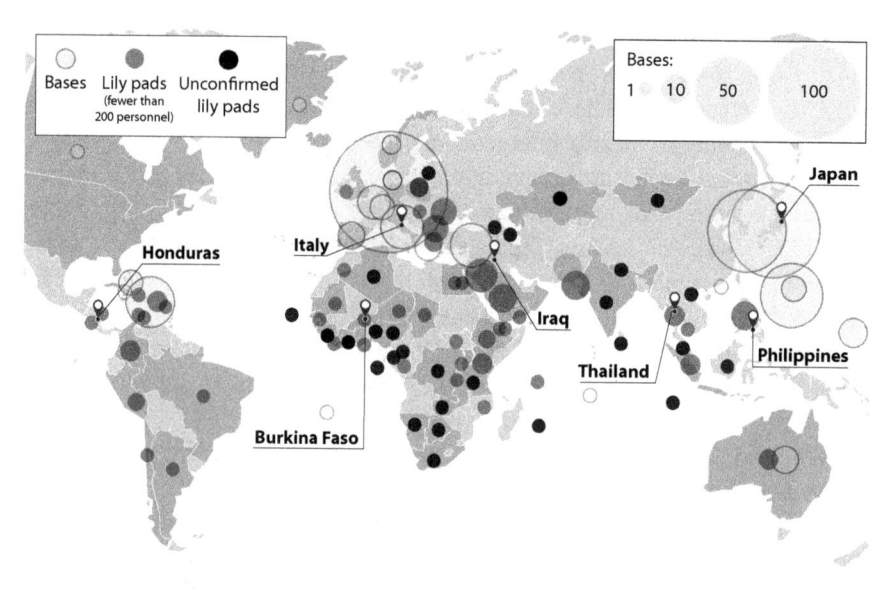

Figure 5.5: United States overseas military bases. Geographical Imaginations, https://geographicalimaginations.com/tag/us-military-bases/.

Global power intervention with the collusion of local elites is changing the socioeconomic, political and cultural landscape of Sri Lanka to the detriment of the ma-

---

[127] Kirinde, Chandani. "Govt Will Not Sign Agreement with US in Its Present Form but is Ready to Negotiate Further Says Bandula Gunawardena; When Asked About SOFA and ACSA, Cabinet Spokesman Says Govt Wont Overturn Signed Agreements." *Dbsjeyaraj.Com* (blog), February 29, 2020. Accessed February 21, 2020. https://dbsjeyaraj.com/dbsj/archives/67847.
[128] Scott-Tyson, Ann. "New US Strategy: 'lily Pad' Bases." *Christian Science Monitor*, August 10, 2004. Accessed July 20, 2022. https://www.csmonitor.com/2004/0810/p06s02-wosc.html; Vine, David. "The Lily-Pad Strategy: How the Pentagon Is Quietly Transforming Its Overseas Base Empire." *Huff-Post*, July 16, 2012. Accessed July 20, 2022. https://www.huffpost.com/entry/us-military-bases_b_1676006.

jority of her people and the natural environment. There is much antipathy towards Chinese and Indian intervention and grabbing of local resources and control of ports and infrastructure. Given the U.S. military record, there is even greater fear of U.S. political and military intervention in Sri Lanka and interference in local governance.

UNHRC Resolution

As earlier noted, in January 2015, a U.S.-backed Sri Lankan government led by President Maithripala Sirisena and Prime Minister Ranil Wickramasinghe replaced the Mahinda Rajapaksa government, which had defeated the LTTE. On October 1, 2015, the United States and the new Sri Lankan government co-sponsored a UNHRC resolution in Geneva,[129] with support from the international Tamil separatist lobby. In effect, the resolution has echoes of the Proclamation of March 2, 1815 – the Kandyan Convention – signed by the British and a faction of the Kandyan aristocracy that turned Sri Lanka into a British colony. Two hundred years later, the UNHRC resolution represents a similar strategy to turn Sri Lanka into a client state where the U.S. and the 'international community' can dictate terms for political reform and internal governance.

The controversial resolution must be understood in the broader context of neocolonialism and external political and economic hegemony. Human rights agendas such as a 'responsibility to protect' can be a basis for U.S. and Western intervention, especially in countries like Sri Lanka where ethno-religious conflicts were deliberately promoted under colonialism.[130] Based on highly contested information[131] the UNHRC Resolution calls for accountability and an international investigation of human rights violations in the final stage of the Sri Lankan armed conflict and international monitoring of transitional justice and reconciliation.[132]

---

129 "Resolution Adopted by the Human Rights Council on 1 October 2015 (A/HRC/RES/30/1)." United Nations General Assembly, October 14, 2015. Available at: https://sangam.org/wp-content/uploads/2015/12/UNHRC-Resolution-30.1-October-1-2015.pdf.

130 Bandarage, Asoka. *The Separatist Conflict in Sri Lanka: Terrorism, Ethnicity, Political Economy.* London: Routledge/Taylor & Francis Group, 2009, Chap. 9.

131 Pieris, G.H. "Encountering 'Death Counts' in the Final Phase of the Eelam War: A review article," *Colombo Telegraph*, February 9, 2014. Accessed February 22, 2014. https://www.colombotelegraph.com/wp-content/uploads/2014/02/here1.pdf.

132 Bandarage, Asoka. "Human Rights, Constitutional Reform and Devolution in Sri Lanka," *Huffington Post*, November 20, 2016. https://www.huffpost.com/entry/human-rights-constitutional-reform-and-devolution_b_58325482e4b08c963e3441a7. Waduge, Shenali. "30 Questions for UNSG & UN Human Rights Council Regarding Sri Lanka." *LankaWeb*, December 31, 2019. Accessed Janu-

Clause 16 of the resolution calls on the Sri Lankan government to devolve power on the basis of the controversial 13th Amendment to the Sri Lankan Constitution. The intention is to facilitate the transition of the country's governance structure from a unitary to a federal state.[133]

If accepted and implemented, constitutional reforms that were proposed under the Sirisena-Wickramasinghe government in response to the UNHRC resolution would allow each province in Sri Lanka to become constitutionally independent with the freedom to secede from a federal union.[134] The political fragmentation and destabilization engendered could result in several warring mini-states, greater foreign political and military intervention and increased external economic control over Sri Lanka's strategic assets and natural resources.

The requirements in the U.S.-sponsored U.N. resolution pressures the Sri Lankan government to set up war crimes courts with foreign judges and an office of missing persons comprised of activist-administrators funded by Western NGOs. This has paved the way for the UNHRC and Western governments and NGOs to interfere in Sri Lanka's judicial and security sectors, moving Sri Lanka in the direction of another failed neocolonial state.[135]

In the name of political settlement, reconciliation and human rights, the UNHRC resolution has been used to pressure the Sri Lankan government to dismiss or imprison intelligence officers and army personnel. Forty intelligence officers who were involved in the anti-LTTE military effort were put in prison apparently "without sound evidence against them."[136] When the 2019 Easter bomb attacks took place, the Sri Lankan government was said to be on the verge of repealing

---

ary 12, 2020. https://www.lankaweb.com/news/items/2019/12/31/30-questions-for-unsg-un-human-rights-council-regarding-sri-lanka-2/.

[133] "Resolution Adopted by the Human Rights Council on 1 October 2015 (A/HRC/RES/30/1)." United Nations General Assembly, October 14, 2015. Available at: https://sangam.org/wp-content/uploads/2015/12/UNHRC-Resolution-30.1-October-1-2015.pdf.

[134] Bandarage, Asoka. "Sovereignty, Territorial Integrity and Constitutional Reform in Sri Lanka," *Huffington Post*, September 27, 2017. https://www.huffpost.com/entry/sovereignty-territorial-integrity-and-constitutional_b_59cbcb67e4b028e6bb0a6746.

[135] Bandarage, Asoka. "The Easter Attacks and Geopolitical Conflict in Sri Lanka," *Critical Asian Studies*, May 16, 2019. https://criticalasianstudies.org/commentary/2019/5/16/201912-asoka-bandarage-the-easter-attacks-and-geopolitical-conflict-in-sri-lanka. Bandarage, Asoka. *The Separatist Conflict in Sri Lanka: Terrorism, Ethnicity, Political Economy.* London: Routledge/Taylor & Francis Group, 2009, Chap. 9; Kurukulasuriya, Lasanda. "How the Jihadi Terror Could Aid USA's Power Plays in the Indian Ocean." *Thuppahi's Blog*, May 6, 2019. Accessed May 10, 2019. https://thuppahis.com/2019/05/06/how-the-jihadi-terror-could-aid-usas-power-plays-in-the-indian-ocean/.

[136] Seneviratne, Kalinga. "Sri Lanka Easter Sunday Attacks Possibly More Than a Religious Conflict – OpEd." Eurasia Review, April 26, 2019. Accessed Aril 28, 2019. https://www.eurasiareview.com/26042019-sri-lanka-easter-sunday-attacks-possibly-more-than-a-religious-conflict-oped/.

the 'Prevention of Terrorism Act of 1979' under the dictates of the West and UNHRC.[137] These measures weakened Sri Lankan intelligence and security and increased the country's dependence on India and the 'international community' to maintain peace and stability.

Easter Sunday Attacks: Political Destabilization

The weakened domestic intelligence and security apparatus helped create the circumstances for the coordinated bomb attacks against Christian Churches and five-star hotels – including the Shangri La Hotel in the Chinese Port City, on Easter Sunday in April 2019. The attacks killed 259 people (including four oceanic scientists from China),[138] convulsing the entire island, and were carried out by local extremist Islamist group *National Towheed Jamaath* and claimed by Islamic State of Iraq and Syria (ISIS).[139]

Despite warnings by Buddhist monks and moderate Muslim leaders prior to the attacks, action was not taken against the spread of extremist Wahabi ideology or *National Towheed Jamaath*.[140] Conflicts were allowed to develop within the Muslim community, and between the Muslim, Buddhist, Christian and other communities. Major factors contributing to the government's failure to curb the spread of radical Islam include the economic and political power wielded by Saudi Arabia and other external forces.[141] Immediately following the Easter attacks, the Sri Lankan Prime Minister and the President called for foreign intelligence and coopera-

---

137 Ibid.
138 *Business Standard India.* "Four Chinese Scientists Killed in Sri Lanka's Suicide Bombings," May 1, 2019. Accessed May 3, 2019. https://www.business-standard.com/article/pti-stories/four-chinese-scientists-killed-in-sri-lanka-s-suicide-bombings-119050100481_1.html.
139 Bandarage, Asoka. "The Easter Attacks and Geopolitical Conflict in Sri Lanka," *Critical Asian Studies*, May 16, 2019. https://criticalasianstudies.org/commentary/2019/5/16/201912-asoka-bandarage-the-easter-attacks-and-geopolitical-conflict-in-sri-lanka.
140 Islamism on rise in Sri Lanka, 'Lanka Riots, A Wahabi Backlash?' https://www.youtube.com/embed/7L0c8oCDd4k accessed March 14, 2023.
141 Bandarage, Asoka. "Roots of Sri Lanka Attacks and a Way Forward." *Other News*, April 24, 2019 https://www.other-news.info/2019/04/roots-of-sri-lanka-attacks-and-a-way-forward/. See also Bandarage, Asoka. "Ethnic and Religious Tension in the World: A Political-Economic Perspective." In *Global Political Economy and the Wealth of Nations: Performance, Institutions, Problems, and Policies*, edited by Phillip Anthony O'Hara, 286–301. Routledge Frontiers of Political Economy. London: Routledge, 2004. Bandarage, Asoka. "Easter Attacks and Geopolitical Conflict over Sri Lanka." *Asia Times*, May 14, 2019. https://asiatimes.com/2019/05/easter-attacks-and-geopolitical-conflict-over-sri-lanka/.

tion to fight the global Islamic threat. Accordingly, the U.S. sent in teams from both the FBI and the U.S. Navy's Indo-Pacific Command.[142]

Many are the perplexing developments surrounding the Easter Sunday bomb attacks. The US Department Defense Indo Pacific Command (INDOPACOM) was involved in renovating Muslim secondary schools in the Eastern Province.[143] Just three days before the attacks, the U.S. Ambassador in Sri Lanka opened two more Muslim schools there funded by the INDOPACOM, at a cost of over US$ 940,000.[144] Indian intelligence passed on information to Sri Lankan authorities of an imminent terrorist attack on April 4. Based on this alert, Sri Lanka's police chief sent out a nationwide alert on April 11 warning of attacks on the Indian High Commission and churches. Indian intelligence again sent warnings on April 20 and about one hour before the bombs started exploding on April 21.[145]

According to a report subsequently denied by Saudi Arabia, it also knew of the impending attacks and advised its mission in Colombo five days before Easter.[146] A Sri Lankan government minister also warned his son of an impending attack. Sri Lankan President Maithripala Sirisena was out of the country and Prime Minister Ranil Wickramasinghe was out of town. The government failed to warn the public and tighten security allowing the carnage to take place.[147]

More than three years after the horrific Easter Bomb Attacks, perpetrators have not been identified. Saying that the massacre now appears to be 'a grand po-

---

[142] Bandarage, Asoka. "Easter Attacks and Geopolitical Conflict over Sri Lanka." *Asia Times*, May 14, 2019. https://asiatimes.com/2019/05/easter-attacks-and-geopolitical-conflict-over-sri-lanka/.

[143] *U.S. Indo-Pacific Command.* "USPACOM Area of Responsibility." Accessed January 3, 2023. https://www.pacom.mil/About-USINDOPACOM/USPACOM-Area-of-Responsibility/.

[144] *U.S. Embassy in Sri Lanka.* "U.S. Government Funds Renovation of Two Schools in Eastern Province," July 9, 2018. Accessed July 20, 2018. https://lk.usembassy.gov/u-s-government-funds-renovation-of-two-schools-in-eastern-province/; *Daily News.* "US Renovates Two Schools in East," February 15, 2019. Accessed February 20, 2019. https://www.dailynews.lk/2019/02/15/local/177625/us-renovates-two-schools-east. Sunday Observer. "US Helps Renovate Two Eastern Schools," April 20, 2019. Accessed April 20, 2019. https://www.sundayobserver.lk/2019/04/21/news/us-helps-renovate-two-eastern-schools.

[145] Janardhanan, Arun, and Nirupama Subramanian. "Easter Attacks: Bombers Had No Crime Record, Sri Lanka Looks at Home Terror Cell." *The Indian Express*, April 23, 2019. Accessed May 20, 2019. https://indianexpress.com/article/world/easter-attacks-bombers-had-no-crime-record-sri-lanka-looks-at-home-terror-cell-5689405/.

[146] *Tamil Guardian.* "Saudi Arabia Warned Its Colombo Envoy of Imminent Attacks," May 4, 2019. https://www.tamilguardian.com/content/saudi-arabia-warned-its-colombo-envoy-imminent-attacks.

[147] Bandarage, Asoka. "Easter Attacks and Geopolitical Conflict over Sri Lanka." *Asia Times*, May 14, 2019. https://asiatimes.com/2019/05/easter-attacks-and-geopolitical-conflict-over-sri-lanka/.

litical plot' the Head of the country's Roman Catholic Church has called on the UNHCR for an investigation.[148]

Developments surrounding the Easter terrorist attacks in Sri Lanka raise complex and challenging questions: is political destabilization a justification for U.S. intervention and establishment of military bases in strategic locations like Sri Lanka? Is extremist Wahabi ideology exported by Saudi Arabia, and the creation of Islamic terrorism in Sri Lanka and other countries, a political tool aiding the geopolitical ambitions of the U.S. and its allies in Asia?[149]

The use of terrorism and destabilization – including the intentional and unintentional creation or inflation of ethno-religious 'enemies' – is a well-established feature of imperialism and their place in the arsenal of imperialism is undeniable. For the powerful, chaos, conflict and war make money, propagate individual and national power, make client states weak and dependent and disable potential challengers to their power.[150] It is well to bear in mind the warning by Ambassador Tamara Kunanayakam:

> There is an undeclared, covert war against Sri Lanka, conducted by a Holy Alliance between Yahapalana, the US Administration, and the corporate world. The result will be more deadly than the almost 30-year-war against LTTE terror and separatism. Failure to resist will result in us losing total control over our territory, wealth, natural resources and economic activity. Our national identity and culture will be dismantled, our ability to determine domestic policy and foreign policy will be lost, and along with it, our independence and sovereignty.[151]

---

148 "Sri Lanka Cardinal Seeks UN Probe into 2019 Easter Bombings." *AlJazeera.com*, March 8, 2022. Accessed March 8, 2022. https://www.aljazeera.com/news/2022/3/8/sri-lanka-cardinal-seeks-un-probe-into-2019-easter-bombings.
149 Ibid. Fmsmnews.com. "Sri Lanka: How Saudi-Backed Terror Targeted China's Allies – FunK MainStream Media News | Alternative Liberty News Sources," May 5, 2019. Accessed May 20, 2019. https://web.archive.org/web/20220311074616/http://fmsmnews.com/sri-lanka-how-saudi-backed-terror-targeted-chinas-allies/. Koenig, Peter. "Sri Lanka, Candidate for a New NATO Base?" *Counter-Currents*, May 1, 2019. Accessed May 20, 2019. https://countercurrents.org/2019/05/sri-lanka-candidate-for-a-new-nato-base-peter-koenig.
150 Klein, Naomi. *The Shock Doctrine*. New York: Henry Holt and Co., 2010.
151 Kunanayakam, Tamara. "Creeping Neo-Liberal Stranglehold on Sri Lanka." *Thuppahi's Blog*, June 27, 2018. Accessed June 19, 2019. https://thuppahis.com/2018/06/27/creeping-neo-liberal-stranglehold-on-sri-lanka/.

Chapter 6:
Debt Colonialism, Inequality and the Crisis of Survival, 2019–2022

Gotabaya Rajapaksa, Sri Lanka's former secretary of defense who championed the military defeat of the Liberation Tigers of Tamil Eelam (LTTE) in 2009 became the President of Sri Lanka on November 16, 2019 in a resounding electoral victory. A dual citizen, he renounced his American citizenship prior to the election. The Parliamentary elections held on August 5, 2020 also gave Rajapaksa's Sri Lanka *Podujana Peramuna* (SLPP) a two-third majority in Parliament. The pro-west opposition party, United National Party (UNP) faced a landslide defeat with the UNP leader and *Yahapalanaya* ("good governance") Prime Minister Ranil Wickremesinghe failing to win a seat in parliament.[1] Gotabaya's brother, Mahinda Rajapaksa, the former President (2005–2015) was appointed Prime Minister on August 9, 2020.

Rajapaksa's massive victories were doubtlessly a response to growing concern over national security following the Easter Bomb attacks of 2019 and widespread opposition to external interventions including the 99-year lease of the Hambantota port to China; the multiple long-term economic and military treaties with the US, including the Acquisition and Cross Servicing Agreement (ACSA), the Status of Forces Agreement (SOFA) and the Millennium Challenge Corporation (MCC) Compact, and the United Nations Human Rights Commission (UNHRC) Resolution during the US-backed *Yahapalanaya* government.

The return of the Rajapaksas was certainly reflective of the fears of the public that interventions of external powers threaten to (further) subordinate their country to economic and military exploitation. Indeed, the National Joint Committee of Sri Lanka, a long-standing consortium of nationalist organizations, expressed the urgent call for the island's non-alignment in a June 2019 letter written to the then Sri Lankan Prime Minister regarding the MCC Agreement:

> [We are] committed to protect and preserve the unity and territorial integrity of our nation. We believe that Sri Lanka should follow a foreign policy of nonalignment. Due to the fact that Sri Lanka is strategically located in the Indian Ocean the country needs to remain nonaligned and refrain from getting involved in the geopolitical confrontation that is developing between

---

[1] *Parliament of Sri Lanka.* "Parliament of Sri Lanka – General Election 2020, Results," August 10, 2020. Accessed August 10, 2020. https://www.parliament.lk/election-2020/. *NewsWire.* "Breaking: Former Prime Minister Ranil Wickramasinghe Defeated," August 6, 2020. Accessed August 6, 2020. https://www.newswire.lk/2020/08/06/breaking-former-prime-minister-ranil-wickramasinghe-defeated/.

America and China, through agreements that would enable these countries to gain a foothold in Sri Lanka.[2]

From the outset, the newly elected Rajapaksa administration was under pressure from both Sri Lanka's nationalist forces that brought him into office and from external powers, especially India and the United States, who wanted to continue pursuing their own geostrategic and economic interests in Sri Lanka.[3] Local activists continued their demands to discard the MCC compact, ACSA, SOFA military agreements and UNHCR Resolution, and to also renegotiate better terms for Sri Lanka on the lease of the Hambantota port and environmental regulation of the Chinese Port City. The demands against Indian projects including the Oil Tank Farm in Trincomalee and the terminal in the Colombo port also persisted.

As noted in Chapter 5 (see page 144), following the report of a special sub-committee, the Sri Lankan government officially withdrew from the MCC Compact in 2020. However, many of the MCC policies regarding land use were continued regardless, and the government continued to welcome US economic projects into the country in line with the MCC Compact. For example, in September 2021, Sri Lanka signed an agreement with New Fortress Energy (NFE), a US-based energy infrastructure company, allowing it to build a terminal for liquefied natural gas off the coast of Colombo. The agreement enables NFE to purchase a 40 percent stake in West Coast Power who owns the *Yugadanavi* 310-megawatt power plant, a significant provider of electricity to the national grid. This deal was signed despite extensive local protests against giving a foreign company "massive controlling power on the country's national security and energy security and with guaranteed exorbitant profits."[4]

On the other hand, in February 2020 the Sri Lankan government defied US authority, and formally withdrew from the 2015 UNHRC resolution co-sponsored by

---

2 National Joint Committee. "Letter Sent by the National Joint Committee to Prime Minister Ranil Wickramasinghe on the Millennium Challenge Corporation Agreement," June 2, 2019. Available at: http://www.sundaytimes.lk/190602/sunday-times-2/the-land-belongs-to-the-people-and-all-living-beings-thou-art-only-the-guardian-of-it-351773.html.
3 Ratnayake, K. "US Official Delivers Trump's Threatening Message to Sri Lankan President." World Socialist Web Site, January 20, 2020. Accessed, January 21, 2020 https://www.wsws.org/en/articles/2020/01/20/slus-j20.html.
4 Bandarage, Asoka. "New Fortress Energy, Sri Lanka, and Planet Earth." *IDN-InDepthNews*, September 30, 2021. https://archive-2017-2022.indepthnews.info/index.php/sustainability/affordable-clean-energy/4769-new-fortress-energy-sri-lanka-and-planet-earth. Pekic, Sanja. "New Fortress to Proceed with Sri Lanka LNG." *Offshore Energy*, March 9, 2022. Visited March 23, 2022. https://www.offshore-energy.biz/new-fortress-to-proceed-with-sri-lanka-lng/#:~:text=Then%2C%20the%20Court%20fully%20dismissed,offshore%20LNG%20terminal%20near%20Colombo.

the *Yahapalanaya* government and the United States.[5] Sri Lankan Foreign Minister Dinesh Gunawardena argued that, "Constitutionally, the resolution seeks to cast upon Sri Lanka obligations that cannot be carried out within its constitutional framework and it infringes the sovereignty of the people of Sri Lanka...."[6]

The UNHRC adopted another resolution on Sri Lanka in 2021, calling for actions including UN intervention to collect evidence on human rights violations during the armed conflict with the LTTE.[7] The Sri Lankan Foreign Minister again rejected the resolution saying that it lacked authority given that the nations that had voted in favor were outnumbered by those that abstained or voted against it. He also complained that the "resolution was brought by countries supported by Western powers that want to dominate the Global South."[8]

Though widely perceived to be 'pro-China', the Rajapaksa regime in fact tried to walk a fine line between the interests of India and the United States on one side, with those of China on the other. While claiming to follow a policy of 'neutrality' in its foreign relations, the administration tried hard to allay the concerns of 'big neighbor' India, much to the chagrin of Sri Lankan nationalists. Keeping with India's 'neighborhood first' policy, Sri Lanka's then foreign secretary Jayanath Colombage declared in August 2020 that Sir Lanka had adopted a new 'India First Policy' and declared that India's strategic security interests would be protected, despite China's increasing presence in Sri Lanka.[9]

Colombage is a close associate of the Pathfinder Foundation, founded by Milinda Moragoda, who was appointed as Sri Lanka's High Commissioner Designate to India in 2021.[10] Moragoda who has held positions in both the UNP and SLFP admin-

---

[5] Francis, Krishan. "UN Rights Chief Regrets Sri Lanka Withdrawal from Resolution." *AP NEWS*, February 27, 2020. https://apnews.com/article/9d6870266f2711b1e005c72ed3e168fc.

[6] Ibid.

[7] "Resolution Adopted by the Human Rights Council on 23 March 2021: 46/1. Promoting Reconciliation, Accountability and Human Rights in Sri Lanka (A/HRC/RES/46/1)." United Nations Human Rights Council, March 26, 2021. https://reliefweb.int/report/sri-lanka/resolution-adopted-human-rights-council-23-march-2021-461-promoting-reconciliation. "OHCHR | A/HRC/51/5: Situation of Human Rights in Sri Lanka – Comprehensive Report of the United Nations High Commissioner for Human Rights." *United Nations High Commissioner for Human Rights*. Accessed January 3, 2023. https://www.ohchr.org/en/documents/reports/ahrc515-situation-human-rights-sri-lanka-comprehensive-report-united-nations-high.

[8] Ibid.

[9] *ThePrint*. "Sri Lanka to Adopt 'India First Approach' as New Policy, Says Foreign Secretary Colombage," August 26, 2020. Accessed November 18, 2021. https://theprint.in/diplomacy/sri-lanka-to-adopt-india-first-approach-as-new-policy-says-foreign-secretary-colombage/489742/.

[10] Weerasooriya, Sahan. "Lanka's First Cabinet Rank High Commissioner in India, Milinda Moragoda, Assumes Duties," August 31, 2021. http://island.lk/lankas-first-cabinet-rank-high-commissioner-in-india-milinda-moragoda-assumes-duties/. *Lanka Sara*. "Milinda Moragoda's Cabinet Rank Delet-

istrations was highly praised by the US embassy in a 2003 cable for his pro-US influence: "A 'big picture' person, Moragoda is also highly aware that the U.S. is the most powerful country in the world, and he feels that it is better that Sri Lanka recognize that fact and work within it."[11]

Ultimately, despite nationalist ideological and political leanings, the Rajapaksa regime never deviated from the neoliberal and authoritarian policies that have dominated Sri Lanka since 1977. Like the UNP and *Yahapalanaya* regimes and the Mahinda regime of 2005–2015, Rajapaksa embraced the highly vulnerable export-import economic model inherited from colonialism. Indeed, all recent regimes have essentially pursued such a 'toxic mix' of trade, privatization, financial liberalization, and a continually increasing dependency on international aid and foreign loans.[12]

Along with most of the world, where neoliberalism dominates and profit rules, such policies are centered on increased consumer spending pursuing a lifestyle financed by more and more personal and national debt with interest payments absorbing future earnings.[13]

Economic Crisis

Beholden to powerful external governments and globalized financial institutions that are the IMF and the World Bank, and internally ridden with extensive corruption, nepotism, mismanagement and ineptitude, successive Sri Lankan regimes have failed to introduce the structural changes and regulations needed for economic resilience in an increasingly volatile and competitive global economy. The current debt, economic and humanitarian crisis in Sri Lanka is not a *de novo*

---

ed in India," September 5, 2021. Accessed September 7, 2021. https://lankasara.com/news/india-mil inda/.

11 Wills, E. Ashley. "03COLOMBO909: SUBJECT: Sri Lanka's Foreign Policy: Prime Minister Tilts toward U.S., but Faces Resistance." WikiLeaks, January 22, 2012. https://web.archive.org/web/20140928080752/http://www.wikileaks.org/plusd/cables/03COLOMBO909_a.html; "WikiLeaks: GL a Pomme, Milinda a Yankee, US cable contends", Colombo Telegraph, Dec. 7, 2011. Accessed March 28, 2023. https://www.colombotelegraph.com/index.php/wikileaks-gl-a-pomme-milinda-a-yankee-us-cable-contends/

12 Kuruvilla, Benny. "Sri Lanka: A Cautionary Tale of Authoritarian Neoliberalism." *Focus on the Global South*, October 17, 2022. Accessed November 3, 2022. https://focusweb.org/sri-lanka-a-cautionary-tale-of-authoritarian-neoliberalism/.

13 Hudson, Michael. "Financial Capitalism v. Industrial Capitalism." *Michael-hudson.com*, September 3, 1998. Accessed November 02, 2022. https://michael-hudson.com/1998/09/financial-capitalism-v-industrial-capitalism/.

one without context; it is the inevitable outcome of decades-old neocolonial, debt-dependent (regressive) development policies.

Yet the amnesiac and attention-deficit narrative in the corporate media, both local and international, is that the debt crisis and the collapse of the Sri Lankan economy in 2022 is due to a confluence of the 2019 Easter bomb attacks, COVID-19 pandemic, the Ukraine War, Chinese loans and widespread corruption and mismanagement in the Rajapaksa administration.[14] Indeed, the US Foreign Relations Committee proposed a resolution adopted in the US Senate on September 14, 2022 that attributes Sri Lanka's crisis to poor governance and economic policy under the Rajapaksas and "predatory loans from the People's Republic of China as part of its debt trap diplomacy."[15]

Here we will discuss factors contributing to the economic crisis, including data, where possible.

The 2019 Easter bomb attacks and the COVID-19 crisis certainly contributed to a sharp drop in the highly unreliable tourist industry. Earnings from tourism, the second largest foreign exchange earner for the Sri Lankan economy, decreased from $4.4 billion in 2018 (before the Easter attacks) to $682 million in 2020 (Figure 6.1). Total employment in tourism, which stood at approximately 403,000 in 2019 is believed to have also decreased drastically.[16]

When COVID-19 cases were first reported in Sri Lanka in March 2020, tourist arrivals were suspended. An island-wide curfew was put in place and the first wave was successfully contained. Unfortunately, there was a rapid increase in cases at the onset of the second wave of infections, and the government resorted to "targeted lockdowns instead of island wide curfews to minimize the impact on economic activity."[17]

However, as the World Bank pointed out, "The COVID-19 pandemic led to Sri Lanka's worst growth performance on record, as is the case for many countries

---

14 Ibid. https://www.youtube.com/watch?v=BT5DI0tyY-A.
15 Menendez, Mr., Mr. Durbin, Mr. Leahy, and Mr. Booker. "117TH Congress, 2nd Session, Senate Resolution Expressing the Sense of the Senate in Support of the Peaceful Democratic and Economic Aspirations of the Sri Lankan People." United States Senate Committee on Foreign Relations, n.d. https://www.foreign.senate.gov/imo/media/doc/sri_lanka_resolution.pdf.
16 Bhowmick, Soumya. "How Tourism in Sri Lanka Went Downhill: Causes and Consequences." *Observer Research Foundation*, June 22, 2022. Accessed June 30, 2022. https://www.orfonline.org/expert-speak/how-tourism-in-sri-lanka-went-downhill/. *Outlook India*. "Sri Lanka Economic Crisis: Lucrative Tourism Industry Bears Major Brunt," July 15, 2022. https://www.outlookindia.com/business/sri-lanka-economic-crisis-lucrative-tourism-industry-bears-major-brunt-news-209545.
17 World Bank. *Sri Lanka Development Update 2021: Economic and Poverty Impact of COVID-19*. World Bank, 2021. https://doi.org/10.1596/35833.

Economic Crisis — 163

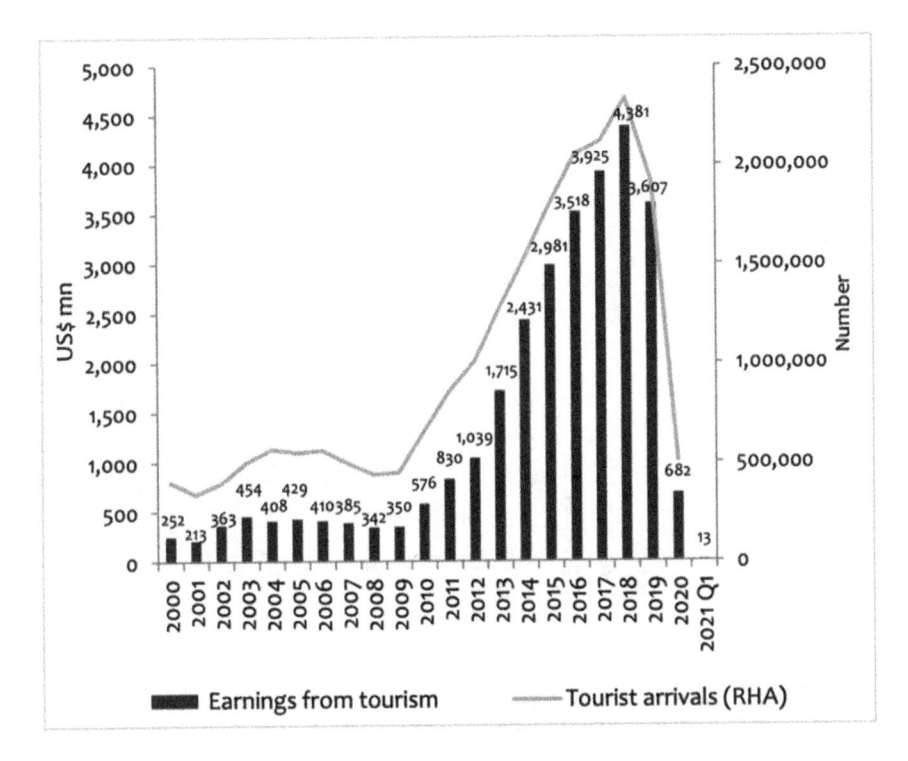

Figure 6.1: Tourist Arrivals and Earnings from Tourism: 2000–2021. Source: Central Bank of Sri Lanka https://www.cbsl.gov.lk/sites/default/files/cbslweb_documents/statistics/mecpac/Chart_Pack_Q1_2021_e.pdf.

around the world."[18] The economy contracted by 3.6 percent in 2020 due to large decreases in construction, manufacturing, tourism, and transport.[19] The acute decline in production in the export-oriented industries such as garment manufacturing and tea, rubber and coconut agriculture, caused significant reductions in export revenue and household income.[20] Imports quickly outpaced exports, widening the trade deficit and contributing to a decline in the Central Banks's foreign reserves from approximately US$ 8 billion in February 2020 to less than US$

---

18 Ibid.
19 Ibid.
20 Ananthavinayagan, Thamil Venthan. "Sri Lanka and the Neocolonialism of the IMF." *The Diplomat*, March 31, 2022. Accessed October 05, 2022. https://thediplomat.com/2022/03/sri-lanka-and-the-neocolonialism-of-the-imf/; *Macrotrends*. "Sri Lanka Trade Balance 1960–2023." Accessed January 3, 2023. https://www.macrotrends.net/countries/LKA/sri-lanka/trade-balance-deficit.

2 billion in August 2022.[21] Many Sri Lankan migrant workers abroad lost jobs and worker remittances – the biggest source of foreign exchange for the economy – declined by more than 20 percent between 2020 and 2021 (Figure 6.2).[22]

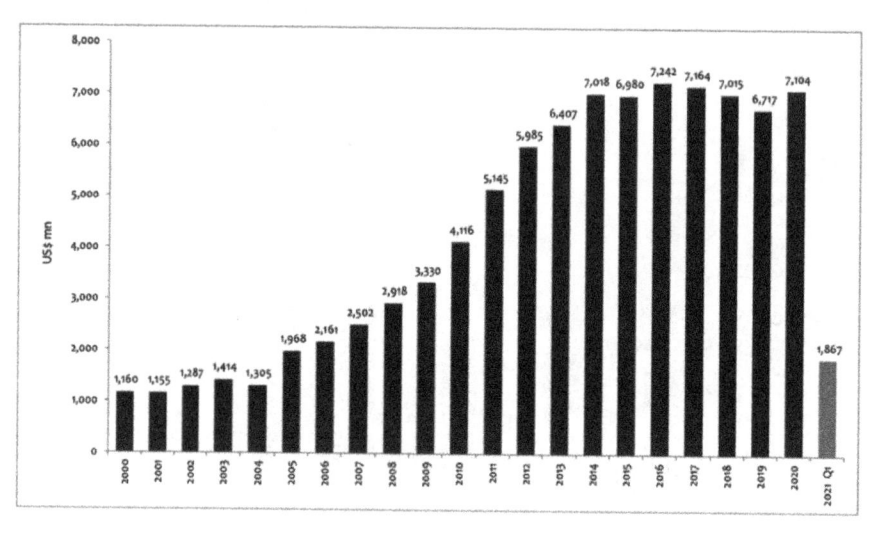

Figure 6.2: Sri Lanka Workers' Remittances: 2000–2021. Source: Central Bank of Sri Lanka, https://www.cbsl.gov.lk/sites/default/files/cbslweb_documents/statistics/mecpac/Chart_Pack_Q1_2021_e.pdf.

Government policies exacerbated the losses in domestic and external revenue. Soon after Gotabaya Rajapaksa's inauguration, in 2019 and 2020, the government introduced deep tax cuts to fulfill an election promise just a few months before the COVID-19 crisis hit. Many direct and indirect taxes were reduced, including the Value Added Tax (VAT), which was reduced from 15 to 8 percent, and the Telecommunication Tariff, which was reduced by 25 percent. This decreased Sri Lan-

---

21 "Spreadsheet: Data Template on International Reserves/Foreign Currency Liquidity." *Central Bank of Sri Lanka.* Accessed November 24, 2022. https://www.cbsl.gov.lk/sites/default/files/cbslweb_documents/statistics/sheets/table2.15.1-20220930_e.xlsx; Quiggin, John, and Thilak Mallawaarachchi. "How Did Sri Lanka Run out of Money? 5 Graphs That Explain Its Economic Crisis." The Conversation. July 26, 2022. Accessed August 3, 2022. http://theconversation.com/how-did-sri-lanka-run-out-of-money-5-graphs-that-explain-its-economic-crisis-187352.

22 Kuruvilla, Benny. "Sri Lanka: A Cautionary Tale of Authoritarian Neoliberalism." *Focus on the Global South,* October 17, 2022. Accessed November 3, 2022. https://focusweb.org/sri-lanka-a-cautionary-tale-of-authoritarian-neoliberalism/. "Sri Lanka: Macroeconomic Developments in Charts: First Quarter 2021." *Central Bank of Sri Lanka, Economic Research Department,* n.d. https://www.cbsl.gov.lk/sites/default/files/cbslweb_documents/statistics/mecpac/Chart_Pack_Q1_2021_e.pdf.

ka's already low tax revenue to GDP ratio from 11.6 percent in 2019 to an abysmal 7.7 percent in 2021, causing a significant loss of government revenue.[23]

Another major policy failure was the sudden ban on imported agrochemicals. The 'revolution' in fertilizer use that Gotabaya Rajapaksa had promised in his election manifesto was expected to take place over a 10-year period. However, in April 2021, he announced an immediate ban on the importation of synthetic fertilizers, justifying it on health and environmental grounds and ignoring the warnings of professional experts.[24] The actual reason for the ban was the desire to save approximately US$ 400 million that Sri Lanka was spending annually on imported synthetic fertilizers and pesticides.[25]

As predicted, the impact of the sudden ban was disastrous for agricultural production, farmer income and food availability. Sri Lankan farmers who had been induced to depend on imported agrochemicals instead of local alternatives for decades, could not suddenly shift to organic farming. Given widespread use of genetically modified seeds requiring use of agrochemicals, in the sudden absence of imported fertilizer and pesticides, agricultural output decreased drastically. Paddy productivity dropped 45 percent, maize output plummeted significantly, and tea production also dropped by 20 percent in 2021–2022.[26] Rice prices skyrocketed, and the government had to import large quantities from other countries adding to the already high import bill. The government withdrew the policy within six months, but in the face of surging commodity prices and stratospheric inflation (Figure 6.3), people's trust in the government was greatly damaged.[27]

---

23 Bhowmick, Soumya. "Understanding the Economic Issues in Sri Lanka's Current Debacle." *ORF Occasional Paper No. 357*. Observer Research Foundation, June 2022. https://www.orfonline.org/wp-content/uploads/2022/06/ORF_OccasionalPaper_357_SriLanka.pdf.

24 Perera, Boniface. "Banning Chemical Fertiliser – Right Thing, Wrong Line." *Daily Mirror* (Sri Lanka), June 21, 2021. Accessed June 22, 2021. https://www.dailymirror.lk/news-features/BANNING-CHEMICAL-FERTILISER-RIGHT-THING-WRONG-LINE/131-214481.

25 Bhowmick, Soumya. "Revisiting Sri Lanka's Abrupt Shift to Organic Farming." *Asia Times*, October 17, 2022. https://asiatimes.com/2022/10/revisiting-sri-lankas-abrupt-shift-to-organic-farming/.

26 Ibid. Dias, Sunimalee. "Fertiliser Policy Worries Ceylon Tea Buyers." *Historyofceylontea.com*, July 11, 2021. https://www.historyofceylontea.com/ceylon-publications/ceylon-tea-articles/fertiliser-policy-worries-ceylon-tea-buyers.html; Claire Robinson, GMO: Myths and Facts, February 2019, https://www.soilassociation.org/media/22505/gmo_myths-and-facts_online.pdf accessed March 20, 2023.

27 Ibid. Kuruvilla, Benny. "Sri Lanka: A Cautionary Tale of Authoritarian Neoliberalism." *Focus on the Global South*, October 17, 2022. Accessed November 3, 2022. https://focusweb.org/sri-lanka-a-cautionary-tale-of-authoritarian-neoliberalism/; *Department of Census and Statistics*. "Inflation and Prices." Accessed January 3, 2023. http://www.statistics.gov.lk/InflationAndPrices/StaticalInformation/MonthlyNCPI.

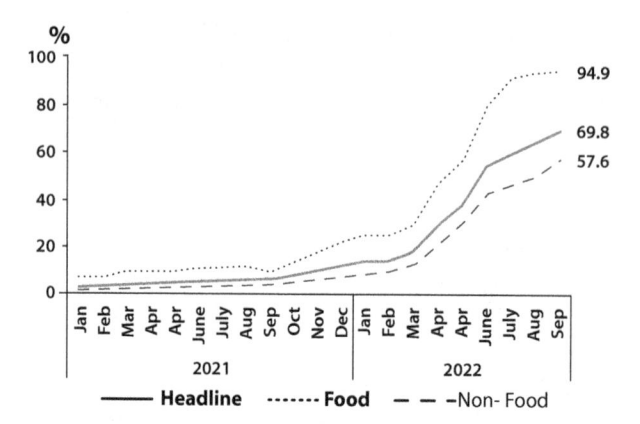

Figure 6.3: Colombo Consumer Price Index (year on year % change). Source: Central Bank of Sri Lanka; http://www.cbsl.gov.lk/sites/default/files/cbslweb_documents/press/pr/press_20220930_infla tion_in_september_2022_ccpi_e.pdf.

Yet another major policy failure of the Gotabaya Rajapaksa administration was the 'deliberate choice' to continue making debt service payments to foreign creditors without using the limited currency reserves to pay for essential imports. The president and his brothers, the Finance Ministers, Mahinda Rajapaksa (August 2019–July 2021) and Basil Rajapaksa (July 2021–April 2022) and top government officials made this decision ignoring worsening economic realities and the advice of many Sri Lankan economists.[28] As financial analyst Umesh Moramudali subsequently observed:

> Even as late as January 2022, while traders were struggling to import essential items, the government decided to repay a $500 million ISB that had matured that month. For context, by January 2022, Sri Lanka's remaining foreign currency reserves were a little over $1 billion. The government decided to use almost half of its remaining reserves to settle the ISB, turning a blind eye to growing shortages of food, medicine, and cooking gas.[29]

---

28 Moramudali, Umesh. "Sri Lanka's Story of Sovereign Default." *The Diplomat*, September 1, 2022. Accessed September 12, 2022. https://thediplomat.com/2022/08/sri-lankas-story-of-sovereign-default/; Jayasinghe, Chanka. "Sri Lanka Stopped from Going to IMF by Attygalle, Jayasundera, Cabraal: Finance Minister." *EconomyNext*, April 12, 2022. Accessed September 12, 2022. https://economynext.com/sri-lanka-stopped-from-going-to-imf-by-attygalle-jayasundera-cabraal-finance-minister-92977; Jayasinghe, Uditha. "Explainer: Sri Lanka on the Edge as Debt Burden Mounts." *Reuters*, January 17, 2022, sec. Rates & Bonds. Accessed September 12, 2022. https://www.reuters.com/markets/rates-bonds/sri-lanka-edge-debt-burden-mounts-2022-01-17/.
29 Moramudali, Umesh. "Sri Lanka's Story of Sovereign Default." *The Diplomat*, September 1, 2022. Accessed September 12, 2022. https://thediplomat.com/2022/08/sri-lankas-story-of-sovereign-default/.

The closest advisors of President Rajapaksa, the Secretary to the Treasury S.R. Artigala, Central Bank governor Ajith Nivard Carbral and president's secretary P.B. Jayasundara have also been blamed for delaying going to the IMF for help when almost all the Ministers of the Cabinet supported doing so at earlier points in the financial meltdown.[30]

Already facing an unprecedented foreign exchange crisis, the Sri Lankan economy further suffered the spillover effects of the war in Ukraine. US led sanctions on oil producing countries, Russia, Iran and Venezuela and speculation in commodity markets led to escalating global commodity prices of energy and food around the world.[31] Lacking foreign currency to import essentials, in March 2022, Sri Lanka fell into a severe shortage of fuel as well as food, medicines, etc. making life miserable in the country.[32] As fuel shortages caused loss of power to the national grid, the state-owned Ceylon Electricity Board imposed regular and extensive power blackouts throughout the country.[33]

Food inflation ballooned to 95 percent in August 2022 in Colombo (Figure 6.3) and hunger, malnutrition and poverty became rampant across the country. In July 2022, the NGO Save The Children reported that "Sri Lanka's 'economic crisis is rapidly becoming a full-blown humanitarian emergency" and that "families are being forced into increasingly desperate measures to survive."[34] In September 2022, the United Nations World Food Program reported:

> 6.3 million people or, over 30 percent of Sri Lanka's population, are 'food insecure' and require humanitarian assistance. Of these, around 5.3 million people are either reducing meals or skipping meals, and at least 65,600 people are severely food insecure. …About 6.7 million people are not consuming an adequate diet and 5.3 million people are reducing the num-

---

30 Jayasinghe, Chanka. "Sri Lanka Stopped from Going to IMF by Attygalle, Jayasundera, Cabraal: Finance Minister." *EconomyNext*, April 12, 2022. Accessed September 12, 2022. https://economynext.com/sri-lanka-stopped-from-going-to-imf-by-attygalle-jayasundera-cabraal-finance-minister-92977.
31 Abeyratne, Sirimal. "Russia-Ukraine War Impact on Sri Lanka." *Sunday Times* (Sri Lanka), March 13, 2022. https://www.sundaytimes.lk/220313/business-times/russia-ukraine-war-impact-on-sri-lanka-476029.html.
32 *Global Voices*. "Sri Lanka in Crisis · Global Voices." Accessed January 3, 2023. https://globalvoices.org/special/sri-lanka-in-crisis/.
33 Aljazeera.com. "Sri Lanka Imposes Rolling Power Cuts as Economic Crisis Worsens," February 23, 2022. Accessed February 24, 2022. https://www.aljazeera.com/news/2022/2/23/sri-lanka-rolling-power-cuts-economic-crisis.
34 *Save the Children International*. "Sri Lanka: More than Two Thirds of Families Struggling to Feed Themselves as Economic Crisis Wipes out Incomes," July 6, 2022. Accessed November 22, 2022. https://www.savethechildren.net/news/sri-lanka-more-two-thirds-families-struggling-feed-themselves-economic-crisis-wipes-out-incomes.

ber of meals partaken during the day while more than 60 percent of families are eating less, cheaper, and less nutritious food.[35]

Despite the gravity of the above examples, Sri Lanka's economic crisis is not entirely due to the corruption and mismanagement of the Rajapaksas, *Yahapalanaya* and previous regimes. As discussed earlier, one must also see the crisis in context of the broader social, political, cultural, and specifically, the economic changes of colonial and neoliberal policies that the island was led to adopt. These policies made Sri Lanka, along with most countries in the Global South, net food importers, with no alternative sources of food. Similar approaches to other essential commodities, namely medicine and fuel, have left the island extremely vulnerable by its dependency on importation, particularly during sudden global price hikes and foreign currency shortages.[36] Emergency financial assistance received from Bangladesh, Japan, China and $3 billion in loans, credit lines and credit swaps from India since January 2022 helped to temporarily ease the situation.[37]

Debt Crisis

The crux of the current economic crisis, the worst ever in Sri Lanka since independence in 1948, is the scarcity of foreign currency.[38] In the past, Sri Lanka has taken pride in paying its external debt service obligations on time which it was able to do by taking more loans.[39] However, the country lost access to international financial markets in 2020, after several downgrades by credit rating agencies in-

---

[35] *Care.org.* "Food Security and Nutrition Crisis in Sri Lanka." September 2022. Accessed January 3, 2023. https://www.care.org/wp-content/uploads/2022/09/Food-Nutrition-Crisis-in-SL-Situation-Update-September2022.pdf.
[36] Ghosh, Jayati, and C. P. ChandrasekharJayati. "A Food Crisis Not of Their Making." *The Hindu Business Line*, September 19, 2022. Accessed September 23, 2022. https://www.thehindubusinessline.com/opinion/a-food-crisis-not-of-their-making/article65911286.ece.
[37] *Outlook India.* "India Extended Assistance Of Over $3 Billion To Debt-Ridden Sri Lanka In 2022," May 3, 2022. Accessed May 12, 2022. https://www.outlookindia.com/business/india-extended-assistance-of-over-3-billion-to-debt-ridden-sri-lanka-in-2022-news-194699.
[38] *The Economic Times.* "Sri Lanka to Repay Debts after Six Months: Governor," May 19, 2022. Accessed May 22, 2022. https://economictimes.indiatimes.com/news/international/world-news/sri-lanka-to-repay-debts-after-six-months-governor/articleshow/91662528.cms?utm_source=contentofinterest&utm_medium=text&utm_campaign=cppst.
[39] *Central Bank of Sri Lanka.* "International Sovereign Bond Issuances of the Government of Sri Lanka," October 31, 2018. Accessed November 12, 2022. https://www.cbsl.gov.lk/en/news/international-sovereign-bond-issuances-of-the-government-of-sri-lanka.

cluding Moody's and Fitch in 2021 and 2022, respectively, making it difficult to borrow more.[40]

Facing a dire situation, the Central Bank of Sri Lanka under its Governor W.D. Lakshman (2019–2021) printed large amounts of money and the Sri Lanka Rupee was floated in March 2022, with the hope of settling its rapid depreciation.[41] Instead, there was a massive depreciation of the Sri Lankan Rupee against the US dollar, 77.8 percent between January and July 2022 making it the world's worst performing currency.[42] Sri Lanka's official reserves dropped to less than US$ 400 million (without counting a currency swap with China for US$ 1.5 billion) in June 2022.[43]

The foreign exchange shortage, inflation and the suffering of the people intensified. In the midst of these worsening economic and social realities, Sri Lanka announced an external debt service suspension on April 12th, 2022 – a default, for the first time in its history.

The Sri Lanka government rejected bilateral financing options available at the time, including Chinese loans of USD 2.5 billion which could have covered commitments.[44] As such, suspicions remain that the default was deliberately 'staged' for geopolitical reasons.[45]

---

[40] Bhat, Swati. "UPDATE 2-Moody's Cuts Sri Lanka's Debt Rating; Govt Says Action Ill-Timed." *Reuters*, October 28, 2021, sec. Bonds News. Accessed November 12, 2022. https://www.reuters.com/article/sri-lanka-ratings-moodys-idUSL4N2RO3D1; *Publicfinance.lk*. "Sri Lanka's Fitch Credit Rating Has Been Downgraded 7 Times during the Last 7-Years (May 2015 – May 2022)," May 25, 2022. Accessed 13 November 2022. https://web.archive.org/web/20220704063120/https://www.publicfinance.lk/en/topics/sri-lanka-s-fitch-credit-rating-has-been-downgraded-7-times-during-the-last-7-years-may-2015-may-2022-1653451955#:~:text=Sri%20Lanka%E2%80%99s%20Fitch%20Credit%20Rating%20has%20been%20downgraded,its%20regional%20peers%20have%20maintained%20their%20credit%20ratings.

[41] Jayasinghe, Chanka. "Sri Lanka Stopped from Going to IMF by Attygalle, Jayasundera, Cabraal: Finance Minister." *EconomyNext*, April 12, 2022. Accessed September 12, 2022. https://economynext.com/sri-lanka-stopped-from-going-to-imf-by-attygalle-jayasundera-cabraal-finance-minister-92977.

[42] World Bank. "The World Bank In Sri Lanka Overview." Text/HTML, October 6, 2022. https://www.worldbank.org/en/country/srilanka/overview.

[43] Ibid.

[44] "China 'sad' that Sri Lanka went to IMF and defaulted: envoy", EconomyNext, April 25, 2022. https://economynext.com/china-sad-that-sri-lanka-went-to-imf-and-defaulted-envoy-93468/ accessed March 15, 2023; "Shock treatment in order to meet IMF deadline", Sunday Times, February 19, 2023. https://www.sundaytimes.lk/230219/columns/shock-treatment-in-order-to-meet-imf-deadline-512393.html accessed March 15, 2023.

[45] Rajasingham-Senanayake, Darini. "A Staged Default: Sri Lanka's Sovereign Bond Debt Trap and IMF's Spring Meetings Amid Hybrid Cold War." IDN-InDepthNews, April 24, 2022. https://archive-2017-2022.indepthnews.info/index.php/the-world/asia-pacific/5249-astaged-default-sri-lanka-s-sovereign-bond-debt-trap-and-imf-s-spring-meetings-amid-hybrid-coldwar-part-1. Accessed May 15, 2022;

Having defaulted and on the brink of bankruptcy, the government hired leading financial and legal advisory firms Lazard and Clifford Chance, for a fee of US$ 5.6 million, to support debt restructuring by the IMF.[46]

Former chief economist of the World Bank, Joseph Stiglitz has identified what he terms 'four steps to damnation' in the IMF assistance strategy for poor countries: privatization of state assets; capital market liberalization; market-based pricing (leading to 'IMF riots'); and free trade.[47]

Both in Sri Lanka and around the world, IMF structural adjustment entails cutbacks of social safety nets and alignment of local economic policy with US and other Western interests, to the further detriment of local working people's standard of living and inevitably leading to more wealth disparity and repeat debt crises.[48]

A History of Debt

Dwindling external receipts, mounting external debt and debt service ratios relative to revenue have been endemic to Sri Lanka's economy since the early years of Independence (Table 3.3, page 78). The country's total foreign debt steadily increased from around US$ 435 million in 1970 to US$ 1.1 billion in 1977, rising sharply after the end of the armed conflict from $US 19.5 in 2009 to US$ 50 billion in 2022 (Figure 6.4).[49]

What happened in 2022, it must be acknowledged, is a magnification of the same vicious cycle that has beleaguered Sri Lanka for decades: a colonially imposed, externally dependent export-import economy; worsening terms of trade; a foreign exchange shortage; debt crisis; food, fuel and other shortages; external

---

Waduge, Shenali, 'IMF puts countries into debt, poverty & inequality but who in Sri Lanka wants IMF – why?', March 18, 2023 https://mail.google.com/mail/u/0/?tab=rm&ogbl#inbox/WhctKKXwqkf RCFXxJKZKdpZjLzTMSzRFxTVMfHsppZWQmhWLWDLtqspwKDwdFvzqTJbWCmb accessed March 20, 2023.

[46] *Business Standard.* "Sri Lanka Picks Lazard, Clifford Chance as Advisers for Debt Restructuring," May 24, 2022. https://www.business-standard.com/article/international/sri-lanka-picks-lazard-clifford-chance-as-advisers-for-debt-restructuring-122052400610_1.html.

[47] Gregory Palast, 'IMF's four steps to damnation' Guardian, April 29, 2001. https://www.theguardian.com/business/2001/apr/29/business.mbas accessed March 15, 2023; see also, Joseph Stiglitz, Globalization and Discontents, New York: W.W.Norton, 2003.

[48] 'IMF and World Bank', Development Economics, http://www.sanandres.esc.edu.ar/secondary/economics20packs/development_economics/page_61.htm accessed March 16, 2023.

[49] Karunatilake, H. N. S. *The Accelerated Mahaweli Programme and Its Impact.* Centre for Demographic and Socio-Economic Studies, 1988, 178–179.

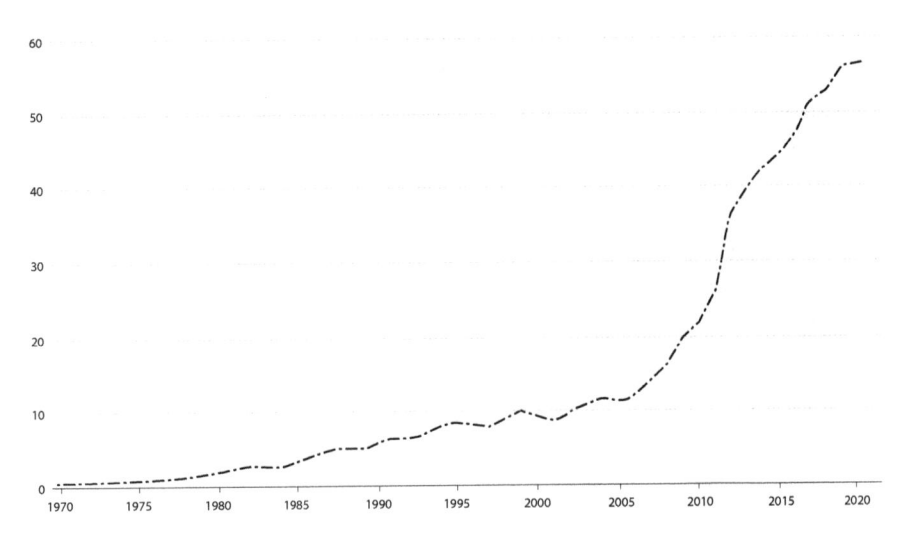

Figure 6.4: Sri Lanka Foreign Debt, 1970–2020. Source: World Bank, https://data.worldbank.org/indicator/DT.DOD.DECT.CD?locations=LK&name_desc=true

political pressure; IMF bail-out and structural adjustment. Faced with balance of payments crises, the country has sought IMF assistance 16 times prior to 2022 (Table 1.1; page 2).

According to World Bank estimates, in January 2022, Sri Lanka owed $15 billion in bonds, mostly dollar-denominated, out of a total of about $50 billion in long-term debt. The country needs $7 billion to $8.6 billion to service its debt load in 2022, whereas it had just US$ 1.6 billion in reserves at the end of March 2022.[50]

Western analysts attribute Sri Lanka's debt crisis largely to loans and a 'debt trap' of China. However, 81 percent of Sri Lanka's external debt is owed to US and European financial institutions and Western allies, Japan and India.[51] China, Sri Lanka's largest bilateral lender, owns about 10 percent of its total foreign debt, followed by Japan, which also owns 10 percent and 2 percent by India. The multilateral Asian Development Bank (ADB) and the World Bank own 13 percent and 9 percent of Sri Lanka's foreign debt respectively (Figure 6.5).

---

[50] Stubbington, Tommy, and Benjamin Parkin. "Sri Lanka on Brink of Sovereign Bond Default, Warn Investors." *Financial Times*, February 8, 2022. Accessed February 10, 2022. https://www.ft.com/content/09e1159f-9c45-4379-b862-98cb5e30a4da; *World Bank*. "International Debt Statistics Online Tables." Accessed January 3, 2023. https://datatopics.worldbank.org/debt/ids/country/LKA.

[51] Norton, Ben. "Real Debt Trap: Sri Lanka Owes Vast Majority to West, Not China." *Multipolarista*, July 11, 2022. Accessed November 10, 2022. https://multipolarista.com/2022/07/11/debt-trap-sri-lanka-west-china/.

About half of Sri Lanka's total foreign debt (47.5 percent) is market borrowings mostly through US- and EU-based ISBs.[52] Asset managers BlackRock and Ashmore Group along with Fidelity, T Rowe Price and TIAA, are among Sri Lanka's main ISB creditors.[53]

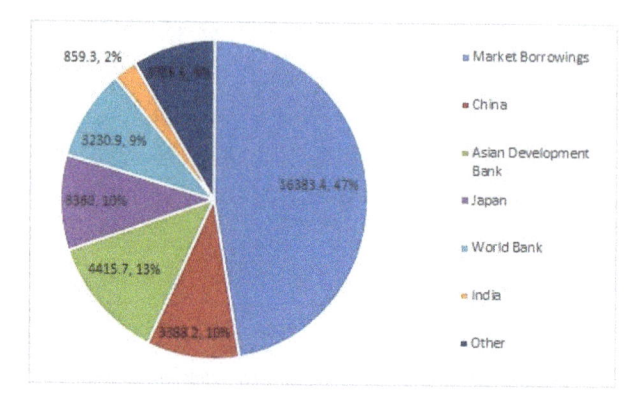

Figure 6.5: Sri Lankan debt stock by major lenders, US$ million. Source: Sri Lanka Department of External Resources, http://www.erd.gov.lk/index.php?option=com_content&view=article&id=102&Itemid=308&lang=en

International Sovereign Bonds

Sri Lanka's severe foreign exchange crisis has brought into focus its issuance of International Sovereign Bonds (ISB). Sri Lanka's first ISB issued in 2007 and two others issued in 2014 were settled through further borrowing.[54] In September 2022 there were outstanding ISBS with a combined total of US$ 11.5 billion, approximate-

---

[52] Vizcaino, Maria Elena, and Sydney Maki. "Fidelity Among Big Sri Lankan Debt Holders Staring Down Risk." *Bloomberg*, April 5, 2022. Accessed April 12, 2022. https://www.bloomberg.com/news/articles/2022-04-05/fidelity-among-big-sri-lankan-debt-holders-staring-down-turmoil.

[53] Campos, Rodrigo, and Jorgelina do Rosario. "Advisers Seek Role with Creditors for $12 Bln Sri Lanka Debt Revamp." Reuters, April 22, 2022, sec. European Currency News. https://www.reuters.com/article/sri-lanka-crisis-debt-talks-idUSL5N2WK371. Vizcaino, Maria Elena, and Sydney Maki. "Fidelity Among Big Sri Lankan Debt Holders Staring Down Risk." *Bloomberg*, April 5, 2022. Accessed April 12, 2022. https://www.bloomberg.com/news/articles/2022-04-05/fidelity-among-big-sri-lankan-debt-holders-staring-down-turmoil.

[54] *Central Bank of Sri Lanka.* "International Sovereign Bond Issuances of the Government of Sri Lanka," October 31, 2018. Accessed November 12, 2022. https://www.cbsl.gov.lk/en/news/international-sovereign-bond-issuances-of-the-government-of-sri-lanka.

ly 36 percent of the country's current foreign debt and the biggest source of foreign funding for Sri Lanka (Table 6.1).[55]

All the currently outstanding ISBs were issued during the *Yahapalanya* regime between 2015 and 2019 and those ISBs will be maturing every year from 2023 to 2030. It is estimated that during the 2020–2025 period, about 50 percent of all Sri Lanka's foreign repayments will be for repaying those ISBs.[56]

Ever since independence, Sri Lanka has been dependent on concessionary loans, mostly from the World Bank, the ADB and the Japanese government to finance development. As per capita income grew, the World Bank classified Sri Lanka as a middle-income country in 1997 and an upper-middle-income country in July 2019.[57] However, as a middle-income country Sri Lanka lost access to concessionary loans provided by the multilateral institutions and became increasingly dependent on ISBs. Thus, non-concessionary borrowing which was only 3 percent in 2005, increased to nearly 50 percent by 2020.[58]

Concessionary loans from multilateral agencies like the IMF, the World Bank and the ADB have low interest rates ranging from 0.25 percent, 2 to 3 percent but they are also subject to "strict conditions like reducing budget deficits, public expenditure, welfare schemes or privatizing loss-making state companies."[59] In contrast, ISBs have few conditions but high interest rates, 5.7 to 7.85 percent and relatively short maturation periods of 5–10 years.[60] Defaulting on ISB payments has subjected beleaguered Sri Lanka to evermore external economic and political pressure including legal battles.

In June 2022, following Sri Lanka's historic default, Hamilton Reserve Bank, based in St. Kitts and Nevis, which holds more than $250 million of Sri Lanka's ISBs due July 25, 2022 filed a suit in New York federal court seeking full repayment of principal and interest. Hamilton Reserve's legal complaint on behalf of the group of creditors holding Sri Lankan ISBs reveals the nature of the relationship

---

55 Jayasinghe, Uditha. "Explainer: Sri Lanka on the Edge as Debt Burden Mounts." *Reuters*, January 17, 2022, sec. Rates & Bonds. Accessed September 12, 2022. https://www.reuters.com/markets/rates-bonds/sri-lanka-edge-debt-burden-mounts-2022-01-17/.
56 Moramudali, Umesh. "Sri Lanka's Story of Sovereign Default." *The Diplomat*, September 1, 2022. Accessed September 12, 2022. https://thediplomat.com/2022/08/sri-lankas-story-of-sovereign-default/.
57 https://www.dailymirror.lk/business/Sri-Lanka-is-and-will-remain-a-middle-income-country/215-246952.
58 Moramudali, Umesh. "Sri Lanka's Story of Sovereign Default." *The Diplomat*, September 1, 2022. Accessed September 12, 2022. https://thediplomat.com/2022/08/sri-lankas-story-of-sovereign-default/.
59 *The Sunday Times* (Sri Lanka). "ISB Repayment Headaches Totalling $14 Billion Stretch until 2030," July 11, 2021. Accessed July 13, 2021. http://www.sundaytimes.lk/210711/business-times/isb-repayment-headaches-totalling-14-billion-stretch-until-2030-448828.html.
60 Ibid.

Table 6.1: Details of outstanding international sovereign bonds as of September 30, 2022.

Maturity Date	Issue Date	Series Name	ISIN for the Rule 144 A Global Bonds	ISIN for the Regulation S Global Bonds	Coupon Rate (%)	Amount (US$ Mn)
18 April 2023	18 April 2018	SRILAN 5.750 04/23	US85227SAV88	USY8137FAK40	5.7500	1,250.00
14 March 2024	14 March 2019	SRILAN 6.850 03/24	US85227SAY28	USY8137FAN88	6.8500	1,000.00
28 June 2024	28 June 2019	SRILAN 6.350 06/24	US85227SBA33	USY8137FAQ10	6.3500	500.00
3 June 2025	3 June 2015	SRILAN 6.125 06/25	US85227SAN62	USY8137FAC24	6.1250	650.00
3 November 2025	3 November 2015	SRILAN 6.850 11/25	US85227SAQ93	USY8137FAE89	6.8500	1,500.00
18 July 2026	18 July 2016	SRILAN 6.825 07/26	US85227SAR76	USY8137FAF54	6.8250	1,000.00
11 May 2027	11 May 2017	SRILAN 6.200 05/27	US85227SAT33	USY8137FAH11	6.2000	1,500.00
18 April 2028	18 April 2018	SRILAN 6.750 04/28	US85227SAW61	USY8137FAL23	6.7500	1,250.00
14 March 2029	14 March 2019	SRILAN 7.850 03/29	US85227SAZ92	USY8137FAP37	7.8500	1,400.00
28 March 2030	28 June 2019	SRILAN 7.550 06/30	US85227SBB16	USY8137FAR92	7.5500	1,500.00
ISBs Outstanding as at 30.09.2022						**11,550.00**

Source: Central Bank of Sri Lanka. Available online at: https://www.cbsl.gov.lk/sites/default/files/cbslweb_documents/about/outstanding_ISBs_as_at_20220930.pdf

creditors have forged between investors in the Global North and long-suffering people in countries in the Global South, in this case, Sri Lanka. The Complaint states:

> ...the Bonds – which are also broadly held by US retirement systems including Fidelity Investments, BlackRock, T. Rowe Price, Lord Abbett, JPMorgan, PIMCO, Neuberger Berman and other US investors – remain indefinitely in default and unpaid, causing American retirees tremendous suffering from potentially massive losses of up to 80% of their original investment value.[61]

As Cephas Lumina, a lawyer from Zambia (another debt-trapped country) and other legal scholars point out, given the lack of an international legal framework for restructuring sovereign debt, predatory private commercial companies, referred to as 'vulture funds' are able to "acquire defaulted sovereign debts at substantial discounts, refuse to participate in debt restructurings and aggressively pursue repayment of the full face value of the debt through litigation, often in multiple jurisdictions."[62] There is a real danger of this happening to the Sri Lankan debt.

Global Debt Crisis

As noted in Chapter 1, the debt and survival crisis is not unique to Sri Lanka, at least 54 countries are currently experiencing a debt crisis, with debt payments undermining the ability of governments to protect basic economic and social rights of their citizens."[63] Economist Michael Hudson's observations on 'debt pollution' are applicable to Sri Lanka as to the increasing number of other debt-stricken countries around the world:

> The most serious problems lie in the financial sphere, where the economy's debt overhead has grown more rapidly than the 'real' economy's ability to carry this debt. One might call

---

61 Dolmetsch, Chris. "Bondholder Sues Sri Lanka in US Court." *Aljazeera.com*, June 22, 2022. Accessed 23 June, 2022. https://www.aljazeera.com/economy/2022/6/22/bondholder-sues-sri-lanka-in-us-court.
62 Lumina, Cephas. "Curbing 'Vulture Fund' Litigation." In *Sovereign Debt and Human Rights*, edited by Ilias Bantekas and Cephas Lumina, 0. Oxford University Press, 2018. https://doi.org/10.1093/oso/9780198810445.003.0027.
63 Jones, Tim. "Growing Global Debt Crisis to Worsen with Interest Rate Rises." *International Debt Charity | Debt Justice (formerly Jubilee Debt Campaign)*, January 23, 2022. Accessed February 19, 2022. https://debtjustice.org.uk/press-release/growing-debt-crisis-to-worsen-with-interest-rate-rises.

its demands for interest and amortization 'debt pollution', stifling the economic environment much as bad air and water plague the earth's biosphere.[64]

Like Sri Lanka, many other countries were already struggling to pay accumulated debts stemming from the expansion of capital flows from the high-income countries to lower-income countries after the 2008 global financial crisis. This financial liberalization was fostered by the IMF and powerful global interests when interest rates dropped in the richer countries. Many low- and middle-income countries were encouraged to liberalize rules, increases external borrowing and open up capital accounts purportedly to attract foreign capital for productive investment.[65] This facilitated borrowing by Sri Lanka and other developing countries from private international capital markets through ISBs, which come with high interest rates and short maturation periods.[66]

Financial liberalization facilitated by the IMF and the developed countries in collaboration with domestic elites of poor countries has created a hierarchical and asymmetrical international financial architecture. As a December 2021 report published by the Bretton Woods Project points out, this unequal framework creates "macroeconomic imbalances, financial fragilities, and exchange-rate instability that can trigger debt and/or currency crises and curb the economic policy autonomy of affected countries to pursue domestic goals."[67]

Deregulation of financial systems and banking occurred with the rise of neoliberalism, creating an economic system based on speculation and financialization with the financial economy increasingly separated from and overtaking the real economy.[68] A major feature of global financial and monetary asymmetry is the

---

[64] Hudson, Michael. "Financial Capitalism v. Industrial Capitalism." *Michael-hudson.com*, September 3, 1998. Accessed November 02, 2022. https://michael-hudson.com/1998/09/financial-capitalism-v-industrial-capitalism/.
[65] Ghosh, Jayati, and C. P. ChandrasekharJayati. "A Food Crisis Not of Their Making." *The Hindu Business Line*, September 19, 2022. Accessed September 23, 2022. https://www.thehindubusinessline.com/opinion/a-food-crisis-not-of-their-making/article65911286.ece.
[66] Vieira, Luiz. "Debt Crisis Prevention: We Need to Talk about Capital Controls." *Bretton Woods Project*, December 9, 2021. March 2, 2022. https://www.brettonwoodsproject.org/2021/12/debt-crisis-prevention-we-need-to-talk-about-capital-controls/.
[67] Ibid.
[68] Hudson, Michael. "Financial Capitalism v. Industrial Capitalism." *Michael-hudson.com*, September 3, 1998. Accessed November 02, 2022. https://michael-hudson.com/1998/09/financial-capitalism-v-industrial-capitalism/.

dominance of the US Federal Reserve and the US dollar.[69] The increase in interest rates by the Federal Reserve in May 2021 forced interest rate hikes in developing countries, like Sri Lanka, exposed to dollar denominated debt. The denomination of a large proportion of their public debt in US dollars has greatly increased the debt burden of countries with depreciating currencies.[70]

As the United Nations Conference on Trade and Development (UNCTAD) 2022 Trade and Development Report points out, the increased cost of credit is bound to "affect the most fragile sectors and regions of the world economy through reduced investment, wages and employment growth, and liquidity stress, hitting hard the unemployed and low and medium wage earners everywhere, as well as firms and governments with elevated external debt in developing countries."[71]

Wealth Transfers

Between 1980 and 2017, developing countries have paid out over $4.2 trillion in interest payments dwarfing the aid that they received from the developed countries during the same period.[72] The massive transfer of financial and resource wealth from poor countries in the Global South to the rich countries in the North has been an enduring feature of both classical and neo-colonialism throughout centuries. A 2021 article published in *New Political Economy* calculated that, between 1960 and 2018, the global South has lost an astounding US$ 152 trillion, accounting for lost growth, due to unequal exchange and lower wages and lower natural resource prices in the global South than in the global North (see Figure 4.2).[73]

---

[69] Costantini, Orsola. "Dollar Dominance Is Financial Dominance." *Institute for New Economic Thinking*, November 23, 2022. https://www.ineteconomics.org/perspectives/blog/dollar-dominance-is-financial-dominance.

[70] Hudson, Michael. "Financial Capitalism v. Industrial Capitalism." *Michael-hudson.com*, September 3, 1998. Accessed November 02, 2022. https://michael-hudson.com/1998/09/financial-capitalism-v-industrial-capitalism/.

[71] "Trade and Development Report 2022." *United Nations Conference on Trade and Development*, 2022. https://unctad.org/system/files/official-document/tdr2022_en.pdf.

[72] Hickel, Jason, Dylan Sullivan, and Huzaifa Zoomkawala. "Plunder in the Post-Colonial Era: Quantifying Drain from the Global South Through Unequal Exchange, 1960–2018." *New Political Economy* 26, no. 6 (November 2, 2021): 1030–1047. https://doi.org/10.1080/13563467.2021.1899153.

[73] Ibid.

Neoliberal globalization has widened wealth and income gaps between the Global North and South and between social classes across the world.[74] Corporate concentration, increasing separation of the financial and real economy and prominence of financial companies in every sector of the global economy have contributed to extreme inequality in wealth and power jeopardizing the survival of humanity and environmental sustainability. BlackRock, the US$ 10 trillion world's largest asset management firm, is one of the main, if not the main, ISB creditor of Sri Lanka. BlackRock is a top shareholder of the extremely profitable food and agrochemical companies as well as energy, media, tech and other sectors.[75]

As Indian economists C. P. Chandrasekhar and Jyoti Ghosh have observed, the food and survival crises facing indebted countries like Sri Lanka today are not entirely of their making but largely due to "market structures, regulations, and trade and finance arrangements that bolster a global corporate-dominated industrial food system and enable market concentration and financial speculation in commodity markets."[76]

Illicit financial flows and offshore tax havens are also a great contributor to foreign exchange crises in the developing countries. A 2016 Study, 'Financial Flows and Tax Havens' by Global Financial Integrity, a think tank that tracks illicit financial flows globally, estimated that 'illicit outflows account for nearly 82 percent of all NRTs (Net Resource Transfers) from developing countries' and that residents of developing countries accounted for US$ 4.4 trillion in assets held in tax havens in 2011.[77]

---

[74] *Tricontinental: Institute for Social Research.* "Dossier No. 57. The Geopolitics of Inequality: Discussing Pathways Towards a More Just World," October 21, 2022. https://thetricontinental.org/dossier-57-geopolitics-of-inequality/.

[75] Mousseau, Frederic. "38 Billion Dollar Question – Who Is Driving the Destructive Industrial Agriculture Model?" *Oaklandinstitute.org*, September 20, 2022. Accessed October 05, 2022. https://www.oaklandinstitute.org/blog/vanguard-blackrock-driving-destructive-industrial-agriculture-model;
Huff, Ethan. "BlackRock and Vanguard Are Taking over Centralized Food Production Technologies and Will Have Near-Total Control over the Future Food Supply in America." Naturalnews.com, May 1, 2022. Accessed June 3, 2022. https://www.naturalnews.com/2022-05-01-blackrock-vanguard-controlling-america-centralized-food-production.html.

[76] Ghosh, Jayati, and C. P. Chandrasekhar. "A Food Crisis Not of Their Making." *The Hindu Business Line*, September 19, 2022. Accessed September 23, 2022. https://www.thehindubusinessline.com/opinion/a-food-crisis-not-of-their-making/article65911286.ece.

[77] "Financial Flows and Tax Havens: Combining to Limit the Lives of Billions of People." *Centre for Applied Research, Norwegian School of Economics; Global Financial Integrity; Jawaharlal Nehru University; Instituto de Estudos Socioeconômicos; Nigerian Institute of Social and Economic Research*, December 2015. Accessed November 2, 2022. https://www.gfintegrity.org/wp-content/uploads/2016/12/Financial_Flows-final.pdf. Bandara, Kapila. "Exporters, Importers Shift Rs 13.2 Trillion Overseas via Dodgy Invoicing." *Sunday Times* (Sri Lanka), July 10, 2022. Accessed November 2, 2022. http://www.

Crony capitalism, which is economic growth through collusion between business and the state rather than through free enterprise, has been common practice in the course of capitalist development in both colonial and imperialist countries. However, it is now taking extreme form around the world.[78] Widespread tax evasion and foreign exchange plunder by an "incestuous business community-politicians-customs nexus" has been a major cause for loss of government revenue during successive governments in Sri Lanka. *Yahapalanaya* advisor Ramalingam Paskeralingam and Rajapaksa relatives Nirupama Rajapaksa and Thirukumar Nadesan are Sri Lankans implicated in the Pandora Papers for foreign currency embezzlement.[79] Global Financial Integrity has reported that Sri Lankan businesses in the import-export trade have 'plundered' US$ 36.833 billion between 2009 and 2017 through "intentional, dodgy invoicing and stashing the foreign exchange earnings offshore" (Table 6.2).[80] Billions in foreign exchange lost every year because of 'value gaps' in trade, due to mis-invoicing -over-invoiced imports and under-invoiced exports -could easily have paid for the country's fuel and food imports.[81]

In December 2022, Sri Lanka's Minister of Justice informed the Parliament that Sri Lanka had lost foreign remittances worth USD 53 billion in the last 12 years, due

---

sundaytimes.lk/220710/news/exporters-importers-shift-rs-13-2-trillion-overseas-via-dodgy-invoicing-488561.html.

78 *Majority Media | Homeland Security & Governmental Affairs Committee | Homeland Security & Governmental Affairs Committee.* "Johnson, Grassley Release Report on Conflicts-of-Interest Investigation," September 23, 2020. Accessed November 12, 2022. http://www.hsgac.senate.gov/. Lockett, Hudson, and Stephanie Findlay. "'Modi's Rockefeller': Gautam Adani and the Concentration of Power in India." *Financial Times*, November 13, 2020. Accessed November 24, 2020. https://www.ft.com/content/474706d6-1243-4f1e-b365-891d4c5d528b.

79 Aponso, Revan. "The Pandora Papers and the Exposure of Sri Lanka's Elite." *The Economics Review*, February 22, 2022. Accessed October 15, 2022 https://theeconreview.com/2022/02/22/the-pandora-papers-and-the-exposure-of-sri-lankas-elite/; Alecci, Scilla. "Sri Lankan Power Couple Piled up Luxury Homes, Artworks and Cash Offshore as Ruling Family Rose and Rose." *The International Consortium of Investigative Journalists*, October 4, 2021. Accessed October 10, 2021. https://www.icij.org/investigations/pandora-papers/sri-lanka-rajapaksa-family-offshore-wealth-power/.

80 "Financial Flows and Tax Havens: Combining to Limit the Lives of Billions of People." *Centre for Applied Research, Norwegian School of Economics; Global Financial Integrity; Jawaharlal Nehru University; Instituto de Estudos Socioeconômicos; Nigerian Institute of Social and Economic Research*, December 2015. Accessed November 2, 2022. https://www.gfintegrity.org/wp-content/uploads/2016/12/Financial_Flows-final.pdf.

81 Ibid.

to some exporters 'depositing their monies in foreign countries', and that the government would formulate new laws to repatriate that money.[82]

Calls are increasing to examine capital flows, through trade mis-invoicing, including import over-invoicing and export under-invoicing. Urgently needed is the amendment of the Foreign Exchange Control Act passed on July 25, 2017 by the Yahapalanaya government which liberalized capital outflows.[83]

Table 6.2: Trade mis-invoicing: value gaps in trade between Sri Lanka and all trading partners, totals and percentages, 2008–2017 (US$ millions).

Year	2008	2009	2010	2011	2012	2013	2014	2015	2016	2017	Average
Value Gap	3,172	2,551	3,277	4,111	3,828	2,989	4,369	4,320	3,871	4,451	3,693
Percent of Total Trade	20.85	21.28	21.86	19.46	19.97	15.68	18.80	19.15	18.20	19.01	22.51

Source: Global Financial Integrity, Trade-Related Illicit Financial Flows in 135 Developing Countries: 2008–2017, March 2020, Tables E and F, 61, 66. https://gfintegrity.org/wp-content/uploads/2020/03/GFI-Trade-IFF-Report-2020-Final.pdf

Sri Lanka has experienced increasing economic inequality since the mid-1980s, following the advent of the 'open economy.' (Figure 1.3). The trend towards inequality is likely to increase further given the unequal impact of the current economic crisis on different classes of people.[84]

As elsewhere, in Sri Lanka, the richest minority who owns and controls the country's largest companies exert tremendous political power through funding the media, political candidates and political campaigns.[85] Whereas some of the richest individuals engage in tax evasion and stashing foreign exchange in tax havens abroad, the migrant labor force – most of them heavily exploited housemaids

---

[82] 'Govt will formulate laws to repatriate USD 53 Billion', Daily News, Dec. 7, 2022. https://www.dailynews.lk/2022/12/07/local/292625/govt-will-formulate-laws-repatriate-usd-53-billion accessed March 16, 2023.

[83] Shamindra Ferdinando, 'All Praise for Lanka's Saviours!', The Island, March 15, 2023. https://island.lk/all-praise-for-lankas-saviours/. Accessed March 16, 2023.

[84] *South Asia@LSE*. "Poverty of Vision: Neglecting Growing Class Inequality in Post-War Sri Lanka?" October 30, 2019. https://blogs.lse.ac.uk/southasia/2019/10/30/poverty-of-vision-neglecting-growing-class-inequality-in-post-war-sri-lanka/. World Bank. "Gini Index – Sri Lanka | Data." Accessed January 3, 2023. https://data.worldbank.org/indicator/SI.POV.GINI?end=2016&locations=LK&start=1985&view=chart.

[85] *Groundviews*. "Income and Wealth Inequality in Sri Lanka," September 3, 2022. https://groundviews.org/2022/09/03/income-and-wealth-inequality-in-sri-lanka/.

and unskilled laborers – keep remitting money to the country helping maintain families and the survival of Sri Lanka's economy. The Central Bank of Sri Lanka acknowledged the value of worker remittances in 2022 amidst of the on-going economic collapse:

> Workers' remittances have been a key pillar of Sri Lanka's foreign currency ...enhancing the external sector resilience of the country... workers' remittances have covered around 80 percent of the annual trade deficit, on average, over the past two decades. Workers' remittances are non-debt creating forex inflows to the country and unlike many merchandise export categories, there is no import content involved in this source of foreign exchange earnings.[86]

Protest and Regime Change

The neoliberal hyperpolarization of wealth inevitably leads to suffering, anger and protest, and in early 2022, protests against the Rajapaksa regime started in different locations among ordinary people facing severe economic hardship, such as farmers affected by the government's fertilizer policy and ordinary people unable to keep up with rising inflation. Their protests did not attract global or even much local media attention. The situation changed, however, when individuals from the westernized urban middle class who were also faced with long power cuts, fuel shortages and other aggravations took to the streets unprecedentedly.[87] They rebranded the protest as *aragalaya* (struggle, in Sinhala) took it to the capital, and situated it in a well-provided for encampment at the exclusive oceanfront Galle Face Green. A wide array of opposition political parties, NGOs, religious and other groups with their own vested interests joined the protest bringing in massive international media coverage.[88]

Blaming the Rajapaksa government's corruption and mismanagement for the country's economic crisis, the angry demonstrators demanded that the president and the Parliament resign. Following intensified protests and violence, the Prime Minister Mahinda Rajapaksa resigned on May 9. Gotabaya Rajapaksa's younger brother, Basil Rajapaksa who was Finance Minister (July 2021–April 2022) and greatly responsible for mismanaging the financial crisis, quit as a lawmaker on June 9. After protestors stormed his official residence on July 9, President

---

[86] *Central Bank of Sri Lanka.* "Workers' Remittances." Accessed January 3, 2023. https://www.cbsl.gov.lk/en/workers-remittances.
[87] Devapriya, Uditha. "A Class Analysis of the Aragalaya." *Ceylon Today,* August 24, 2022. Accessed September 3, 2022. https://ceylontoday.lk/2022/08/25/a-class-analysis-of-the-aragalaya/.
[88] Waduge, Shenali. "Sri Lanka's Crisis: Scenarios & Options." *Shenali Waduge,* July 12, 2022. Accessed July 22, 2022. https://www.shenaliwaduge.com/sri-lankas-crisis-scenarios-options/.

Gotabaya Rajapaksa fled the country and resigned on July 14. The powerful Rajapaksas, considered to be nationalists and allies of China, were brought down. Except for the charge of embezzlement of one Rajapaksa relative, a former ambassador to the United States, the many other financial allegations against them, including those prior to 2015, remain to be proven.[89]

Long-time US collaborator Ranil Wickramasinghe, who was rejected by the public in the Parliamentary elections of 2020 and who is accountable for the 2015 Central Bank bond scam, was appointed Acting President by Gotabaya Rajapaksa before his resignation. Most members of the Sri Lankan parliament sought to preserve their own power and positions without risking fundamental political change. They elected Wickramasinghe as President on July 20 violating the democratic will of the electorate, revealing the collusion between seemingly rival political parties and shared support for the neoliberal agenda. Thus, despite a change at the top, the rest of the corrupt and ineffective regime remained in a "confused and pathetic state" with "lawmakers, representing 15 political parties ...pulling in different directions."[90]

In contrast, the *aragalaya* was celebrated internationally as a peaceful, democratic and exemplary endeavor despite reports of extensive violence committed by the protestors. As political analyst Shenali Waduge observed, cheered by *aragalaya* supporters, some of the protestors were

> breaking barricades, scaling walls & illegally entering public places & ransacking contents, destroying & stealing, misusing and abusing state property, burning down homes, destroying vehicles, burning books, manhandling people even armed forces/police, attacking people and even killing them.[91]

---

[89] Reuters. "Sri Lanka Says Mahinda Rajapaksa Officials Hid More than $2bn in Dubai." *The Guardian*, March 20, 2015, sec. World news. Accessed November 12, 2022. https://www.theguardian.com/world/2015/mar/20/sri-lanka-says-mahinda-rajapaksa-officials-hid-more-than-2bn-in-dubai. Bastians, Darisha. "Former Sri Lankan Minister Is Charged With Misuse of Public Funds." *The New York Times*, April 23, 2014. https://www.nytimes.com/2015/04/23/world/asia/sri-lanka-basil-rajapaksa-charged-with-misuse-of-public-funds.html. Pundir, Pallavi. "Why This Rich and Powerful Family Is Blamed for All of Sri Lanka's Money Problems." *Vice*, June 8, 2022. Accessed June 12, 2022. https://www.vice.com/en/article/93a9ke/rajapaksa-wealth-politics-sri-lanka-economic-crisis. Ferdinando, Shamindra. "Sri Lanka's Foreign Policy Dilemma." *The Island*, November 9, 2022. November 9, 2022. http://island.lk/sri-lankas-foreign-policy-dilemma/.

[90] Ferdinando, Shamindra. "Sri Lanka's Foreign Policy Dilemma." *The Island*, November 9, 2022. November 9, 2022. http://island.lk/sri-lankas-foreign-policy-dilemma/.

[91] Ibid.; Ghoshal, Devjyot, and Uditha Jayasinghe. "How a Band of Activists Helped Bring down Sri Lanka's Government." *Reuters*, July 12, 2022, sec. Asia Pacific. Accessed July 13, 2022. https://www.reuters.com/world/asia-pacific/how-band-activists-helped-bring-down-sri-lankas-government-2022-07-11/.

As Waduge asked, why is it that those charging corruption against the Rajapaksa regime, not take their "campaign to the Courts to file legal action which is the right democratic path to take?"[92]

Middle class *aragalaya* protesters and their foreign supporters gushed over their courageous activism.[93] The Asia Foundation, for example, published a piece titled "Notes from the Field: Sri Lanka's Revolutionary "Aragalaya.""[94]

However, many questions about the *aragalaya* remain unanswered.[95] Why did local and foreign interests guiding the protests only want the removal of the Rajapaksas but not seek to challenge the root causes of Sri Lanka's debt colonialism (i.e., domination via foreign debt) and digital colonialism (i.e., domination via digital technology)?[96] Why did they not encourage the youthful protesters to join global movements for much-needed debt cancellation, debt swaps and regulation of capital market borrowing?[97] As in many previous youth-led 'color revolutions', the energy of protest, through ignorance or narrative control, seems to be focused away from challenging global systems of trade, finance and dominance that are doubtlessly major causes of the recurring crises.

While the young, technologically savvy data strategists and market professionals were able to mobilize large numbers of protesters using WhatsApp, Facebook and other social media, they were uninformed and misled regarding the historical and geopolitical dimensions of their country's economic crisis. Lacking this context, they also lacked any vision beyond neoliberalism, that might build towards collective and sustainable alternatives.[98]

---

92 Waduge, Shenali. "Sri Lanka's Protestors Have given an Ugly Example to the World." *Shenali Waduge*, August 13, 2022. Accessed November 1, 2022. https://www.shenaliwaduge.com/sri-lankas-protestors-have-given-an-ugly-example-to-the-world/.
93 Senanayake, Devana. "Inside Sri Lanka's Unprecedented Mass Protests." *Foreign Policy*, April 26, 2022. Accessed April 27, 2022. https://foreignpolicy.com/2022/04/26/sri-lanka-protests-rajapaksa-economic-crisis-colombo/.
94 Ranaraja, Maljini. "Notes from the Field: Sri Lanka's Revolutionary 'Aragalaya.'" *The Asia Foundation*, July 20, 2022. https://asiafoundation.org/2022/07/20/notes-from-the-field-sri-lankas-revolutionary-aragalaya/.
95 Ibid.
96 Kwet, Michael. "Digital Colonialism: The Evolution of US Empire." *Transnational Institute*, March 4, 2021. Accessed June 12, 2022. https://longreads.tni.org/digital-colonialism-the-evolution-of-us-empire.
97 *International Debt Charity | Debt Justice (formerly Jubilee Debt Campaign)*. "300 Organisations Demand Debt Cancellation," October 9, 2022. Accessed October 20, 2022. https://debtjustice.org.uk/wp-content/uploads/2022/09/Give-BlackRock-a-Call.png.
98 Ghoshal, Devjyot, and Uditha Jayasinghe. "How a Band of Activists Helped Bring down Sri Lanka's Government." *Reuters*, July 12, 2022, sec. Asia Pacific. Accessed July 13, 2022. https://www.reu

Despite common dismissal as 'conspiracy theory', there is evidence that some aspects of the *aragalaya* that led to the 2022 regime change in Sri Lanka were, if not orchestrated, backed by powerful external forces. These include the US National Endowment for Democracy (NED), which is widely known for its 'soft power' regime change operations around the world. NED has distributed money to hundreds of NGOs and civil society groups in Sri Lanka for 'democracy building' through intervention in local government, electoral processes, youth and women's leadership, research and journalism, and influencing local thinking and behavior for many years (Table 6.3).[99] Between 2017 and 2021, for example, the NED states that they funded 89 such projects in Sri Lanka, with a total expenditure of $6,827,898.[100]

Table 6.3: National Endowment for Democracy (NED) Funding for Sri Lanka, 2017–2021.

Organization Name	Award Amount				
Projects	2017	2018	2019	2020	2021
Accountability Tracking Transnational Economic Crimes	–	–	–	–	$106,556
Adayaalam Centre for Policy Research Tools for Civic and Political Engagement in the North and East	$15,900	–	–	–	–
Youth Social Justice Program	–	–	–	$19,000	–
AFRIEL Promoting Political Participation and National Reconciliation	$70,000	$74,300	$84,300	$139,024	–
Gathering and Archiving Women's Experiences	–	–	–	$60,000	–
Human Rights Archiving and Analysis	–	–	–	$105,000	–
Human Rights Advocacy	–	–	$62,198	$2,198	–

---

ters.com/world/asia-pacific/how-band-activists-helped-bring-down-sri-lankas-government-2022-07-11/.

99 *Ned.org.* "Sri Lanka 2021 – National Endowment for Democracy," September 24, 2022. Accessed September 24, 2022. https://web.archive.org/web/20220924152609/https://www.ned.org/region/asia/sri-lanka-2021/./. Leelarathna, Hassina. "CIA NED IRI in Sri Lanka." *SriLankaexpress.org*, December 2017. https://srilankaexpress.org/cia-ned-iri-in-sri-lanka.

100 *National Endowment for Democracy.* "NED Grant Search." Accessed December 9, 2022. https://www.ned.org/wp-content/themes/ned/search/grant-search.php?organizationName=&region=ASIA&projectCountry=Sri+Lanka&amount=&fromDate=2017&toDate=2021&projectFocus%5B%5D=&search=&maxCount=100&orderBy=Year&start=1&sbmt=1.

Table 6.3: National Endowment for Democracy (NED) Funding for Sri Lanka, 2017–2021. *(Continued)*

Organization Name Projects	Award Amount				
	2017	2018	2019	2020	2021
Aham Humanitarian Resource Center Developing a Forum for Democratic Actors in the Eastern Province	–	–	–	–	$30,000
Alliance Development Trust Youth Leadership Development	–	$37,542	$40,000	$40,000	–
Centre for Environmental Justice (Guarantee) Limited Citizen Participation in Monitoring Economic Development	–	$36,000	$36,000	$36,000	$36,000
Centre for Human Rights and Development Seeking Redress for Victims of Human Rights Violations	$54,278	$60,000	$60,000	$60,000	–
Center for International Private Enterprise (CIPE) Jumpstarting Democratic Reforms Through Increased Access to Information	–	$190,013	–	–	–
Increasing Transparency and Accountability in Public Finance	–	–	$311,355	–	–
Protecting Democratic Space through Dialogue on Economic Policy	–	–	–	$669,607	–
Redressing Victim Communities through Legal Assistance & Advocacy	–	–	–	–	$70,000
Strengthening Democracy through Increased Citizen Engagement in the Reform Process	$242,216	–	–	–	–
Centre for Justice and Change Leadership Development for the Promotion and Protection of Human Rights	–	$30,000	$34,200	$4,200	$30,000
Centre for Policy Alternatives, (Guarantee) Ltd. Promoting Freedom of Expression through Citizen Journalism	$80,000	–	$77,000	$77,000	–
Raising Public Awareness on Politics and Governance	–	–	–	$80,000	–

Table 6.3: National Endowment for Democracy (NED) Funding for Sri Lanka, 2017–2021. *(Continued)*

Organization Name / Projects	Award Amount 2017	2018	2019	2020	2021
Families of the Disappeared Mobilize Families of the Disappeared in Support of Reconciliation and Justice	$30,000	$30,000	$30,000	–	–
Human Rights Documentation and Advocacy	$109,007	$60,000	–	–	–
Freedom of Expression Promoting Freedom of Expression and Access to Independent Journalism	–	–	–	$75,000	$100,000
International Republican Institute (IRI) Supporting Subnational Governance	$524,000	–	–	–	–
Improving Local Engagement for Democratic Actors	–	–	$430,000	–	–
Janawaboda Kendraya Civic Engagement for Sustained Collective Action	–	$41,000	$41,000	$41,500	$41,500
Community Mobilization and Political Participation	$68,000	$65,911	$68,000	$68,000	–
Public Education for Informed Citizen Engagement	$40,500	–	–	–	–
The International Working Group on Sri Lanka Ltd. Seeking Transitional Justice, Reform, and Reconciliation in Post-War Sri Lanka	$140,000	$140,000	$90,000	$50,000	$14,460
Law and Society Trust Improving Legal Literacy on Land Rights	$47,114	$70,000	$499,983	$85,340	$50,000
National Democratic Institute for International Affairs (NDI) Promoting Grassroots Youth Leadership And Participatory Governance	–	–	$475,000	–	$325,000
Right to Life Human Rights Center Protecting Democracy and Human Rights through Journalism	–	–	–	$38,000	–
Rights Now – Collective for Democracy Raising Awareness on Human Rights and Democracy	–	–	$25,604	$45,000	–

Table 6.3: National Endowment for Democracy (NED) Funding for Sri Lanka, 2017–2021. *(Continued)*

Organization Name Projects	Award Amount				
	2017	2018	2019	2020	2021
Social Scientists' Association Enhancing Civic Education for High School Students	–	$50,000	$50,000	–	–
Revisiting Democracy in Sri Lanka	–	–	$51,000	–	–
The Social Architects Promoting Youth Involvement in Reconciliation	$40,000	$55,090	$15,090	–	–
Creating a Community of Practitioners for Social Accountability to Strengthen Democratic Process.	–	–	$50,000		
Trincomalee District Youth Development – AHAM Strengthening Youth Leadership and Civic Participation in Eastern Sri Lanka	–	$30,000	$30,000	–	–
Uva Shakthi Foundation Promoting Citizen Participation and Local Government Accountability in Estate Tamil Communities	$20,000	$20,000	$20,000	$20,000	$29,500
Promoting Freedom of Expression and Access to Independent Journalism	–	–	–	$75,000	–
Vattrapalai International Institute of Art and Film Participatory Democracy through Artistic Expression	–	–	–	$30,000	–
Verite Research Pvt. Ltd. Parliamentary Tracking Tool for Accountability and Good Governance	$58,000	$63,428	–	$75,000	$75,000
Viluthu Strengthening Civil Society Networks for Active Political Participation	$60,000	$70,000	–	$60,000	$60,000

Source: Adapted from National Endowment for Democracy's Grants to Sri Lanka, 2017–2021. Available online at: https://www.ned.org/wp-content/themes/ned/search/grant-search.php

Aware of these realities and arguing that India 'must keep an eye on the neo-colonial conspiracy in its backyard,' former Indian Foreign Service Ambassador, M.K. Bhadrakumar, stated in July 2022:

The US typically forms small groups in such situations, based on 'common values', to leverage global governance as a tool for geopolitical games. Its game plan is to gain control over Colombo's economic and foreign policies and to integrate Sri Lanka into its military-strategic offensive against China. There is no question that powerful forces are backing the protesters.[101]

A Sri Lankan data strategist, Chameera Dedduwage, a 'volunteer' for a NED funded 'election organization' in Sri Lanka was a key organizer of the *aragalaya* action that led to the storming of the President's official residence on July 9.[102] His group's involvement has been called a "carbon copy of events that unfolded during the 2011 US-supported 'Arab Spring.'"[103] It is also interesting to note that the US Under Secretary for State, Victoria Nuland, known as the mastermind of the regime change in Ukraine in 2014 was in Sri Lanka in March 2022 during the protests to bring down the Rajapaksa regime.[104]

According to shocking revelations made by leader of the National Freedom Front political party Wimal Weerawansa on November 15, 2022, US Ambassador Julie Chung was intimately involved in a psychological operation leading to regime change.[105] Weerawansa stated that during the last days of the *aragalaya*, Ambassador Chung met with President Gotabaya almost every day, telling him to invoke the blessings of God saying, "Mr. President, you are a Buddhist. I am Catholic. I want

---

101 Bhadrakumar, MK. "India Passive on Sri Lanka." *Tribuneindia News Service*. Accessed January 4, 2023. https://www.tribuneindia.com/news/comment/india-passive-on-sri-lanka-415338.
102 "US Fingerprints Found Behind Sri Lanka Unrest." *The New Atlas/Brian Berletic*, 2022. https://www.youtube.com/watch?v=Ysy6qrXi0m0; Ferdinando, Shamindra. "Post-War National Reconciliation: Diaspora Sets Prerequisites." *The Island*, November 23, 2022. Accessed November 23, 2022 http://island.lk/post-war-national-reconciliation-diaspora-sets-prerequisites/.
103 *Thuppahi's Blog*. "USA Machinations Behind Aragalaya?" July 15, 2022. Accessed August 1, 2022. https://thuppahis.com/2022/07/15/63710/. *Red Fire*. "Sri Lanka: US Backed Colour Revolution in Colombo," July 20, 2022. Accessed July 25, 2022. https://redfireonline.com/2022/07/20/sri-lanka-us-backed-colour-revolution-in-colombo/.
104 Parry, Robert. "The Mess That Nuland Made." *Consortium News*, July 13, 2015. Accessed February 27, 2022. https://consortiumnews.com/2015/07/13/the-mess-that-nuland-made/. *U.S. Embassy in Sri Lanka*. "U.S. Under Secretary of State for Political Affairs Victoria Nuland Travels to Colombo for Bilateral U.S.-Sri Lanka Talks," March 22, 2022. Accessed July 23, 2022. https://lk.usembassy.gov/u-s-under-secretary-of-state-for-political-affairs-victoria-nuland-travels-to-colombo-for-bilateral-u-s-sri-lanka-talks/.
105 "Wimal Comes out with Shocking Details of Gotabaya's Narrow Shave as Angry Crowds Stormed the Presidential Palace on July 9.," November 15, 2022. Accessed November 15, 2022. https://lankasara.com/news/wimal-comes-out-with-shocking-details-of-gotabayas-narrow-shave-as-angry-crowds-stormed-the-presidential-palace-on-july-9/. Weerasooriya, Sahan. "US Ambassador Influenced Prez GR as Part of Its Regime Change Plot – Wimal." *The Island*, August 3, 2022. Accessed August 5, 2022. http://island.lk/us-ambassador-influenced-prez-gr-as-part-of-its-regime-change-plot-wimal/.

you to pray when you are in trouble."[106] According to Weerawansa, the President "misread these sentiments in a romantic way."[107] The President was also in constant touch with the Inspector General of Police, Army Commander and intelligence chiefs meeting with them all continuously.[108] Weerawansa further said:

> As a result, mental barriers were formed. One of the entrances to the President's office was blocked by activists. When the President decided to open it, it was the US ambassador who persuaded him saying that the IMF would not give money and there would be human rights issues. She, therefore, advised him not to do it...
>
> When the activists surrounded the president's house, he was inside with a family member. Security guards had been monitoring the CCTV system and telling the President there was no problem and that the situation was under control.
>
> The President just picked up the remote control of a TV and turned on a private channel on the television. Then it was observed that the gates of the presidential palace were broken, and people were pouring in.
>
> That's when he ran out the back door. He would have suffered a similar fate to Gaddafi in Libya if he stayed back. Why did the security forces fail to inform him of this? These are things that need to be investigated.[109]

Unfortunately, it is unlikely that the alleged regime change operation, like the 2015 bond scam and the 2019 Easter bomb attacks, will be subjected to an impartial judicial investigation. In the context of Sri Lanka as a tense theater of geopolitical rivalry, the debt crisis cannot be understood simply as an economic crisis. Was it, in fact, a 'staged default' designed to push Sri Lanka into an IMF bailout to complete the island's subservience to the US-dominated economic, political and military agenda?[110] In this regard, it is useful to quote again from the US State Department's 'Integrated Country Strategy', issued on April 6, 2022 in the midst of Sri Lanka's financial meltdown:

> In line with the Administration's Interim National Security Strategic Guidance and 2022 Indo Pacific Strategy, Mission Colombo seeks to advance America's national interests by building a

---

[106] "Wimal Comes out with Shocking Details of Gotabaya's Narrow Shave as Angry Crowds Stormed the Presidential Palace on July 9.," November 15, 2022. Accessed November 15, 2022. https://lankasara.com/news/wimal-comes-out-with-shocking-details-of-gotabayas-narrow-shave-as-angry-crowds-stormed-the-presidential-palace-on-july-9/.

[107] Ibid.

[108] Ibid.

[109] Ibid.

[110] Rajasingham-Senanayake, Darini. "A Staged Default: Sri Lanka's Sovereign Bond Debt Trap and IMF's Spring Meetings Amid Hybrid Cold War." *IDN-InDepthNews*, April 24, 2022. Accessed May 15, 2022. https://archive-2017-2022.indepthnews.info/index.php/the-world/asia-pacific/5249-a-staged-default-sri-lanka-s-sovereign-bond-debt-trap-and-imf-s-spring-meetings-amid-hybrid-cold-war-part-1.

strong, long-term partnership with Sri Lanka, . ..[which] can serve as a lynchpin for the sustainment of a free, open, connected, and secure Indo-Pacific... Mission Colombo will work to ... support ...{Sri Lanka's} ability to protect its sovereignty from malign regional actors ... We remain committed to defending our strategic interests and values in Sri Lanka – the fulcrum of the Indo-Pacific region.[111]

It is clear that for the US, strategic interests prevail over concern for the survival of Sri Lankan people. While more and more local people are seeking economic self-reliance and import substitution as the path to survival, the US 'Integrated Country Strategy' argues that "Policies focused on import substitution and self-reliance may prevent the Sri Lankan Government from adhering to economic reforms in line with international best practices" and states that the US Embassy will engage with the Sri Lankan government, to "refrain from import substitution practices."[112] Clearly the US wants to keep Sri Lanka tethered to the IMF-dependent economic model. The modern Golden Rule is that those with the gold make the rules.

Widening Disparities

On September 1, 2022 Sri Lanka reached a preliminary agreement with the IMF for a 48-month Extended Fund Facility (EEF) of US$ 2.9 billion.[113] As the IMF agreement requires prior debt restructuring with all external and private creditors, the timeline of the IMF loan is still in question.[114] On September 2, the powerful Paris Club representing the interests of the creditor countries issued a statement supporting the IMF restructuring process.[115] The Paris Club was established in 1956 (in Paris, of course) and is considered "a strategic instrument of developed countries for maintaining their grip on the world's economy."[116] It is dedicated

---

111 "Integrated Country Strategy Sri Lanka." *United States Department of State*, April 6, 2022, 1. https://www.state.gov/wp-content/uploads/2022/06/ICS_SCA_Sri-Lanka_Public.pdf.
112 Ibid., 19.
113 *IMF.* "Press Release No. 22/295 IMF Staff Reaches Staff-Level Agreement on an Extended Fund Facility Arrangement with Sri Lanka," September 1, 2022. Accessed September 3, 2022. https://www.imf.org/en/News/Articles/2022/09/01/pr22295-imf-reaches-staff-level-agreement-on-an-extended-fund-facility-arrangement-with-sri-lanka.
114 Bhowmick, Soumya. "Sri Lanka's IMF Saga." *The Diplomat*, October 4, 2022. Accessed October 4, 2022. https://thediplomat.com/2022/10/sri-lankas-imf-saga/.
115 *Club de Paris / Paris Club.* "Paris Club Statement on Sri Lanka," September 2, 2022. Accessed October 4, 2022. https://clubdeparis.org/en/communications/press-release/paris-club-statement-on-sri-lanka-02-09-2022.
116 *The Morning.* "What Do We Know about the Paris Club?" Accessed September 4, 2023. https://themorning.lk//articles/217620.

to recovering the highest possible repayment of loans for creditor countries from debtor countries.[117]

In addition to the Paris Club, the financial advisory group Lazard, hired by the Sri Lankan government to represent it in the restructuring process, has started talks with competing regional powers, India, China and Japan to find common ground on reducing the debt they are owed by Sri Lanka.[118] While external institutions are discussing Sri Lanka's debt restructuring behind closed doors, the contents of the IMF Agreement and the IMF's *Debt Sustainability Analysis Report on Sri Lanka* have not been released to the Sri Lankan public who would clearly bear the impact of the 'shock treatment' accompanying restructuring.[119]

Even before the finalization of the IMF bail-out, political and economic pressures on the country are increasing as internal and external interests with their own agendas seek to benefit from the country's downtrodden situation. With IMF intervention and India's US$ 3 billion 2022 loan assistance, the US and India have tightened their economic and political grip on the country. Apparently, the ruling party in the Sri Lankan parliament made a declaration before the passing of the 21st Amendment to the constitution (limiting Presidential powers and disallowing dual citizenship for parliamentarians) that the US$ 2.9 billion IMF loan facility would be in jeopardy unless the Amendment was enacted.

As veteran journalist Shamindra Ferdinando asks, "Should Constitutional Amendments be subjected to foreign interference?"[120] Likewise, the lifting of the ban on six Tamil diaspora groups by Ranil Wickramasinghe in August 2022 is believed to be motivated by the hope of attracting much-needed foreign exchange reserves.[121] The 2022 UNHRC Resolution on Sri Lanka also uses the economic crisis to extend its mandate over Sri Lanka to include 'monitoring and reporting ... on the

---

[117] Ibid.
[118] *Business Standard.* "Lazard in Talks with China, India, Japan on Restructuring Sri Lanka's Debt," September 13, 2022. https://www.business-standard.com/article/international/lazard-in-talks-with-china-india-japan-on-restructuring-sri-lanka-s-debt-122091300694_1.html; *CNBC.* "Sri Lanka to Present Debt Restructuring, IMF Bailout Plans to Creditors on Friday," September 18, 2022. https://www.cnbc.com/2022/09/19/sri-lanka-to-present-debt-restructuring-imf-bailout-plans-to-creditors.html.
[119] *IMF.* "Sri Lanka and the IMF." Accessed January 4, 2023. https://web.archive.org/web/20230103203208/https://www.imf.org/en/Countries/LKA.
[120] Ferdinando, Shamindra. "Sri Lanka's Foreign Policy Dilemma." *The Island*, November 9, 2022. November 9, 2022. http://island.lk/sri-lankas-foreign-policy-dilemma/.
[121] *Telegraph India.* "Sri Lanka Lifts Ban on Six Tamil Diaspora Groups, 316 Individuals," August 14, 2022. Accessed August 16, 2022. https://www.telegraphindia.com/world/sri-lanka-lifts-ban-on-six-tamil-diaspora-groups-and-316-individuals/cid/1880190.

impact of the economic crisis and corruption on human rights' in addition to its calls for constitutional reform and devolution of political authority.[122]

President Ranil Wickremesinghe, an ardent promoter of neoliberal economics, is also the finance minister of Sri Lanka. In fact, he is an associate of the Mont Pelerin Society established by the father figures of the neo-liberal project, Fredrich Von Hyak, Milton Friedman and Allan Waters in 1947.[123] In November 2022, Wickramasinghe presented his 'IMF –friendly' 2023 austerity budget for Sri Lanka focused on 'boosting revenue, implementing tax reforms and fiscal consolidation' in order to secure the IMF bailout package.[124]

Among other questionable items, the Budget proposes to establish "a special committee to explore the cultivation of marijuana for export purposes."[125] In response to the accusation that the budget fails to provide 'any economic relief to the public who have been hit by high inflation', Tourism Minister Harin Fernando remarked, "This is not the time we could afford sugar coated pills, we have to turn this country next year so that we can start paying our debts."[126]

---

[122] "Resolution on Sri Lanka Passed at UNHRC." *Colombo Gazette*, October 6, 2022. Accessed October 6, 2022. https://colombogazette.com/2022/10/06/resolution-on-sri-lanka-passed-at-unhrc/.

[123] *Sinhalanet*. "Foreign Think Tanks Influence Sri Lanka: Mont Pelerin Society – ADVOCATA – Institute of Policy Studies," August 2, 2022. Accessed August 4, 2022. https://www.sinhalanet.net/foreign-think-tanks-influence-sri-lanka-mont-pelerin-society-advocata-institute-of-policy-studies. Waduge, Shenali. "Tamara Kunanayagam at Viyathmaga Forum: Selling Sri Lanka to Foreign Companies." *Lankaweb*, May 17, 2018. Accessed June 12, 2018. https://www.lankaweb.com/news/items/2018/05/17/tamara-kunanayagam-at-viyathmaga-forum-selling-sri-lanka-to-foreign-companies/.

[124] Jayasinghe, Uditha. "Sri Lanka's 2023 Budget Aims To Put Crisis-Hit Economy Back On Track." *International Business Times*, November 10, 2022. Accessed November 12, 2022. https://www.ibtimes.com/sri-lankas-2023-budget-aims-put-crisis-hit-economy-back-track-3634313; *The Financial Express*. "Sri Lanka's 'IMF-Friendly' Budget 2023 Gains Parliamentary Nod," November 22, 2022. Accessed November 22, 2022. https://www.financialexpress.com/economy/sri-lankas-imf-friendly-budget-2023-gains-parliamentary-nod/2886236/.

[125] *NewsWire*. "Live Updates : Budget 2023," November 14, 2022. November 22, 2022. https://www.newswire.lk/2022/11/14/live-updates-budget-2023/.

[126] Jayasinghe, Uditha. "Sri Lanka's 2023 Budget Aims To Put Crisis-Hit Economy Back On Track." *International Business Times*, November 10, 2022. Accessed November 12, 2022. https://www.ibtimes.com/sri-lankas-2023-budget-aims-put-crisis-hit-economy-back-track-3634313; *The Financial Express*. "Sri Lanka's 'IMF-Friendly' Budget 2023 Gains Parliamentary Nod," November 22, 2022. Accessed November 22, 2022. https://www.financialexpress.com/economy/sri-lankas-imf-friendly-budget-2023-gains-parliamentary-nod/2886236/.

Privatization

The most important source for generating state revenue identified in the 2023 Sri Lanka budget is the privatization of State-owned enterprises (SOEs), which is a primary strategy of IMF Structural Adjustment and neoliberal economics. The Sri Lanka 2023 Budget states:

> The government is currently maintaining 420 State-owned enterprises. 52 of these generate over Rs. 86 Billion in losses... A Unit has now been established at the Ministry of Finance with the specific task of restructuring SOEs. Initially, measures will be taken to restructure Sri Lankan Airlines, Sri Lanka Telecom, Colombo Hilton, Waters Edge, and Sri Lanka Insurance Corporation (SLIC) along with its subsidiaries, the proceeds of which will be used to strengthen foreign exchange reserves of the country, and strengthening the Rupee.[127]

As discussed in Chapter 3 (page 84), the left-wing Bandaranaike governments established a large number of SOEs between the mid- 1950s and the mid- 1970s, many of them import substitution industries. As discussed in Chapter 4, after the introduction of the Open Economy many SOEs were privatized. The process of privatization or commercialization has continued steadily since then with successive governments selling SOEs outright or turning them into Public Private Partnerships (PPP). The process of commoditizing state-owned land discussed throughout this book is a major aspect of privatization in Sri Lanka.

Not only the land, but water, indispensable for survival of life on Earth, is threatened by privatization and commoditization in Sri Lanka and around the world.[128] It is perplexing why the 2023 Sri Lanka budget includes a sentence without any explanation: "Safety stickers are to be introduced for drinking water bottles."[129] Is this a ploy to encourage people to drink store-bought water?

There are three categories of SOEs in Sri Lanka: 55 strategic SOEs, 287 SOEs with commercial interests and 185 SOEs with non-commercial interests.[130] The

---

127 *NewsWire*. "Live Updates: Budget 2023," November 14, 2022. November 22, 2022. https://www.newswire.lk/2022/11/14/live-updates-budget-2023/.
128 Petrella, Ricardo. "THE RIGHT TO WATER IN PERDITION?" *Other News*, November 28, 2022. Accessed November 30, 2022. https://www.other-news.info/the-right-to-water-in-perdition/. Waduge, Shenali. "LankaWeb – Sri Lanka's Water Should NOT Be Privatized." LankaWeb, November 26, 2022. Accessed November 30, 2022. https://www.lankaweb.com/news/items/2022/11/26/sri-lankas-water-should-not-be-privatized/.
129 *NewsWire*. "Live Updates: Budget 2023," November 14, 2022. November 22, 2022. https://www.newswire.lk/2022/11/14/live-updates-budget-2023/.
130 *The Island*. "It's High Time Sri Lanka Brought SOE Privatisation to the Policy Table: Advocata," December 20, 2021. Accessed January 30, 2022. http://island.lk/its-high-time-sri-lanka-brought-soe-privatisation-to-the-policy-table-advocata/. Rodrigo, Migara. "Sri Lanka's State-Owned Enterprises:

55 strategically important SOEs are estimated to employ around 1.9 percent of the country's labor force. The total state sector workforce is estimated to be about 1.4 million people, which accounts for over one in six of the country's total workforce. Given retirement and other benefits, many Sri Lankans prefer to work for the government sector instead of the private sector where such benefits are rarely available.[131] Given these realities, there is concern, that:

> ...privatization can result in retrenchment, high employee turnover, and lower salaries, causing further socioeconomic problems in communities. Many SOEs enjoy monopolies and privatizing them can result in corporations making decisions based on profits rather than on public benefit.[132]

There are also serious concerns over the outcome of past Sri Lankan privatizations, for example, the government owned paper manufacturing plants and textile mills. After privatization these industries were closed, and much foreign exchange was used for imports putting the country in an utterly dependent situation. For example, during the 2022 economic crisis, among fuel, food and cooking gas shortages, there was a severe shortage of paper needed for printing school textbooks, term test papers and newspapers.[133]

Unlike the private sector, many of the SOEs in Sri Lanka have powerful trade unions (with workers at different skill and professional levels) which have fought for workers' rights and the country's sovereignty for decades. Privatization is likely to lead to the elimination of many trade unions, strikes and other forms of labor resistance. In November 2022 union workers of The Government Press plant, targeted for privatization and "attacks on wages, conditions and jobs" went on strike.[134] In October 2022, Ceylon Petroleum Corporation (CPC) workers also held a protest strike against privatization of the CPC.[135]

A Major Crisis in the Making." *The Island*, January 1, 2022. Accessed January 30, 2022. http://island.lk/sri-lankas-state-owned-enterprises/.
131 Rafi, Talal. "Sri Lanka's State-Owned Enterprises Are a Big Part of Its Economic Problems." *The Diplomat*, July 27, 2022. Accessed July 28, 2022. https://thediplomat.com/2022/07/sri-lankas-state-owned-enterprises-are-a-big-part-of-its-economic-problems/.
132 Ibid.
133 Kuruwita, Rathindra. "JVP Leader Questions Wisdom of Promoting Privatisation." *The Island*, September 9, 2022. Accessed September 10, 2022. http://island.lk/jvp-leader-questions-wisdom-of-promoting-privatisation/.
134 Fernando, Lakshman, and W. A. Sunil. "Sri Lankan Unions Shut down Government Press Workers' Strike." *World Socialist Web Site*, November 23, 2022. https://www.wsws.org/en/articles/2022/11/24/zixp-n24.html.

The CPC, a vital enterprise pertaining to the island's oil supply and security has been identified for privatization under the IMF restructuring program and Lanka India Oil Company (LIOC), China's Sinopec, Petroleum Development Oman and Shell have expressed interest in this privatization deal.[136] It is important to note that in the name of privatization, the CPC is being handed over to SOEs of powerful foreign countries. The parent company of LIOC is the Indian Oil Corporation Limited (IOC) which is owned by the Ministry of Petroleum and Natural Gas of India. Sinopec Group is the world's largest oil refining, gas and petrochemical conglomerate and is wholly owned by the Chinese state. Petroleum Development Oman is owned by the Government of Oman, Royal Dutch Shell, Total Energies and Partex.[137]

Lessons from privatization in other parts of the world are relevant to Sri Lanka. According to a 2016 study, *The Privatising Industry in Europe* by the Transnational Institute in Amsterdam, in Europe, privatization has failed to produce the expected revenue as only "profitable firms are being sold and consistently at undervalued prices."[138] The study notes that according to research by the IMF and European universities, privatized firms are no more efficient than state-owned firms and that under the rubric of privatization, many European energy companies in Portugal, Greece and Italy, have been sold off to state-owned corporations from China. The Study also states that privatization in Europe has 'encouraged a growth in corruption, with frequent cases of nepotism and conflicts of interest' in Greece, Italy, Spain, Portugal and the UK.[139]

Considering the profitability of their consulting, the firms Clifford Chance and Lazard, hired by the Sri Lankan government to help with debt restructuring, warrant scrutiny for conflicts of interest. *The Privatising Industry in Europe*, for example, lists Clifford Chance as part of a small group of privatization advisory law firms, with annual revenues of more than a billion Euros, "reaping huge profits from the new wave of crisis-prompted privatizations."[140]

---

135 Sunil, W. A. "Sri Lankan Petroleum Workers Strike against Privatisation, Defying Essential Services Laws." *World Socialist Web Site*, October 18, 2022. https://www.wsws.org/en/articles/2022/10/19/yhmm-o19.html.
136 Ibid.
137 *IndianOil*. "Indian Oil Corporation Ltd. : IndianOil – The Energy of India." Accessed January 4, 2023. https://iocl.com/; http://www.sinopecgroup.com/group/en/. *Petroleum Development Oman*. "PDO." Accessed January 4, 2023. https://www.pdo.co.om/en.
138 *Transnational Institute*. "The Privatising Industry in Europe," February 17, 2016. Accessed November 21, 2022. https://www.tni.org/en/publication/the-privatising-industry-in-europe.
139 Ibid., 17.
140 Ibid., 11.

Lazard is reputed to be both "the number one sovereign advisory firm" and the "world's largest privatization advisory player." Lazard's operational global headquarters are in New York City, but the company is officially incorporated in the capital of Bermuda. When contracted as an advisor, Lazard has taken advantage of its prominent position by involving itself not only its advisory services branch, but also its asset management branch.[141] According to the Transnational Institute study,

> Upon the Initial Public Offering (IPO) of important state companies, Lazard has on a number of occasions undervalued the price of a company, which has allowed its asset management branch to buy up the stock at low prices which have then been sold for considerable profit when stock prices soared.[142]

The practice of both advising on privatization and then profiting from that advice raises ethical questions about Lazard. Questions should also be raised about the entire ecosystem of neoliberal global financial and political-economic institutions responsible for both creating debt crises in the first place, and then subsequently finding devious ways to benefit from them, all at the expense of ordinary people.[143] As whistleblower General Smedley Butler described war in his seminal 1935 polemic against imperialism, global finance is also a global racket "conducted for the benefit of the very few, at the expense of the very many. Out of war a few people make huge fortunes."[144]

Despite such serious concerns over privatization, there is now an enormous push by local and international actors advocating to privatize the remaining SOEs as the solution to Sri Lanka's debt and economic crises.[145] The Advocata Institute in Colombo, which is closely associated with the Mont Pelerin Society, The Atlas Network and their neoliberal agenda, is spearheading a major campaign to convince the public that privatization of SOEs is the path to 'reset Sri Lanka' for

---

141 Ibid., 17.
142 Ibid., 10.
143 Ibid.
144 Smedley D. Butler, *War Is a Racket: The Antiwar Classic by America's Most Decorated Soldier* (New York: Skyhorse Publishing, 2016), 1.
145 *The Island.* "It's High Time Sri Lanka Brought SOE Privatisation to the Policy Table: Advocata," December 20, 2021. Accessed January 30, 2022. http://island.lk/its-high-time-sri-lanka-brought-soe-privatisation-to-the-policy-table-advocata/. *Sinhalanet.* "Foreign Think Tanks Influence Sri Lanka: Mont Pelerin Society – ADVOCATA – Institute of Policy Studies," August 2, 2022. Accessed August 4, 2022. https://www.sinhalanet.net/foreign-think-tanks-influence-sri-lanka-mont-pelerin-society-advocata-institute-of-policy-studies.

solvency and prosperity.[146] The 'great Sri Lanka fire sale' of its SOEs and strategic assets is now on, with huge returns expected for colluding local and global financial and corporate elites and pauperization for ordinary people.[147] John Perkins, the author of *Confessions of an Economic Hit Man*, described the combination of "debt, enforced austerity, underinvestment, privatization, and the undermining of democratically elected governments" that also applies to what is happening in Sri Lanka.[148]

Undermining of democracy and sovereignty are particular concerns in the case of the new CBSL (Central Bank of Sri Lanka) Monetary Bill approved by the Sri Lanka Cabinet in accordance with IMF conditionalities.[149] If enacted, this Bill would essentially privatize the Central Bank of Sri Lanka making it an independent institution without accountability to the democratically elected government of the country.[150] Lalithasiri Gunaruwan, Professor in the Department of Economics at the Colombo University elaborates:

> if ... "Monetary Policy", is detached and "removed" away from the reach of the "people's sovereign representatives" ... the possibility of the CBSL becoming an organ functioning "under the advice of international bodies", could not be excluded, ... the Bill violates people's sovereignty ..., when ... authorisation of any other currency than Sri Lankan rupee for transactions within Sri Lanka, or in any part of the country, could be effected by the CBSL with no approval

---

146 *Advocata Institute.* "#ReformNow Conference – Let's Reset Sri Lanka," December 9, 2022. https://web.archive.org/web/20221209060942/https://www.reformnow.advocata.org/. *The Island.* "It's High Time Sri Lanka Brought SOE Privatisation to the Policy Table: Advocata," December 20, 2021. Accessed January 30, 2022. http://island.lk/its-high-time-sri-lanka-brought-soe-privatisation-to-the-policy-table-advocata/. *Atlas Network.* "Reforming and Privatizing State-Owned Enterprises in Sri Lanka," December 23, 2016. https://www.atlasnetwork.org/articles/reforming-and-privatizing-state-owned-enterprises-in-sri-lanka.

147 Pollard, Ruth. "Analysis | Is the Great Sri Lanka Fire Sale About to Begin?" *Washington Post*, May 30, 2022. Accessed May 31, 2022. https://www.washingtonpost.com/business/energy/is-the-great-sri-lanka-fire-sale-about-to-begin/2022/05/29/e187bc68-dfa3-11ec-ae64-6b23e5155b62_story.html.

148 Gelder, Sarah van. "More Confessions of an Economic Hit Man: This Time, They're Coming for Your Democracy." *YES! Magazine*, March 18, 2016. Accessed November 2, 2022. https://www.yesmagazine.org/economy/2016/03/18/more-confessions-of-an-economic-hit-man-this-time-theyre-coming-for-your-democracy.

149 'Cabinet Nod for New Draft Bill of CBSL Act', Daily FT, 21 December 2022. https://www.ft.lk/top-story/Cabinet-nod-for-draft-bill-of-new-CBSL-Act/26-743331 accessed March 16, 2023.

150 'A Closer Look at the IMF', Face the Nation, 1 March 2023. https://www.youtube.com/watch?v=_AWg6VvTj9g accessed March 16, 2023; State of the Nation, Episode 20, 29 January 2023. https://www.youtube.com/watch?v=SonHtrZT2jc&t=80s accessed March 17, 2023.

sought, or no intervention made, by their democratic agents, namely the Parliament or Cabinet of Ministers ...[151]

Even before the IMF package and the new CBSL Monetary Bill are formally adopted, back door deals are under way to authorize use of Indian currency in Sri Lanka. The many serious concerns over the CBSL Bill have led to the filing of four petitions in the Sri Lanka Supreme Court challenging the draft bill as unconstitutional.[152]

A Multifaceted Collapse

Sri Lanka's downfall is not only economic but political as well as cultural and psychological. Forces of global financial and corporate power are not leaving any room for the survival of a local economy or a national government that can meet the needs of its people.[153] The multifaceted crisis is leading to the demise of Sri Lanka's sovereignty turning the country into a mere shell of a state, wide open for more and more external political, economic and military exploitation. A politician rejected in democratic elections was made president following a controversial protest movement and a regime change operation. While a change was made at the top, the parliament responsible for the neocolonial crisis remains in place, fractured and subservient local collaborators to external masters.

Soon after the change of government, several incidents took place in 2022 drawing Sri Lanka into geopolitical confrontations which are not of its own making. In June, for example, Sri Lanka banned a Russian-operated plane from leaving the island and Russia, in turn, cancelled all Aeroflot flights to the country. Although the flights were later restored, the controversy is suspected to be related to western sanctions imposed on Russia due to its invasion of Ukraine.[154] Another incident took place over the berthing of the Chinese ship Yuan and Wang at the Hambantota

---

151 T. Lalithasiri Gunaruwan. "Proposed Central Bank of Sri Lanka Bill". Lanka Lead News, March 12, 2023. https://www.lankaleadnews.com/?p=125631. Accessed March 16, 2023.
152 "Four petitions filed in the Supreme Court challenging the Central Bank of Sri Lanka draft Bill". ColomboPage, Mar 14, 2023. http://www.colombopage.com/archive_23A/Mar14_1678771657CH.php Accessed March 16, 2023.
153 Hudson, Michael. "Financial Capitalism v. Industrial Capitalism." *Michael-hudson.com*, September 3, 1998. Accessed November 02, 2022. https://michael-hudson.com/1998/09/financial-capitalism-v-industrial-capitalism/.
154 Press Trust of India. "Detention of Russia Aircraft Is Private Legal Issue, Says Sri Lanka." *Business Standard*, June 6, 2022. Accessed June 12, 2022. https://www.business-standard.com/article/international/detention-of-russia-aircraft-is-private-legal-issue-says-sri-lanka-122060600030_1.html.

port in August. India raised objections shared by the US that the ship which is "used for space and satellite tracking, with specific usage in intercontinental ballistic missile launches" is a dual-use 'spy ship'.[155] After much controversy, Sri Lanka allowed the ship to be birthed at Hambantota, laying bear Sri Lanka's victimization by geopolitical rivalry over its strategic location.

While external forces are reaping economic and political benefits from the country, ordinary people are struggling to survive. The garment export sector which is suffering from reduced production has slashed jobs and wages.[156] Tourist arrivals following the worst of the financial crisis, are "still nowhere near government aspirations" and workers in that sector are experiencing continued unemployment and loss of income.[157] Sri Lanka's tea exports dropped to a historic low level bringing down wages of many workers in the process.[158]

However, migrant workers' remittances – the "key pillar of Sri Lanka's foreign currency earnings" –increased by 16 percent in September 2022, from US$ 279 million in July to US$ 325 million in August, with over 200,000 people going abroad for work. Sri Lanka's Labor and Foreign Employment Minister has expressed gratitude to expatriate workers for legally sending money through the banking system and supporting the country.[159] Slashing of jobs, wages, welfare benefits, access to land and other resources for survival associated with the IMF austerity agenda is likely to increase labor migration abroad in the coming years despite the slave conditions endured by many a housemaid or unskilled migrant laborer.

Sri Lanka, which scored high on the PQLI index in the past, is now experiencing "its highest poverty rate since 2009, and an erosion of the steady gains in wel-

---

155 Colombo had initially denied permission to the Chinese spy ship Yuan Wang 5 to berth at the Hambantota port. Srinivasan, Meera, and Suhasini Haidar. "Colombo Denies Reports on Chinese Ship." *The Hindu*, July 28, 2022, Accessed July 30, 2022 sec. World. https://www.thehindu.com/news/international/sri-lanka-denies-chinese-ship-is-headed-for-hambantota/article65695210.ece.
156 Perera, Wimal. "Sri Lankan Apparel Workers Hit by Major Jobs and Wages Cuts." *World Socialist Web Site*, November 17, 2022. https://www.wsws.org/en/articles/2022/11/17/wraf-n17.html.
157 Abeysinghe, Arundathie. "Sri Lanka's Tourism Industry Revives Despite Public Protests." *The Diplomat*, November 8, 2022. Accessed November 11, 2022 https://thediplomat.com/2022/11/sri-lankas-tourism-industry-revives-despite-public-protests/.
158 *France 24*. "Sri Lanka Tea Exports Lowest in 23 Years," May 4, 2022. Accessed May 12, 2022. https://www.france24.com/en/live-news/20220504-sri-lanka-tea-exports-lowest-in-23-years; Thevarajah, M., and K. Kandipan. "Sri Lanka: Glenugie Estate Workers Return after Union Betrays Strike." *World Socialist Web Site*, November 17, 2022. Accessed November 21, 2022. https://www.wsws.org/en/articles/2022/11/18/zocd-n18.html.
159 *Central Bank of Sri Lanka*. "Workers' Remittances." Accessed January 3, 2023. https://www.cbsl.gov.lk/en/workers-remittances; *ColomboPage*. "Sri Lanka: Migrant Workers' Remittances up by 16%, over 200,000 People Have Gone Abroad for Work," September 11, 2022. September 16, 2022. http://www.colombopage.com/archive_22B/Sep11_1662879267CH.php.

fare made between 2006 and 2019, according to a World Bank statement of October 2022."[160] The worsening economic condition is accompanied by increasing government authoritarianism and repression. A medical doctor who revealed extreme child malnutrition based on a survey in the Hambantota District, for example, was suspended from work.[161] A more political example was the threatening of the protest strike against privatization of the CPC with the repressive Essential Public Services Act.

In the face of growing opposition, in November 2022, President Ranil Wickremesinghe threatened to take police state action to suppress anti-government protests using the armed forces and a state of emergency.[162] The Ranil Wickremesinghe government introduced a new repressive Bureau of Rehabilitation bill which was approved by cabinet and presented to parliament on September 23. Civil society activists and parliamentary opposition MPs have filed petitions arguing that the bill is unconstitutional.[163] Should this bill be enforced, it would give authorities broad powers to detain people accused of crimes without court orders in military-run 'rehabilitation' centers, placing them at great risk of abuse including torture and being force-fed drugs.[164]

Amidst the multifaceted turmoil still more controversies are being added in the name of helping victims of price hikes and the financial crisis. One example of this is the effort to change the custom of state sector female workers, in particular schoolteachers, from wearing saris to work. While the rationale of the proponents is that saris are more expensive and more inconvenient than modern attire, opponents argue that saris are cheaper and a symbol of national tradition and re-

---

[160] Srinivasan, Meera. "Urban Poverty Triples in Sri Lanka amid Enduring Crisis." *The Hindu*, October 11, 2022, sec. World. Accessed October 13, 2022. https://www.thehindu.com/news/international/urban-poverty-triples-in-sri-lanka-amid-enduring-crisis/article65997513.ece.

[161] Wijesiriwardena, Pani. "Sri Lankan Government Suspends Doctor for Revealing Extreme Levels of Child Malnutrition." *World Socialist Web Site*, November 8, 2022. Accessed November 12, 2022. https://www.wsws.org/en/articles/2022/11/09/btii-n09.html.

[162] Gunadasa, Saman. "Sri Lankan President Threatens to Crush Anti-Government Struggles." *World Socialist Web Site*, November 25, 2022. Accessed November 28, 2022. https://www.wsws.org/en/articles/2022/11/26/tsgl-n26.html.

[163] Dewage, Naveen. "Sri Lankan Cabinet Tables Repressive 'Rehabilitation' Bureau Bill." *World Socialist Web Site*, October 5, 2022. Accessed November 28, 2022. https://www.wsws.org/en/articles/2022/10/06/zznq-o06.html.

[164] *Human Rights Watch*. "Sri Lanka: Draft 'Rehabilitation' Law Would Spur Abuse," October 17, 2022. Accessed November 28, 2022. https://www.hrw.org/news/2022/10/17/sri-lanka-draft-rehabilitation-law-would-spur-abuse. "Swasthika Arulingam- Attorney at Law," Uploaded October 10, 2022. https://www.youtube.com/watch?v=juDfoHdhLnE.

spect, much needed values in a social and cultural environment being quickly eroded by globalization and external intervention.[165]

The island's unique culture and identity are threatened by the Sri Lankan government's lack of finances and the interventions of external powers with their own agendas offering funds. Using its crisis-enhanced economic leverage, India, for example, is asserting kinship with Sri Lanka and developing large-scale 'spiritual tourism' into the island based on Hindu mythology. This could further Sri Lanka's incorporation into the Indian Hindu cultural milieu, threatening the distinct Buddhist identity maintained over the centuries.[166]

For much of the populace, the economic crisis has threatened physical and mental health in numerous ways, aggravating dissatisfaction with life, lack of hope for the country's future and causing despair among large segments of the population.[167] Many seek to leave the country, while others might resort to crime or substance abuse. In fact, drug addiction, which was already high among the youth including secondary school children, is reported to be increasing.[168]

Is this a familiar echo of the rise in alcohol and opium abuse that accompanied the colonial era, when such neutralizing vices were promoted by the colonial authorities and local elite?

What is needed is not such cynical counterinsurgency, or the proposed repressive Bureau of Rehabilitation for drug users and political protestors, but a humane economy that provides opportunities for survival and fulfilling lives for all.

---

[165] Perera, Neshella. "Sri Lanka's Economic Crisis Forces Public Sector to Let Saree Go as Office Attire." *EconomyNext*, September 23, 2022. Accepted November 3, 2022. https://economynext.com/sri-lankas-economic-crisis-forces-public-sector-to-let-saree-go-as-office-attire-100230; Waduge, Shenali. "Teachers' Aragalaya against Sarees Must Be Nipped in the Bud." *The Morning*, November 23, 2022. November 25, 2022. https://web.archive.org/web/20221125034643/https://www.themorning.lk/teachers-aragalaya-against-sarees-must-be-nipped-in-the-bud/.

[166] 'Blood is thicker than water': S. Jaishankar on India-Sri Lanka, Hindustan Times, March 18, 2023. www.hindustantimes.com/india-news/blood-is-thicker-than-water-s-jaishankar-on-india-sri-lanka-relations-101679090180927.html. Accessed March 24, 2023; 'Sri Lanka to concentrate on promoting Ramayana trail to Indian tourists'. The Hindu, August 19, 2022. https://www.thehindu.com/news/national/sri-lanka-to-concentrate-on-promoting-ramayana-trail-to-indian-tourists-tourism-envoy-jayasuriya/article65750481.ece. Accessed March 24.

[167] Matthias, Anne Thushara, and Saroj Jayasinghe. "Worsening Economic Crisis in Sri Lanka: Impacts on Health." *The Lancet Global Health* 10, no. 7 (July 2022): e959. https://doi.org/10.1016/S2214-109X(22)00234-0; *Verité Research*. "Mood of the Nation – October 2022." Accessed January 4, 2023. https://web.archive.org/web/20221101140447/https://www.veriteresearch.org/insight/mood-of-the-nation-oct-2022/.

[168] Range, Irangika. "Government to Eradicate Drug Abuse, Anti-Social Activities in Urban Areas – Minister." *Daily News*, August 9, 2022. August 18, 2022. https://www.dailynews.lk/2022/08/09/local/284650/government-eradicate-drug-abuse-anti-social-activities-urban-areas-minister.

Chapter 7:
Ecological and Collective Alternatives to Neoliberal Globalization

The Buddha's teaching, the Dhamma, has been preserved in Sri Lanka over the centuries, and encompasses the fundamental teaching: All experiences are preceded by thought, having mind as their master, and being created by mind.[1] In this concluding chapter, we turn to this fundamental truth on which to build a framework for collective and ecological alternatives to the globalized system underlying perennial socioeconomic, cultural and political crises; war and refugee crises; leading us to an existential crisis.

Globally, corporate controlled media, academia, publishing, entertainment and school systems have propagated the dominant free market ideology to such an extent that capitalism has become a form of fundamentalism, an unquestioned sacrosanct belief. Driven by profit and power, with leaders resembling sociopaths addicted to and corrupted by power, the guiding myth of our age pervades the Global North and the South, including countries with seemingly different political and cultural systems, such as 'Communist' China, Russia, India and the Islamic states.

This dominant worldview is a myth that equates economic and technological growth with development, advancing an illusion of progress and freedom that belies the overflowing evidence of the destruction that this ideology has wrought; environmental and social collapse, poverty and destitution, war and death, and the mental and physical ill-health that pervades our fractured societies.[2] There is scarce room for questioning this dominant thinking, let alone for maintaining an alternative life style outside the corporate and technologically controlled status-quo. The rebellious peasants, intellectuals and political leaders who defied colonialism and neocolonialism in Sri Lanka and elsewhere paid, and continue to pay, a heavy price with their livelihoods and lives.

According to a 2017 Report from Credit Suisse, the richest one percent of the world own 50 percent of the global wealth; in contrast, 70 percent of the world's working age population, have a mere 2.7 percent of global wealth.[3] A handful of

---

[1] *The Dhammapada: Verses and Stories.* "Dhammapada Verse 1, Cakkhupalatthera Vatthu." Accessed January 4, 2023. https://www.tipitaka.net/tipitaka/dhp/verseload.php?verse=001.
[2] Bandarage, Asoka. *Sustainability and Well-Being: The Middle Path to Environment, Society and the Economy.* Basingstoke: Palgrave Macmillan, 2013, 4–6.
[3] Neate, Rupert, and Rupert Neate Wealth correspondent. "Richest 1% Own Half the World's Wealth, Study Finds." *The Guardian*, November 14, 2017, sec. Inequality. Accessed November 15,

mega corporations and asset management companies like BlackRock control every sector of the global economy. In individual countries including in Sri Lanka, the top one percent control a disproportionate share of the wealth. Together, this global and local elite maintain and control the economic and financial system, using governments, propaganda, debt and other means of exploitation and counter-insurgency to both profit from and control populations. Indeed, as demonstrated throughout this book, the elites are overwhelmingly responsible for the debt, hunger and energy crises decimating the poorer classes in Sri Lanka, a common situation around the world. As the NGO, War on Want puts it: "More [IMF] debt won't solve Sri Lanka's debt Crisis."[4]

Transformation of Consciousness

As discussed in the book's introduction, the search for sustainable alternatives must start in the human mind with the transformation of consciousness. Mindfulness – the cultivation of present-moment awareness and equanimity – is a valuable tool for finding the much-needed inner solace and guidance for these challenging times; it is also a foundation for cultural change from dualism, domination and violence to one of unity, quality and peace. In Buddhist teaching, mindfulness is inextricably tied to an ethical approach to life that upholds virtuous, non-violent action.[5]

Unsurprisingly, the corporate individualist and consumerist approaches to mindfulness popular in the west, do not offer direction or tools to create sustainable and socially just development. In truth, like any movement co-opted and subverted by the dominant and dominating narratives of imperialism and profit-motive, it weakens interest in social-change activism and social transformation.[6]

In the face of vast and unrelenting counter-insurgency to maintain the global status quo, we need to explore the many ways that the inner transition of awareness, compassion and resilience – from mindfulness and other practices, such as

---

2017. https://www.theguardian.com/inequality/2017/nov/14/worlds-richest-wealth-credit-suisse; Lehmann, Axel P. "Global Wealth Report 2022." *Credit Suisse Research Institute*, 2022. https://www.credit-suisse.com/media/assets/corporate/docs/about-us/research/publications/global-wealth-report-2022-en.pdf.
4 *War on Want*. "More Debt Won't Solve Sri Lanka's Debt Crisis," July 29, 2022. Accessed August 3, 2022. https://www.waronwant.org/news-analysis/more-debt-wont-solve-sri-lankas-debt-crisis.
5 Walpola Rāhula. *What the Buddha Taught*. Rev. ed. London: G. Fraser, 1978.
6 Bandarage, Asoka. "Mindfulness, Social Action in Covid-19 Crisis." *Asia Times*, April 6, 2020. https://asiatimes.com/2020/04/mindfulness-social-action-in-covid-19-crisis/.

communion with nature, prayer and chanting – can be applied to an outer political and economic transition in order to meet the unprecedented challenges of our time.

The first step on the only path that can save humanity and the planet is for more and more people to become aware of the purpose and irrationality of the current global political-economic and cultural system, and to understand its historical and psychological roots in domination and exploitation.

Domination and the Market Paradigm

Domination, both individual and collective, is based on a psychology of dualism: mind versus matter, subject versus object, self versus other. Dualisms, in turn, give rise to structures of social domination, such as anthropocentrism (humans over nature); sexism (male over female); capitalism (capital over labor); imperialism (center over periphery/ North over South); feudalism (lords over serfs); and ethnocentrism (races and ethnic groups over each other). Dualism cultivates the delusion of the self as separate and in opposition to the other. This in turn gives rise to the erroneous notion that the wellbeing of the self requires domination and victory over, even annihilation of, the other. At the root of domination lies egoism, an excessive attachment to the separate self.[7]

Today, 'ego consciousness' and its ethics of individualism, domination, and competition is the central force of individuals, groups, societies and the economic systems and in how humans relate toward nature and the natural world. This myopic consciousness causes increasing and massive destruction of the environment, widening economic disparities, and social conflicts.

In fact, the myopia of the attempt by modern science and technology to conquer nature is arguably driven by human existential insecurity, ultimately the fear of impermanence and death.[8]

The ideology of materialist development that emerged under mercantilism 500 years ago, and advanced greatly during the Industrial Revolution some 250 years later, came to integrate the entire world within a single interconnected market and technological framework. Its origin lies in the ideas of the Scientific

---

7 Bandarage, Asoka. *Women, Population and Global Crisis: A Political-Economic Analysis.* London: Zed Books, 1997, Part 3; Eisler, Riane. *The Chalice and the Blade: Our History, Our Future.* 1st ed. Cambridge [Mass.]: Harper & Row, 1987.
8 Bandarage, Asoka. *Sustainability and Well-Being: The Middle Path to Environment, Society and the Economy.* Basingstoke: Palgrave Macmillan, 2013, 75.

Revolution in Europe championed by the likes of Francis Bacon and René Descartes in the 17th century.[9]

In contrast to the eco-centric vision of life found in earlier and many concurrent indigenous societies, the new rationalist worldview promoted a linear, quantitative and mechanistic outlook on human and non-human life. It undermined traditional community relations and, globally, people have been increasingly pitted against each other and against the natural world.[10] Reductionist and materialistic, the capitalist and communist concepts of life both approach nature as an inanimate object to be technologically conquered and exploited for purposes of economic growth.

Admittedly, capitalism is an inherently dynamic economic system. It promises freedom from the bondage of tradition and the limits of nature. It presumes that maximization of individual benefit would lead to the common good. Fueled by private accumulation of natural, financial and productive resources, capital constantly expands to new frontiers, appropriating all regions of the Earth and sectors of life: production, reproduction, and even consciousness. Capital and technological expansion constitutes a single process, 'technocapitalism'. It expands restlessly and near exponentially, increasingly through the technological edge even more than the competitive advantage of labor exploitation.[11]

Social, environmental, and moral and ethical standards are irrelevant in capitalist decision-making. Adam Smith, the author of the 1776 *The Wealth of Nations*, considered the 'father of capitalism', envisaged that the pursuit of private interest in the Free Market would lead to public good. A moral philosopher, Smith was interested in provisions for social and productive accountability and the creation of 'virtuous citizens.'[12] Unfortunately, it quickly transpired that unrestrained neoliberal capitalism has all the morality and sanity of a runaway train gaining speed on its insatiable desire for energy, resources and profit. Profit maximization, the 'bottom line', has become the 'good', the end in itself; an end with no end. Simultaneously, to feed and protect this insatiable appetite as it spreads, military activity

---

[9] Merchant, Carolyn. *The Death of Nature: Women, Ecology, and the Scientific Revolution.* Science/Women's Studies. New York: Harper & Row, 1989.
[10] Bandarage, Asoka. *Sustainability and Well-Being: The Middle Path to Environment, Society and the Economy.* Basingstoke: Palgrave Macmillan, 2013, 38–40.
[11] Ibid., 40.
[12] Griswold, Charles L. "Adam Smith: Conscience of Capitalism." *The Wilson Quarterly* (1976–) 15, no. 3 (1991): 53–61.

has become a 'direct production component' of international trade, "as necessary for imports as are pipelines and supertankers."[13]

The result is a system devoid of compassion and wisdom, where industries producing negative use values, such as the military, dominate amidst enormous environmental devastation, biodiversity loss and human suffering. Human livelihoods and environmental sustainability are extraneous to capitalist planning and production, made clear, for example, by the increasing displacement of workers by artificial intelligence (30 percent of global workforce estimated to be automated by 2030)[14] and continued use of fossil fuel for US military activity (the "largest single institutional consumer of hydrocarbons in the world")[15] and coal for economic production.[16]

The modern economy disrupts and dissects the natural integration of planetary life, seeking instead to reintegrate, recreate, and control society and the environment through modern science, technology, and the market (Figure 7.1) The extremism of this approach is evident in current technological and market developments to redesign life and to create what some scientists call a 'post-nature' and 'post-human' world.[17] According to Fidelity Investments which promotes synthetic biology, in less than fifty years, there could be more lab-created forms of

---

13 *Science Daily.* "Military Greenhouse Gas Emissions: EPA Should Recognize Environmental Impact of Protecting Foreign Oil, Researchers Urge," July 22, 2010. Accessed November 9, 2022. https://www.sciencedaily.com/releases/2010/07/100721121657.htm. Bandarage, Asoka. *Sustainability and Well-Being: The Middle Path to Environment, Society and the Economy.* Basingstoke: Palgrave Macmillan, 2013, 22–23.
14 Galeon, Dom. "McKinsey Finds Automation Could Eradicate a Third of America's Workforce by 2030." *Futurism,* December 1, 2017. Accessed November 12, 2022. https://futurism.com/mckinsey-finds-automation-eradicate-third-americas-workforce-2030.
15 Nuttall, W., C. Samaras, and M. Bazilian. "Energy and the Military: Convergence of Security, Economic, and Environmental Decision-Making." [Working Paper]. University of Cambridge, November 20, 2017. https://doi.org/10.17863/CAM.17547.
16 McClelland, Calum. "The Impact of Artificial Intelligence – Widespread Job Losses." *IoT For All,* July 1, 2020. Accessed November 1, 2022. https://www.iotforall.com/impact-of-artificial-intelligence-job-losses/; Rapier, Robert. "Global Coal Consumption Surged In 2021." *Forbes,* August 9, 2022. Accessed November 1, 2022. https://www.forbes.com/sites/rrapier/2022/08/09/global-coal-consumption-surged-in-2021/.
17 *Z33.be.* "Alter Nature: Designing Nature – Designing Human Life – Owning Life," February 18, 2011. Accessed November 22, 2022. https://web.archive.org/web/20160412131539/http://www.z33.be/en/projects/alter-nature-designing-nature-designing-human-life-owning-life. Bandarage, Asoka. *Sustainability and Well-Being: The Middle Path to Environment, Society and the Economy.* Basingstoke: Palgrave Macmillan, 2013, 43.

plant and animal life on the planet than those identified in nature.[18] In agriculture, earth-based people such as the rice cultivating peasantry in Sri Lanka are being displaced by commoditization of land for agribusiness. Meanwhile, genetic engineering, robotics, artificial intelligence, and other new types of cognitive tools are being employed by corporate-funded scientists to design a new 'transhuman' species merged with technology.[19]

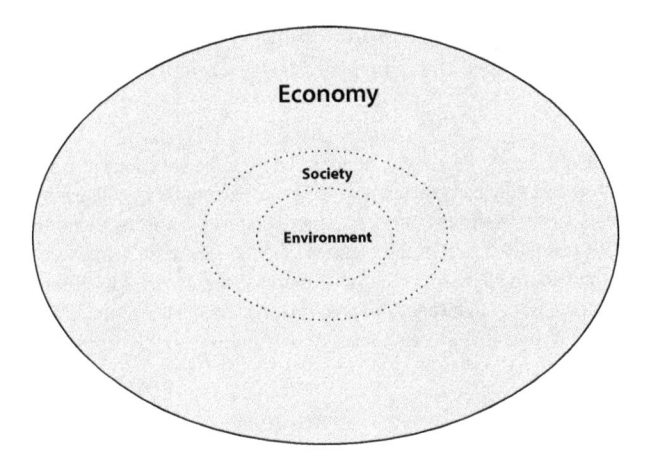

Figure 7.1: Domination and the Market Paradigm. Source: Asoka Bandarage, *Sustainability and Well-Being*. Basingstoke: Palgrave Macmillan, 2013, 6.

As humanity and the environment increasingly become mere appendages of technology and the economy, we face an existential crisis of what it means to be human in nature. As more and more people are displaced from land, community and employment and unable to purchase goods and services, they become superfluous to the economic machine and therefore more expendable.

The corporate-scientific visions of technological domination over nature also fail to address the fact that if the climate is not stabilized, we will unleash long term planetary forces far beyond our capacity to control. Human induced natural forces, such as droughts, wildfires, and floods will come to dominate and radically curtail activities – as they are doing already, in Sri Lanka and around the world. Karl Polyani warned in 1944 in *The Great Transformation:* "To allow the market

---

18 https://vimeo.com/60287475. Bandarage, Asoka. *Sustainability and Well-Being: The Middle Path to Environment, Society and the Economy.* Basingstoke: Palgrave Macmillan, 2013, 44.
19 Ibid., 43.

mechanism to be the sole director of the fate of human beings and their natural environment... would result in the demolition of society."[20]

In *Brave New World* published in 1931, Aldous Huxley warned how unknowingly people come to love their oppression and adore the very technology and consumerism that undo their capacities to think and feel.[21] Are we are on the cusp of that Brave New World and/or the apocalypse?

The language of neoliberalism is that of freedom, democracy and human rights. The growing disparity between language and reality, however, is leading to the domination of consciousness best described by George Orwell in *Nineteen Eight Four*:

> Reality control...Newspeak, doublethink,...To know and not to know, to be conscious of complete truthfulness while telling carefully constructed lies...to repudiate morality while laying claim to it, to believe that democracy was impossible ...to forget, whatever it was necessary to forget, then to draw it back to memory again in the moment when it was needed, and then promptly to forget it again, and above all, to apply the same process to the process itself that was the ultimate subtlety: consciously to induce unconsciousness, and then, once again, to become unconscious of the act of hypnosis...just performed.[22]

Partnership and the Ecological Paradigm

To repeat the famous quote attributed to Albert Einstein, "We cannot solve our problems with the same level of thinking that created them." The problems created by neoliberalism and extreme market domination cannot be solved within that paradigm, and a new paradigm is desperately needed.

The alternative to ego consciousness, rooted in the psychology of fear and a 'self vs. other' mentality, is a universal consciousness grounded in the truth of unity within diversity. This higher consciousness sees the other as an extension

---

20 Polanyi, Karl. Great Transformation: The Political and Economic Origins of Our Time. Boston: Beacon Press, 2001, 76. Available at: https://archive.org/details/greattransformat00karl.
21 Huxley, Aldous. *Brave New World*. New York: Harper & Bros., 1946. Available at: https://archive.org/details/bravenewworld00huxl.
22 Cited in Asoka Bandarage, *Women, Population and Global Crisis: A Political-Economic Analysis*, London: Zed Books, 1997, 298; Orwell, George. *1984*. Signet Books. New York: The New American Library, 1949.

of the self and the well-being of the self and the other as inherently interdependent. It weakens dualism and contributes to partnership ethics.[23]

The environment—planet Earth—encompasses human society and the economy within its fold. The economy, the production and distribution of the material means of existence, is only one subsystem of society. The environment – Mother Nature – has primacy over the human-created spheres of society and the economy. The natural world does not need humanity for its survival, but humanity cannot survive without the natural environment, the soil, water, air, sunlight, etc. The ecological worldview, subscribed to by indigenous thinking, eastern spirituality (especially Buddhism) and some fields within western science such as evolutionary biology and ecology, recognizes that we are part of the Earth, not apart and separate from it (Figure 7.2).[24]

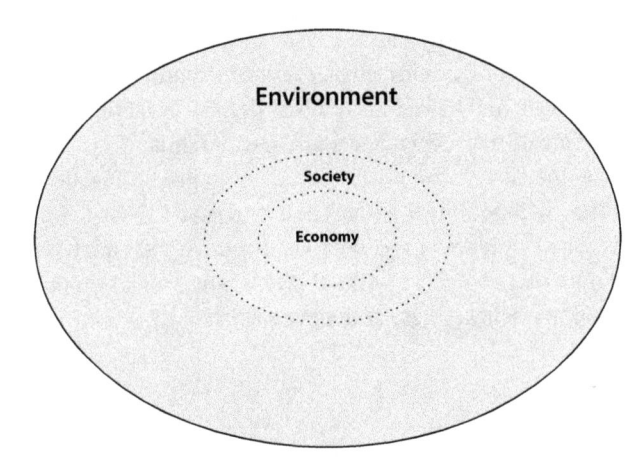

Figure 7.2: Partnership and the Ecological Paradigm. Source: Asoka Bandarage, *Sustainability and Well-Being*. Basingstoke: Palgrave Macmillan, 2013, 6.

Instead of attempting to dominate and subsume society and the environment within the logic of unbridled, exploitative economic growth, the components of the economy – technology, property relations, the market, and finance – must be redesigned to serve the needs of environmental sustainability and human well-being. Likewise, rather than upholding and extending the extremist growth-oriented eco-

---

23 Eisler, Riane Tennenhaus. *The Chalice and the Blade: Our History, Our Future*. 1st ed. Cambridge [Mass.]: Harper & Row, 1987; Bandarage, Asoka. *Sustainability and Well-Being: The Middle Path to Environment, Society and the Economy*. Basingstoke: Palgrave Macmillan, 2013, 73–76.
24 Ibid., 5; Mander, Jerry. *In the Absence of the Sacred: The Failure of Technology and the Survival of the Indian Nations*. Sierra Club books pbk. ed. San Francisco: Sierra Club Books, 1992.

nomic system through new technological and market-based strategies, such as geo-engineering and carbon trading, the world's economic structures must be transformed so that the exploitation of people and plunder of the Earth are replaced by systems that honor environmental sustainability and social justice (The Earth Charter, Appendix 3).

Although competition, domination, and conflict seem to characterize today's world, altruism and cooperation, not exploitation and oppression, have been the defining ethics of human history. After dualism itself, there is a convenient and cynical second fallacy maintained by those in power wishing to hold their position: that dualism is an innate and inevitable human trait. But as anthropologist David Graeber said in *The Utopia of Rules*, "The ultimate, hidden truth of the world is that it is something that we make, and could just as easily make differently."[25]

Even Charles Darwin, who popularized the idea of the survival of the fittest, paid homage to the importance of empathy and altruism in human evolution.[26] Given the capacity of the human mind for consciousness transformation, it is possible for us to shift from fear, anger, and hatred to a path of psycho-social development grounded on a global ethic of interdependence and partnership.[27]

Clearly, we cannot rely on the current neoliberal paradigm to produce leaders who will lead this change. They will not bite the hand that guides and feeds them, as poisonous as the food is. Dualism leaves us as only victims or aggressors, with no Middle Path of love. The only reality to those without love is power and, without innocence or goodness, they don't believe these traits even exist.

The Balanced Middle Path

The Middle Path derives from the Buddha's teaching and is directed towards the cultivation of mental equilibrium, morality, and individual liberation. It can also be applied to social and economic transformation and is a path to nurturing peace and harmony in the world.[28]

---

[25] Graeber, David. *The Utopia of Rules: On Technology, Stupidity, and the Secret Joys of Bureaucracy.* Brooklyn: Melville House, 2015, 89.
[26] Ekman, Paul. "Darwin's Compassionate View of Human Nature." *JAMA* 303, no. 6 (February 10, 2010): 557–558. https://doi.org/10.1001/jama.2010.101.
[27] Bandarage, Asoka. "Ethical Path to Ecological and Social Survival." In *Globalism and Localization: Emergent Solutions to Ecological and Social Crises*, edited by Jeanine Canty. New York: Routledge, 2019. https://doi.org/10.4324/9780429274145.
[28] Walpola Rāhula. *What the Buddha Taught.* Rev. ed. London: G. Fraser, 1978.

Grounded in inner tranquility, the Middle Path is a non-violent alternative to extremism of all types, including ethno-religious fundamentalism and the economic fundamentalism of neoliberalism. It opposes, the craving, aversion, and selfishness of extremism, with the righteous intention of generosity, compassion, and wisdom.

Economist E.F. Schumacher envisioned a road map for the transformation of the global economic system in what he called "Buddhist economics."[29] The terminology is not important as are the ethical principles it promotes: rational use of natural resources, appropriate technology, balanced consumption, equitable distribution of wealth, and livelihoods for all. These principles are also shared by the newer field of Ecological Economics which distinguishes itself from conventional economics, designed to uphold the status-quo.[30]

The ethical approach to the economy shows that the alleviation of suffering of human beings and other animals would need to take priority over unregulated market and technological growth and the extreme accumulation of wealth by a tiny minority. Production of harmful or negative use values – fossil fuel combustion, nuclear and conventional weapons – violates the ethics of partnership. Renewable and clean sources of energy and appropriate technology based on solar, wind, and biomass instead of fossil fuels would become the basis of the economy.

Agribusiness changes the environment through ecologically and socially damaging petrochemicals and genetic engineering. In contrast, entrepreneurs, across the world, are now designing approaches to organic agriculture that adapt human needs to fit the land. Permaculture, a revolutionary agro-ecological approach founded in the late 1970s on the ethics of 'earth care, people care and fair share', studies nature and emulates nature's models in agriculture and related fields, such as water resource management and architecture.[31]

The Middle Path does not disavow all quantitative growth, the roles of corporations, or the state. Nor does it call for a complete delinking from the global market or modern technology.[32] It is not possible or necessary to return to the stagnation that characterized some pre-capitalist societies or abandon economic growth and technological innovation altogether. However, to restore both ecological and

---

[29] Schumacher, E. F. *Small Is Beautiful: Economics as If People Mattered.* New York: HarperCollins, 2010.
[30] Daly, Herman E. *Beyond Growth: The Economics of Sustainable Development.* Boston: Beacon Press, 1996.
[31] *Deep Green Permaculture.* "Deep Green Permaculture: Connecting People to Nature, Empowering People to Live Sustainably." Accessed January 4, 2023. https://deepgreenpermaculture.com/.
[32] Asoka Bandarage, *Women, Population and Global Crisis: A Political-Economic Analysis,* London: Zed Books, 1997, 327.

social balance, extreme homogenization and globalization need to be countered with stronger local and intermediate socioeconomic structures and cultural practices. Community-level economic systems are vital for the survival of local ecosystems, cultures, ethnic groups, neighborhoods, and livelihoods.

As futurist Hazel Henderson noted, the demand for bioregionalism and decentralization carries within it a critique of monopoly capitalism and unsustainable technological growth.[33] Bioregionalism honors local self-sufficiency as well as community control over water, land, and other natural resources, including plant and seed varieties. Calls for economic decentralization or Schumacher's *Small is beautiful* approach do not entail complete autarky or abandoning the need for a global social and ecological agenda.

However, sustainable development calls for limiting privatization and changes in property relations, not just changes in technologies of production. Transnational corporations and nation states should be regulated in their appropriation and exploitation of natural resources, weapons production, and the deployment and monetary transactions of large banks and financial institutions. The Middle Path and other ethical teachings encourage us to question the ethical intentions of such institutions. Do they generate tolerance and moderation or domination and new forms of inequality and environmental destruction?

As Schumacher explained, the Buddhist Middle Path is by no means "antagonistic to physical well-being."[34] However, it is more important than ever to learn to distinguish between human needs and wants, between what is sufficient for human and planetary wellbeing and what constitutes greed and domination over nature and people. The sustainable and compassionate approach upholds intergenerational justice that honors the needs of the present while ensuring that resources are available for future generations of humans and other species.[35]

Excessive material consumption tends to decrease overall human well-being leading to natural resource depletion, human alienation from nature, and spiritual emptiness. Extreme economic inequalities exacerbate fear, hatred, and social volatility. As the Middle Path Equilibrium Curve illustrates, a balanced Middle Path between extreme over-consumption by the rich and extreme under-consumption

---

[33] Henderson, Hazel. *Paradigms in Progress: Life beyond Economics*. 1st Berrett-Koehler ed. San Francisco: Berrett-Koehler Publishers, 1995.

[34] Schumacher, E. F. *Small Is Beautiful: Economics as If People Mattered*. New York: HarperCollins, 2010, 60.

[35] *Deep Green Permaculture*. "Deep Green Permaculture: Connecting People to Nature, Empowering People to Live Sustainably." Accessed January 4, 2023. https://deepgreenpermaculture.com/.

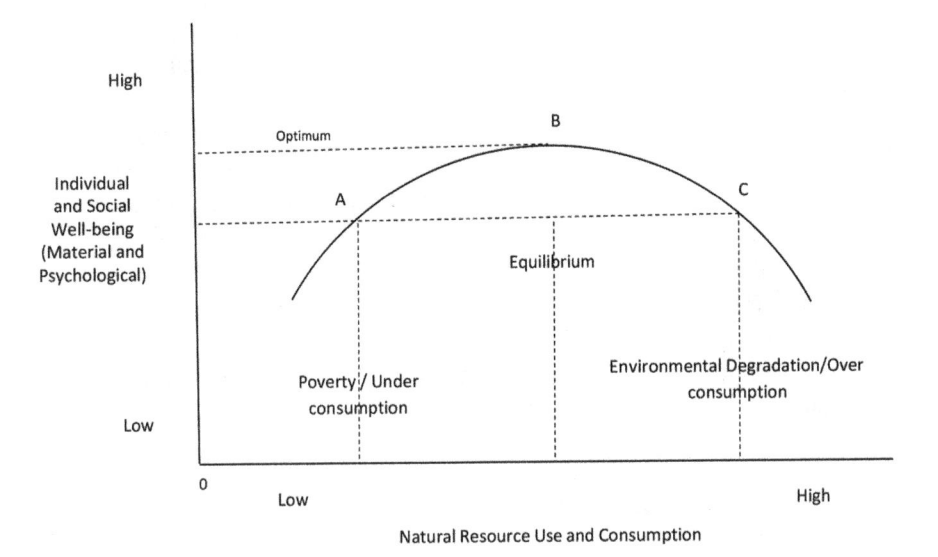

Figure 7.3: Middle Path Equilibrium Curve. Source: Adapted from Patrick Mendis, "Buddhist Equilibrium: The Theory of the Middle Path for Sustainable Development", Staff Paper P93–2 Department of Agriculture and Applied Economics, University of Minnesota, January 1993, 28. https://ageconsearch.umn.edu/record/13948/files/p93-02.pdf.

by the poor would maximize overall human and social well-being providing room for environmental regeneration.[36] (Figure 7.3).

Instead of speaking of a collective 'we', it is necessary to explore the differential responsibilities and burdens borne by different communities for climate disruption, social inequality and related problems.

The conflict over climate mitigation targets and policies between the countries of the global North and South must not be used to ignore the need for improved access to food, water, shelter, health care, and education for the poor and malnourished in Sri Lanka and elsewhere.[37] The world's resources are, indeed, limited, and increased consumption by the poor can only be achieved by reducing overconsumption by the wealthy. It is the privileged groups, especially those at the top

---

[36] Bandarage, Asoka. *Sustainability and Well-Being: The Middle Path to Environment, Society and the Economy.* Basingstoke: Palgrave Macmillan, 2013, 83.
[37] Friends of the Earth International. "Report: How Nature Based Solutions Threaten Food Sovereignty," November 3, 2022. Accessed November 30, 2022. https://www.foei.org/publication/double-jeopardy-report-nature-based-solutions/.

of the global social hierarchy that need to shift away from their egotistical consciousness and consumption habits and share more within the global commons.[38]

Privileged global and national elites try to deflect attention from economic inequality by inciting ethno-religious and other forms of social polarization as has been the case in Sri Lanka throughout the colonial and neocolonial periods. Vigilance is needed to ensure that eco-fascist views and extremist social movements do not gain ground as economic conditions deteriorate and social and environmental dislocations, population displacements, and refugee crises worsen around the world.[39] The shift towards renewable energy and environmental sustainability has to be accompanied with social justice- democratic changes in the control over resources and production and access to economic opportunities for wider groups of people.

Resistance to Economic Domination

In the 1930s, in the era of the Great Depression, Keynesian economic thought, state intervention and social democratic reforms, such as US President Franklin D. Roosevelt's New Deal helped deter a complete a breakdown of the capitalist world economy.[40] The benevolent capitalism and the popularity of socialism in that period had far-reaching effects. In Sri Lanka the Donoughmore Reforms of 1933 introduced the framework for social democracy and the welfare state. As discussed earlier (see page 82), this eventually led to Sri Lanka achieving high scores on the Physical Quality of Life Index (a composite of literacy, infant mortality and life expectancy indicators) compared to most other colonies.

In the current era of neoliberal extremism, the corporate dominated world order is increasingly integrated in a tight web of financial, technological and market control. Although capitalism is built inherently on competition, monopolistic corporations and seemingly rival national states, such as, the USA and China work together to maintain the status-quo. Ironically, the U.S. is the biggest debtor nation in the world and China is its creditor. The United Nations, which was originally created to represent the rights of all nations, is also increasingly subjected to corporate interests. For example, the Global Compact, the United Nations initiative to encourage transnational corporations to adopt environmentally and socially re-

---

[38] Bandarage, Asoka. *Sustainability and Well-Being: The Middle Path to Environment, Society and the Economy.* Basingstoke: Palgrave Macmillan, 2013, 83.
[39] Ibid., 54–56.
[40] *Britanica.Com.* "Great Depression – Marxism and the Great Depression." Accessed January 4, 2023. https://www.britannica.com/event/Great-Depression/Political-movements-and-social-change.

sponsible policies have failed with Corporate Social Responsibility being reduced to philanthropy and green marketing by megalithic corporations.[41] Transnational corporations have entered every area of global governance including the United Nations setting the agendas for global initiatives including climate mitigation.[42]

Given the globalized nature of power and control, transformation also requires a global analysis and collective action rather than simply individual efforts by separate countries. In the early decades of decolonization, developing countries led by United Nations Conference on Trade and Development (UNCTAD), the Group of 77 and the Non-Alignment Movement initiated major efforts, such as the Declaration New International Economic Order (Appendix 1) to improve their collective position in the global political economy. These initiatives are more relevant than ever given worsening Global North-South disparities and the new Cold War. The Declaration of the Indian Ocean as a Zone of Peace of 1971, which Sri Lanka championed, too is entirely valid given rising geopolitical rivalry in the Indian Ocean (Appendix 2).

Another important regional mechanism is the Asian Clearing Union (ACU) established in 1974 as an initiative of the United Nations Economic and Social Commission for Asia and the Pacific. The ACU payment arrangement was designed to facilitate payments among participating regional countries (Sri Lanka, Bangladesh, Bhutan, India, Iran, Myanmar, Nepal, Pakistan, Maldives), economize on use of foreign reserves and transfer costs and promote trade and banking transactions among them. However, Sri Lanka left the long-standing south-to south cooperative ACU mechanism in October 2022 prompting Bangladesh to halt transactions with Sri Lanka, raising the question if Sri Lanka was prompted to do so by the IMF debt restructuring process.[43]

Since the 1970s, major collaborative initiatives have been continued by developing countries and global NGOs to reform the global economic and financial system. Examples are the efforts of UNCTAD to develop a multilateral legal framework for sovereign debt restructuring processes.[44] Yet given opposition of creditors

---

41 *Transnational Institute.* "United Nations and Transnational Corporations: A Deadly Association," April 4, 2007. Accessed January 4, 2023. https://www.tni.org/en/article/united-nations-and-transnational-corporations-a-deadly-association. Bandarage, Asoka. *Sustainability and Well-Being: The Middle Path to Environment, Society and the Economy.* Basingstoke: Palgrave Macmillan, 2013, 62.
42 Interview with Harris Gleckman, Transnational Institute, 21 November 2019, https://www.tni.org/en/article/the-un-is-being-turned-into-a-public-private-partnership.
43 *The Asian Age.* "Sri Lanka Quits ACU," October 28, 2022. http://dailyasianage.com/news/295902/?regenerate.
44 UNCTAD. "Sovereign Debt Restructuring." Accessed January 4, 2023. https://unctad.org/topic/debt-and-finance/sovereign-debt-restructuring.

and the protection given them by the advanced countries and multilateral institutions, the U.N. has failed to uphold its commitment and implement a debt restructuring mechanism.[45]

Still, countries in the Global South are keeping up their demands for meaningful participation in international institutions over debt restructuring, climate mitigation and other important and divisive issues. As the locus of global power shifts away from the west and a multipolar world arises, new multilateral partnerships are emerging for development financing, such as, the New Development Bank (NDB), formerly referred to as the BRICS (Brazil, Russia, India, China and South Africa) Bank and the Asian Infrastructure Development Bank as alternatives to the Bretton Woods and other western dominated financial institutions.[46] Whether the BRICS countries provide genuine partnership over new forms of domination need to be questioned in the context of their aggression against small neighboring countries, as in the case between India and Sri Lanka.

Debt Jubilee (now Debt Justice) which approaches debt 'through the lens of power and colonialism' works with activist groups across the global south and the north to cancel debt, especially 'odious' or illegitimate debts incurred by despotic regimes of poor countries.[47] In Sri Lanka too, a number of activist groups including a network of farmers' organizations across the island are calling for debt cancellation.[48] A moratorium on borrowing from private financial markets is also called for to enable the country to extricate itself from the current debt trap caused by such borrowing.[49] A statement released by 182 international economists

---

[45] Gallagher, Kevin, and Richard Kozul-Wright. *The Case for a New Bretton Woods. Case for Series*. Cambridge, UK: Polity, 2022.

[46] McNair, David. "Global Economic Turmoil Calls for a Modernized Global Financial Architecture to Address Needs of the Most Vulnerable Countries." *Carnegie Endowment for International Peace*, November 15, 2022. Accessed December 4, 2022. https://carnegieendowment.org/2022/11/15/global-economic-turmoil-calls-for-modernized-global-financial-architecture-to-address-needs-of-most-vulnerable-countries-pub-88400. *New Development Bank*. "NDB." Accessed January 4, 2023. https://www.ndb.int/; Asian Infrastructure Investment Bank. "AIIB – Asian Infrastructure Investment Bank." Accessed January 4, 2023. https://www.aiib.org/en/index.html.

[47] *International Debt Charity | Debt Justice*. "Colonialism and Debt." Accessed January 4, 2023. https://debtjustice.org.uk/wp-content/uploads/2022/08/Bishop-photo.jpg.

[48] *IDN-InDepthNews*. "A New Coalition Issues a Statement on the Crisis in Sri Lanka," July 3, 2022. https://www.indepthnews.net/index.php/the-world/asia-pacific/5427-a-new-coalition-issues-a-statement-on-the-crisis-in-sri-lanka. *War on Want*. "More Debt Won't Solve Sri Lanka's Debt Crisis," July 29, 2022. Accessed August 2, 2022. https://www.waronwant.org/news-analysis/more-debt-wont-solve-sri-lankas-debt-crisis.

[49] Rajaisngham-Senanayake, Darini. "'Make The Economy Scream:' Whither the Asian 21st Century?" *Countercurrents*, October 21, 2022. Accessed November 2, 2022. https://countercurrents.org/2022/10/make-the-economy-scream-whither-the-asian-21st-century/.

and other experts on 8 January 2023, points out that only debt cancellation would allow economic recovery for Sri Lanka but that private investors, especially hedge funds owning Sri Lanka's debt are obstructing debt relief for Sri Lanka.[50] In affirming the thesis of this book that the Sri Lankan crisis is illustrative of a global crisis, the experts' Statement elaborates that

> The Sri Lankan case will provide an important indicator of whether the world – and the international financial system in particular – is equipped to deal with the increasingly urgent questions of sovereign debt relief and sustainability; and to ensure a modicum of justice in international debt negotiations. It is therefore crucial not only for the people of Sri Lanka, but to restore any faith in a multilateral system that is already under fire for its lack of legitimacy and basic viability.[51]

Civic Engagement and Grassroots Struggles

The struggle against finance capital is the tip of the iceberg. As corporate dominance expands, the struggles to stop deforestation and the building of massive infrastructural projects, the commoditization and grabbing of land and resources which threaten local ecosystems and communities are intensifying. This can be seen across the world, in the United States, Canada, the Amazon, South Asia, Sri Lanka and other regions.[52]

Valiant efforts are being made to safeguard food sovereignty and resist the introduction of GMOs (genetically modified organisms) in agriculture.[53] Bolivia, which experienced a historic popular victory against privatization and control of water by the Bechtel corporation more than fifteen years ago introduced water as a common good in the Bolivian constitution. However, the struggle over water use between corporate interests and consumers, persists in Bolivia as in Sri Lanka and many other countries.[54]

---

50 Larry Elliott, *The Guardian*, January 8, 2023, https://www.theguardian.com/business/2023/jan/08/hedge-funds-holding-up-vital-debt-relief-for-crisis-hit-sri-lanka-warn-economists.
51 Ibid.
52 Bandarage, Asoka. "No to the Keystone Pipeline." *HuffPost*, March 21, 2013. https://www.huffpost.com/entry/no-to-the-keystone_b_2927453; *Friends of the Earth International*. "Friends of the Earth International – FOEI – Ngo." Accessed January 4, 2023. https://www.foei.org/.
53 Norero, Daniel. "Ecuador Passes Law Allowing GMO Crop Research." *Genetic Literacy Project*, June 20, 2017. Accessed October 5, 2021. https://geneticliteracyproject.org/2017/06/20/ecuador-passes-law-allowing-gmo-crop-research/.
54 López, Aldo Orellana. "Bolivia, 15 Years on from the Water War." *Narco News*, April 23, 2015. Accessed July 6, 2018. http://narconews.com/Issue67/article4799.html.

Resistance to environmental and community destruction takes divergent cultural forms in different locales. In South East Asia, 'forest monks' lead efforts against deforestation by symbolically 'ordaining' trees. In anointing the trees as sacred, they uphold the Buddhist precept of non-violence to keep loggers away.[55] In line with its Buddhist culture, the small Himalayan kingdom of Bhutan has committed itself to a carbon neutral policy in its constitution.[56] In Latin America, *buen vivir*, the indigenous philosophy on good living, is evoked to resist corporate globalization and encourage a more balanced ethical way of living. Ecuador added rights of nature and *buen vivir* to its constitution which states, "We … hereby decide to build a new form of public coexistence, in diversity and in harmony with nature, to achieve the good way of living."[57]

Today, environmental justice organizations are building bridges to strengthen their collective efforts, using non-violent education campaigns, civil obedience, and legislative action at the local, national, and global levels. A leading network involving some 5,000 local activist groups in 75 national member groups to challenge 'the current model of economic and corporate globalization' is Friends of the Earth International (FOEI).[58] FOEI and an alliance of other organizations are campaigning for a UN Binding Treaty to regulate the human rights violations committed by transnational corporations.[59]

Globalizing civic engagement is challenging in a world where corporate control is widening, and inequality is deepening. Due to differences in social class and cultural backgrounds, financial needs, and attempts at cooptation by dominant interests, conflicts over ideological perspectives and strategies are inevitable. Still,

---

[55] Yi, Fred. "Forest Monks | Religion & Ethics NewsWeekly." *PBS*, January 15, 2010. Accessed January 3, 2023. https://www.pbs.org/wnet/religionandethics/2010/01/15/january-15-2010-forest-monks/5472/.

[56] "Tshering Tobgay: This Country Isn't Just Carbon Neutral – It's Carbon Negative." TED Talk. Accessed January 4, 2023. https://www.ted.com/talks/tshering_tobgay_this_country_isn_t_just_carbon_neutral_it_s_carbon_negative.

[57] Berros, María Valeria. "The Constitution of the Republic of Ecuador: Pachamama Has Rights." *Environment & Society Portal*, n.d. Accessed January 3, 2023. https://www.environmentandsociety.org/arcadia/constitution-republic-ecuador-pachamama-has-rights.

[58] *Friends of the Earth International.* "Economic Justice Resisting Neoliberalism." Accessed January 4, 2023. https://www.foei.org/what-we-do/economic-justice-and-resisting-neoliberalism/.

[59] *Friends of the Earth International.* "Why a UN Binding Treaty on Corporations and Human Rights?" October 21, 2022. https://www.foei.org/un-binding-treaty-important/.

given the urgency of ecological and social protection, transnational activism is soaring.[60]

Bioregionalism and Localization

Most local and transnational movements are compelled to focus their activities on resistance against dominant policies and activities rather than on renewal and regeneration of communities and the environment. While efforts to reform the neoliberal capitalist system are much needed, the depth of the current crisis calls for deeper questioning and transformation towards an ecological consciousness and an ecologically based human civilization.

Recognizing that the basis for sustainability and human well-being lies in bioregionalism and strong local communities, some global advocacy groups are actively promoting 'a systemic shift away from economic globalization towards localization'. A leader in this effort is the International Alliance for Localization (IAL) which joins people and groups from 58 countries. Using the Himalayan community of Ladakh as a case study, IAL is seeking to both resist economic globalization and encourage local renewal through education and community building at the local level.[61]

An inspiring movement with a plan for transitioning from the current centralized oil, gas, and coal economy to smaller, local self-reliant economies and communities is the Transition Network. According to the book description of *The Transition Handbook*:

> Rebuilding local agriculture and food production, localizing energy production, rethinking healthcare, rediscovering local building materials in the context of zero energy building, rethinking how we manage our waste, all build resilience and offer the potential for an extraordinary renaissance – economic, cultural, spiritual...[62]

---

60 Martinez-Alier, Joan, Leah Temper, Daniela Del Bene, and Arnim Scheidel. "Is There a Global Environmental Justice Movement?" *The Journal of Peasant Studies* 43, no. 3 (May 3, 2016): 731–755. https://doi.org/10.1080/03066150.2016.1141198.
61 *The Economics of Happiness*. Documentary, News. International Society for Ecology & Culture (ISEC), n.d. Available at: https://vimeo.com/492145296. *Local Futures*. "The Economics of Happiness Film." Accessed January 4, 2023. https://www.localfutures.org/programs/the-economics-of-happiness/. Bandarage, Asoka. "Voices of Hope in a Time of Crisis." *HuffPost*, November 11, 2014. https://www.huffpost.com/entry/voices-of-hope-in-a-time-_b_6137040. See also, Norberg-Hodge, Helena. *Ancient Futures: Learning from Ladakh*. San Francisco: Sierra Club Books, 1991.
62 Hopkins, Rob. *The Transition Handbook: From Oil Dependency to Local Resilience*. Chelsea Green Publishing, 2008, 15.

Since 2005, the Transition Towns network has spread to more than 50 countries, in thousands of groups, towns, villages, cities, universities, schools and other local institutions in Europe, the United States, and beyond. It is considered the fastest growing environmental movement in the global North.[63] The criticisms of Transition that de-carbonization and local resilience cannot be achieved merely at the grassroots level are important ones. Indeed, the roots of social and ecological crises that lie in capitalism need to be confronted at the national and global levels in addition to the local level.

Despite limits and shortcomings, the Transition model does hold promise for non-violent, local level regional, and global change. Transition could well be a viable path for renewal and regeneration for communities devastated by climate related wildfires, hurricanes, floods, and landslides in Sri Lanka and elsewhere. The strength of the Transition approach is rooted in the values and principles it upholds: respect for resource limits and resilience; inclusivity and social justice, balance, sharing ideas and power, positive visioning and creativity.

Transition is grounded on what is termed 'Inner Transition' the exploration of processes taking place within the individual, resembling Buddhist and other ethical approaches to psycho-social change.

> The nature of our relationship with our inner life determines how able we are to make the practical lifestyle, relational and cultural changes needed for Transition – as well, bringing precious depth, texture and meaning into our everyday lives.[64]

Human beings have the capacity to make the inner transition needed to move the world to a balanced path of environmental and social sustainability. We can do so from our diverse cultural, class, and other social and professional and social roles. The future of humankind does not lie in corporate-controlled transhumanism as claimed by the techno-utopians. The future lies in deepening our innate ethical intelligence – wisdom and compassion – and its application to social action as outlined in the 2000 Earth Charter (Appendix 3).[65] This requires practical changes in the global capitalist economic system.

---

[63] Sage, Colin. "The Transition Movement and Food Sovereignty: From Local Resilience to Global Engagement in Food System Transformation." *Journal of Consumer Culture* 14, no. 2 (July 1, 2014): 254–275. https://doi.org/10.1177/1469540514526281.

[64] *Transition Network*. "Inner Transition | Connection with Ourselves, Others and the Natural World," July 28, 2016. https://transitionnetwork.org/do-transition/inner/.

[65] "The Earth Charter." *Earth Charter Commission*, March 2000. https://earthcharter.org/wp-content/uploads/2020/03/echarter_english.pdf?x90804.

Sri Lanka and other countries faced with debt, food, fuel and health crises need radical reorientation of their economies to avoid IMF restructuring policies of adversity and repeat debt cycles. A comprehensive shift from the export-import model towards food sovereignty and economic democracy, a shift that goes beyond narrow economic and technocratic terms, is called for.[66] As economic analyst Devaka Gunawardena shows, the challenge of import substitution alone raises the need for integrated political, economic and cultural transformation:

> If we talk about substituting food imports, for example, how would it shape people's habits and diets, including the potential impact of a public distribution system? If we talk about reducing oil imports, a proxy for energy consumption, how would this require changes in the design of the built environment and public transportation? If we talk about reducing pharmaceutical imports, how would this generate new questions about ways in which to remove pressures within people's livelihoods, including confronting the social determinants of health?[67]

System Change in Sri Lanka

Alternatives to the IMF debt trap do exist. Numerous plans for developing resources including the island's vast ocean resources have been put forward if policy makers would take them up.[68] The 53 billion dollar political and ethical question facing Sri Lanka today is why the country is subjecting itself to IMF forced privatization of state assets and other stringent policies over a miniscule $2.9 billion loan when Sri Lanka can pay up its entire foreign debt of US$ 50 billion if the Sri Lankan government formulates new laws (e.g. amendment of the Foreign Exchange Control Act of 2017) to repatriate the US$ 53 billion held in foreign countries by Sri Lanka's exporters.[69]

---

[66] Waduge, Shenali. "Sri Lanka: Stop Living off Loans – Austerity for Rich & Stimulus for Middle Class & Poor." *Shenali Waduge*, December 18, 2022. Accessed December 22, 2022. https://www.shenaliwaduge.com/sri-lanka-stop-living-off-loans-austerity-for-rich-stimulus-for-middle-class-poor/.

[67] Gunawardena, Devaka. "Sri Lanka: Crisis of Neoliberalism and the Progressive Alternative – The Bullet." *Socialist Project*, May 31, 2022. December 22, 2022. https://socialistproject.ca/2022/05/sri-lanka-crisis-of-neoliberalism-and-progressive-alternative/.

[68] Sanath Nanayakkara, 'A Rescue and Reset Plan' June 25, 2022, The Island https://island.lk/a-rescue-and-reset-plan-for-sri-lanka/ accessed March 17, 2023.

[69] Kuruwita, Rathindra. "Govt. Says Selling State Assets Only Way to Build Reserves and Prevent Crippling Shortages." *The Island*. Accessed January 4, 2023. http://island.lk/govt-says-selling-state-assets-only-way-to-build-reserves-and-prevent-crippling-shortages/. *Daily News*. "Govt Will Formulate Laws to Repatriate USD 53 Billion," December 7, 2022. Accessed December 22, 2022. https://www.dailynews.lk/2022/12/07/local/292625/govt-will-formulate-laws-repatriate-usd-53-billion. https://

A collective representing trade union and civil society in Sri Lanka are calling for 'tangible measures to tackle the well-organized influential public–private sector partnership engaged in 'over invoicing' and 'under invoicing' of imports/exports, with the blessing of successive governments.[70] Still others are asking "why can't the policy makers negotiate with those who hold Sri Lanka's export earnings to remit the funds in installments of 10 billion dollars beginning from March onwards"?[71]

Challenging the local-global political-economic nexus, environmental and social justice activists have resisted the wide array of controversial external interventions including the Hambantota Port deal and the Port City with China, the leasing of the Colombo Port terminal and the Trincomalee oil tank to India and the Millennium Challenge Corporation (MCC) compacts, New Fortress Energy deal and Acquisition and Cross-Servicing Agreement (ACSA) and State of Forces Agreement (SOFA) with the United States. The resistance continues against IMF-led privatization of SOES like the Ceylon Petroleum Corporation (CPC) and the Ceylon Government Press. These efforts need global exposure and support given that they are aspects of the worldwide struggle for environmental sustainability, economic democracy and political sovereignty.

Sri Lankans concerned about the implications of an IMF bail-out and the push for greater external intervention point out that the island is rich with valuable natural resources and human capital and that if the land and ocean and the graphite, ilmenite and the other valuable mineral resources are used wisely, Sri Lanka can be economically self-sufficient and prosperous. As earlier noted, the Committee on Public Accounts revealed that there are fuel and natural gas deposits in the Mannar Basin; enough to meet the entire country's needs for 60 years.[72] The control of these valuable resources need to be considered in finalizing the provisional approval given to India's Adani Group to develop wind power projects in Mannar.

If the abundant mineral, solar and wind power are also locally controlled and sustainably employed, Sri Lanka can become not only energy self-sufficient, but a

---

www.ipsnews.net/2022/12/imf-led-privatization-land-resource-grab-sri-lanka/. https://island.lk/repatriation-of-export-earnings/.

70 Shamnidra Ferdinando, 'All Praide for Sri Lanka's Saviours!', The Island, March 15, 2023 https://island.lk/all-praise-for-lankas-saviours/ accessed March 17, 2023.

71 Ranjith Soysa, 'Bring Back those dollars', The Island, March 3, 2023, https://island.lk/bring-back-those-dollars/. accessed March 17, 2023; see also, Ladduwahetty, Neville "Repatriation of Export Earnings" The Island, 12 December 2022, https://island.lk/repatriation-of-export-earnings/accessed March 17, 2023.

72 *ColomboPage*. "Sri Lanka: COPA Focuses on Failure to Develop a Formal Program to Explore Oil and Natural Gas in the Mannar Basin," May 6, 2022. Accessed June 22, 2022. http://www.colombopage.com/archive_22A/May06_1651842024CH.php.

net exporter of energy as well. The same applies to many of today's debt-ridden 'poor' countries in Africa and elsewhere. For this to happen, the rampant corruption and mismanagement must be replaced by ethically based systems of governance and resource use, at *both* the local and global levels.[73]

Solutions that go beyond IMF debt restructuring and corporate greenwashing are needed in Sri Lanka and other indebted countries. As those opposed to selling strategic assets and profitable ventures to wealthy local and foreign interests suggest, some of Sri Lanka's state-owned enterprises (SOEs), such as the CPC that are making profits should be re-organized and maintained.[74] They also point out that instead of selling off the country's valuable SOEs in the name of debt restructuring, some of them can be turned into profitable cooperatives with creative use of finance and technology.[75]

As discussed in this book, colonial and neo-colonial policies and corruption and mismanagement by local elites have turned Sri Lanka into a country indebted and subservient simultaneously to several external masters. Sri Lanka, like much of the rest of the world requires system change from the neoliberal model towards an ethical, just and sustainable path of development. The change is needed at all levels, from the personal to the national and international and in all sectors from education to politics and economics. Key is the education of the young away from the materialist, competitive and individualist trajectory towards a more wholistic, collective and environmentally responsible path. A similar change of direction is essential in the political leadership and administration and the economy.

While fundamental psycho-social change may seem utopian to many, it is necessary to remember that though Sri Lanka today is a poverty-stricken nation and broken society, it is a land with a rich multicultural heritage, an enlightened ecological and social philosophy drawn from Buddhism, and a system of sustainable agriculture based on the most advanced irrigational complex in the ancient world. From this source, Sri Lanka can not only learn from her own past, but she also has much to contribute to transforming the course of global development to a new direction that can sustain, protect and honor life.

---

73 Bandarage, Asoka. "Ethical Path to Ecological and Social Survival." In *Globalism and Localization: Emergent Solutions to Ecological and Social Crises*, edited by Jeanine Canty. New York: Routledge, 2019, https://doi.org/10.4324/9780429274145.

74 Kuruwita, Rathindra. "JVP Leader Questions Wisdom of Promoting Privatisation." *The Island*, September 9, 2022. Accessed September 10, 2022. http://island.lk/jvp-leader-questions-wisdom-of-promoting-privatisation/.

75 Ibid.

A shift away from the technologically centralized global economy towards localization, including bioregionalism, economic democracy, food and energy sovereignty, would provide the way to a sustainable future for Sri Lanka and other debt trapped countries.[76] The Sarvodaya Movement, which includes 10,000 villages in Sri Lanka is considered the largest village-centered eco-social development effort in the world. Its social and economic philosophy is drawn from Buddhist teaching, and its sustainable energy and agricultural efforts as well as social justice and inter-cultural initiatives have great potential for the entire world.[77] The relative weaknesses of the movement, especially its dependence on foreign aid and its potential for change need serious consideration if such movements are to succeed.

Sri Lanka is an island of great beauty and resources and a society of generous, creative and resilient people. To overcome the current crisis, local populations need to come together and put ecological and human survival before narrow interests of corporations, individualism, profit or concepts of domination or ethnoreligious or cultural superiority. Ultimately, the values of dualism – self vs. the other – and domination and ethno-cultural superiority that underlie capitalism need to be challenged on all fronts; to be replaced with the values of interdependence and human partnership with nature and each other.

Ecological and collective consciousness needs to prevail if we are to survive in an island and a world worth living in.

---

[76] Bandarage, Asoka. *Sustainability and Well-Being: The Middle Path to Environment, Society and the Economy.* Basingstoke: Palgrave Macmillan, 2013. http://www.dawsonera.com/depp/reader/protected/external/AbstractView/S9781137308993.

[77] *Sarvodaya.* "Sri Lanka's Sarvodaya Shramadana Movement." Accessed January 4, 2023. https://www.sarvodaya.org/. Macy, Joanna. *Dharma and Development: Religion as Resource in the Sarvodaya Self-Help Movement.* Kumarian Press, 1985; Taylor, Debbie. "SRI LANKA The Sarvodaya Peoples Movement: Too Much Too Soon." *New Internationalist,* November 1981. https://newint.org/features/1981/11/01/much.

Appendices

1. Declaration on the Establishment of New International Economic Order, 1974 / A_RES_3201(S-VI)-EN.pdf

https://digitallibrary.un.org/record/218450?ln=en

United Nations   A/RES/S-6/3201

General Assembly   Distr: General
                                                   1 May 1974

Sixth Special session
Agenda item 7

Resolution adopted by the General Assembly

3201 (S-VI). Declaration on the Establishment of a New International Economic Order

The General Assembly

Adopts the following Declaration:

Declaration on the Establishment of a New International Economic Order

We, the Members of the United Nations,

Having convened a special session of the General Assembly to study for the first time the problems of raw materials and development, devoted to the consideration of the most important economic problems facing the world community,

Bearing in mind the spirit, purposes and principles of the *Charter of the United Nations* to promote the economic advancement and social progress of all peoples,

Solemnly proclaim our united determination to work urgently for the Establishment of a New International Economic Order based on equity, sovereign equality, interdependence, common interest and cooperation among all States, irrespective of their economic and social systems which shall correct inequalities and redress existing injustices, make it possible to eliminate the widening gap between the developed and the developing countries and ensure steadily accelerating economic and social development and peace and justice for present and future generations, and, to that end, declare:

    1. The greatest and most significant achievement during the last decades has been the independence from colonial and alien domination of a large number of peoples and nations which has enabled them to become members of the community of free peoples. Technological progress has also been made in all spheres of economic activities in the last three decades, thus providing a solid potential for improving the well-being of all peoples. However, the remaining vestiges of alien and colonial domination, foreign occupation, racial discrimination, apartheid and neo-colonialism in all its forms continue to be among the greatest obstacles to the full emancipation and progress of the developing countries and all the peoples involved. The benefits of technological progress are not shared equitably by all members of the international community. The developing countries, which constitute 70 per cent of the world's population, account for only 30 per cent of the worlds income. It has proved impossible to achieve an even and balanced development of the international community under the existing international economic order. The gap between the developed and the developing countries continues to widen in a system which was established at a time when most of the developing countries did not even exist as independent States and which perpetuates inequality.

    2. The present international economic order is in direct conflict with current

developments in international political and economic relations. Since 1970 the world economy has experienced a series of grave crises which have had severe repercussions, especially on the developing countries because of their generally greater vulnerability to external economic impulses. The developing world has become a powerful factor that makes its influence felt in all fields of international activity. These irreversible changes in the relationship of forces in the world necessitate the active, full and equal participation of the developing countries in the formulation and application of all decisions that concern the international community.

3. All these changes have thrust into prominence the reality of interdependence of all the members of the world community. Current events have brought into sharp focus the realization that the interests of the developed countries and those of the developing countries can no longer be isolated from each other, that there is a close interrelationship between the prosperity of the developed countries and the growth and development of the developing countries, and that the prosperity of the international community as a whole depends upon the prosperity of its constituent parts. International co-operation for development is the shared goal and common duty of all countries. Thus the political, economic and social well-being of present and future generations depends more than ever on co-operation between all the members of the international community on the basis of sovereign equality and the removal of the disequilibrium that exists between them.

4. The new international economic order should be founded on full respect for the following principles:

   a. Sovereign equality of States, self-determination of all peoples, inadmissibility of the acquisition of territories by force, territorial integrity and non-interference in the internal affairs of other States;

   b. The broadest co-operation of all the States members of the international community, based on equity, whereby the prevailing disparities in the world may be banished and prosperity secured for all;

   c. Full and effective participation on the basis of equality of all countries in the solving of world economic problems in the common interest of all countries, bearing in mind the necessity to ensure the accelerated development of all the developing countries, while devoting particular attention to the adoption of special measures in favour of the least developed land-locked and island developing countries as well as those developing countries most seriously affected by economic crises and natural calamities, without losing sight of the interests of other developing countries;

   d. The right of every country to adopt the economic and social system that it deems the most appropriate for its own development and not to be subjected to discrimination of any kind as a result;

   e. Full permanent sovereignty of every State over its natural resources and all economic activities. In order to safeguard these resources, each State is entitled to exercise effective control over them and their exploitation with means suitable to its own situation, including the right to nationalization or transfer of ownership to its nationals, this right being an expression of the full permanent sovereignty of the State. No State may be subjected to economic, political or any other type of coercion to prevent the free and full exercise of this inalienable right;

   f. The right of all States, territories and peoples under foreign occupation, alien and colonial domination or apartheid to restitution and full compensation for the exploitation arid depletion of, and damages to, the natural resources and all other resources of those States, territories and peoples;

   g. Regulation and supervision of the activities of transnational corporations by taking measures in the interest of the national economies of the countries where such transnational corporations operate on the basis of the full sovereignty of those countries;

h. The right of the developing countries and the peoples of territories under colonial and racial domination and foreign occupation to achieve their liberation and to regain effective control over their natural resources and economic activities;

i. The extending of assistance to developing countries, peoples and territories which are under colonial and alien domination, foreign occupation, racial discrimination or apartheid or are subjected to economic, political or any other type of coercive measures to obtain from them the subordination of the exercise of their sovereign rights and to secure from them advantages of any kind, and to neo colonialism in all its forms, and which have established or are endeavouring to establish effective control over their natural resources and economic activities that have been or are still under foreign control;

j. Just and equitable relationship between the prices of raw materials, primary commodities, manufactured and semi-manufactured goods exported by developing countries and the prices of raw materials, primary commodities, manufactures, capital goods and equipment imported by them with the aim of bringing about sustained improvement in their unsatisfactory terms of trade and the expansion of the world economy;

k. Extension of active assistance to developing countries by the whole international community, free of any political or military conditions;

l. Ensuring that one of the main aims of the reformed international monetary system shall be the promotion of the development of the developing countries and the adequate flow of real resources to them;

m. Improving the competitiveness of natural materials facing competition from synthetic substitutes;

n. Preferential and non-reciprocal treatment for developing countries, wherever feasible, in all fields of international economic co-operation whenever possible;

o. Securing favourable conditions for the transfer of financial resources to developing countries.

p. Giving to the developing countries access to the achievements of modern science and technology, and promoting the transfer of technology and the creation of indigenous technology for the benefit of the developing countries in forms and in accordance with procedures which are suited to their economies;

q. The need for all States to put an end to the waste of natural resources, including food products;

r. The need for developing countries to concentrate all their resources for the cause of development;

s. The strengthening, through individual and collective actions, of mutual economic, trade, financial and technical co-operation among the developing countries, mainly on a preferential basis;

t. Facilitating the role which producers' associations may play within the framework of international co-operation and, in pursuance of their aims, inter alia assisting in the promotion of sustained growth of the world economy and accelerating the development of developing countries.

5. The unanimous adoption of the International Development Strategy for the Second United Nations Development Decade (Resolution 2626 (XXV)) was an important step in the promotion of international economic co-operation on a just and equitable basis. The accelerated implementation of obligations and commitments assumed by the international community within the framework of the Strategy, particularly those concerning imperative development needs of developing countries, would contribute significantly to the fulfilment of the aims and objectives of the present Declaration.

6. The United Nations as a universal organization should be capable of dealing with problems of international economic co-operation in a comprehensive manner and ensuring equally the interests of all countries. It must have an even greater role in the establishment of a new international economic order. The Charter of Economic Rights and Duties of States, for the preparation of which the present Declaration will provide an additional source of inspiration, will constitute a significant contribution in this respect. All the States Members of the United Nations are therefore called upon to exert maximum efforts with a view to securing the implementation of the present Declaration, which is one of the principal guarantees for the creation of better conditions for all peoples to reach a life worthy of human dignity.

7. The present Declaration on the Establishment of a New International Economic Order shall be one of the most important bases of economic relations between all peoples and all nations.

2229th plenary meeting
1 May 1974

2. 2832 Declaration of the Indian Ocean as a Zone of Peace, 1971 / A_RES_2832(XXVI)-EN.pdf

https://digitallibrary.un.org/record/192075?ln=en

1. *Welcomes with satisfaction* the report of the Secretary-General on the economic and social consequences of the arms race and of military expenditures[23] and expresses the hope that it will help to focus future disarmament negotiations on nuclear disarmament and on the goal of general and complete disarmament under effective international control;

2. *Extends its thanks* to the Secretary-General and to the consultant experts as well as to the Governments and international organizations that have rendered assistance in the preparation of the report;

3. *Requests* the Secretary-General to arrange for the reproduction of the report as a United Nations publication and to give it the widest possible publicity in as many languages as is considered desirable and practicable;

4. *Recommends* to all Governments the widest possible distribution of the report so as to acquaint public opinion in their countries with its contents, and invites the specialized agencies as well as intergovernmental, national and non-governmental organizations to use their facilities to make the report widely known;

5. *Recommends* that the conclusions of the report of the Secretary-General on the economic and social consequences of the arms race and of military expenditures should be taken into account in future disarmament negotiations;

6. *Calls upon* all States to intensify their efforts during the Disarmament Decade with a view to promoting negotiations on effective measures for the cessation of the nuclear arms race at the earliest possible date and for nuclear disarmament, as well as on a treaty on general and complete disarmament under strict and effective international control;

7. *Decides* to keep the item entitled "Economic and social consequences of the armaments race and its extremely harmful effects on world peace and security" under constant review and to place it on the provisional agenda of its twenty-eighth session.

2022nd plenary meeting,
16 December 1971.

2832 (XXVI). Declaration of the Indian Ocean as a zone of peace

The General Assembly,

Conscious of the determination of the peoples of the littoral and hinterland States of the Indian Ocean to preserve their independence, sovereignty and territorial integrity, and to resolve their political, economic and social problems under conditions of peace and tranquillity,

Recalling the Declaration of the Third Conference of Heads of State or Government of Non-Aligned Countries, held at Lusaka from 8 to 10 September 1970, calling upon all States to consider and respect the Indian Ocean as a zone of peace from which great Power rivalries and competition as well as bases conceived in the context of such rivalries and competition should be excluded, and declaring that the area should also be free of nuclear weapons,

Convinced of the desirability of ensuring the maintenance of such conditions in the Indian Ocean area by means other than military alliances, as such alliances entail financial and other obligations that call for the diversion of the limited resources of the States of the area from the more compelling and productive task of economic and social reconstruction and could further involve them in the rivalries of power blocs in a manner prejudicial to their independence and freedom of action, thereby increasing international tensions,

Concerned at recent developments that portend the extension of the arms race into the Indian Ocean area, thereby posing a serious threat to the maintenance of such conditions in the area,

Convinced that the establishment of a zone of peace in the Indian Ocean would contribute towards arresting such developments, relaxing international tensions and strengthening international peace and security,

Convinced further that the establishment of a zone of peace in an extensive geographical area in one region could have a beneficial influence on the establishment of permanent universal peace based on equal rights and justice for all, in accordance with the purposes and principles of the Charter of the United Nations,

1. *Solemnly declares* that the Indian Ocean, within limits to be determined, together with the air space above and the ocean floor subjacent thereto, is hereby designated for all time as a zone of peace;

2. *Calls upon* the great Powers, in conformity with this Declaration, to enter into immediate consultations with the littoral States of the Indian Ocean with a view to:

(a) Halting the further escalation and expansion of their military presence in the Indian Ocean;

(b) Eliminating from the Indian Ocean all bases, military installations and logistical supply facilities, the disposition of nuclear weapons and weapons of mass destruction and any manifestation of great Power military presence in the Indian Ocean conceived in the context of great Power rivalry;

3. *Calls upon* the littoral and hinterland States of the Indian Ocean, the permanent members of the Security Council and other major maritime users of the Indian Ocean, in pursuit of the objective of establishing a system of universal collective security without military alliances and strengthening international security through regional and other co-operation, to enter into consultations with a view to the implementation of this Declaration and such action as may be necessary to ensure that:

(a) Warships and military aircraft may not use the Indian Ocean for any threat or use of force against the sovereignty, territorial integrity and independence of any littoral or hinterland State of the Indian Ocean in contravention of the purposes and principles of the Charter of the United Nations;

(b) Subject to the foregoing and to the norms and principles of international law, the right to free and unimpeded use of the zone by the vessels of all nations is unaffected;

(c) Appropriate arrangements are made to give effect to any international agreement that may ultimately be reached for the maintenance of the Indian Ocean as a zone of peace;

4. *Requests* the Secretary-General to report to the General Assembly at its twenty-seventh session on the progress that has been made with regard to the implementation of this Declaration;

---

[23] A/8469 and Add.1.

5. *Decides* to include in the provisional agenda of its twenty-seventh session an item entitled "Declaration of the Indian Ocean as a zone of peace".

2022nd plenary meeting,
16 December 1971.

2880 (XXVI). Implementation of the Declaration on the Strengthening of International Security

The General Assembly,

Bearing in mind the Declaration on the Strengthening of International Security contained in General Assembly resolution 2734 (XXV) of 16 December 1970,

Noting that some positive results conducive to the strengthening of international peace and security have been achieved through negotiations and co-operation among States,

Convinced that bilateral and regional efforts towards achieving international security should be strictly in accordance with the purposes and principles of the United Nations,

Convinced further that such efforts should be complemented by collective measures adopted by the competent organs of the United Nations, in order to ensure the complete implementation of the Declaration,

Deeply concerned at the persistence of armed conflicts and other situations resulting therefrom which threaten international peace and security,

Convinced that the United Nations, as a centre for harmonizing the actions of nations, bears the responsibility for promoting, through all its principal and subsidiary organs, full respect for the Preamble and the purposes and principles of the Charter of the United Nations,

Emphasizing that the Declaration, which constitutes an organic whole, needs to be implemented in its entirety, through the full use of United Nations machinery and capabilities, including those provided for in Chapters VI and VII of the Charter and the dispatch of special missions by the Security Council,

Expressing its conviction that the lack of substantial progress in solving issues relating to international peace and security, economic development and independence, disarmament, colonialism, *apartheid* and racial discrimination, human rights and fundamental freedoms is a constant source of tension and a threat to the security of nations,

Convinced that a broad exchange of views on the question of the strengthening of international security, undertaken annually, will make it possible to review the changing international situation and to seek areas of negotiation and agreement, thereby helping to improve the prospects for peace and international security,

Believing that the achievement of universality in the United Nations, in accordance with the Charter, would increase the effectiveness of the Organization in the strengthening of international peace and security,

Taking note of the report of the Secretary-General[24] and having considered the item entitled "Implementation of the Declaration on the Strengthening of International Security",

1. *Solemnly reaffirms* all the principles and provisions contained in the Declaration on the Strengthening of International Security and strongly appeals to all States to take effective measures to implement the Declaration in its entirety;

2. *Calls upon* all States to contribute towards resolving existing conflicts and situations likely to endanger international peace and security, in accordance with the purposes and principles of the Charter of the United Nations and in keeping with the Declaration;

3. *Calls upon* all States to respect the national unity, political independence and territorial integrity of every State, to refrain from the threat or use of force and to observe fully the principle that the territory of a State shall not be the object of military occupation resulting from the use of force in violation of the Charter and the principle that the acquisition of territories by force is inadmissible;

4. *Declares* that the termination of coercive acts which deprive peoples of their inalienable rights to self-determination, freedom and independence, the implementation of relevant United Nations resolutions concerning colonialism, racism and *apartheid*, and the elimination of serious and systematic violations of human rights and fundamental freedoms, which should be respected by all States, are essential elements for the strengthening of international peace and security;

5. *Invites* the Security Council to consider all appropriate means and procedures for ensuring the strict and full implementation of its resolutions relating to international peace and security;

6. *Urges* the early undertaking of a broad review of all aspects of the concept of peace-keeping operations in order to determine, in accordance with the Charter, appropriate guidelines for its application and to establish appropriate and effective machinery capable of preserving and restoring peace;

7. *Calls* for an early agreement on the definition of aggression, which would assist the United Nations in its fundamental task of maintaining international peace and security;

8. *Declares* that, in view of the close connexion between the strengthening of international security, disarmament and development, the United Nations should evolve a concept of collective economic security designed to promote the sustained development and expansion of national economies and, moreover, affirms that a substantial portion of the savings derived from measures in the field of disarmament should be devoted to promoting economic and social development, particularly in the developing countries;

9. *Declares* that any measure or pressure directed against any State while exercising its sovereign right freely to dispose of its natural resources constitutes a flagrant violation of the principles of self-determination of peoples and non-intervention, as set forth in the Charter, which, if pursued, could constitute a threat to international peace and security;

10. *Invites* all Member States, in particular the more developed countries, to adopt all appropriate measures to normalize the financial situation of the United Nations and to provide it with the means of effectively achieving its goals;

11. *Requests* the Secretary-General to submit to the General Assembly at its twenty-seventh session a report on measures adopted in pursuance of the Declaration, containing, *inter alia*:

---
[24] A/8431 and Add.1-5.

3. Earth Charter, 2000 / echarter_english.pdf
https://earthcharter.org/wp-content/uploads/2020/03/echarter_english.pdf?x90804

THE EARTH CHARTER

PREAMBLE

We stand at a critical moment in Earth's history, a time when humanity must choose its future. As the world becomes increasingly interdependent and fragile, the future at once holds great peril and great promise. To move forward we must recognize that in the midst of a magnificent diversity of cultures and life forms we are one human family and one Earth community with a common destiny. We must join together to bring forth a sustainable global society founded on respect for nature, universal human rights, economic justice, and a culture of peace. Towards this end, it is imperative that we, the peoples of Earth, declare our responsibility to one another, to the greater community of life, and to future generations.

Earth, Our Home
Humanity is part of a vast evolving universe. Earth, our home, is alive with a unique community of life. The forces of nature make existence a demanding and uncertain adventure, but Earth has provided the conditions essential to life's evolution. The resilience of the community of life and the well-being of humanity depend upon preserving a healthy biosphere with all its ecological systems, a rich variety of plants and animals, fertile soils, pure waters, and clean air. The global environment with its finite resources is a common concern of all peoples. The protection of Earth's vitality, diversity, and beauty is a sacred trust.

The Global Situation
The dominant patterns of production and consumption are causing environmental devastation, the depletion of resources, and a massive extinction of species. Communities are being undermined. The benefits of development are not shared equitably and the gap between rich and poor is widening. Injustice, poverty, ignorance, and violent conflict are widespread and the cause of great suffering. An unprecedented rise in human population has overburdened ecological and social systems. The foundations of global security are threatened. These trends are perilous—but not inevitable.

The Challenges Ahead
The choice is ours: form a global partnership to care for Earth and one another or risk the destruction of ourselves and the diversity of life. Fundamental changes are needed in our values, institutions, and ways of living. We must realize that when basic needs have been met, human development is primarily about being more, not having more. We have the knowledge and technology to provide for all and to reduce our impacts on the environment. The emergence of a global civil society is creating new opportunities to build a democratic and humane world. Our environmental, economic, political, social, and spiritual challenges are interconnected, and together we can forge inclusive solutions.

Universal Responsibility
To realize these aspirations, we must decide to live with a sense of universal responsibility, identifying ourselves with the whole Earth community as well as our local communities. We are at once citizens of different nations and of one world in which the local and global are linked. Everyone shares responsibility for the present and future well-being of the human family and the larger living world. The spirit of human solidarity and kinship with all life is strengthened when we live with reverence for the mystery of being, gratitude for the gift of life, and humility regarding the human place in nature.

We urgently need a shared vision of basic values to provide an ethical foundation for the emerging world community. Therefore, together in hope we affirm the following interdependent principles for a sustainable way of life as a common standard by which the conduct of all individuals, organizations, businesses, governments, and transnational institutions is to be guided and assessed.

The Earth Charter

PRINCIPLES

I. RESPECT AND CARE FOR THE COMMUNITY OF LIFE

1. Respect Earth and life in all its diversity.
a. Recognize that all beings are interdependent and every form of life has value regardless of its worth to human beings.
b. Affirm faith in the inherent dignity of all human beings and in the intellectual, artistic, ethical, and spiritual potential of humanity.

2. Care for the community of life with understanding, compassion, and love.
a. Accept that with the right to own, manage, and use natural resources comes the duty to prevent environmental harm and to protect the rights of people.
b. Affirm that with increased freedom, knowledge, and power comes increased responsibility to promote the common good.

3. Build democratic societies that are just, participatory, sustainable, and peaceful.
a. Ensure that communities at all levels guarantee human rights and fundamental freedoms and provide everyone an opportunity to realize his or her full potential.
b. Promote social and economic justice, enabling all to achieve a secure and meaningful livelihood that is ecologically responsible.

4. Secure Earth's bounty and beauty for present and future generations.
a. Recognize that the freedom of action of each generation is qualified by the needs of future generations.
b. Transmit to future generations values, traditions, and institutions that support the long-term flourishing of Earth's human and ecological communities. In order to fulfill these four broad commitments, it is necessary to:

II. ECOLOGICAL INTEGRITY

5. Protect and restore the integrity of Earth's ecological systems, with special concern for biological diversity and the natural processes that sustain life.
a. Adopt at all levels sustainable development plans and regulations that make environmental conservation and rehabilitation integral to all development initiatives.
b. Establish and safeguard viable nature and biosphere reserves, including wild lands and marine areas, to protect Earth's life support systems, maintain biodiversity, and preserve our natural heritage.
c. Promote the recovery of endangered species and ecosystems.
d. Control and eradicate non-native or genetically modified organisms harmful to native species and the environment, and prevent introduction of such harmful organisms.
e. Manage the use of renewable resources such as water, soil, forest products, and marine life in ways that do not exceed rates of regeneration and that protect the health of ecosystems.
f. Manage the extraction and use of non-renewable resources such as minerals and fossil fuels in ways that minimize depletion and cause no serious environmental damage.

6. Prevent harm as the best method of environmental protection and, when knowledge is limited, apply a precautionary approach.
a. Take action to avoid the possibility of serious or irreversible environmental harm even when scientific knowledge is incomplete or inconclusive.
b. Place the burden of proof on those who argue that a proposed activity will not cause significant harm, and make the responsible parties liable for environmental harm.
c. Ensure that decision making addresses the cumulative, long-term, indirect, long distance, and global consequences of human activities.
d. Prevent pollution of any part of the environment and allow no build-up of radioactive, toxic, or other hazardous substances.
e. Avoid military activities damaging to the environment.

7. Adopt patterns of production, consumption, and reproduction that safeguard Earth's regenerative capacities, human rights, and community well-being.
a. Reduce, reuse, and recycle the materials used in production and consumption systems, and ensure that residual waste can be assimilated by ecological systems.
b. Act with restraint and efficiency when using energy, and rely increasingly on renewable energy sources such as solar and wind.
c. Promote the development, adoption, and equitable transfer of environmentally sound technologies.

The Earth Charter

d. Internalize the full environmental and social costs of goods and services in the selling price, and enable consumers to identify products that meet the highest social and environmental standards.
e. Ensure universal access to health care that fosters reproductive health and responsible reproduction.
f. Adopt lifestyles that emphasize the quality of life and material sufficiency in a finite world.

8. Advance the study of ecological sustainability and promote the open exchange and wide application of the knowledge acquired.
a. Support international scientific and technical cooperation on sustainability, with special attention to the needs of developing nations.
b. Recognize and preserve the traditional knowledge and spiritual wisdom in all cultures that contribute to environmental protection and human well-being.
c. Ensure that information of vital importance to human health and environmental protection, including genetic information, remains available in the public domain.

III. SOCIAL AND ECONOMIC JUSTICE

9. Eradicate poverty as an ethical, social, and environmental imperative.
a. Guarantee the right to potable water, clean air, food security, uncontaminated soil, shelter, and safe sanitation, allocating the national and international resources required.
b. Empower every human being with the education and resources to secure a sustainable livelihood, and provide social security and safety nets for those who are unable to support themselves.
c. Recognize the ignored, protect the vulnerable, serve those who suffer, and enable them to develop their capacities and to pursue their aspirations.

10. Ensure that economic activities and institutions at all levels promote human development in an equitable and sustainable manner.
a. Promote the equitable distribution of wealth within nations and among nations.
b. Enhance the intellectual, financial, technical, and social resources of developing nations, and relieve them of onerous international debt.
c. Ensure that all trade supports sustainable resource use, environmental protection, and progressive labor standards.
d. Require multinational corporations and international financial organizations to act transparently in the public good, and hold them accountable for the consequences of their activities.

11. Affirm gender equality and equity as prerequisites to sustainable development and ensure universal access to education, health care, and economic opportunity.
a. Secure the human rights of women and girls and end all violence against them.
b. Promote the active participation of women in all aspects of economic, political, civil, social, and cultural life as full and equal partners, decision makers, leaders, and beneficiaries.
c. Strengthen families and ensure the safety and loving nurture of all family members.

12. Uphold the right of all, without discrimination, to a natural and social environment supportive of human dignity, bodily health, and spiritual well-being, with special attention to the rights of indigenous peoples and minorities.
a. Eliminate discrimination in all its forms, such as that based on race, color, sex, sexual orientation, religion, language, and national, ethnic or social origin.
b. Affirm the right of indigenous peoples to their spirituality, knowledge, lands and resources and to their related practice of sustainable livelihoods.
c. Honor and support the young people of our communities, enabling them to fulfill their essential role in creating sustainable societies.
d. Protect and restore outstanding places of cultural and spiritual significance.

IV. DEMOCRACY, NONVIOLENCE, AND PEACE

13. Strengthen democratic institutions at all levels, and provide transparency and accountability in governance, inclusive participation in decision making, and access to justice.
a. Uphold the right of everyone to receive clear and timely information on environmental matters and all development plans and activities which are likely to affect them or in which they have an interest.
b. Support local, regional and global civil society, and promote the meaningful participation of all interested individuals and organizations in decision making.
c. Protect the rights to freedom of opinion, expression, peaceful assembly, association, and dissent.
d. Institute effective and efficient access to administrative and independent judicial procedures, including remedies

The Earth Charter

and redress for environmental harm and the threat of such harm.
e. Eliminate corruption in all public and private institutions.
f. Strengthen local communities, enabling them to care for their environments, and assign environmental responsibilities to the levels of government where they can be carried out most effectively.

14. Integrate into formal education and life-long learning the knowledge, values, and skills needed for a sustainable way of life.
a. Provide all, especially children and youth, with educational opportunities that empower them to contribute actively to sustainable development.
b. Promote the contribution of the arts and humanities as well as the sciences in sustainability education.
c. Enhance the role of the mass media in raising awareness of ecological and social challenges.
d. Recognize the importance of moral and spiritual education for sustainable living.

15. Treat all living beings with respect and consideration.
a. Prevent cruelty to animals kept in human societies and protect them from suffering.
b. Protect wild animals from methods of hunting, trapping, and fishing that cause extreme, prolonged, or avoidable suffering.
c. Avoid or eliminate to the full extent possible the taking or destruction of non-targeted species.

16. Promote a culture of tolerance, nonviolence, and peace.
a. Encourage and support mutual understanding, solidarity, and cooperation among all peoples and within and among nations.
b. Implement comprehensive strategies to prevent violent conflict and use collaborative problem solving to manage and resolve environmental conflicts and other disputes.
c. Demilitarize national security systems to the level of a non-provocative defense posture, and convert military resources to peaceful purposes, including ecological restoration.
d. Eliminate nuclear, biological, and toxic weapons and other weapons of mass destruction.
e. Ensure that the use of orbital and outer space supports environmental protection and peace.
f. Recognize that peace is the wholeness created by right relationships with oneself, other persons, other cultures, other life, Earth, and the larger whole of which all are a part.

THE WAY FORWARD

As never before in history, common destiny beckons us to seek a new beginning. Such renewal is the promise of these Earth Charter principles. To fulfill this promise, we must commit ourselves to adopt and promote the values and objectives of the Charter.

This requires a change of mind and heart. It requires a new sense of global interdependence and universal responsibility. We must imaginatively develop and apply the vision of a sustainable way of life locally, nationally, regionally, and globally. Our cultural diversity is a precious heritage and different cultures will find their own distinctive ways to realize the vision. We must deepen and expand the global dialogue that generated the Earth Charter, for we have much to learn from the ongoing collaborative search for truth and wisdom.

Life often involves tensions between important values. This can mean difficult choices. However, we must find ways to harmonize diversity with unity, the exercise of freedom with the common good, short-term objectives with long-term goals. Every individual, family, organization, and community has a vital role to play. The arts, sciences, religions, educational institutions, media, businesses, nongovernmental organizations, and governments are all called to offer creative leadership. The partnership of government, civil society, and business is essential for effective governance.

In order to build a sustainable global community, the nations of the world must renew their commitment to the United Nations, fulfill their obligations under existing international agreements, and support the implementation of Earth Charter principles with an international legally binding instrument on environment and development.

Let ours be a time remembered for the awakening of a new reverence for life, the firm resolve to achieve sustainability, the quickening of the struggle for justice and peace, and the joyful celebration of life.

ORIGIN OF THE EARTH CHARTER
The Earth Charter was created by the independent Earth Charter Commission, which was convened as a follow-up to the 1992 Earth Summit in order to produce a global consensus statement of values and principles for a sustainable future. The document was developed over nearly a decade through an extensive process of international consultation, to which over five thousand people contributed. The Charter has been formally endorsed by thousands of organizations, including UNESCO and the IUCN (World Conservation Union). For more information, please visit www.EarthCharter.org.

Selected Bibliography

"300 Organisations Demand Debt Cancellation." Debt Justice (formerly Jubilee Debt Campaign), October 9, 2022. https://debtjustice.org.uk/press-release/300orgs

"A New Coalition Issues a Statement on the Crisis in Sri Lanka." IDN-InDepthNews, July 3, 2022. https://www.indepthnews.net/index.php/the-world/asia-pacific/5427-a-new-coalition-issues-a-statement-on-the-crisis-in-sri-lanka

Abeyratne, Sirimal. "Economic Roots of Political Conflict: The Case of Sri Lanka." *The World Economy* 27, no. 8 (2004): 1295–1314. https://doi.org/10.1111/j.1467-9701.2004.00645.x

Ali, Ameer. "Badi Revolution and Its Disappointing Aftermath." DailyFT, July 27, 2018. https://www.ft.lk/columns/Badi-revolution-and-its-disappointing-aftermath/4-659815

Ames, Glenn Joseph. *The Globe Encompassed: The Age of European Discovery, 1500–1700.* Upper Saddle River, N.J.: Pearson Prentice Hall, 2008. http://catdir.loc.gov/catdir/toc/ecip078/2007001935.html

Ananthavinayagan, Thamil Venthan. "Sri Lanka and the Neocolonialism of the IMF." The Diplomat, March 31, 2022. https://thediplomat.com/2022/03/sri-lanka-and-the-neocolonialism-of-the-imf/

Apaydin, Veysel (ed.). *Critical Perspectives on Cultural Memory and Heritage: Construction, Transformation and Destruction.*

Apaydin, Veysel (ed.).UCL Press, London 2020. http://library.oapen.org/handle/20.500.12657/22337

Aponso, Revan. "The Pandora Papers and the Exposure of Sri Lanka's Elite." The Economics Review, February 22, 2022. https://theeconreview.com/2022/02/22/the-pandora-papers-and-the-exposure-of-sri-lankas-elite/

Appuhamy, Durand. *The Kandyans' Last Stand against the British.* 1st ed. Colombo: M.D. Gunasena & Co., 1995.

Athukorala, Prema-Chandra, and Sarath Rajapatirana. "Liberalization and Industrial Transformation: Lessons from the Sri Lankan Experience." *Economic Development and Cultural Change* 48, no. 3 (2000): 543–572. https://doi.org/10.1086/452610

Balachandran, P. K. "The Execution That Triggered the Struggle for Self-Rule." Ceylon Today, July 7, 2012. https://web.archive.org/web/20141221192706/http://www.ceylontoday.lk/59-9199-news-detail-the-execution-that-triggered-the-struggle-for-self-rule.html

Bandara, J. M. R. S., H. V. P. Wijewardena, Y. M. a. Y. Bandara, R. G. P. T. Jayasooriya, and H. Rajapaksha. "Pollution of River Mahaweli and Farmlands under Irrigation by Cadmium from Agricultural Inputs Leading to a Chronic Renal Failure Epidemic among Farmers in NCP, Sri Lanka." *Environmental Geochemistry and Health* 33, no. 5 (October 2011): 439–453. https://doi.org/10.1007/s10653-010-9344-4

Bandara, Kapila. "Exporters, Importers Shift Rs 13.2 Trillion Overseas via Dodgy Invoicing." Sunday Times (Sri Lanka), July 10, 2022. http://www.sundaytimes.lk/220710/news/exporters-importers-shift-rs-13-2-trillion-overseas-via-dodgy-invoicing-488561.html

Bandarage, Asoka. *Colonialism in Sri Lanka: The Political Economy of the Kandyan Highlands, 1833–1886.* New Babylon, Studies in the Social Sciences. Berlin: Mouton, 1983.

Bandarage, Asoka. "Victims of Development." *The Women's Review of Books* 5, no. 1 (October 1987): 1. https://doi.org/10.2307/4020177

Bandarage, Asoka. "Women and Capitalist Development in Sri Lanka, 1977–87." *Bulletin of Concerned Asian Scholars* 20, no. 2 (June 1, 1988): 57–81. https://doi.org/10.1080/14672715.1988.10404449

Bandarage, Asoka. *Women, Population and Global Crisis: A Political-Economic Analysis.* London: Zed Books, 1997. https://archive.org/details/womenpopulationg0000band

Bandarage, Asoka. "Ethno-Religious Evolution in Pre-Colonial Sri Lanka." *Ethnic Studies Report* XXI, no. 2 (July 2003): 103–147.

Bandarage, Asoka. "Ethnic and Religious Tension in the World: A Political-Economic Perspective." In *Global Political Economy and the Wealth of Nations: Performance, Institutions, Problems, and Policies*, edited by Phillip Anthony O'Hara, 286–301. Routledge Frontiers of Political Economy. London: Routledge, 2004. http://catdir.loc.gov/catdir/enhancements/fy1102/2003058686-b.html

Bandarage, Asoka. *The Separatist Conflict in Sri Lanka: Terrorism, Ethnicity, Political Economy.* London: Routledge/Taylor & Francis Group, 2009.

Bandarage, Asoka. *Sustainability and Well-Being: The Middle Path to Environment, Society and the Economy.* Basingstoke: Palgrave Macmillan, 2013. https://doi.org/10.1080/14672715.1982.10412654

Bandarage, Asoka. "Ethical Path to Ecological and Social Survival." In *Globalism and Localization: Emergent Solutions to Ecological and Social Crises*, edited by Jeanine Canty. New York: Routledge, 2019. https://doi.org/10.4324/9780429274145

Bandarage, Asoka. "New Fortress Energy, Sri Lanka, and Planet Earth." IDN-InDepthNews, September 30, 2021. https://archive-2017-2022.indepthnews.info/index.php/sustainability/affordable-clean-energy/4769-new-fortress-energy-sri-lanka-and-planet-earth

Bandarage, Asoka. "Women in Development: Liberalism, Marxism and Marxist-Feminism", *Development and Change*, vol. 15, no. 4, 1984, pp. 495–515.

Bello, Walden. "How the IMF and World Bank Turned a Pandemic into a Public Relations Stunt – FPIF." Foreign Policy In Focus, October 12, 2020. https://fpif.org/how-the-imf-and-world-bank-turned-a-pandemic-into-a-public-relations-stunt/

Bhowmick, Soumya. "Understanding the Economic Issues in Sri Lanka's Current Debacle." Observer Research Foundation, June 2022. https://www.orfonline.org/wp-content/uploads/2022/06/ORF_OccasionalPaper_357_SriLanka.pdf

Boas, Taylor C., and Jordan Gans-Morse. "Neoliberalism: From New Liberal Philosophy to Anti-Liberal Slogan." *Studies in Comparative International Development* 44, no. 2 (June 1, 2009): 137–161. https://doi.org/10.1007/s12116-009-9040-5

"Bond Scam: Expose of the Largest Financial Scam in the History of SL." Sri Lanka News – Newsfirst, February 3, 2018. https://www.newsfirst.lk/2018/02/03/bond-scam-expose-largest-financial-scam-history-sl/

"Bolivia, 15 Years on from the Water War." Narco News, accessed January 4, 2023. http://narconews.com/Issue67/article4799.html

Bookchin, Murray. *The Ecology of Freedom: The Emergence and Dissolution of Hierarchy.* Black Rose Books, 1991.

Breuste, Jürgen, and Lalitha Dissanayake. "Socio-Economic and Environmental Change of Sri Lanka's Central Highlands Responses and Adaptation." In *Impact of Global Changes on Mountains*, 11–31. CRC Press, 2019.

Byrne, George. "There Is No Alternative." Sociology Lens, January 21, 2015. https://www.sociologylens.net/article-types/opinion/there-is-no-alternative/14356

Central Bank of Sri Lanka "Spreadsheet: Data Template on International Reserves/Foreign Currency Liquidity." Accessed November 24, 2022. https://www.cbsl.gov.lk/sites/default/files/cbslweb_documents/statistics/sheets/table2.15.1-20220930_e.xlsx

Central Intelligence Agency "Special Report Left-Leaning Regime in Ceylon Faces Elections." CIA Special Report, March 12, 1965. https://www.cia.gov/readingroom/document/cia-rdp79-00927a004800050002-5 Clapp, Jennifer. "The Rise of Financial Investment and Common

Ownership in Global Agrifood Firms." *Review of International Political Economy* 26, no. 4 (July 4, 2019): 604–629. https://doi.org/10.1080/09692290.2019.1597755

"Compact: Sri Lanka Compact." Millennium Challenge Corporation, December 29, 2020. https://www.mcc.gov/where-we-work/program/sri-lanka-compact

Costantini, Orsola. "Dollar Dominance Is Financial Dominance." Institute for New Economic Thinking, November 23, 2022. https://www.ineteconomics.org/perspectives/blog/dollar-dominance-is-financial-dominance

Club de Paris / Paris Club. "Paris Club Statement on Sri Lanka." September 2, 2022. https://clubdeparis.org/en/communications/press-release/paris-club-statement-on-sri-lanka-02-09-2022

Daly, Herman E. *Beyond Growth: The Economics of Sustainable Development*. Boston: Beacon Press, 1996.

Dasgupta, KumKum. "A Gulf of Trouble for Mannar, India's Climate Change Hotspot." Hindustan Times, November 29, 2015. https://www.hindustantimes.com/india/climate-change-choking-gulf-of-mannar-hurting-marine-treasure/story-dVQF5q97EbNoxONs8o9EEN.html

De Silva, Kingsley M. "Education and Social Change, 1832 to c. 1900." In *History of Ceylon: From the Beginning of the Nineteenth Century to 1948*, Vol. 3. Colombo: Ceylon University Press, 1959.

De Silva, Kingsley M.. "The Rebellion of 1848 in Ceylon." *Ceylon Journal of Historical and Social Studies* 7, no. 2 (July 1964): 144–170.

De Silva, Kingsley M., and H. C. Ray. *History of Ceylon*. Vol. 2. Colombo: Ceylon University Press, 1960.

DeSilva, Chandra Richard. *The Portuguese in Ceylon, 1617–1638*. H. W. Cave, 1972.

DeVotta, Neil. "Sri Lanka's Road to Ruin Was Political, Not Economic." Foreign Policy, July 12, 2022. https://foreignpolicy.com/2022/07/12/sri-lanka-crisis-politics-economics-rajapaksa-protest/

Dewaraja, Lorna Srimathie. *The Kandyan Kingdom of Sri Lanka, 1707–1782*. Colombo: Lake House Investments, 1988.

The Dhammapada: Verses and Stories. "Dhammapada Verse 1, Cakkhupalatthera Vatthu." https://www.tipitaka.net/tipitaka/dhp/verseload.php?verse=001

Dharmapala, Anagarika. *Return to Righteousness: A Collection of Speeches, Essays, and Letters of the Anagarika Dharmapala*. Edited by Ananda W. P. Guruge. Anagarika Dharmapala Birth Centenary Committee, Ministry of Education and Cultural Affairs, Ceylon, 1965.

Dissanaike, Tharuka. "Sale or Sell out? Sri Lanka's Farmers and Land Reform." Panos London, March 27, 2006. https://panoslondon.panosnetwork.org/features/sale-or-sell-out-sri-lankas-farmers-and-land-reform/

"Document 137. Memorandum of a Conversation, Colombo, March 11, 1956." In *Foreign Relations of the United States, 1955–1957, South Asia*, Vol. VII. Office of the Historian, Bureau of Public Affairs, U.S. Department of State, 2018. https://history.state.gov/historicaldocuments/frus1955-57v08

"Documents of the Fifth Conference of Heads of State or Government of Non-Aligned Countries, Held at Colombo from 16 to 19 August 1976." Accessed January 2, 2023. http://cns.miis.edu/nam/documents/Official_Document/5th_Summit_FD_Sri_Lanka_Declaration_1976_Whole.pdf

"Dossier No. 57. The Geopolitics of Inequality: Discussing Pathways Towards a More Just World." Tricontinental: Institute for Social Research, October 21, 2022. https://thetricontinental.org/dossier-57-geopolitics-of-inequality/

"Dossier on the Adani Group's Environmental and Social Record." AdaniWatch, Bob Brown Foundation, September 2020. https://www.banktrack.org/download/dossier_on_the_adani_group_s_environmental_and_social_record/adani_dossier_preliminary_sept2020_intermediate_21.pdf

Dunham, David, and Saman Kelegama. "Stabilisation and Adjustment: Sri Lankan Experience, 1977–1993." *Economic and Political Weekly* 33, no. 24 (1998): 1475–1482. https://www.jstor.org/stable/4406883

"Economic Justice Resisting Neoliberalism – Friends of the Earth." Friends of the Earth International. https://www.foei.org/what-we-do/economic-justice-and-resisting-neoliberalism/

Eisler, Riane Tennenhaus. *The Chalice and the Blade: Our History, Our Future.* 1st ed. Cambridge [Mass.]: Harper & Row, 1987.

Ekman, Paul. "Darwin's Compassionate View of Human Nature." *JAMA* 303, no. 6 (February 10, 2010): 557–558. https://doi.org/10.1001/jama.2010.101

Ellman, Antony O. *Land Settlement in Sri Lanka, 1840–1975: A Review of the Major Writings on the Subject.* Colombo: Agrarian Research and Training Institute, 1976. https://search.library.wisc.edu/catalog/999501363202121

Evers, Hans-Dieter. "Buddhism and British Colonial Policy in Ceylon, 1815–1875." *Journal of Asian Studies* 11, no. 3 (December 1964).

Fakhri, Michael. "Interim Report of the Special Rapporteur on the Right to Food." United Nations General Assembly, July 18, 2022. https://documents-dds-ny.un.org/doc/UNDOC/GEN/N22/428/88/PDF/N2242888.pdf?OpenElement

Ferdinando, Shamindra. "Sri Lanka's Foreign Policy Dilemma." The Island, November 9, 2022. http://island.lk/sri-lankas-foreign-policy-dilemma/

Fernando, P. T. M. "The British Raj and the 1915 Communal Riots in Ceylon." *Modern Asian Studies* 3, no. 3 (1969): 245–255. https://www.jstor.org/stable/311950

"Financial Flows and Tax Havens: Combining to Limit the Lives of Billions of People." Centre for Applied Research, Norwegian School of Economics; Global Financial Integrity; Jawaharlal Nehru University; Instituto de Estudos Socioeconômicos; Nigerian Institute of Social and Economic Research, December 2015. https://www.gfintegrity.org/wp-content/uploads/2016/12/Financial_Flows-final.pdf

Fisher, Mark. *Capitalist Realism: Is There No Alternative?* Zero Books. Winchester, UK; Washington, USA: Zero Books, 2009.

"Food Security and Nutrition Crisis in Sri Lanka." Care.org, accessed January 3, 2023. https://www.care.org/wp-content/uploads/2022/09/Food-Nutrition-Crisis-in-SL-Situation-Update-September2022.pdf

"Foreign Think Tanks Influence Sri Lanka: Mont Pelerin Society – ADVOCATA – Institute of Policy Studies." Sinhalanet, August 2, 2022. https://www.sinhalanet.net/foreign-think-tanks-influence-sri-lanka-mont-pelerin-society-advocata-institute-of-policy-studies

Gallagher, Kevin, and Richard Kozul-Wright. *The Case for a New Bretton Woods.* Case for Series. Cambridge, UK: Polity, 2022.

Gamage, Daya. "US-India Tie Strongest Military Knot on Indo-Pacific: Small Nations Tagged in." Asian Tribune, December 25, 2019. https://web.archive.org/web/20200226001718/http://asiantribune.com/node/93295

Gelder, Sarah van. "More Confessions of an Economic Hit Man: This Time, They're Coming for Your Democracy." YES! Magazine, March 18, 2016. https://www.yesmagazine.org/economy/2016/03/18/more-confessions-of-an-economic-hit-man-this-time-theyre-coming-for-your-democracy

Ghosh, Jayati, and C. P. Chandrasekhar. "A Food Crisis Not of Their Making." The Hindu Business Line, September 19, 2022. https://www.thehindubusinessline.com/opinion/a-food-crisis-not-of-their-making/article65911286.ece

Ghoshal, Devjyot, and Uditha Jayasinghe. "How a Band of Activists Helped Bring down Sri Lanka's Government." Reuters, sec. Asia Pacific, July 12, 2022. https://www.reuters.com/world/asia-pacific/how-band-activists-helped-bring-down-sri-lankas-government-2022-07-11

Global Trade Negotiations Homepage, Center for International Development at Harvard University. "Washington Consensus."Internet Archive Wayback Machine, April 2003. https://web.archive.org/web/20170715151421/http://www.cid.harvard.edu/cidtrade/issues/washington.html

Goonatilake, Susantha. *Recolonisation: Foreign Funded NGOs in Sri Lanka.* SAGE Publishing India, 2006.

Goonewardena, K. W. *The Foundation of Dutch Power in Ceylon, 1638–1658.* Djambatan: Netherlands Institute for International Cultural Relations, 1958.

"Govt Will Formulate Laws to Repatriate USD 53 Billion." Daily News, December 7, 2022. https://www.dailynews.lk/2022/12/07/local/292625/govt-will-formulate-laws-repatriate-usd-53-billion

Griswold, Charles L. "Adam Smith: Conscience of Capitalism." *The Wilson Quarterly (1976–)* 15, no. 3 (1991): 53–61. https://www.jstor.org/stable/40258121

Gunaratna, Rohan. *Sri Lanka, a Lost Revolution? The inside Story of the JVP.* Kandy, Sri Lanka: Institute of Fundamental Studies, 1990.

Halliday, Fred. "The Ceylonese Insurrection." *New Left Review*, no. 69 (October 1971). https://newleftreview.org/issues/i69/articles/fred-halliday-the-ceylonese-insurrection

Harvey, David. *A Brief History of Neoliberalism.* Oxford University Press, 2007.

Henderson, Hazel. *Paradigms in Progress: Life beyond Economics.* 1st Berrett-Koehler ed. San Francisco: Berrett-Koehler Publishers, 1995.

Herring, Ronald J. "Economic Liberalisation Policies in Sri Lanka: International Pressures, Constraints and Supports." *Economic and Political Weekly* 22, no. 8 (1987): 325–333. https://www.jstor.org/stable/4376706

Hickel, Jason, Dylan Sullivan, and Huzaifa Zoomkawala. "Plunder in the Post-Colonial Era: Quantifying Drain from the Global South Through Unequal Exchange, 1960–2018." *New Political Economy* 26, no. 6 (November 2, 2021): 1030–1047. https://doi.org/10.1080/13563467.2021.1899153

Hoffman, Philip T. *Why Did Europe Conquer the World?* Princeton University Press, 2015.

Hopkins, Rob. *The Transition Handbook: From Oil Dependency to Local Resilience.* Chelsea Green Publishing, 2008.

Huff, Ethan. "BlackRock and Vanguard Are Taking over Centralized Food Production Technologies and Will Have Near-Total Control over the Future Food Supply in America." Naturalnews.com, May 1, 2022. https://www.naturalnews.com/2022-05-01-blackrock-vanguard-controlling-america-centralized-food-production.html

"Human Development Report 1990: Concept and Measurement of Human Development." Human Development Reports. New York: UNDP (United Nations Development Programme), 1990. https://hdr.undp.org/content/human-development-report-1990

Huxley, Aldous. *Brave New World.* New York: Harper & Bros., 1946.

"Indigenous Activist Urges the Vatican to Revoke 500-Year-Old Documents." CBC Radio, December 14, 2018. https://www.cbc.ca/radio/tapestry/why-religion-1.4934033/indigenous-activist-urges-the-vatican-to-revoke-500-year-old-documents-1.4940937

"Inside Story of How Sri Lanka Fell into the ACSA-SOFA Trap." The Sunday Times (Sri Lanka), July 7, 2019. http://www.sundaytimes.lk/190707/columns/inside-story-of-how-sri-lanka-fell-into-the-acsa-sofa-trap-357287.html

Indrapala, Karthigesu. "Dravidian Settlements in Ceylon and the Beginnings of the Kingdom of Jaffna." PhD, University of London, 1965.

International Monetary Fund, Communications Department. "Press Release No. 22/295 IMF Staff Reaches Staff-Level Agreement on an Extended Fund Facility Arrangement with Sri Lanka." IMF, September 1, 2022. https://www.imf.org/en/News/Articles/2022/09/01/pr22295-imf-reaches-staff-level-agreement-on-an-extended-fund-facility-arrangement-with-sri-lanka

International Science and Technology Institute Inc. "Mahaweli Enterprise Development, MED/EIED Project, MED/EIED 1992 Workplan." United States Agency International Development, 1992. https://pdf.usaid.gov/pdf_docs/PDABD752.pdf

Iriyagolle, Gamini. *The Kandyan Convention: A Conditional Treaty of Cession between the Sinhalese and the British, 2nd March 1815.* Sinhala Veera Vidahana, 2000.

Irwin, Douglas. "Import Substitution Is Making an Unwelcome Comeback." Peterson Institute for International Economics, July 8, 2020. https://www.piie.com/blogs/trade-and-investment-policy-watch/import-substitution-making-unwelcome-comeback

"It's High Time Sri Lanka Brought SOE Privatisation to the Policy Table: Advocata." The Island, December 20, 2021. http://island.lk/its-high-time-sri-lanka-brought-soe-privatisation-to-the-policy-table-advocata/

Jacques, Martin. *When China Rules the World: The Rise of the Middle Kingdom and the End of the Western World.* London: Allen Lane, 2009.

Jayanthakumaran, Kangesu. "Trade Liberalization and Performance: The Impact of Trade Reform on Manufacturing Sector Performance: Sri Lanka 1977–89." PhD Thesis, University of Bradford, United Kingdom, 1994.

Joseph, Gilbert M., and Greg Grandin. *A Century of Revolution: Insurgent and Counterinsurgent Violence during Latin America's Long Cold War.* Duke University Press, 2010.

Joshi, Gopal (ed.). *Privatization in South Asia: Minimizing Negative Social Effects through Restructuring.* New Delhi: South Asia Multi Disciplinary Advisory Team (SAAT), International Labor Organization (ILO), 2000. http://www.ilo.org/global/publications/ilo-bookstore/order-online/books/WCMS_PUBL_9221119017_EN/lang-en/index.htm

Kadirgamar, Ahilan, and Devaka Gunawardena. "Sri Lanka's Crisis: The Disaster of Economic Dependency." Deccan Herald, April 6, 2022. https://www.deccanherald.com/opinion/sri-lankas-crisis-the-disaster-of-economic-dependency-1098125.html

Kamal, Baher. "Market Lords, Much More than a War, Behind World's Food Crisis." Inter Press Service, November 11, 2022. https://www.ipsnews.net/2022/11/market-lords-much-war-behind-worlds-food-crisis/

Karunatilake, H. N. S. *The Accelerated Mahaweli Programme and Its Impact.* Centre for Demographic and Socio-Economic Studies, 1988.

Keerawella, Gamini. "Contraction of Democratic Structures after 1977 – Gamini Keerawella." Sri Lanka Brief, January 16, 2020. https://srilankabrief.org/contraction-of-democratic-structures-after-1977-gamini-keerawella/

Kelegama, Saman. *Privatization in Sri Lanka: The Experience During the Early Years of Implementation.* Sri Lanka Economic Association, 1993.

Kelegama, Saman, and Gamani Corea. *Economic Policy in Sri Lanka: Issues and Debates.* Thousand Oaks, CA: Sage Publications, 2004. http://catdir.loc.gov/catdir/toc/ecip0419/2004014911.html

Kerry, John F., Christopher J. Dodd, Russell D. Feingold, Barbara Boxer, Robert Menendez, Benjamin L. Cardin, Robert P. Casey, et al. *Sri Lanka: Recharting U.S. Strategy After the War, Committee on Foreign Relations, United States Senate, One Hundred Eleventh Congress, First Session, December 7, 2009.* Washington D.C.: U.S. Government Printing Office, 2009.

Kessel, Andrew. "Debt-for-Nature Swaps: A Critical Approach." 2006. https://www.macalester.edu/geography/wp-content/uploads/sites/18/2012/03/kessel.pdf

Kinzer, Stephen. *Overthrow: America's Century of Regime Change from Hawaii to Iraq.* 1st ed. New York: Times Books/Henry Holt, 2006.

Klein, Naomi. *The Shock Doctrine.* Henry Holt and Co., 2010.

Knox, Robert. *An Historical Relation of Ceylon.* 1st ed. Ceylon Historical Journal, v. 6, July 1956-April 1957, nos. 1–4. Maharagama, Ceylon: Printed at Saman Press, 1958.

Kunanayakam, Tamara. "Creeping Neo-Liberal Stranglehold on Sri Lanka." Thuppahi's Blog, June 27, 2018. https://thuppahis.com/2018/06/27/creeping-neo-liberal-stranglehold-on-sri-lanka/

Kurukulasuriya, Lasanda. "Factum Perspective: The President Elaborates on the Geopolitics of Two Oceans." NewsWire, October 2, 2022. https://www.newswire.lk/2022/10/02/factum-perspective-the-president-elaborates-on-the-geopolitics-of-two-oceans/

Kuruvilla, Benny. "Sri Lanka: A Cautionary Tale of Authoritarian Neoliberalism." Focus on the Global South, October 17, 2022. https://focusweb.org/sri-lanka-a-cautionary-tale-of-authoritarian-neoliberalism/

Kuruwita, Rathindra. "Govt. Says Selling State Assets Only Way to Build Reserves and Prevent Crippling Shortages." The Island, January 4, 2023. http://island.lk/govt-says-selling-state-assets-only-way-to-build-reserves-and-prevent-crippling-shortages/

Kuruwita, Rathindra. "MONLAR: Land given to the Poor Will End up with Multinationals."LankaWeb, July 8th, 2019, January 3, 2023. https://www.lankaweb.com/news/items/2019/07/08/monlar-land-given-to-the-poor-will-end-up-with-multinationals/

Kwet, Michael. "Digital Colonialism: The Evolution of US Empire." Transnational Institute, March 4, 2021. https://longreads.tni.org/digital-colonialism-the-evolution-of-us-empire

Ladduwahetty, Neville "Repatriation of Export Earnings" The Island, 12 December 2022. https://island.lk/repatriation-of-export-earnings/

Lakshman, W. D. "The IMF-World Bank Intervention in Sri Lankan Economic Policy: Historical Trends and Patterns." *Social Scientist* 13, no. 2 (1985): 3–29. https://doi.org/10.2307/3520187

Leelarathna, Hassina. "CIA NED IRI in Sri Lanka." SriLankaexpress.org, December 2017. https://srilankaexpress.org/cia-ned-iri-in-sri-lanka

Lehmann, Axel P. "Global Wealth Report 2022." Credit Suisse Research Institute, 2022. https://www.credit-suisse.com/media/assets/corporate/docs/about-us/research/publications/global-wealth-report-2022-en.pdf

Lepore, Jill. "The Elephant Who Could Be a Person." The Atlantic, November 16, 2021. https://www.theatlantic.com/ideas/archive/2021/11/happy-elephant-bronx-zoo-nhrp-lawsuit/620672/

"Living Wage, A Wage That Covers a Workers' Basic Needs Is a Human Right." Labour Behind the Label, accessed January 3, 2023. https://labourbehindthelabel.org/living-wage/

Lockett, Hudson, and Stephanie Findlay. "'Modi's Rockefeller': Gautam Adani and the Concentration of Power in India." Financial Times, November 13, 2020. https://www.ft.com/content/474706d6-1243-4f1e-b365-891d4c5d528b

López, Aldo Orellana. "Bolivia, 15 Years on from the Water War." Narco News, April 23, 2015. http://narconews.com/Issue67/article4799.html

Lumina, Cephas. "Curbing 'Vulture Fund' Litigation." In *Sovereign Debt and Human Rights*, edited by Ilias Bantekas and Cephas Lumina. Oxford University Press, 2018. https://doi.org/10.1093/oso/9780198810445.003.0027

Mackintosh, Craig. "Letters from Sri Lanka – The World's Largest Water Harvesting Earthworks Project." The Permaculture Research Institute, August 10, 2009. https://www.permaculturenews.org/2009/08/10/the-worlds-largest-water-harvesting-earthworks-project/

Macy, Joanna. *Dharma and Development: Religion as Resource in the Sarvodaya Self-Help Movement.* Kumarian Press, 1985.

Magdoff, Harry. "Colonialism (c. 1450-c.1970)." In *The New Encyclopaedia Britannica,* 15th edition, 890. Chicago: Encyclopaedia Britannica, 1992.

Malalasekera, G. P. *The Pāli Literature of Ceylon.* Kandy, Sri Lanka: Buddhist Publication Society, 1994.

Mander, Jerry. *In the Absence of the Sacred: The Failure of Technology and the Survival of the Indian Nations.* Sierra Club books pbk. ed. San Francisco: Sierra Club Books, 1992.

Mander, Jerry. *The Capitalism Papers: Fatal Flaws of an Obsolete System.* Berkeley, CA: Counter Point, 2012.

Manifesto. "UN Declaration: New International Economic Order." STEPS Centre, August 10, 2009. https://steps-centre.org/general/un-declaration-new-international-economic-order/

Marirajan, T., and Vineeta Hoon. "Socio Economic Monitoring for Coastal Managers of South Asia: Field Trials and Baseline Surveys in Gulf of Mannar Region, South Tamilnadu, India Project Completion Report: NA10NOS4630055." India: Peoples Action for Development (PAD), The Centre for Action Research on Environment Science and Society (CARESS), May 2012. https://www.ncei.noaa.gov/data/oceans/coris/library/NOAA/CRCP/other/grants/International_FY10_Products/NA10NOS4630055_MannarGulf_Socmon.pdf

Mawdsley, Emma. "The Millennium Challenge Account: Neo-Liberalism, Poverty and Security." *Review of International Political Economy* 14, no. 3 (July 4, 2007): 487–509. https://doi.org/10.1080/09692290701395742

McNair, David. "Global Economic Turmoil Calls for a Modernized Global Financial Architecture to Address Needs of the Most Vulnerable Countries." Carnegie Endowment for International Peace, November 15, 2022. https://carnegieendowment.org/2022/11/15/global-economic-turmoil-calls-for-modernized-global-financial-architecture-to-address-needs-of-most-vulnerable-countries-pub-88400

Mendis, D. L. O. *Eppawala: Destruction of Cultural Heritage in the Name of Development.* 1st ed. Colombo: Sri Lanka Pugwash Group, 1999.

Menendez, Mr, Mr Durbin, Mr Leahy, and Mr Booker. "117th Congress, 2nd Session, Senate Resolution Expressing the Sense of the Senate in Support of the Peaceful Democratic and Economic Aspirations of the Sri Lankan People." United States Senate Committee on Foreign Relations, n.d. https://www.foreign.senate.gov/imo/media/doc/sri_lanka_resolution.pdf

Merchant, Carolyn. *The Death of Nature: Women, Ecology, and the Scientific Revolution.* Science/Women's Studies. New York: Harper & Row, 1989. http://www.h-net.org/review/hrev-a0b7n6-aa

"Mihintale Sanctuary: The First Wildlife Sanctuary in the World." AmazingLanka.com, February 22, 2014. https://amazinglanka.com/wp/mihintale-sanctuary/

Millenium Challenge Corporation. "Sri Lanka Constraints Analysis Report 2017." 2017. https://assets.mcc.gov/content/uploads/constraints-analysis-sri-lanka.pdf

Ministry of External Affairs, Government of India. "Media Center: Statements: Bilateral/Multilateral Documents: Agreement on Persons of Indian Origin in Ceylon."October 30, 1964. https://mea.gov.in/bilateral-documents.htm?dtl/6426/Agreement+on+Persons+of+Indian+Origin+in+Ceylon

Mittal, Janhavi. "Land Privatization: Why Sri Lanka Must Reject the MCC Compact." Oaklandinstitute.org, August 17, 2020. https://www.oaklandinstitute.org/blog/privatizing-state-land-sri-lanka

Monbiot, George. "Neoliberalism – the Ideology at the Root of All Our Problems." The Guardian, sec. Books, April 15, 2016. https://www.theguardian.com/books/2016/apr/15/neoliberalism-ideology-problem-george-monbiot

Moore, Mick. *Economic Liberalisation, Growth, and Poverty: Sri Lanka in Long Run Perspective.* Discussion Paper (Institute of Development Studies (Brighton, England)). Brighton, England: Institute of Development Studies at the University of Sussex, 1990. http://www.ids.ac.uk/publications/ids-series-titles

Moosa, Imad A., and Nisreen Moosa. *Eliminating the IMF: An Analysis of the Debate to Keep, Reform or Abolish the Fund.* Cham: Springer International Publishing, 2019. https://doi.org/10.1007/978-3-030-05761-9

Moramudali, Umesh. "Is Sri Lanka Really a Victim of China's 'Debt Trap'?" The Diplomat, May 14, 2019. https://thediplomat.com/2019/05/is-sri-lanka-really-a-victim-of-chinas-debt-trap/

Mousseau, Frederic. "38 Billion Dollar Question – Who Is Driving the Destructive Industrial Agriculture Model?" oaklandinstitute.org, September 20, 2022. https://www.oaklandinstitute.org/blog/vanguard-blackrock-driving-destructive-industrial-agriculture-model

National Joint Committee. "Letter Sent by the National Joint Committee to Prime Minister Ranil Wickramasinghe on the Millennium Challenge Corporation Agreement." The Sunday Times, June 2, 2019. http://www.sundaytimes.lk/190602/sunday-times-2/the-land-belongs-to-the-people-and-all-living-beings-thou-art-only-the-guardian-of-it-351773.html

Neate, Rupert. "Richest 1% Own Half the World's Wealth, Study Finds." The Guardian, sec. Inequality, November 14, 2017. https://www.theguardian.com/inequality/2017/nov/14/worlds-richest-wealth-credit-suiss

Noble, A., P. Amerasinghe, H. Manthrithilake, and S. Arasalingam. "Review of Literature on Chronic Kidney Disease of Unknown Etiology (CKDu) in Sri Lanka." International Water Management Institute (IWMI), 2014. https://doi.org/10.5337/2014.206

Norberg-Hodge, Helena. *Ancient Futures: Learning from Ladakh.* San Francisco: Sierra Club Books, 1991.

Norton, Ben. "IMF Warns of 'wave of Debt Crises' Coming in Global South, with War, Interest Rate Hikes, Overvalued Dollar." Multipolarista, November 13, 2022. https://multipolarista.com/2022/11/13/imf-debt-crises-global-south-interest-dollar/

Nuttall, W., C. Samaras, and M. Bazilian. "Energy and the Military: Convergence of Security, Economic, and Environmental Decision-Making." Working Paper. University of Cambridge, November 20, 2017. https://doi.org/10.17863/CAM.17547

Orwell, George. *1984.* Signet Books. New York: The New American Library, 1949.

"Over 120 Global Companies Adopt ESG Reporting Metrics." World Economic Forum, accessed December 25, 2022. https://www.weforum.org/impact/stakeholder-capitalism-esg-reporting-metrics/

Oxfam. "Profiting From Pain: The Urgency of Taxing the Rich amid a Surge in Billionaire Wealth and a Global Cost-of-Living Crisis." Press Release. Oxfam, May 23, 2022. https://oi-files-d8-prod.s3.eu-west-2.amazonaws.com/s3fs-public/2022-05/Oxfam%20Media%20Brief%20-%20EN%20-%20Profiting%20From%20Pain%2C%20Davos%202022%20Part%202.pdf

Paranavitana, K. D. "Suppression of Buddhism and Aspects of Indigenous Culture under the Portuguese and the Dutch." *Journal of the Royal Asiatic Society of Sri Lanka* 49 (2004): 1–14. https://www.jstor.org/stable/23732424

Parfentev, Mikhail. "WTO and Neoliberalism: Summary." Mikhailparfentev.Medium.Com (blog), January 31, 2016. https://mikhailparfentev.medium.com/wto-and-neo-liberalism-summary-70701ef8df51

"Prashad, Vijay. Part 2: A Manual for Regime Change 8. A Study of Assassination." In *Washington Bullets*. New York: Monthly Review Press, 2020.

Pattisson, Pete, Niamh McIntyre, and Imran Mukhtar. "Revealed: 6,500 Migrant Workers Have Died in Qatar since World Cup Awarded." The Guardian, sec. Global development, February 23, 2021. https://www.theguardian.com/global-development/2021/feb/23/revealed-migrant-worker-deaths-qatar-fifa-world-cup-2022

Peebles, Patrick. "Colonization and Ethnic Conflict in the Dry Zone of Sri Lanka." *The Journal of Asian Studies* 49, no. 1 (1990): 30–55. https://doi.org/10.2307/2058432

Peiris, G. H. *Sri Lanka: Land Policy for Sustainable Development to Strengthen the Struggle for Survival*. 1st edition. Boralasgamuwa: Visidunu Publication, 2017.

Perera, Bawantha. "The Destruction of Tropical Forests in Sri Lanka." Lankapura, accessed December 27, 2022. https://lankapura.com/2011/01/destruction-tropical-forests-sri-lanka/

Perera, Sasanka. *New Evangelical Movements and Conflict in South Asia: Sri Lanka and Nepal in Perspective*. RCSS Policy Studies. Colombo: Regional Centre for Strategic Studies, 1998.

Polanyi, Karl. *Great Transformation: The Political and Economic Origins of Our Time*. Boston: Beacon Press, 2001. http://site.ebrary.com/id/10014733

Pollard, Ruth. "Analysis | Is the Great Sri Lanka Fire Sale About to Begin?" Washington Post, May 30, 2022. https://www.washingtonpost.com/business/energy/is-the-great-sri-lanka-fire-sale-about-to-begin/2022/05/29/e187bc68-dfa3-11ec-ae64-6b23e5155b62_story.html

"Poverty of Vision: Neglecting Growing Class Inequality in Post-War Sri Lanka?" South Asia@LSE, October 30, 2019. https://blogs.lse.ac.uk/southasia/2019/10/30/poverty-of-vision-neglecting-growing-class-inequality-in-post-war-sri-lanka/

Povoledo, Elisabetta, and Ian Austen. "Pope Apologizes to Indigenous People of Canada." nytimes.com, April 1, 2022. https://www.nytimes.com/2022/04/01/world/europe/pope-apology-indigenous-people-canada.html

Qinhua, Xi. "The BRI Is the Most Ambitious Infrastructure Project in History." CGTN, January 23, 2019. https://news.cgtn.com/news/3d3d514e77496a4d32457a6333566d54/index.html

"QUAD Is 'Dangerous', Akin To NATO's Eastward Expansion In Europe: China." Outlook India, March 20, 2022. https://www.outlookindia.com/international/quad-is-dangerous-akin-to-nato-s-eastward-expansion-in-europe-china-news-187758

Quiggin, John, and Thilak Mallawaarachchi. "How Did Sri Lanka Run out of Money? 5 Graphs That Explain Its Economic Crisis." The Conversation, July 26, 2022. http://theconversation.com/how-did-sri-lanka-run-out-of-money-5-graphs-that-explain-its-economic-crisis-187352

Rajapathirana, Ranjith. "Judicial Assassination of Patriot Edward Henry Pedris." Sunday Observer, August 7, 2020. https://www.sundayobserver.lk/2020/08/09/spectrum/judicial-assassination-patriot-edward-henry-pedris

Rajasingham-Senanayake, Darini. "A Staged Default: Sri Lanka's Sovereign Bond Debt Trap and IMF's Spring Meetings Amid Hybrid Cold War." IDN-InDepthNews, April 24, 2022. https://archive-2017-2022.indepthnews.info/index.php/the-world/asia-pacific/5249-a-staged-default-sri-lanka-s-sovereign-bond-debt-trap-and-imf-s-spring-meetings-amid-hybrid-cold-war-part-1

Ranaraja, Maljini. "Notes from the Field: Sri Lanka's Revolutionary 'Aragalaya.'" The Asia Foundation, July 20, 2022. https://asiafoundation.org/2022/07/20/notes-from-the-field-sri-lankas-revolutionary-aragalaya/

Ratnayake, K. "Evidence of India's Involvement in Regime Change in Sri Lanka." World Socialist Web Site, January 21, 2015. https://www.wsws.org/en/articles/2015/01/21/sril-j21.html

Ratnayake, K.. "More Evidence of US Involvement in Sri Lankan Regime-Change." World Socialist Web Site, February 16, 2015. https://www.wsws.org/en/articles/2015/02/16/slus-f16.html

"#ReformNow Conference – Let's Reset Sri Lanka." Advocata Institute, December 9, 2022. https://web.archive.org/web/20221209060942/https://www.reformnow.advocata.org/

"Report: How Nature Based Solutions Threaten Food Sovereignty." Friends of the Earth International, November 3, 2022. https://www.foei.org/publication/double-jeopardy-report-nature-based-solutions/

Roberts, Michael. *Caste Conflict and Elite Formation: The Rise of a Karāva Elite in Sri Lanka, 1500–1931.* Cambridge South Asian Studies. Cambridge: Cambridge University Press, 1982. http://catdir.loc.gov/catdir/enhancements/fy0803/80041243-t.html

Russell, Jane. "Complexities of Governance and Policy: 90th Anniversary of Universal Franchise in Sri Lanka." Awarelogue Initiative, Colombo, January 1, 2021. https://www.academia.edu/49945173/COMPLEXITIES_OF_GOVERNANCE_AND_POLICY_90th_Anniversary_of_Universal_Franchise_in_Sri_Lanka

Sage, Colin. "The Transition Movement and Food Sovereignty: From Local Resilience to Global Engagement in Food System Transformation." *Journal of Consumer Culture* 14, no. 2 (July 1, 2014): 254–275. https://doi.org/10.1177/1469540514526281

Salih, Rozana. "Privatisation in Sri Lanka-Economic and Social Effects." In *Privatization in South Asia: Minimizing Negative Social Effects through Restructuring*, edited by Gopal Joshi. New Delhi: South Asia Multi Disciplinary Advisory Team (SAAT), International Labor Organization (ILO), 2000. http://www.ilo.org/global/publications/ilo-bookstore/order-online/books/WCMS_PUBL_9221119017_EN/lang-en/index.htm

Sallay, Alvin. "Bleak Outlook for What Was Once the 'Granary of the East.'" The Sunday Times Sri Lanka, February 5, 2017. http://www.sundaytimes.lk/170205/business-times/bleak-outlook-for-what-was-once-the-granary-of-the-east-227053.html

Sanmugathasan, N. *A Marxist Looks at the History of Ceylon.* Colombo: Sarasavi Printers, 1972. https://www.marxists.org/history/erol/sri-lanka/ceylon-history/index.htm

"Saudi Arabia Warned Its Colombo Envoy of Imminent Attacks." Tamil Guardian, May 4, 2019. https://www.tamilguardian.com/content/saudi-arabia-warned-its-colombo-envoy-imminent-attacks

Schiavenza, Matt. "What Exactly Does It Mean That the U.S. Is Pivoting to Asia?" The Atlantic, April 15, 2013. https://www.theatlantic.com/china/archive/2013/04/what-exactly-does-it-mean-that-the-us-is-pivoting-to-asia/274936/

Schumacher, E. F. *Small Is Beautiful: Economics as If People Mattered.* HarperCollins, 2010.

Scott-Tyson, Ann. "New US Strategy: 'lily Pad' Bases." Christian Science Monitor, August 10, 2004. https://www.csmonitor.com/2004/0810/p06s02-wosc.html

Senanayake, Devana. "Inside Sri Lanka's Unprecedented Mass Protests." Foreign Policy, April 26, 2022. https://foreignpolicy.com/2022/04/26/sri-lanka-protests-rajapaksa-economic-crisis-colombo/

Seneviratne, Kalinga. *The Scourge of Poverty and Proselytism: Socio-Economic and Cultural Challenges Facing Buddhist Communities in Asia: A Case Study of Sri Lanka.* Singapore: Lotus Communication Network, 2017.

Shiva, Vandana. *Oneness vs the 1%: Shattering Illusions, Seeding Freedom.* North Geelong, Victoria: Spinifex Press, 2018.

Siddiqui, Kalim. "The 'Import-Substitution' Policy in Post-Colonial Countries: A Review." The World Financial Review, November 29, 2021. https://worldfinancialreview.com/the-import-substitution-policy-in-post-colonial-countries-a-review/

Simhala Komisan Sabhava. *Report of the Sinhala Commission*. 1st ed. Vol. 1. Colombo: National Joint Committee, 1998.

Skanthakumar, B. "Growth with Inequality: The Political Economy of Neoliberalism in Sri Lanka." Country Paper for Crises, Vulnerability and Poverty in South Asia 2013 report. South Asia Alliance for Poverty Eradication (SAAPE), 2013. http://www.sacw.net/IMG/pdf/Skanthakumar_Growth_with_Inequality_The_Political_Economy_of_Neoliberalism_in_Sri_Lanka_Aug_2013.pdf

Soederberg, Susanne. "American Empire and 'Excluded States': The Millennium Challenge Account and the Shift to Pre-Emptive Development." *Third World Quarterly* 25, no. 2 (March 1, 2004): 279–302. https://doi.org/10.1080/0143659042000174815

Somasunderam, Ramesh. *Strategic Significance of Srilanka*. Pannipitiya, Sri Lanka: Stamford Lake Publication, 2005.

Sorg, Christoph. *Social Movements and the Politics of Debt: Transnational Resistance against Debt on Three Continents. Protest and Social Movements*. Amsterdam: Amsterdam University Press, 2022.

"Sri Lanka." WID – World Inequality Database, accessed December 25, 2022. https://wid.world/country/sri-lanka/

"Sri Lanka: How Saudi-Backed Terror Targeted China's Allies." FunK MainStream Media News, Alternative Liberty News Sources, Fmsmnews.com, May 5, 2019. https://web.archive.org/web/20220311074616/http://fmsmnews.com/sri-lanka-how-saudi-backed-terror-targeted-chinas-allies/

"Sri Lanka in Crisis." Global Voices, accessed January 3, 2023. https://globalvoices.org/special/sri-lanka-in-crisis/

"Sri Lanka: Migrant Workers' Remittances up by 16%, over 200,000 People Have Gone Abroad for Work." ColomboPage, September 11, 2022. http://www.colombopage.com/archive_22B/Sep11_1662879267CH.php

"Sri Lanka: More than Two Thirds of Families Struggling to Feed Themselves as Economic Crisis Wipes out Incomes." Save the Children International, July 6, 2022. https://www.savethechildren.net/news/sri-lanka-more-two-thirds-families-struggling-feed-themselves-economic-crisis-wipes-out-incomes

"Sri Lanka to Adopt 'India First Approach' as New Policy, Says Foreign Secretary Colombage." ThePrint, August 26, 2020. https://theprint.in/diplomacy/sri-lanka-to-adopt-india-first-approach-as-new-policy-says-foreign-secretary-colombage/489742/

"Sri Lanka to Present Debt Restructuring, IMF Bailout Plans to Creditors on Friday." CNBC, September 18, 2022. https://www.cnbc.com/2022/09/19/sri-lanka-to-present-debt-restructuring-imf-bailout-plans-to-creditors.html

Sri Lanka Government. "Regaining Sri Lanka: Vision and Strategy for Accelerated Development." December 2002. https://planipolis.iiep.unesco.org/sites/default/files/ressources/sri_lanka_prsp_2002.pdf

Sri Lanka Ministry for Foreign Employment Promotion and Welfare. "National Labour Migration Policy for Sri Lanka." International Labour Organization, October 2008. https://www.ilo.org/dyn/migpractice/docs/268/Policy.pdf

Sri Lanka National Physical Planning Department. "National Physical Planning Policy & The Plan – 2017–2050." Battaramulla, Sri Lanka, June 2019. https://nppd.gov.lk/images/National_Physical_Plans/National_Physical%20Planning%20Policy%20and%20The%20Plan%202050.pdf

Srinivasan, Meera. "Urban Poverty Triples in Sri Lanka amid Enduring Crisis." The Hindu, sec. World, October 11, 2022. https://www.thehindu.com/news/international/urban-poverty-triples-in-sri-lanka-amid-enduring-crisis/article65997513.ece

Steinmetz-Jenkins, Daniel. "The Rotten Roots of the IMF and the World Bank." The Nation, June 15, 2022. https://www.thenation.com/article/culture/the-rotten-roots-of-global-economic-governance/

Stiglitz, Joseph E. "The End of Neoliberalism and the Rebirth of History" Project Syndicate, November 4, 2019. https://www.project-syndicate.org/commentary/end-of-neoliberalism-unfettered-markets-fail-by-joseph-e-stiglitz-2019-11

"The Adani Files, A Short History of Corruption, Destruction and Criminal Activity." Adani Files, accessed January 3, 2023. http://adanifiles.com.au

"The Doctrine of Discovery, 1493." Gilder Lehrman Institute of American History, accessed December 25, 2022. https://tinyurl.com/4ffem99u

"The Dynamics of Distress and Debt in Emerging Markets: Sri Lanka's Struggling Economy." ECornell Keynotes, 2022. https://www.youtube.com/watch?v=0CX_odCq20I

"The Economics of Happiness." Documentary, News. International Society for Ecology & Culture (ISEC), n.d. https://vimeo.com/492145296

"The Human Dimension to Sri Lanka's Economic Crisis." Himal Southasian, October 14, 2022. https://www.himalmag.com/sonali-deraniyagala-human-dimension-to-sri-lankas-economic-crisis-2022/

Tolisano, Jim, Pia Abeygunewardene, Tissa Athukorala, Craig Davis, William Fleming, Kapila Goonesekera, and Tamara Rusinow. "An Environmental Evaluation of the Accelerated Mahaweli Development Program: Lessons Learned and Donor Opportunities for Improved Assistance." Bethesda, Maryland: DAI / U.S. Agency for International Development, May 1993.

"Trade-Related Illicit Financial Flows in 135 Developing Countries: 2008–2017." Global Financial Integrity, March 2020. https://secureservercdn.net/45.40.149.159/34n.8bd.myftpupload.com/wp-content/uploads/2020/03/GFI-Trade-IFF-Report-2020-Final.pdf?time=1583347870

Transnational Institute. "The Privatising Industry in Europe." tni.org, February 17, 2016. https://www.tni.org/en/publication/the-privatising-industry-in-europe

Transnational Institute. "United Nations and Transnational Corporations: A Deadly Association." tni.org, April 4, 2007. https://www.tni.org/en/article/united-nations-and-transnational-corporations-a-deadly-association

United Nations Conference on Trade and Development. "'True Champion of the South' Gamani Corea Honored at Tribute Seminar." UNCTAD, March 26, 2014. https://unctad.org/news/true-champion-south-gamani-corea-honored-tribute-seminar

United Nations News. "Sri Lanka's Economic Crisis Pushes Health System to Brink of Collapse." UN News, August 17, 2022. https://news.un.org/en/story/2022/08/1124842

Unites States Congress. "The Hickenlooper Amendment Limits U.S. Aid to Latin America." SHEC: Resources for Teachers, accessed January 2, 2023. https://shec.ashp.cuny.edu/items/show/799

Unites States Department of Defense. "Indo-Pacific Strategy Report: Preparedness, Partnerships, and Promoting a Networked Region." June 1, 2019. https://media.defense.gov/2019/Jul/01/2002152311/-1/-1/1/DEPARTMENT-OF-DEFENSE-INDO-PACIFIC-STRATEGY-REPORT-2019.PDF

United States Department of State. "Integrated Country Strategy Sri Lanka." April 6, 2022. https://www.state.gov/wp-content/uploads/2022/06/ICS_SCA_Sri-Lanka_Public.pdf

United States Department of State, Office of the Historian, Bureau of Public Affairs. "Milestones: 1945–1952: Decolonization of Asia and Africa, 1945–1960." Accessed December 31, 2022. https://history.state.gov/milestones/1945-1952/asia-and-africa

United States Embassy in Sri Lanka. "U.S. Government Funds Renovation of Two Schools in Eastern Province." July 9, 2018. https://lk.usembassy.gov/u-s-government-funds-renovation-of-two-schools-in-eastern-province/

"US Fingerprints Found Behind Sri Lanka Unrest." The New Atlas, 2022. https://www.youtube.com/watch?v=Ysy6qrXi0m0

"US House of Representatives to Work with Sri Lanka Parliament." Daily News, September 17, 2016. https://www.dailynews.lk/2016/09/17/local/93425

"U.S. Strategic Framework for the Indo-Pacific." Trumpwhitehouse.archives.gov, accessed January 3, 2023. https://trumpwhitehouse.archives.gov/wp-content/uploads/2021/01/IPS-Final-Declass.pdf

"USA Machinations Behind Aragalaya?" Thuppahi's Blog, July 15, 2022. https://thuppahis.com/2022/07/15/63710/

U.S. Indo-Pacific Command. "USPACOM Area of Responsibility." Accessed January 3, 2023. https://www.pacom.mil/About-USINDOPACOM/USPACOM-Area-of-Responsibility/

Vaughan, Aron. "BlackRock Is the Biggest Company You've Never Heard Of." Innovation & Tech Today, July 8, 2022. https://innotechtoday.com/blackrock-is-the-biggest-company-youve-never-heard-of/

Vieira, Luiz. "Debt Crisis Prevention: We Need to Talk about Capital Controls." Bretton Woods Project, December 9, 2021. https://www.brettonwoodsproject.org/2021/12/debt-crisis-prevention-we-need-to-talk-about-capital-controls/

Vimalananda, Tennakoon. *Buddhism in Ceylon Under the Christian Powers and the Educational and Religious Policy of the British Government in Ceylon, 1797–1832*. M.D. Gunasena & Company Limited, 1963.

Vine, David. "The Lily-Pad Strategy: How the Pentagon Is Quietly Transforming Its Overseas Base Empire." HuffPost, July 16, 2012. https://www.huffpost.com/entry/us-military-bases_b_1676006

Vitali, Stefania, James B. Glattfelder, and Stefano Battiston. "The Network of Global Corporate Control." *PloS One* 6, no. 10 (2011): e25995. https://doi.org/10.1371/journal.pone.0025995

Vizcaino, Maria Elena, and Sydney Maki. "Fidelity Among Big Sri Lankan Debt Holders Staring Down Risk." Bloomberg, April 5, 2022. https://www.bloomberg.com/news/articles/2022-04-05/fidelity-among-big-sri-lankan-debt-holders-staring-down-turmoil

Waduge, Shenali, 'IMF puts countries into debt, poverty & inequality but who in Sri Lanka wants IMF – why?', March 18, 2023 https://mail.google.com/mail/u/0/?tab=rm&ogbl#inbox/WhctKKXwqkfRCFXxJKZKdpZjLzTMSzRFxTVMfHsppZWQmhWLWDLtqspwKDwdFvzqTJbWCmb accessed March 20, 2023.

Waduge, Shenali. "Sri Lanka's Protestors Have given an Ugly Example to the World." Shenali Waduge, August 13, 2022.

Waduge, Shenali. "US in Sri Lanka since 2015 – Turning Sri Lanka into a Neo-Colonial Military Base." LankaWeb, accessed January 2, 2023. https://www.lankaweb.com/news/items/2019/11/01/us-in-sri-lanka-since-2015-turning-sri-lanka-into-a-neo-colonial-military-base/

Walpola Rāhula. *What the Buddha Taught*. Rev. ed. London: G. Fraser, 1978.

Wasala, Rohana R. "Empowerment or Entrapment? The Millennium Challenge Corporation Compact and the Message of the Fasting Monk." LankaWeb, November 10, 2019. https://www.lankaweb.com/news/items/2019/11/10/empowerment-or-entrapment-the-millennium-challenge-corporation-compact-and-the-message-of-the-fasting-monk/

Watson, Ian Bruce, and Siri Gamage. *Conflict and Community in Contemporary Sri Lanka: "Pearl of the East" or "the Island of Tears."* Studies on Contemporary South Asia. New Delhi: Sage Publications, 1999. http://catdir.loc.gov/catdir/enhancements/fy0657/99036872-t.html

Weeraratna, Senaka. "Portuguese Era Dark Chapter in Sri Lanka's History." *Sunday Observer*, April 16, 2021. https://www.sundayobserver.lk/2021/04/18/impact/portuguese-era-dark-chapter-sri-lanka%E2%80%99s-history

Wijeyawickrema, C. "Paskaralingam, Charith & Malik." *LankaWeb*, October 5, 2018. https://www.lankaweb.com/news/items/2018/10/05/paskaralingam-charith-malik/

Wills, E. Ashley. "03COLOMBO909: SUBJECT: Sri Lanka's Foreign Policy: Prime Minister Tilts toward U.S., but Faces Resistance." *WikiLeaks*, January 22, 2012. https://web.archive.org/web/20120122012246/http://wikileaks.org/cable/2003/05/03COLOMBO909.html

World Bank. *Sri Lanka Development Update 2021: Economic and Poverty Impact of COVID-19*. World Bank, 2021. https://doi.org/10.1596/35833

World Economic Forum. "The Great Reset." Accessed December 25, 2022. https://www.weforum.org/great-reset/

CPSIA information can be obtained
at www.ICGtesting.com
Printed in the USA
LVHW060229030623
748745LV00001B/24